Ford Cortina 1600XL StationWagon — 1972

Ford Cortina Saloon — 1975

Ford Cortina GT 2000 — 1975

Ford Cortina 1300 — 1972

Ford Cortina 1600 GT — 1972

Printed by Times Printers Sdn Bhd., Singapore.

S.P.
WORKSHOP MANUAL SERIES No. 60
CORTINA MK3

S.P.
WORKSHOP MANUAL SERIES No. 60

CORTINA MK3
1300, 1600, 1600 GT 4 Cylinder OHV
1600, 2000 4 Cylinder OHC

With Specifications,
Repair and Maintenance Data

MURRAY BOOK DISTRIBUTORS Pty Ltd
SYDNEY • LONDON

An SP Workshop Manual Series No. 60
Published by
Murray Book Distributors Pty. Ltd.
Durham UK — Sydney, Australia

Edited and Photographed at the company's
workshops at:—

"The Hub" Building,   Unit 4
89–97 Jones St.,   Hetton Lyons Industrial Estate
ULTIMO. 2007.   Hetton-Le-Hole
AUSTRALIA.   Tyne & Wear DH5 ORH
                            ENGLAND.

First Edition: August, 1973
Reprinted: May, 1974
Second Edition: May, 1976
Reprinted: October, 1977

National Library of Australia Registry Number
SBN 85566 180 I

The information in this manual is derived from the latest models available for our workshop research, and from other available sources at the time of writing. Any subsequent modifications will need to be taken into consideration by the operator.

While every precaution is taken to ensure the accuracy of the contents, onus can not be accepted for any misinterpretation of the described repair operations or for any errors or omissions inadvertently made.

ACKNOWLEDGEMENT

Scientific Publications wishes to thank the National Roads and Motorists Association, Car Repairs Pty Ltd, Lidcombe, for their help in various aspects of preparing this manual.

OVERSEAS REPRESENTATIVES

New Zealand: M.E.P. Bookshop, 82 Taranaki St., Wellington.
Publishers Services, 13 Eden St. Newmarket, Auckland.
E.Sime and Co., 82 Tory St., Wellington; and 140 Target Rd, Glenfield Auckland.
South Africa: Australian Industries (Export) Pty Ltd, PO Box 2016, Johannesburg.
South East Asia: Repco (S.E. Asia) Pty. Ltd., 47 West Coast Road, Singapore.
United Kingdom: Alltech Distributors, 15 High St., Humpton, Middlesex,
Frederick Muller Ltd., Victoria Works, Edgware Road, London
Scientific Publications, Unit 4, Hetton Lyons Industrial Estate,
HETTON-LE-HOLE, TYNE and WEAR, DH5 0RH.

S P. MANUAL SERIES

MOTOR VEHICLES

	Book No.	Pages	Illustrations
Austin			
Austin 1100, 1300	148	184	249
Austin Maxi	149	192	298
Allegro OHV			
1100, 1300 (1973-76)	25	192	327
Allegro OHC			
1500, 1750 (1973-76)	51	200	329
Chrysler/Mitsubishi			
Galant/GA-GB/Colt			
1300, 1600 (1971-74)	05	192	202
Galant GC-GD/Colt			
1600 (1774-77)	17	176	232
Lancer LA-LB	162		
Datsun			
1000, 1200	87	224	208
510: 1300, 1400, 1600			
(1968-72)	88	256	241
180B, 160B	110	224	208
Sunny. 120Y	111	224	278
Ford			
Capri Mk I	82	173	108
Capri Mk II	09*		
Consul/Zephyr Mk II			
(1956-62)	08	184	124
Cortina 1200, 1500			
1600, Mk I & II			
(1964-71)	68	288	192
Cortina Mk III 1600,			
2000 (1971-74)	60	240	239
Cortina Mk III, 6 cyl.			
(1972-74)	59	176	135
Cortina IV 4 Cyl	158*		
Excort Mk I	81	192	172
Escort Mk II	20	192	240
Falcon XK to XW			
6 cyl. (1960-70)	62	290	188
Falcon XY to XB			
6 cyl. (1970-76)	155	272	226
Falcon XR to XY			
V8 (1966-71)	154	272	190
Falcon XA and XB			
V8 (1971-76)	156	240	327
Fiesta	159*	144	224
Hillman			
Avenger	80	176	267
Hunter	79	188	121
New Hunter	37	224	312
Holden			
Gemini	113	160	215
FX, FJ, FE, FC, FB.			
EK, EJ, EH, HD,			
HR (1948-68)	67	286	128
HK, HT, HG V8			
(1968-71)	85	272	215
HK, HT, HG 6 cyl.			
(1968-71)	86	224	188
HQ, HJ 6 cyl.	146	208	194
HQ, HJ V8	147	256	240
Torana LC, LJ 6 cyl.			
(1969-74)	84	192	172
Torana LH, LX 6 cyl.			
(1974-76)	58	192	200
Torana HB	72	192	120
Torana LC, LJ, TA			
4 cyl. (1969-75) ohv	56	196	287
Torana LC, LJ, TA			
4 cyl. (1969-75) ohc	145	196	295
Torana LH, LX 4 cyl.			
(1974-76)	16	180	197
Honda			
Civic Hondamatic	139	176	350
Civic Manual	140	176	339

	Book No.	Pages	Illustrations
Leyland			
Allegro OHV			
1100, 1300 (1973-76)	25	192	327
Allegro OHC			
1500, 1750 (1973-76)	51	200	329
Marina 1.3, 1.8			
(1971-75)	142	192	277
Marina 1500, 1750	03	160	291
P76: V8	04	180	274
P76: 6 cyl.	141	180	324
BL 1100, 1300	148	184	245
Mazda			
Capella 616: 1600			
(1970-73)	89	160	134
1500, 1800	90	212	196
RX2, R100 Rotaries	91	200	199
1000/1300	92	160	305
MG			
TC to MGB Mk I	70	320	204
Morris			
Minor 1000	24	96	96
Marina see Leyland			
Mini (1959-72)	64	236	187
Mini (1971-76)	02	224	276
1100	65	146	106
1800 Mk I, Mk II	66a	224	174
Peugeot			
403, 404	31	122	171
Renault			
12	32	160	317
Dauphine	34	134	158
R8 and R10	74	164	97
Toyota			
Corolla 1100	73	176	107
Corolla 1200	122	240	217
Corona 2R	83	224	186
Corona 2000 16R, 18R	120	176	256
Corona 12R, RT80/81	123	160	220
Valiant			
AP6, VC, VE, VF			
V8 (1965-70)	69	174	95
R, S, AP5, AP6, VC,			
VE, VF 6 cyl.			
(1962-70)	78	280	145
Hemi VG, VH,			
6 cyl. (1970-74)	52	224	183
Galant: see under Chrysler			
VJ-VK see also Chrysler	157		
Vauxhall			
Viva HA, HB, 90	76	200	140
Viva HC, OHV	57	192	309
Chevette 1256 cc	114	160	239
Volkswagen			
"Superbug" 1302S, 1600			
(1971-73)	45	224	188
Beetle 1100, 1200,			
1200A, 1300, 1500			
(1954-71)	46	260	240
Fastback Type 3, 1600	47	232	167
Transporter (1954-72)	48	272	205
Type 2, 1700			
1800, 2000	151	168	240
Passat 1300			
1500, 1600	152	168	235
Golf 1500, 1600	153	160	254

	Book No.	Pages	Illustrations
Volvo Series 140			
With Carbies	53	212	172
With Fuel Inject.	54	196	147

HARD TO GET AND VINTAGE MANUALS

	Book No.	Pages	Illustrations
Austin			
A40 Devon, Dorset	00	106	89
A40 Somerset	01	100	84
Jaguar			
Mks VII, VIII, IX,			
XK 120, 140, 150	21	274	237
Mk I, II: 2.4, 3.4, 3.8	22	274	281
E Type 3.8, 4.2			
(1962-69)	77	202	124
Standard			
8-14 (1939-46)	40	82	51
Ten (1955-58)	41	148	134
Spacemaster II	42	126	105
TR2, TR3, TR4	44	168	130

MOWERS AND SMALL ENGINES

	Book No.	Pages	Illustrations
Rover Series to 1977	99*		
Small Engines	112	160	231
Victa Series to 1977	103*	128	138
Scott Bonnar (1976-77)	97*		
Victa twin and	161	72	120
85cc to 1978			

MOTOR CYCLES

	Book No.	Pages	Illustrations
Honda			
QA50 Minibike	129	64	95
SL70, CT90	130	128	224
C/S: 50, 65, 70	131	96	182
Street/Trail 175	132	112	341
125 Vertical Twin	133	112	346
250, 350	134	128	376
100-125 Vertical Single	135	112	374

OUTBOARDS

	Book No.	Pages	Illustrations
Evinrude-Johnson			
3-4 hp (1964-72)	105	64	92
5-6 hp (1965-74)	106	96	177
9½ hp (1964-73)	107	80	198
18, 20, 25 hp (1960-73)	108	112	260
18, 20, 25 hp (1960-73)	108	112	260
33-40 hp (1965-74)	109	128	300
40 hp Lark (1965-74)	104	112	250

*MANUALS IN PRODUCTION

	Book No.
Austin 1100, 1300	148
Valiant VJ-VK	157
Golf 1500/1600	153
Rovers Mowers	99
Scott Bonnar Mowers	97
Capri Mk II	09
Cortina IV 4 Cyl.	158
Lancer LA-LB	162

ENGINE
PART I: OHV ENGINES
SPECIFICATIONS

ENGINE ASSEMBLY

Type	4 cyl – ohv
Models and capacity:	
1300	1263 cc
1600	1588 cc
1600 GT	1588 cc
Bore	80.98 cc
Stroke:	
1300	62.99 mm
1600 and 1600 GT	77.62 mm
Compression ratio:	
1300 LC and 1600	
LC	8.0:1
1300 HC, 1600 HC and	
1600 GT	9.0:1
Engine idle speed:	
1300 and 1600	680 – 720 rpm
1600 GT	780 – 820 rpm
Firing order	1-2-4-3

CYLINDER HEAD

Type	Cross flow
Combustion chamber	Machined in piston crown
Valve guides	Machined directly in cylinder head
Valve seat angle	44 deg 30 min – 45 deg
Valve seat width	1.5875 – 1.9844 mm
Valve guide bore diameter	7.907 – 7.937 mm

VALVES

Head diameter:	
Inlet – 1300	38.28 – 38.02 mm
– 1600 and 1600 GT .	39.60 – 39.40 mm
Exhaust – 1300	31.60 – 31.30 mm
– 1600 and 1600 GT .	34.00 – 33.80 mm
Stem diameter:	
Inlet	7.868 – 7.886 mm
Exhaust	7.863 – 7.846 mm
Available oversizes	0.076 or 0.381 mm
Stem to guide clearance:	
Inlet	0.020 – 0.068 mm
Exhaust	0.043 – 0.091 mm
Valve length:	
Inlet	105.8 – 106.2 mm
Exhaust	105.8 – 106.0 mm
Valve timing – except GT:	
Inlet opens	23 deg btdc
Inlet closes	53 deg abdc
Exhaust opens	53 deg bbdc
Exhaust closes	23 deg atdc
Valve timing – GT:	
Inlet opens	27 deg btdc
Inlet closes	65 deg abdc
Exhaust opens	65 deg bbdc
Exhaust closes	27 deg atdc
Valve clearance:	
Inlet	0.25 mm
Exhaust	0.50 mm
Valve spring:	
Free length	37.59 mm
Fitted length	32.08 mm

CYLINDER BLOCK

Standard bore grades:	
8 gradings	80.947 mm to 81.008 mm
Crankshaft journal bore:	
Standard	57.683 – 57.626 mm
Oversize	58.064 – 58.077 mm
Camshaft journal bore:	
Standard	42.888 – 42.913 mm
Oversize	43.421 mm

PISTONS

Material	Aluminium alloy
Standard diameter grades:	
Selective fit to suit graded bores	8 grades
Oversizes available in service	0.064, 0.380 and 0.760 mm
Piston clearance in cylinder bore:	
1300	0.048 – 0.064 mm
1600 and 1600 GT	0.041 – 0.056 mm

PISTON RINGS

Number of rings	Two compression and one oil control
Ring end gap	0.23 – 0.36 mm
Ring clearance in piston groove:	
Compression	0.041 – 0.091 mm
Oil control	0.046 – 0.097 mm

GUDGEON PINS

Type	Full floating
Retained by	Circlips in piston
Length	71.12 – 71.37 mm
Diameter:	
1 . . .	20.622 – 20.625
2 . . .	20.625 – 20.627
3 . . .	20.627 – 20.630
4 . . .	20.630 – 20.632
Clearance in small end bush	0.003 – 0.008 mm
Interference fit in piston	0.003 – 0.008 mm

CRANKSHAFT AND BEARINGS

Main bearing journal diameter:
Standard — red .... 53.993 – 54.003 mm
       — blue .... 53.983 – 53.993 mm
*Regrind undersize —
       — 1 ... 0.254 mm
       — 2 ... 0.508 mm
       — 3 ... 0.762 mm
Main bearing clearance:
Standard — red .... 0.013 – 0.048 mm
       — blue .... 0.010 – 0.046 mm
Crankpin diameter:
Standard .... 49.195 – 49.215 mm
**Regrind undersizes —
       — 1 .. 0.254 mm
       — 2 .. 0.508 mm
       — 3 .. 0.762 mm
       — 4 .. 1.016 mm
Crankpin bearing clearance .... 0.010 – 0.060 mm
Crankshaft end-float .... 0.075 – 0.280 mm

* Undersize main bearings available to suit regrind sizes.
** Undersize big end bearings available to suit regrind sizes.

CONNECTING ROD

Type .... H section forged steel
Small end .... Bushed
Big end bore .... 52.900 – 52.910 mm
Bearing inside diamiater:
Standard .... 49.238 – 49.268 mm
Undersizes .... 0.051 mm, 0.254 mm, 0.508 mm, 0.762 mm, 1.016 mm

Big end bearing clearance .... 0.010 – 0.060 mm

CAMSHAFT AND BEARINGS

Drive .... Tensioned chain
Tensioner type .... Spring loaded cam and pad
Camshaft end float .... 0.06 – 0.20 mm
Thrust plate thickness .... 4.46 – 4.51 mm
Cam lift — except 1600 GT:
Inlet lobe .... 5.985 mm
Exhaust lobe .... 6.158 mm
Cam lift 1600 GT:
Inlet lobe .... 5.865 mm
Exhaust lobe .... 5.895 mm
Journal diameter .... 39.637 – 39.616 mm
Bearing diameter inside ... 39.662 – 39.675 mm

LUBRICATION

Pump type .... Eccentric rotor
Outer rotor to housing clearance .... 0.25 mm max.

Inner rotor tip clearance .... 0.15 mm max.
Rotor to cover clearance .... 0.13 mm max.
Oil pressure:
At 700 rpm .... 0.35 – 0.50 kg/cm^2
At 1500 rpm .... 2.45 – 2.80 kg/cm^2
Relief valve setting .... 2.45 – 2.80 kg/cm^2
Oil capacity:
Without filter .... 3.0 litres
With filter .... 3.5 litres

TORQUE WRENCH SETTINGS

Main bearing cap .... 9.7 kg/m
Cylinder head bolts:
Stage 1 .... 5.5 kg/m
Stage 2 .... 7.0 kg/m
Stage 3 .... 9.7 kg/m
Flywheel .... 7.6 kg/m
Camshaft sprocket ...... 6.2 kg/m
Connecting rod .... 5.5 kg/m
Timing cover .... 0.9 kg/m
Rocker pedestal .... 4.0 kg/m
Spark plugs .... 4.0 kg/m
Crankshaft pulley bolt ..... 3.8 kg/m
Sump drain plug .... 2.7 kg/m
Oil pump bolts .... 2.0 kg/m
Intake manifold .... 2.0 kg/m
Exhaust manifold .... 1.6 kg/m
Engine sump:
Stage 1 .... 0.7 kg/m
Stage 2 .... 1.3 kg/m
Oil pump cover .... 0.9 kg/m
Timing cover .... 0.9 kg/m

1. DESCRIPTION

The four cylinder overhead valve in line engine has a cast iron cylinder block. The cylinder head is also cast iron with the valve guides cast integral with the head.

Each valve has its individual port and is operated by tappet, pushrod and rocker arm from the camshaft.

Main bearing shells in all engines must not be adjusted by filing or scraping.

Crankshaft end float is controlled by two half-thrust washers at each side of the centre main bearing. The five main bearings are replaceable.

Oil leaks from the front and rear of the crankshaft are prevented by seals pressed into the front cover and rear oil seal carrier. The front seal runs on the crankshaft pulley hub and the rear seal runs on the crankshaft flange.

On manual transmission models a clutch spigot bearing is provided at the rear end of the crankshaft and the flywheel is mounted on the crankshaft flange.

On automatic transmission models a drive plate fitted to the crankshaft flange couples the engine to the torque converter.

Connecting rods are H section forgings with replaceable big end bearing shells.

Right Hand Side View of Engine and Transmission Assembly. Typical.

The solid skirt aluminium alloy pistons have combustion chambers machined in the piston crowns.

The pistons have two compression rings and one scraper type oil ring.

Gudgeon pins are fully floating and retained by circlips in the piston bosses.

The oil pump is the eccentric bi-rotor type and is driven by a skew gear from the camshaft.

The oil pressure relief valve is a non-adjustable plunger and spring type, incorporated in the oil pump body.

The camshaft runs in three bearings and is driven by a single roller chain from the crankshaft sprocket. Chain tension is controlled by an automatic mechanical tensioner. Camshaft end float is controlled by the locating plate at the front bearing. The integral skew gear on the camshaft also drives the distributor in addition to the oil pump. An eccentric also integral with the camshaft operates the fuel pump.

On the GT engines special inlet and exhaust manifolds are used, with the inlet manifold incorporating a four stud mounting flange to accommodate a dual barrel Weber carburettor.

2. ENGINE ASSEMBLY

TO REMOVE

(1) Raise the bonnet and fit fender covers to both front fenders.

(2) Mark around the bonnet hinge plates on the bonnet with a soft lead pencil to facilitate correct replacement.

(3) Detach the windscreen washer hose and remove the bonnet.

(4) Drain the cooling system at the drain plugs on the lower radiator tank and the side of the cylinder block.

(5) Instal and securely tighten the cooling system drain plugs after draining.

(6) Disconnect the leads at the terminals of the battery and the earth strap from the engine.

(7) Disconnect the upper and lower radiator hoses and remove the radiator from the vehicle.

(8) Remove the heater hoses from the water pump and inlet manifold and where fitted disconnect the automatic choke hoses.

(9) Disconnect the throttle shaft linkage and down shift cable on automatic transmission models. Disconnect the fuel and vacuum pipes at the carburettor.

(10) Detach the accelerator inner and outer cable from the throttle shaft and bracket.

(11) Disconnect the choke control cable at the carburettor (not applicable when automatic choke is used) and unclip the vent pipe (except GT models).

(12) Remove the carburettor from the inlet manifold.

NOTE: If the inlet manifold is not being removed plug the carburettor mounting flange on the manifold to prevent entry of dirt or foreign matter.

(13) Raise the front of the vehicle and support on

chassis stands at the forward jacking points. Remove the sump shield if fitted. Remove the sump drain plug and drain the engine oil.

(14) Unscrew the exhaust pipe nuts and disconnect the exhaust pipe from the manifold.

(15) Remove the engine breather pipe at the manifold and disconnect the fuel supply pipe at the fuel pump.

NOTE: It may be necessary to plug the fuel supply pipe to prevent fuel running out.

(16) Disconnect the high tension leads at the spark plugs and the coil, release the retaining clips and remove the distributor cap and high tension leads. Withdraw the distributor rotor.

(17) Disconnect the low tension lead.

(18) Disconnect the temperature gauge sender unit lead and the generator or alternator leads.

(19) Disconnect the starter motor leads at the starter, take out the securing bolts and remove the starter from the engine.

(20) Remove the lower clutch housing bolts, disconnect the reinforcing bracket and remove the cover.

(21) On automatic models — crank the engine as necessary by hand and remove the drive plate to torque converter retaining bolts through the starter motor aperture.

NOTE: Lever the torque converter towards the transmission to separate it from the drive plate.

(22) Lower the vehicle to the ground and support the transmission on a jack.

(23) Unscrew the clutch housing to engine securing bolts.

(24) Using a suitable sling and lifting tackle take the weight of the engine from above.

(25) Take out the bolts securing each engine side mounting to the front crossmember.

(26) Raise the engine slightly, draw it forward off the input shaft or torque converter and lift the engine up and out through the bonnet opening.

NOTE: On automatic transmission models fully lever the torque converter off the drive plate as the engine is withdrawn.

TO INSTAL

Installation is a reversal of the removal procedure with attention to the following points:

(1) On manual transmission models rotate the crankshaft, with the transmission in gear, to align the splines of the input shaft with the clutch plate hub splines as necessary.

(2) Ensure that the engine is correctly installed and securely mounted before connecting the various components.

(3) Before installing the radiator flush it out with compressed air and water in the opposite direction to the normal circulation of the water.

(4) Refill the engine with the correct grade and quantity of oil.

(5) Refill the cooling system and check the fan belt tension. See COOLING SYSTEM.

(6) Start and run the engine until it reaches normal operating temperature while checking for oil, water and fuel leaks.

(7) When the engine has cooled sufficiently recheck the cooling system and the engine oil level and top up as necessary.

3. ROCKER ARMS AND SHAFT

TO REMOVE AND INSTAL

(1) Remove the carburettor air cleaner.

(2) Remove the distributor cap and high tension leads.

(3) Disconnect the throttle shaft from the carburettor and the accelerator inner and outer cable from the throttle shaft and throttle shaft bracket.

(4) Remove the rocker cover and discard the cover gasket.

(5) Progressively loosen and remove the rocker pedestal securing bolts and remove the rocker arm and shaft assembly from the engine.

(6) Take out the push rods and place them in a rack so that they are kept in their original position for reassembly.

Installation is a reversal of the removal procedure with attention to the following points:

(1) Check that the ends of the valve stems are flat and true. Valves with stem ends that are worn excessively should be renewed.

(2) Tighten the rocker pedestal securing bolts evenly and progressively to the specified torque.

(3) Check and adjust rocker arm to valve stem clearance.

(4) Use a new rocker cover gasket on installation.

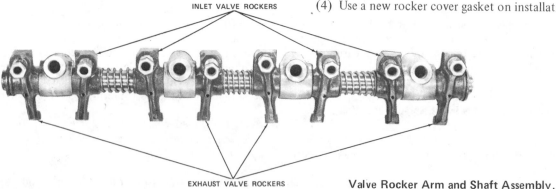

INLET VALVE ROCKERS

EXHAUST VALVE ROCKERS   **Valve Rocker Arm and Shaft Assembly.**

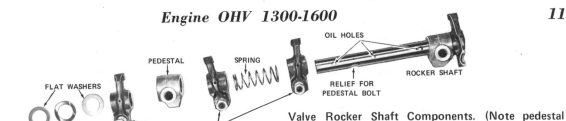

Valve Rocker Shaft Components. (Note pedestal bolt holes on same side as rocker arm adjusting nuts and rocker arm pads inclined towards pedestals.)

TO DISMANTLE AND ASSEMBLE

(1) Remove the rocker arm and shaft assembly as previously described.

(2) Take out the split pin from one end of the rocker shaft, withdraw the flat washer, followed by the waved washer and second flat washer. Note that the second flat washer is positioned adjacent to the end of the rocker arm.

(3) Slide off each rocker arm, pedestal and spring and the flat and waved washers adjacent to the split pin on the opposite end of the shaft.

Keep each component in its respective dismantling order so that it can be assembled in exactly the same location on the shaft from which it was removed.

Assembly procedure is a reversal of the dismantling operation with particular attention to the following points:

(1) Check the valve stem contact faces on the rocker arm pads for wear and renew the rocker arms as necessary.

(2) Check and renew the rocker arms and shaft if wear is excessive in the rocker arm bores or on the rocker shaft.

(3) Check that the lubrication holes in the shaft are free from any carbon or sludge.

(4) Position the rocker arms and pedestals on the shaft so that the bolt holes in the pedestals are on the same side

as the rocker arm adjusting screws.

(5) It should be noted that each rocker arm is offset, and upon assembly both rockers, either side of the pedestal should have its pad end offset towards the pedestal concerned.

4. CYLINDER HEAD

TO REMOVE AND INSTAL

(1) Raise the engine bonnet and fit fender covers to both front fenders.

(2) Drain the cooling system at the taps on the lower radiator tank and the left hand side of the cylinder block.

(3) Remove the carburettor air cleaner.

(4) Remove the top radiator hose.

(5) Detach the vacuum hose and heater hoses from the inlet manifold. Where fitted detach the automatic choke hoses.

(6) Undo the nuts and disconnect the exhaust pipe from the exhaust manifold.

(7) Disconnect the crankcase ventilation hose from the inlet manifold.

(8) Disconnect the temperature gauge wire at the sender unit on the cylinder head, unscrew and remove the unit to avoid damage when the cylinder head is removed.

(9) Disconnect the fuel line and the vacuum advance line at the carburettor.

(10) Detach the accelerator inner and outer cable from the throttle shaft and bracket and disconnect the throttle shaft from the carburettor.

(11) Disconnect the choke control from the carburettor and the downshift cable on automatic transmission models.

View of Cylinder Head with Valves Installed.

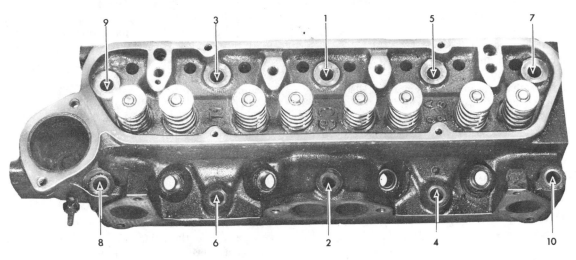

Sequence for Tightening Cylinder Head Bolts.

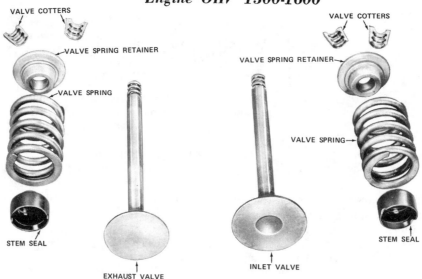

Valve and Spring Components.

(12) Disconnect the high tension leads from the spark plugs and centre terminal on the ignition coil, release the retaining clips and remove the distributor cap and leads.

(13) Remove the spark plugs from the cylinder head and unclip the carburettor ventilation pipe from the rocker cover where fitted.

(14) Take out the securing screws and remove the rocker cover and gasket from the cylinder head. Discard the gasket.

(15) Release the rocker pedestal securing bolts evenly and progressively until the rocker assembly can be removed from the cylinder head.

(16) Withdraw the push rods from the engine assembly and place them aside so that they may be re-installed in the exact positions from which they were removed.

(17) Release the cylinder head securing bolts evenly and progressively in the reverse order of tightening and lift the cylinder head from the cylinder block.

(18) Remove and discard the cylinder head gasket.

Installation is a reversal of the removal procedure with attention to the following points:

(1) Use new gaskets throughout when assembling.

(2) Use guide studs screwed into diagonal holes at opposite ends of the block face to position both the cylinder head and gasket.

(3) Instal and tighten the cylinder head bolts evenly and progressively in the order shown to the specified torque, see Specifications.

(4) Ensure that the push rods are installed in the position from which they were removed.

(5) Check and adjust the rocker arm to valve stem clearance and recheck after the engine has attained its operating temperature.

(6) Check and adjust the carburettor idling mixture and engine idling speed as necessary.

(7) Check for engine oil or water leaks.

TO DISMANTLE

(1) Remove the cylinder head from the engine as previously described.

(2) Remove the exhaust manifold retaining nuts and

set bolts and lift the manifold from the cylinder head. Discard the gasket.

(3) Remove the inlet manifold retaining nuts and set bolts and lift the manifold from the cylinder head. Discard the gasket.

(4) Using a suitable valve spring compressor, compress each valve spring in turn to remove the valve retaining cotters and remove the compressor.

(5) Lift off the valve spring retainers and springs and remove the valve stem oil seal from each valve. Discard the oil seals.

(6) Remove any burrs on the valve stem cotter grooves to prevent damage to the valve guides when the valves are removed.

(7) Remove the valves from the cylinder head and place them with their springs, retainers and cotters in a rack so that they can be installed in their original positions when assembling the cylinder head.

TO CLEAN AND INSPECT

(1) Remove all traces of carbon from the combustion chambers and exhaust ports. Clean the manifold mating surfaces of the cylinder head.

(2) Remove the deposits from the water passages.

(3) Insert a valve into its mating guide in the cylinder head and check for wear between the valve stem and the guide by moving the valve sideways. Check the wear in different positions by lifting the valve to assimilate an opening valve position.

(4) When a point of maximum movement (wear) is observed support the valve in this position.

(5) Mount a dial gauge onto the cylinder head with the pointer bearing on the side of the valve head.

(6) Hold the valve against one side of the guide, zero the dial scale and move the valve to the other side of the guide. Note the scale reading and compare the reading (wear) to Specifications.

(7) If the wear is in excess of that specified insert a new valve into the guide and recheck the reading, if it is now within specification instal the new valve.

(8) If the wear exceeds specifications the valve guide

will have to be reamed to the next oversize and the next oversize valve fitted.

(9) Repeat the wear checking procedure on the remaining valves.

(10) Inspect the valve seats for damage and wear. If necessary the seats should be recut to the specified angle and width, see Specifications.

If the valve seats are worn to the extent that they are not serviceable new valve seat inserts may be installed by an automotive engine reconditioning shop.

(11) Inspect the valve faces for damage or wear. Reface the exhaust valve faces as necessary after cleaning off all carbon deposits.

(12) Lap the exhaust valves into the cylinder head seats with a suitable lapping compound.

IMPORTANT: The aluminium coated inlet valves must not be refaced or lapped on to the valve seat. When this type of valve becomes pitted or worn it must be discarded and a new valve fitted. Exhaust valves may be refaced on a valve refacing machine and lapped to the seat.

(13) Ensure that the lapped mark on the valve face is in the centre of the face. If necessary, recut crown and throat the exhaust valve seat in the cylinder head to centralise the lap marking on the valve face.

NOTE: If the seat is recut after lapping, lightly reface the valve face before relapping to check the seat to face position.

(14) When the exhaust valves have been correctly seated sparingly smear the seat face with 'Prussian Blue' (or similar) and insert each valve into the cylinder head evenly. Do not rotate the valve. Withdraw the valve and check the marking on the valve face. The marking must be true and concentric.

(15) With the valves correctly positioned in their seats remove all traces of 'Prussian Blue' (or similar) and insert the valves into the cylinder head lubricating the stems and faces with engine oil.

(16) Measure the free length of the valve springs and check the tension of the valve springs as follows.

Place the two springs end to end, with a thin plate between them instal the assembly between the jaws of a vice. When the vice is closed approximately 12.7 mm the original spring should be within five per cent of the length of the new spring when measured from the plate to the vice jaw. Check the remaining springs and renew as necessary.

TO ASSEMBLE

Assembly is a reversal of the dismantling procedure with attention to the following points:

(1) Lubricate the valve stems with oil before assembling.

(2) The shroud type valve stem seals should be installed just below the spring retainers and with the open end of the seals facing the cylinder head.

(3) Use care when compressing the valve springs to avoid damage to the seals.

(4) Ensure that the valve retaining cotters are fully seating in the valve stem grooves as the spring compressor is released.

TO ADJUST VALVE CLEARANCE

(1) If the valve and rocker mechanism has been removed or dismantled, assemble and adjust the valve stem to rocker arm clearance with the engine cold and recheck after completing the assembling with the engine at operating temperature.

NOTE: It is important that the valve being adjusted is in the fully closed position. Rotate the engine by hand observing each pair of opening valves as follows:

Turn the engine in the direction of rotation until the 6 deg ignition timing marks are aligned, check that both valves of No. 4 cylinder are at the rock position by moving the crankshaft pulley back and forth a small amount. Should the valves not be at the rock position turn the engine one complete turn and recheck No. 4 cylinder valves for rock.

With the valves of No. 4 cylinder at the rock position adjust both valves of No. 1 cylinder.

Adjust the valves of No. 2 cylinder with No. 3 valves rocking.

Adjust the valves of No. 4 cylinder with No. 1 valves rocking.

Adjust the valves of No. 3 cylinder with No. 2 valves rocking.

NOTE: Adjust the valve clearances in the sequence of the firing order of the engine using the timing mark and rotor position to determine the firing point of each cylinder.

Provision for adjusting the clearance is made in the rocker arm by an adjustable self locking screw.

(2) If the valve clearance is to be adjusted with the engine hot, ensure that the engine is in fact at normal operating temperature, if necessary run the engine at a fast idle to obtain the correct temperature.

(3) Remove the air cleaner and rocker cover.

(4) Carry out the adjustment procedure in the order already described.

(5) Instal the rocker cover using a new gasket and instal the air cleaner. Check for oil leaks around the rocker cover gasket after running the engine.

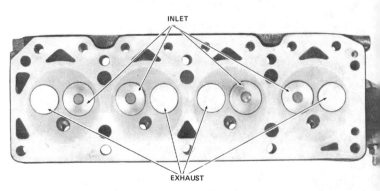

Cylinder Head Facing Showing Valve Arrangement and Water Circulation Holes. Typical.

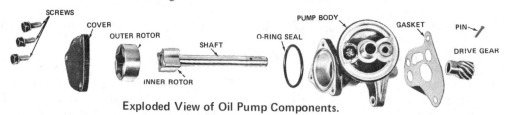

Exploded View of Oil Pump Components.

5. ENGINE SUMP

TO REMOVE AND INSTAL

(1) Remove the engine from the vehicle as previously described.

(2) With the engine mounted on a suitable workstand or work bench clean around the joining surfaces of the sump to cylinder block.

(3) Remove the sump retaining bolts and lift the sump off the cylinder block.

(4) Thoroughly clean all traces of the old gasket from the cylinder block ensuring that no pieces fall into the engine.

(5) Thoroughly clean the sump removing all traces of the old gasket, sludge and impurities.

(6) Place the two pieces of gasket onto the sump and check that the holes are correctly aligned. As necessary soak the gaskets in warm water to expand them or place them under a strong hot light to shrink them.

(7) Coat the gasket seating surfaces of the cylinder block with a suitable type sealant.

(8) Place the two curved seals in position on the front and rear of the engine.

(9) Place the two sections of gasket onto the engine block sliding the ends of the gasket under the ends of the curved seals.

(10) Using a suitable type sealant coat the gasket mating surfaces of the sump.

(11) Position the sump over the gaskets, aligning the bolt holes as the sump is lowered into position on the engine.

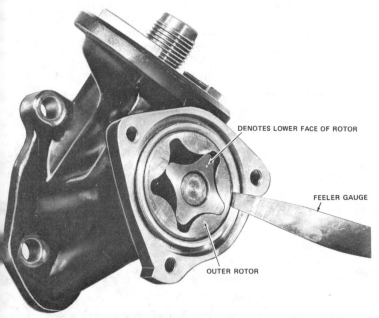

Measuring Clearance Between Outer Rotor and Pump Body.

(12) Instal all bolts finger tight.

(13) Torque the bolts to specifications in several stages working in a diagonal sequence starting at the centre bolts.

(14) Instal the engine as previously described.

6. OIL PUMP

TO REMOVE AND INSTAL

(1) Place a tray directly under the oil pump to catch oil leakage when the pump is removed.

(2) Take out the three retaining bolts and washers and withdraw the oil pump and filter assembly from the crankcase.

(3) Remove and discard the gasket installed between the pump body and engine.

Installation is a reversal of the removal procedure with attention to the following points:

(1) Use a new gasket on installation.

(2) Check the engine oil level after the engine has run for a few minutes and add as necessary.

TO DISMANTLE

(1) Remove the bolt and special washer securing the filter container to the body assembly and lift off the container and filter element assembly. Discard the element.

(2) Lift out the ring, sealing the open end of the filter container to the body assembly and discard the ring.

NOTE: Where a disposal type oil filter is fitted unscrew the filter from the pump body and discard the filter and sealing ring.

(3) Scribe a light mark across the flange of the pump body and end cover, take out the four retaining bolts and remove the pump end cover.

(4) Remove the O-ring seal from the groove in the pump body and discard the O-ring.

(5) Clean the lower face of the outer rotor and mark it so that it can be installed correctly on assembly.

(6) Normally the pump relief valve or the filter relief valve will not require removing unless either has been proved defective, when a new oil pump should be installed. Both these valves are a press fit in the pump and filter body assembly.

(7) If further dismantling is required, use a pin punch to drive the retaining pin out of the skew gear and shaft, press the skew gear off the shaft and withdraw the inner rotor and shaft assembly from the pump body. Do not remove the inner rotor from the pump shaft.

TO CHECK AND INSPECT

(1) Check the clearance between the outer rotor and the housing. Maximum clearance should not exceed specifications.

(2) Check the clearance between the tips of the inner rotor and the shoulders of the outer rotor. See Specifications for maximum clearance.

NOTE: Both rotors in the oil pump are supplied as a matched pair. If rotor tip clearance is found to be excessive both rotors will have to be renewed.

(3) Instal both rotors in the pump housing and place a straight edge across the end face of the pump housing, using a feeler gauge measure the clearance between the end of both rotors and the straight edge. See Specifications for maximum clearance.

(4) Check the pump end cover for wear or scoring.

(5) Check the pump shaft for wear in the housing and renew as required.

(6) Check the skew gear teeth for wear or damage and renew the gear if necessary.

(7) Check the pressure relief valve and the filter relief

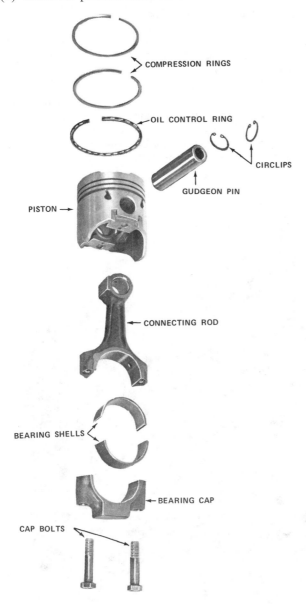

Exploded View of Piston and Connecting Rod.

valve assemblies for a weak or broken spring, if oil pressure is not satisfactory.

Renew any assembly that is found to be defective.

TO ASSEMBLE

(1) Having cleaned all components and effected replacements as necessary, lightly oil the components with engine oil and insert the inner rotor and shaft in the pump housing. Press on the skew gear and secure with a new retaining pin by peening each end of the pin.

NOTE: When pressing on the skew gear, support the assembly on the opposite end of the pump shaft to avoid damaging the inner rotor retaining pin.

(2) Position the outer rotor to mesh with the inner rotor and instal it in the pump body according to the mark made on dismantling.

NOTE: Ensure that the chamfered face of the rotor is to the inner end of the pump body.

(3) Place a new rubber O-ring in the groove in the end of the pump body and position the cover plate according to the scribe mark made on dismantling.

(4) Instal the four cover plate retaining bolts and tighten securely.

(5) When an element type filter is used place a new oil filter O-ring seal in the groove in the pump body assembly and press it in evenly at alternate points to fully seat it in the groove. Do not stretch the O-ring as it may cause an oil leak.

Place a new oil filter element in the filter container so that it is located on the spring loaded seat, position the filter and element on the pump body and tighten the securing bolt.

(6) When a disposal type filter is used lightly grease the sealing ring and screw the filter onto the pump body, only use hand pressure to tighten the filter.

7. PISTONS AND CONNECTING RODS

TO REMOVE AND DISMANTLE

(1) With the engine removed from the vehicle remove the cylinder head and sump as previously described.

(2) Rotate the crankshaft until number one piston is on the bottom of its stroke.

(3) Using a suitable ridge removing tool remove the ridge from the top of the cylinder where necessary. Raise the piston to tdc and wipe the top of the piston clean.

(4) Remove the ridge from the remaining cylinders in turn where necessary, in the same manner.

(5) If the connecting rods and big end bearing caps are not numbered, then mark the caps in relation to the connecting rods. Also number the connecting rods and piston assemblies in relation to the cylinders in which they are installed.

(6) Rotate the crankshaft until the first connecting rod and piston to be removed is at the bdc position with the cap bolts accessible.

(7) Withdraw the big end bearing cap bolts and

withdraw the bearing cap and lower bearing shell from the connecting rod.

(8) Using a suitable piece of wood or a hammer handle and being careful not to damage the upper bearing shell in the connecting rod, push the connecting rod and piston assembly through the top of the cylinder bore and remove it from the engine.

(9) Check that the upper bearing shell has remained in the connecting rod, otherwise remove it from the crankpin and position it correctly in the connecting rod, align the marks and instal the cap, fit and tighten the bolts finger tight.

(10) Remove the remaining pistons and connecting rod assemblies in the same manner.

(11) Remove the piston rings over the top of the pistons and discard the rings.

(12) Using a piece of broken ring of an appropriate length clean the carbon deposit from the ring grooves. Avoid damaging the ring lands when scraping.

NOTE: An ideal method of removing carbon deposit from pistons is to immerse the piston in a tank of chemical cleaner. After soaking, the carbon can be hosed off with water.

This method minimises the chances of damage through scraping, particularly with aluminium alloy pistons.

(13) Thoroughly clean the top of the piston, wash the assembly and blow it dry with compressed air.

(14) Remove the gudgeon pin retaining circlips from the piston bosses, push out the gudgeon pin and remove the piston from the connecting rod.

NOTE: As the gudgeon pin is offset towards the thrust side of the engine, the arrow cast in the piston crown must point to the front of the engine, when the piston is correctly installed. The word FRONT on the connecting rod must face towards the front of the engine.

(15) Refer to the following section — PISTONS AND CYLINDER BORES, and proceed as necessary before attempting to assemble and instal the piston and connecting rod assemblies.

TO FIT NEW PISTON RINGS

(1) Place each piston ring in the relatively unworn portion of the cylinder bore to which it is to be fitted and align it squarely with the cylinder wall. This can be done by inserting an inverted piston from above and pushing the ring down the bore to its required position.

(2) Withdraw the piston and measure the gap in the ring with a feeler gauge. If necessary, adjust the gap by filing to the dimension given in the Specifications.

Treat each ring and cylinder bore individually and ensure that rings are assembled to the respective piston for the cylinder bore in which they were fitted for end gap check.

(3) Check the piston ring to groove clearance and, using a suitable ring expanding tool, fit the rings to the pistons.

NOTE: The compression rings are marked TOP to facilitate correct installation.

(4) Apply a liberal coat of engine oil to the piston assembly, space the ring gaps 120 deg apart with the top ring gap away from the exhaust valve position.

(5) Use a ring compressor to compress the rings and instal each piston assembly in its respective cylinder bore.

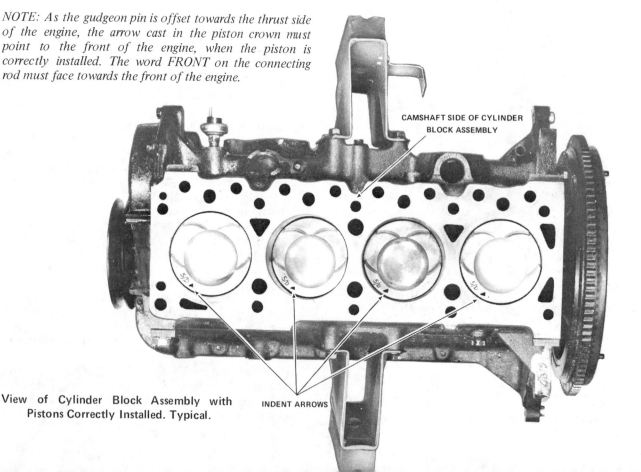

CAMSHAFT SIDE OF CYLINDER BLOCK ASSEMBLY

INDENT ARROWS

View of Cylinder Block Assembly with Pistons Correctly Installed. Typical.

TO ASSEMBLE AND INSTAL

(1) Assemble the piston to the connecting rod so that the word FRONT on the connecting rod is on the same side of the assembly as the arrow on the piston crown.

(2) With the gudgeon pin lightly coated with engine oil, heat the piston in hot water or oil and slide the gudgeon pin into position through the piston bosses and the connecting rod small end.

(3) Instal a new circlip in each piston boss and ensure that it is correctly seated in its groove.

(4) If new piston rings are being installed, check the clearance of each ring in its groove and, using a ring expanding tool, instal the rings on the piston.

NOTE: Ensure that the rings being installed on each piston have been fitted in the cylinder for that particular piston and the ring gap correctly adjusted.

(5) Position the ring gap 120 deg apart, with the gap in the top compression ring away from the exhaust valve position.

(6) Liberally coat the piston assembly with engine oil and insert it into its correct cylinder bore, allowing the oil control ring to contact the top of the cylinder block.

NOTE: Ensure that the arrow on the piston crown points to the front of the engine.

(7) Using a ring compressor to compress the rings, press the piston assembly down into the cylinder bore.

(8) Apply oil to the crankpin and bearing upper shell in the connecting rod and with a piece of wood or hammer handle tap the piston down the bore until the connecting rod and upper bearing shell seat correctly on the crankpin.

(9) Instal the big end bearing cap and lower half bearing so that the dowels in the connecting rod register with the dowel holes in the cap.

(10) Instal the big end cap retaining bolts and tighten the bolts to the specified torque, see Specifications.

(11) Rotate the crankshaft after each piston and connecting rod assembly has been installed to check for freeness.

NOTE: When fitting new big end bearing shells, ensure that the small tang on each bearing fits into the machined groove in the connecting rod or cap.

Bearings must not be adjusted by filing or scraping.

See Specifications for undersizes, which are available for standard crankshafts and for reground crankshafts.

(12) Instal the cylinder head and sump as described earlier.

(13) Instal the engine to the vehicle as previously described.

8. PISTONS AND CYLINDER BORES

TO CHECK CYLINDER BORES

Check each cylinder bore for wear, including taper and ovality and the cylinder walls for scuffing or scoring.

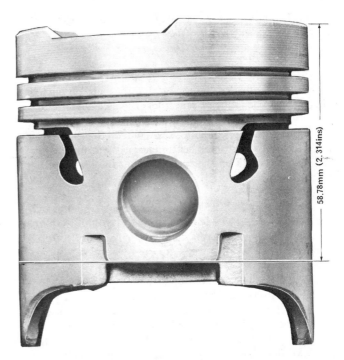

Piston Grade Point. (Calculated by measuring the piston skirt at right angles to the gudgeon pin. 58.78 mm down from the piston crown.)

Cylinders with any of the above characteristics should be honed or rebored and oversize pistons and rings fitted.

NOTE: After honing check the fit of old pistons in the cylinder bores and renew as necessary.

TO MEASURE AND FIT PISTONS

In production, standard pistons are graded into eight grades and are fitted selectively. See Specifications. The piston grade number is stamped on the piston crown and on the block face, adjacent to the cylinder bore concerned.

Oversize pistons are also available for reboring. See Specifications.

When measuring or checking pistons for fit in the cylinder bores, ensure that all measurements are taken at right angles to the gudgeon pin axis and 59 mm from the piston crown. This is important, as the pistons are cam ground and slightly tapered towards the top of the skirt.

Pistons should be fitted to individual bores by measurement and then checked with a feeler strip and a spring pull scale to measure the fit of the piston in the bore.

Use the following procedure when checking piston fit in the cylinder bore.

(1) Select a feeler strip the correct thickness and width and long enough to extend the full length of the piston and to the top of the cylinder bore when the piston is fully inserted in the bore.

(2) Position the feeler strip for its full length in the cylinder bore, insert the piston into the top of the bore so that the feeler strip is located lengthwise between the cylinder wall and the piston skirt at 90 deg to the gudgeon pin axis in the piston and on the thrust side of the cylinder bore.

NOTE: The piston must be installed into the bore with its crown facing downwards when piston measurements are being taken.

(3) With the piston positioned approximately 38.0 mm below the top of the cylinder bore and the gudgeon pin axis parallel to the lengthwise centre line of the cylinder block, attach a spring scale to the top end of the feeler strip.

(4) Hold the piston and slowly pull on the spring scale in a plane parallel to the centre line of the cylinder bore, noting the reading on the spring scale as the feeler strip is withdrawn.

NOTE: A pull of 3.2 – 5.0 kg is desired on a 12.7 mm wide and 0.0508 mm thick feeler strip to ensure that the working clearance between the cylinder bore and piston is correct.

(5) If the pull required to withdraw the feeler strip is within the limits specified, then the clearance of the piston in the cylinder is correct. If not, check the original measurements of the piston and bore, check the piston skirt for high spots, and if necessary, select another piston from the next higher or lower grade range, whichever is the case.

(6) Follow the same procedure to fit the other pistons to their respective cylinder bores.

9. CRANKSHAFT AND BEARINGS

TO REMOVE

(1) Remove the engine from the vehicle as previously described.

(2) Position the engine on an engine stand or suitable work bench.

(3) Detach the fan belt and remove the fan from the water pump.

(4) Remove the sump and the oil suction pipe and strainer.

(5) Remove the crankshaft pulley retaining bolt and washer and withdraw the pulley from the crankshaft.

(6) Take out the retaining bolts and remove the timing cover and gasket from the front of the engine.

(7) Detach the oil slinger from the front end of the crankshaft.

(8) Undo the two retaining bolts and remove the timing chain tensioner bracket. Remove the tensioner arm assembly from the pivot pin.

(9) Release the lock plate and remove the camshaft sprocket retaining bolts.

(10) Ease the camshaft sprocket off the camshaft flange, disengage the chain from the crankshaft sprocket and remove the camshaft sprocket and chain from the engine.

NOTE: There is a dowel in the camshaft flange to ensure that the timing sprocket is installed correctly in relation to the timing mark position.

(11) Remove the big end bolts and withdraw the big end caps with half of the bearing shells. Note the locating dowel on the connecting rod face and the numbers on the rod and cap. The connecting rods are marked FRONT for correct installation.

(12) Carefully push each connecting rod and piston up the cylinder bore as far as possible without exceeding the upper limits of the piston stroke.

(13) Check the crankshaft end float, either with a feeler gauge at the centre main bearing or by attaching a dial indicator gauge to the front face of the cylinder block so that its plunger bears on the front face of the crankshaft sprocket, or on the end of the crankshaft.

(14) Prise the crankshaft rearwards, and zero the gauge.

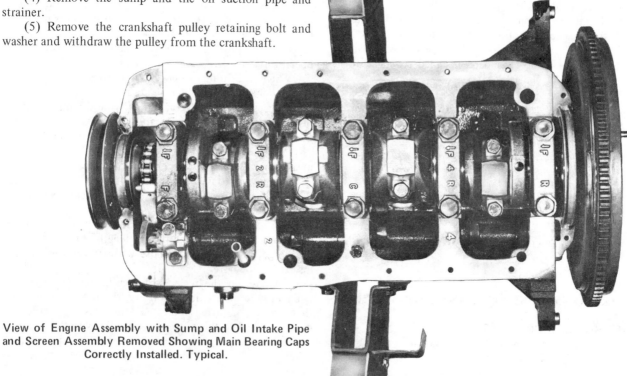

View of Engine Assembly with Sump and Oil Intake Pipe and Screen Assembly Removed Showing Main Bearing Caps Correctly Installed. Typical.

Checking Crankshaft End-Float with Feeler Gauge at the Thrust Washer.

(15) Next, prise the crankshaft forward as far as it will go and check the reading on the dial gauge. If the main bearing thrust washers are serviceable, the gauge reading will be within the limits specified.

(16) Remove the clutch pressure plate assembly and the clutch driven plate.

(17) Bend back the lock tabs, unscrew the flywheel retaining bolts and withdraw the flywheel from the rear of the crankshaft. (On automatic transmission remove the torque converter drive plate with spacer and reinforcing plate.)

(18) Check that the main bearing caps are marked in relation to their location in the engine and note that the caps are marked with an arrow, which must point to the front of the engine when correctly installed.

(19) Unscrew each main bearing cap bolt and withdraw each cap and bearing half shell. Note the end thrust half-washers on the centre main bearing cap and keep each cap and half shell so that they can be installed in their original positions.

(20) Remove the rear crankshaft oil seal carrier retaining bolts and separate the carrier from the crankcase.

NOTE: *Before removing the crankshaft, bearing clearance may be determined by using the Plastigage method as follows:*

(a) Remove one bearing cap and with a piece of fluffless rag wipe the journal and bearing clean.

(b) Position a piece of Plastigage, the approximate length of the bearing width, and slightly off centre on to the bearing surface of the crankshaft journal.

(c) Instal the bearing cap and tighten the cap bolts to the specified torque.

(d) Remove the cap bolts and carefully detach the cap and lower half bearing.

(e) With the Plastigage scale measure the compressed Plastigage strip to determine the oil clearance.

Cylinder Block and Crankshaft with Centre Main Bearing Cap Removed Showing End-Float Thrust Washer. (Grooves in Thrust Washers Must Face Crankshaft Web.)

(f) The widest point of the strip will indicate the minimum clearance and the narrowest point the maximum clearance.

(g) The remaining bearings can be checked in turn using the same procedure.

IMPORTANT: *Do not revolve the crankshaft while the Plastigage is in position.*

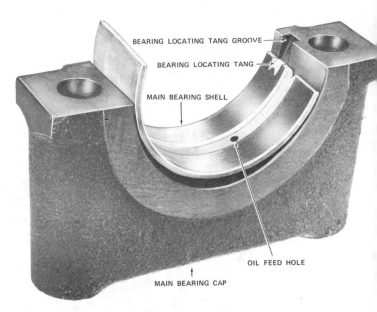

Main Bearing Cap and Bearing Shell Showing Locating Tang and Groove.

(21) Carefully lift the crankshaft from the crankcase using care not to dislodge or damage the upper halves of the main bearing shells if they are to be used again.

(22) If new bearing shells are to be installed, remove the upper halves of the bearings from the crankcase.

TO CHECK AND INSPECT

(1) Check and measure the main bearing journals and crankpins for wear, taper and scoring. If wear is excessive, the journals and crankpins should be reground to accommodate the nearest undersize bearing shells. One worn or damaged journal will necessitate the grinding of all journals and crankpins or the fitting of a new or reconditioned crankshaft and new shells.

(2) Check the thrust washers for pitting or wear. Oversize thrust washers are available for service but normally new standard thrust washers will bring crankshaft end float back to specifications.

(3) Always instal a new rear crankshaft oil seal, which is located in the seal carrier, the seal can be readily driven out and renewed.

(4) Check the timing cover seal and renew if necessary. Renew the timing cover gasket.

(5) Ensure that the oilway drillings to the main bearings in the crankcase and crankshaft are clean and free of carbon or sludge.

TO INSTAL

(1) Place the upper half of each main bearing in position in the crankcase so that the locating tang on the bearing engages the groove in the bearing housing and the oil feed holes in the bearing and bearing housing coincide.

(2) Ensure that the main bearing journals of the crankshaft are clean and lubricate them and the upper half of the bearings with clean engine oil.

(3) Carefully place the crankshaft into position in the

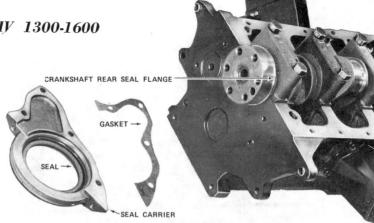

CRANKSHAFT REAR SEAL FLANGE

GASKET

SEAL

SEAL CARRIER

Cylinder Block and Crankshaft Assembly with Rear Crankshaft Seal Carrier and Gasket Removed.

crankcase and instal the end float thrust washer to each side of the centre main bearing web.

NOTE: The oil grooves in the side of each thrust washer must face towards the crankshaft web.

(4) Place the lower half of each bearing in its appropriate bearing cap so that the locating tang on the bearing engages with the groove in the bearing cap.

(5) Lubricate the bearing cap and shell assembly with clean engine oil, and position each cap assembly in its correct location according to the marks noted during removal and with the arrows on the caps pointing to the front of the engine.

(6) Instal the bearing retaining bolts and tighten progressively to the specified torque, occasionally rotating the crankshaft to ensure that it is not binding. Again check the crankshaft end-float as detailed earlier.

(7) Using a smear of sealer on the periphery of the new oil seal, press the seal into the carrier so that the lip face of the seal faces toward the rear main bearing. Ensure that the

BELOW:

Big End and Main Bearing Caps Correctly Installed to Engine. (The intermediate front and the intermediate rear main bearing caps are identical but should not be interchanged.)

TIMING MARKS

Timing Marks on Crankshaft and Camshaft Sprockets for Correct Valve Timing.

seal has been previously dipped in oil.

(8) Using a new gasket position the seal carrier over the crankshaft against the rear crankcase, align the bolt holes and secure the seal carrier to the crankcase.

(9) Instal the flywheel to the rear of the crankshaft making sure that it is seating squarely upon the crankshaft flange.

(10) Fit and tighten the flywheel securing bolts with new lock plates to the specified torque and lock by turning up the edge of the lock plates.

(On automatic transmission fit the torque converter drive plate with spacer and reinforcing plate and fit and tighten the retaining bolts to the specified torque.)

(11) Draw each connecting rod down into position on the crankpin and install the big end bearing with clean engine oil. Rotate the crankshaft to ensure that none of the bearings are binding.

(12) Temporarily fit the camshaft sprocket on to the camshaft flange and rotate both the camshaft and crankshaft until the timing marks on each sprocket are in line with each other and with the centre of each shaft. Note that the camshaft sprocket is correctly located by a dowel in the camshaft flange.

(13) Remove the camshaft sprocket, engage it in the timing chain, loop the chain around the crankshaft sprocket so that the timing chain marks will be in alignment and position the camshaft sprocket on the camshaft flange. Instal and tighten the sprocket retaining bolts using a new lock plate.

(14) Turn the crankshaft through two complete revolutions and again check that the timing marks on the sprockets are in alignment with each other and a line taken through the centre of both shafts. Turn up the lock plates to lock both bolts.

(15) Position the timing chain tensioner arm on the pivot pin located on the front main bearing cap and secure the tensioner cam and bracket assembly to the cylinder block with the two bolts and spring washers.

NOTE: Tension on the cam spring should be approximately 2.5 turns of the spring from the free position.

(16) Instal the oil slinger on the front end of the crankshaft with its convex side facing the timing sprocket.

(17) Carefully withdraw the old seal from the timing cover and instal a new seal so that the lip of the seal will face towards the oil slinger.

(18) Using a new cover gasket, position the timing cover over the timing chain and secure with the bolts and spring washers.

NOTE: Special aligning tools are available to centralise the timing cover and rear crankshaft oil seals. These tools should be used when installing the respective assemblies to the engine, to minimise the chance of oil leaking at these points.

(19) Lubricate the boss of the crankshaft pulley with

engine oil or light grease, instal the pulley on to the crankshaft and secure with the bolt and retaining washer.

(20) Further installation is a reversal of the removal procedure, but it will be necessary to align the clutch plate with the spiggot bearings on manual transmission models using a spare input shaft.

10. TIMING CHAIN, TENSIONER AND SPROCKETS

TO REMOVE

(1) With the engine removed from the vehicle, remove the sump as described earlier.

(2) Remove the securing bolt and washer and withdraw the crankshaft pulley from the front end of the crankshaft.

(3) Take out the retaining bolts and remove the timing cover and gasket from the front of the engine.

(4) Remove the oil slinger from the front end of the crankshaft.

(5) Undo and remove the two retaining bolts and remove the timing chain tensioner and bracket assembly.

(6) Withdraw the tensioner arm from the pivot pin on the front main bearing cap.

(7) Release the lock plate and remove the two bolts securing the camshaft sprocket to the camshaft flange.

(8) Ease the camshaft sprocket off the camshaft flange, disengage the chain from the crankshaft sprocket and remove the camshaft sprocket and chain from the engine.

NOTE: The dowel in the camshaft flange ensures that the sprocket cannot be installed incorrectly.

(9) Using a suitable puller, withdraw the crankshaft sprocket from the end of the crankshaft.

NOTE: The crankshaft sprocket has an identification groove on the forward end of the sprocket boss.

(10) Check that the timing chain lubrication hole in the front face of the cylinder block is clear.

TO INSTAL

(1) Using a suitable tubular drift, drive the crankshaft sprocket on the end of the crankshaft to abut the shoulder of the front main bearing journal. Note that the identification mark on the sprocket boss and the valve timing mark on sprocket must face forward.

(2) Temporarily instal the camshaft sprocket on the camshaft flange and tighten the securing bolts.

(3) Check the alignment of the two sprockets by placing a straight edge across the forward edge of the sprocket teeth. If necessary, instal shim washers between the crankshaft sprocket and the abutment face on the crankshaft to correct any misalignment between the sprockets.

(4) Rotate the crankshaft and camshaft until the timing marks on the sprockets are in line with each other and with the centre of each shaft. Note that the camshaft sprocket is correctly located by a dowel in the camshaft flange.

(5) Remove the camshaft sprocket, engage it in the timing chain, loop the chain around the crankshaft sprocket so that the timing marks will remain in alignment and

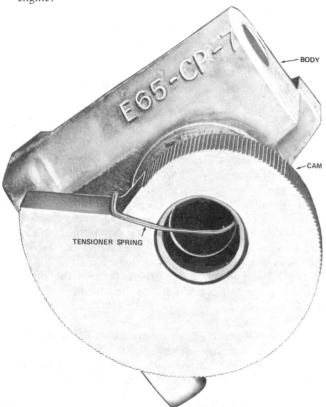

Timing Chain Tensioner Cam Assembly.

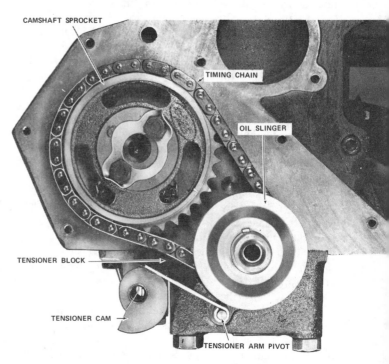

Timing Chain and Tensioner Assembly.

position the camshaft sprocket on the camshaft flange. Using a new lock plate, instal and tighten the sprocket retaining bolts.

(6) Turn the crankshaft through two complete revolutions and again check that the timing marks on the sprockets are in alignment with each other and a line taken through the centre of both shafts. Turn up the lock plate to lock the camshaft bolts.

(7) Position the timing chain tensioner arm on the pivot located on the front main bearing cap and secure the tensioner cam and bracket assembly to the cylinder block with the two bolts and spring washers.

NOTE: Tension on the cam spring should be approximately 2.5 turns of the spring from the free position.

(8) Instal the oil slinger on the front end of the crankshaft with its convex side facing the crankshaft sprocket.

(9) Carefully withdraw the old oil seal from the timing cover and install a new seal so that the lip of the seal will face the inside of the timing cover.

(10) Using a new cover gasket, position the timing cover and seal aligning tool on the front of the engine and secure with the bolts and spring washers. Remove the seal aligning tool.

(11) Lubricate the boss of the crankshaft pulley with engine oil, install the pulley on the crankshaft and secure with bolt and retaining washer.

(12) Further installation is a reversal of the removal procedure.

11. CAMSHAFT AND TAPPETS

TO REMOVE

(1) With the engine removed from the vehicle, remove the rocker assembly and push rods as described earlier, keeping the push rods in order so that they can be installed in their original positions on assembly.

(2) Scribe a mark on the distributor clamp plate and a corresponding mark on the crankcase to facilitate assembly. Remove the adjustment bolt securing the clamp plate to the crankcase and withdraw the distributor from the engine. Do not remove the clamp plate screw and nut.

(3) Remove the two securing bolts and withdraw the fuel pump and gasket from the engine.

(4) Undo and remove the three securing screws and withdraw the oil pump and filter assembly from the right hand side of the engine.

(5) Turn the engine upside down and remove the sump.

(6) Remove the crankshaft pulley, timing cover, chain tensioner and camshaft sprocket and chain from the front of the engine.

(7) Measure the camshaft end-float, using a feeler gauge between the thrust plate and the rear face of the camshaft flange. As an alternative, use a dial indicator mounted on the front face of the engine with the gauge plunger bearing on the front face of the camshaft flange. When using this method, push the camshaft as far as it will go towards the rear of the engine and zero the dial gauge.

Checking Camshaft End-Float.

Then gently prise the rear face of the camshaft flange to bring the camshaft forward against the rear face of the thrust plate and check and record the gauge reading.

(8) Release the lock plate tabs and undo and remove the two bolts securing the thrust plate to the cylinder block and withdraw the thrust plate.

(9) With the engine still turned upside down, push each tappet down as far as it will go.

(10) Carefully withdraw the camshaft out through the front and remove it from the engine.

NOTE: Use care when removing the camshaft to avoid damaging the camshaft bearings with the sharp edge of the cams.

(11) Remove the tappets from the crankcase, keeping them in their correct order so that they can be installed in their original bores.

(12) If it is necessary to remove the camshaft bearings for renewal, remove the rear main bearing oil seal retaining cover from the rear of the cylinder block and using special tool and adaptors available for this purpose withdraw each camshaft bearing bush from the crankcase.

NOTE: The camshaft bearing bushes are pre-sized and new bushes do not require line boring after they are fitted. Ensure that the oil holes in the bushes and cylinder block are aligned and instal the bushes with the split to the top of the cylinder block but inclined outwards 45 deg from the vertical.

TO CHECK AND TEST

(1) Check the camshaft bearing bushes and journals for wear or scoring. If the journals are excessively worn or scored, the camshaft should be renewed and new bearings

Camshaft Identification for OHV Engines. 1300 Plain, 1600 as Shown, 1600 GT 116E.

installed. Check the oil ways in the crankcase for freedom from dirt or sludge.

(2) Check the camshaft thrust plate for wear or scoring and renew the plate as required. See Specifications for standard thrust plate thickness.

(3) Check the fit of the tappets in the cylinder block bores. Clean the tappets and tappet bores thoroughly. They are a selective fit when new and should just fall in the bore when lubricated with light engine oil at room temperature.

TO INSTAL

(1) If the camshaft bearings have been removed for renewal, use special tool and adaptors to instal the new bushes and ensure that the oil holes in the bushes coincide with the holes in the cylinder block.

NOTE: The camshaft bearing bushes are pre-sized and do not require line boring or reaming after installation. Ensure that the oil holes in the bushes and cylinder block are aligned and instal the bushes with the split to the top of the cylinder block but inclined outwards 45 deg from the vertical.

(2) Lubricate the tappets and tappet bores with clean engine oil and insert each tappet in its bore from the crankcase side with the engine upside down.

NOTE: Ensure that each tappet is replaced in its original bore from which it was removed.

(3) Lubricate the camshaft journals, skew gear and fuel pump drive eccentric with clean engine oil and insert it in the bushes from the front, taking care not to damage the bushes with the sharp edges of the cams.

(4) Position the camshaft thrust plate between the camshaft flange and front bearing journal, and using a new lock plate, instal and tighten the two bolts and lock plate. Lock the bolts by turning up the ends of the lock plate. Rotate the camshaft to ensure that it turns freely and recheck the camshaft end-float.

(5) ·Using a new gasket lightly coated with suitable sealing compound, instal the crankshaft rear oil seal retainer and secure with bolts and spring washers.

NOTE: When installing the rear oil seal retainer and timing cover use the correct seal aligning tool, for both assemblies, to minimise the chance of oil leaking from these points.

(6) Temporarily instal the camshaft sprocket on the flange of the camshaft, rotate the crankshaft and camshaft until the timing marks on the sprockets are in line with each other and the centre of each shaft. Note that the camshaft sprocket is correctly located by a dowel in the camshaft flange.

(7) Remove the camshaft sprocket, engage it in the timing chain, loop the chain around the crankshaft sprocket so that the timing marks will remain in alignment and position the camshaft sprocket on the camshaft flange. Using a new lock plate, instal and tighten the sprocket retaining bolts.

(8) Turn the crankshaft through two complete revolutions and again check that the timing marks on the sprockets are in alignment with each other and a line taken through the centre of both shafts. Turn up the lock plate to lock the camshaft bolts.

(9) Instal the timing chain tensioner, timing cover and crankshaft pulley as described in TIMING CHAIN TENSIONER AND SPROCKETS – To Instal.

(10) Instal the sump as described in ENGINE SUMP – To Instal.

(11) Instal the distributor as described in DISTRIBUTOR – To Instal and Time Ignition.

(12) Instal the fuel pump and oil pump and filter assembly.

12. INLET AND EXHAUST MANIFOLDS

INLET MANIFOLD
To Remove and Instal

(1) Raise the bonnet and fit fender covers to both front fenders.

(2) Drain the cooling system from the drain plug on the lower radiator tank sufficiently to lower the water level below the inlet manifold.

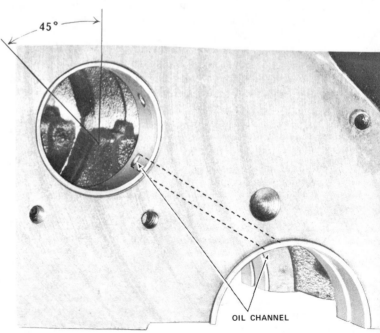

Camshaft Bearing Location. Note: Camshaft Bearing to be Installed with Split in Bearing 45 deg to the Vertical.

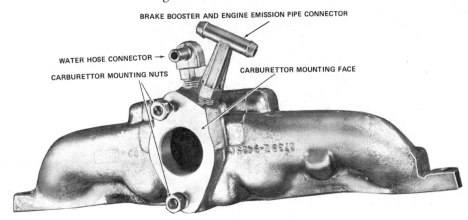

BRAKE BOOSTER AND ENGINE EMISSION PIPE CONNECTOR

WATER HOSE CONNECTOR →

CARBURETTOR MOUNTING NUTS

CARBURETTOR MOUNTING FACE

View of Inlet Manifold. Typical.

(3) Remove the carburettor air cleaner.

(4) Disconnect the water heater hose, the crankcase ventilation hose and the brake servo vacuum pipe (where fitted) at the inlet manifold.

(5) Detach the distributor high tension leads from the spark plugs and the coil tower.

(6) Unclip the distributor cap and remove the cap with HT leads from the engine.

(7) Disconnect the fuel feed pipe and vacuum advance pipe from the carburettor.

(8) Disconnect the choke control cable at the carburettor (not applicable when automatic choke is used).

(9) Detach the automatic choke hoses (where fitted).

(10) Unclip the throttle shaft from the carburettor throttle lever.

(11) Unscrew the carburettor to manifold securing nuts and remove the carburettor from the manifold.

(12) Remove the manifold to cylinder head retaining bolts and withdraw the inlet manifold and gasket from the cylinder head.

Installation is a reversal of the removal procedure with attention to the following points:

(1) Remove any carbon deposits from the manifold and cylinder head ports and passages. Do not use any tool that will score the inlet ports and passages.

(2) Ensure that the mounting faces of the cylinder head and manifold are clean of old gaskets and free of any burrs.

(3) Check the manifold mounting face with a steel straight edge for warpage. If warpage is excessive the manifold will have to be surface ground.

(4) Always instal new manifold and carburettor gaskets when assembling the manifold and carburettor to the engine.

EXHAUST MANIFOLD
To Remove and Instal

(1) Raise the engine bonnet and fit fender covers to both front fenders.

(2) Remove the exhaust pipe clamp bolts and detach the exhaust pipe clamp and pipe from the exhaust manifold.

(3) Unscrew the exhaust manifold to cylinder head retaining nuts and withdraw the manifold and gasket from the studs.

Installation is a reversal of the removal procedure with attention to the following points:

(1) Remove any carbon deposits from the manifold and cylinder head ports and passages.

(2) Check the exhaust manifold for excessive warpage, and if found necessary, rectify by surface grinding.

(3) Ensure that the mounting faces of the cylinder head and manifold are clean and free of any burrs.

(4) Always instal new manifold gaskets when assembling the manifold to the engine.

13. DISTRIBUTOR

TO REMOVE

(1) Disconnect the high tension leads from the spark plugs by pulling on the connectors of the leads.

(2) Disconnect the coil high tension lead, disconnect number one cylinder spark plug lead from the distributor cap for identification purposes.

(3) Rotate the engine by hand and align the timing mark on the pulley with the 6 deg. mark on the timing case.

(4) Lift the distributor cap up slightly and observe to which spark plug connection the rotor button points. If it does not point towards number one cylinder plug connection, then rotate the engine one complete turn and again align the timing marks on the pulley and timing case.

(5) Place the distributor cap aside and mark the centre-end of the rotor button and place a corresponding mark on the distributor body.

(6) Disconnect the low tension lead and the vacuum line from the distributor.

(7) Scribe a line across the distributor retaining clamp and the cylinder block to ensure correct assembly.

(8) Remove the bolt retaining the distributor and the clamp to the cylinder block and lift the distributor and clamp from the engine. Mark the rotor button position on the distributor body.

NOTE: Do not loosen or remove the bolt retaining the clamp to the distributor. If possible avoid turning the engine while the distributor assembly is removed.

TO INSTAL DISTRIBUTOR AND TIME IGNITION

(1) If the ignition timing has been upset by turning the engine with the distributor removed, remove number one

DEGREE GRADUATIONS

NOTCH IN PULLEY

Ignition Timing Marks. Degrees Shown are Before Top Dead Centre.

spark plug and rotate the crankshaft until number one piston is approaching top dead centre on the compression stroke, check that the timing notch on the crankshaft pulley is in line with the 6 deg. timing mark on the timing cover.

With the timing marks correctly positioned instal and tighten number one spark plug.

(2) Rotate the rotor until the mark on the centre-end of the rotor button is in line with the mark made after the distributor was removed.

(3) With the distributor held above its orifice in the cylinder block, rotate the distributor body slightly until the centre line of the vacuum advance unit faces towards the rear of the engine at an angle of 45 deg.

(4) Insert the distributor and align the scribed lines across the clamp and the cylinder block.

(5) As the distributor was installed the rotor button was turned clockwise by the camshaft gear, the rotor button and distributor body marks should now be aligned.

(6) If the rotor and body marks are not aligned, lift the distributor and rotate the rotor button in the required direction.

Instal the distributor again aligning the clamp plate marks and check that the rotor and distributor body marks are aligned.

NOTE: Should only a small adjustment be required to align the marks loosen the distributor body clamp bolt and turn the distributor body the required amount and tighten the clamp bolt.

(7) Instal the distributor clamp plate bolt finger tight and rotate the distributor body anti-clockwise until the contact breaker points are closed, then rotate the distributor body clockwise until the points are just commencing to open and tighten the clamp bolt securely.

(8) Connect the low tension lead to the distributor and the vacuum pipe to the advance unit on the distributor body.

(9) Instal the distributor cap and connect the high tension leads to the spark plugs, ignition coil, and distributor cap.

(10) The engine is now timed to enable it to be started and it is recommended that a suitable timing light be used to recheck the ignition timing at idling speed.

14. ENGINE VENTILATION SYSTEM

DESCRIPTION

With the engine running ventilating air is drawn through the engine by the reduced pressure in the inlet manifold. The volume of air drawn through the engine is dependent on engine loadings (reduced pressure in the manifold) and is controlled by the regulator valve.

Fresh air is drawn in through the oil filler cap into the crankcase then through the oil separator, regulator valve (mounted on the top of the oil separator), the connecting hose between the regulator valve and into the inlet manifold.

The crankcase fumes are drawn into the cylinders and mixed and burnt with the fuel air mixture.

TO CLEAN REGULATOR VALVE

(1) Raise the engine bonnet and fit a fender cover to the right front fender.

(2) Remove the air cleaner from the engine.

(3) Disconnect the manifold hose from the regulator valve.

VENTILATION VALVE →

GROMMET →

OIL SEPARATOR

Crankcase Ventilation System Components.

(4) Remove the regulator valve from the oil separator.

(5) Clean the regulator valve in a suitable cleaning solvent and then blow it dry with compressed air.

(6) Instal the regulator valve into the oil separator and reconnect the manifold hose.

(7) Install the air cleaner and remove the fender cover and close the bonnet.

15. ENGINE MOUNTINGS

TO REMOVE AND INSTAL
Front

(1) Raise the front of the vehicle and support on stands placed beneath the lower control arms as close as practicable to the road wheels.

(2) Interpose a block of wood between the engine sump and a jack. Position the jack so that it will raise the side of the engine from which the mounting is being removed.

(3) Take the weight of the engine slightly with the jack.

(4) Remove the engine mounting top and bottom retaining nuts and washers.

(5) Raise the jack sufficiently to enable the engine mounting to be withdrawn from the mounting brackets.

NOTE: If both engine mountings are to be renewed renew one side at a time to avoid the possibility of the engine tilting causing damage to other components.

Installation is a reversal of the removal procedure allowing the full weight of the engine to bear on the mounting before tightening the retaining nuts.

Rear

(1) Raise the rear of the vehicle and support it on stands placed beneath the rear axle housing as close as practicable to the road wheels.

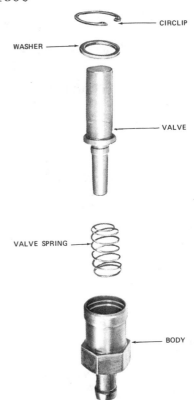

Exploded View of Crankcase Vent Valve.

(2) Interpose a block of wood between a jack and the transmission, take the weight of the engine and transmission on the jack.

(3) Remove the rear cross-member to side frame bolts.

(4) Remove the centre bolt and withdraw the cross-member from the vehicle.

(5) Remove the retaining bolts and lift the engine mounting from the cross-member.

Installation is a reversal of the removal procedure.

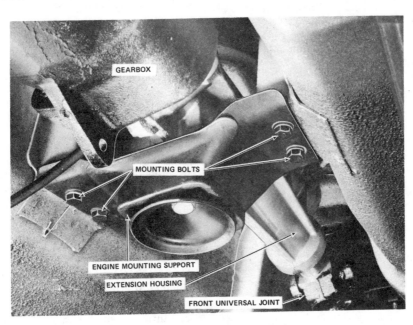

Rear Engine Mounting. Typical.

PART II OHC ENGINE

For 1600 OHC Specification Differences from the 2000 OHC Engine—please see page 234

ENGINE ASSEMBLY

Type	4 cyl in line – ohc
Firing order	1–3–4–2
Compression ratio	9.2:1
Bore	90.80 mm
Stroke	76.95 mm
Capacity	1,979 cc
Idle speed	680 – 720 rpm
Ignition timing –	
static	4 deg. btdc

CYLINDER HEAD

Material	Cast iron
Type	Cross flow
Valve seat angle	44 deg 30 min – 45 deg
Valve seat width	1.6 – 2.0 mm
Valve seat crowning angle	35 deg cutter
Valve seat throating angle	65 deg cutter
Valve guide inside diameter:	
Standard	8.063 – 8.088 mm
Oversize – 1st	0.20 mm
– 2nd	0.40 mm

VALVES

Head diameter:	
Inlet	41.8 – 42.2 mm
Exhaust	35.8 – 36.2 mm
Stem diameter:	
Inlet – standard	8.043 – 8.025 mm
– 1st oversize	0.20 mm
– 2nd oversize	0.40 mm
Exhaust – standard	8.017 – 7.999 mm
– 1st oversize	0.20 mm
– 2nd oversize ...	0.40 mm
Stem to guide clearance:	
Inlet	0.020 – 0.063 mm
Exhaust	0.086 – 0.089 mm
Length:	
Inlet	111.15 mm
Exhaust	110.5 – 111.5 mm
Refacing angle:	
Inlet	Not refaceable
Exhaust	45 deg
Valve timing:	
Inlet opens	18 deg btdc
Inlet closes	70 deg abdc
Exhaust opens	64 deg bbdc
Exhaust closes	24 deg atdc
Valve clearance:	
Inlet	0.20 mm
Exhaust	0.25 mm

VALVE SPRINGS

Free length	44.0 mm
Compressed length	24.0 mm
Assembled spring load:	
Open	77 – 83 kg
Closed	29 – 33 kg

CYLINDER BLOCK

Type	4 cyl in line
Material	Cast iron
Standard bore	90.830 – 90.840 mm
Cylinder rebore sizes:	
1st oversize	0.50 mm
2nd oversize	1.00 mm
Cylinder bore:	
Maximum ovality	0.1270 mm
Maximum taper	0.2032 mm

PISTONS

Material	Aluminium alloy
Standard grade	90.780 – 90.805 mm
Oversize Pistons:	
1st oversize	0.50 mm
2nd oversize	1.00 mm
Piston to bore clearance	0.025 – 0.060 mm

PISTON RINGS

Side clearance in grooves:	
Compression rings	0.041 – 0.091 mm
Oil control ring	0.046 – 0.097 mm
End gap:	
Compression rings	0.38 – 0.58 mm
Oil control ring	0.40 – 1.40 mm

GUDGEON PIN

Type	Selective fit
Length	72.0 – 72.8 mm
Securing	Interference fit in connecting rod
Serviced	With piston as a matched set

CRANKSHAFT AND BEARINGS

Material	Cast iron
Number of main bearings	5
End thrust taken at	Centre main bearing
End float	0.08 – 0.28 mm

Main bearing journal dia-
meter:

Standard — red	57.000 — 56.990 mm
— blue	56.990 — 56.980 mm

Regrind undersize:

1st	0.25 mm
2nd	0.50 mm
3rd	0.75 mm
4th	1.00 mm

Main bearing clear-ance	0.014 — 0.048 mm

Thrust washer thickness:

Standard	2.30 — 2.35 mm
Oversize	2.50 — 2.55 mm

Crankpin diameter:

Standard — red	52.000 — 51.990 mm
— blue	51.990 — 51.980mm

Regrind undersize:

1st	0.25 mm
2nd	0.50 mm
3rd	0.75 mm

Crankpin bearing clearance:

Standard	0.014 — 0.048 mm
Undersize	0.014 — 0.058 mm

CONNECTING ROD AND BEARINGS

Connecting rod type	Forged H section

Crankpin bearing bore

— red	55.00 — 55.01 mm
— blue	55.01 — 55.02 mm
Gudgeon pin bore	23.964 — 23.976 mm
Bearing type	Steel backed aluminium/ tin or lead/bronze in-serts

*Bearing inside diameter:

Standard — red	52.014 — 52.038 mm
— blue	52.004 — 52.028 mm

Regrind undersize:

1st	0.25 mm
2nd	0.50 mm
3rd	0.75 mm
4th	1.00 mm

Crankpin bearing clearance:

Standard	0.014 — 0.048 mm
Undersize	0.014 — 0.058 mm

NOTE: Bearing shells must be installed in the assembled connecting rod with the cap nuts torqued to specifications.

CAMSHAFT AND BEARINGS

Drive	Toothed belt
Toothed belt tension	30 — 37 kg

Thrust plate thickness:

Selective	3.98 or 4.01 mm
End float	0.05 — 0.09 mm

Journal diameter:

Front	42.01 — 41.99 mm
Centre	44.72 — 44.52 mm
Rear	45.01 — 44.99 mm

Bearing inside diameter:

Front	42.055 — 42.035 mm
Centre	44.675 — 44.655 mm
Rear	45.055 — 45.035 mm

LUBRICATION

Pump type	Eccentric rotor
Rotor to body clear-ance	0.15 — 0.30 mm
Rotor to rotor tip clear-ance	0.05 — 0.20 mm
Rotor to cover (end float)	0.03 — 0.10 mm

Minimum oil pressure:

At idle (700 rpm)	1.1 kg/cm^2
At 1500 rpm	2.5 kg/cm^2
Oil light illuminating pressure	0.4 kg/cm^2
Relief valve opens at	4.0 — 4.7 kg/cm^2

Oil change — capacity:

With filter	3.5 litres
Without filter	3.0 litres

TORQUE WRENCH SETTINGS

Cylinder head bolts:

1st stage	4.0 kg/m
2nd stage	6.0 kg/m
3rd stage	11.0 kg/m
Main bearing cap bolts	10.0 kg/m
Big end cap bolts	4.5 kg/m
Camshaft gear bolt	4.8 kg/m
Camshaft thrust plate bolts	1.0 kg/m
Crankshaft pulley bolt	5.5 kg/m
Carburettor to manifold nut	2.0 kg/m
Distributor clamp bolt	2.0 kg/m
Drive plate bolts	7.0 kg/m
Auxiliary gear bolt	4.8 kg/m
Auxiliary shaft thrust plate screws	1.0 kg/m
Exhaust manifold bolts/ nuts	2.0 kg/m
Flywheel bolts	7.0 kg/m
Fuel pump bolts	2.0 kg/m
Inlet manifold bolts/ nuts	2.0 kg/m
Oil pump bolts	2.0 kg/m
Oil pump cover screws	1.0 kg/m
Oil pump pick up pipe screws	1.0 kg/m

Rocker cover bolts:

Bolts 1 to 6	0.70 kg/m
Bolts 7 and 8	0.25 kg/m
Bolts 9 and 10	0.70 kg/m
Bolts 7 and 8	0.70 kg/m

Sump bolts:
1st stage	0.2 kg/m
2nd stage	0.8 kg/m
3rd stage	0.8 kg/m
Sump drain plug	2.8 kg/m
Toothed drive belt	
tension	See text
Toothed drive belt tensioner	
pivot bolt	2.0 kg/m
Thermostat housing	
bolts	2.0 kg/m

1. DESCRIPTION

The 2000 overhead camshaft engine is a four cylinder, in line, four stroke engine with a cross-flow cylinder head.

The camshaft runs in three bearings which are a press fit into three in line machined tunnels which are cast integrally with the cylinder head. The camshaft is located centrally above the cam followers and is driven by a toothed belt.

The fuel pump, oil pump and distributor are driven by an auxiliary shaft. Drive to the auxiliary shaft and the camshaft is from the crankshaft via the toothed belt.

The cast iron crankshaft is carried in five replaceable bearings, with crankshaft end-float being controlled by the centre main bearing. The bearings are steel backed lead/bronze or aluminium/tin inserts.

Oil leakage from the front and rear of the crankshaft is prevented by seals which are installed in the crankshaft cover and over the rear of the crankshaft into the recess of the rear main bearing.

The connecting rods are H-section forgings with replaceable big end inserts. The bearings are steel backed aluminium/tin or lead/bronze inserts.

The aluminium alloy three ring pistons are of the flat top type having a full skirt with a steel expander strut. Both the upper and lower compression rings are cast iron. The upper compression ring is chrome plated. The oil control ring consists of a spacer and two chromed segments.

The gudgeon pin is an interference fit in the connecting rod. The gudgeon pin and piston are renewed as an assembly.

The inlet and exhaust valves are operated by cam followers which pivot on an adjustable pivot. The pivots are adjustable to provide the specified clearance between the upper face of the cam follower and the camshaft lobe. A spring retains the cam follower to the adjustable pivot.

The camshaft toothed belt is protected by a cover. The alternator and water pump are driven by a vee belt from a pulley in front of the camshaft toothed belt cover.

CAUTION: To prevent the toothed belt from jumping one or more teeth ensure that the engine is always turned in the normal direction of rotation.

2. ENGINE ASSEMBLY

TO REMOVE AND INSTAL

(1) Raise the engine bonnet and fit covers to both front fenders.

(2) Mark around the bonnet hinge plates with a soft lead pencil to ensure correct positioning on installation and remove the engine bonnet.

(3) Disconnect the battery earth strap.

(4) Drain the cooling system by removing the drain plug from the bottom of the radiator and the right hand side of the engine block.

(5) When the cooling system has drained instal and securely tighten the drain plugs.

(6) Remove the top and bottom radiator hoses.

(7) Remove the radiator retaining bolts and lift the radiator from the engine compartment.

NOTE: Because there is a possibility of internal deposits becoming lodged in the waterways as the core dries out, the radiator should be laid flat with its connections up and cap on, then filled with water, until ready for installation.

(8) Remove the engine pipe to exhaust manifold flange nuts.

(9) Remove the air cleaner mounting bolts and remove the air cleaner from the engine.

(10) Disconnect the heater hoses and the power brake hose.

(11) Disconnect the accelerator cable from the carburettor and remove the cable retaining link from the accelerator linkage.

(12) Disconnect the fuel line from the fuel tank at the fuel pump. Instal a suitable plug into the fuel line.

(13) Disconnect the wires from the starter motor and the alternator.

(14) Disconnect the wires from the oil pressure and water temperature switches.

(15) Remove the high tension lead from between the coil and distributor and disconnect the low tension wire from the distributor.

(16) Raise the front of the vehicle and support it on stands.

(17) Drain the engine oil into a suitable container. Instal the sump drain plug and torque the drain plug to specifications when the oil has been drained from the sump.

(18) Remove the starter motor retaining bolts and remove the starter motor from the vehicle.

(19) Remove the bolts from the bracket between the clutch/torque converter housing and the cylinder block. Withdraw the bracket.

(20) Remove the engine mounting nuts.

(21) Support the transmission with a jack and a block of wood.

(22) Remove the cylinder block to clutch/torque converter housing retaining bolts.

(23) On automatic transmission models remove the flywheel cover plate and remove the torque converter to drive plate retaining bolts through the starter motor aperture.

NOTE: Turn the engine in the direction of rotation to gain access to the torque converter retaining nuts.

(24) With suitable lifting tackle installed to the engine manoeuvre the engine from the engine compartment.

NOTE: On automatic transmission models as the engine is withdrawn from the transmission lever the torque converter

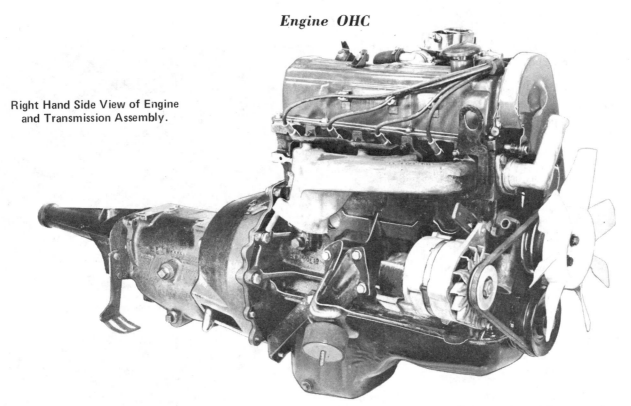

Right Hand Side View of Engine and Transmission Assembly.

off the drive plate to ensure that the torque converter remains correctly coupled with the input shaft of the transmission.

(25) If the engine is to be dismantled, remove the engine mounting brackets and place the engine on a work bench or suitable engine stand.

Installation is a reversal of the removal procedure with attention to the following points:

(1) If it is necessary to rotate the engine to align the input shaft of the manual transmission with the clutch plate splines, rotate the engine in the normal direction of rotation only.

(2) Ensure that the engine is correctly installed and securely mounted before connecting the various components.

(3) Before installing the radiator flush it out with compressed air and water in the opposite direction to the normal circulation of the coolant.

(4) Refill the engine with the correct grade and quantity of engine oil.

(5) Refill the cooling system and check the fan belt tension.

(6) Start and run the engine until it reaches normal operating temperature while checking for oil, water and fuel leaks. Adjust the carburettor and ignition timing as necessary.

(7) When the engine has cooled sufficiently recheck the cooling system and the engine oil level and top up as necessary.

3. MINOR SUB-ASSEMBLIES

This section refers to the removal, installation and servicing where applicable of the minor sub-assemblies without the necessity of removing the engine from the vehicle.

Removal, installation and servicing procedures of the major sub-assemblies are covered separately under their appropriate headings.

ALTERNATOR
To Remove and Instal

(1) If the engine is installed in the vehicle disconnect the battery earth strap and the wires from the alternator.

(2) Slacken the alternator adjusting and mounting bolts.

(3) Move the alternator towards the engine and remove the drive belt.

(4) Remove the adjusting and mounting bolts then lift the alternator from the vehicle.

Installation is a reversal of the removal procedure ensuring that the fan belt has a deflection of 13 mm between the alternator and fan pulleys when correctly adjusted.

DISTRIBUTOR
To Remove

(1) Remove the oil filler cap from the rocker cover and rotate the engine in the normal direction of rotation.

(2) Align the 4 deg. advance mark on the crankshaft pulley with the pointer. Looking into the oil filler neck of the rocker cover inspect the position of the two cam lobes on number one cylinder.

(3) If both the cam lobes are not facing upwards, then turn the engine one full turn clockwise and again align the 4 deg. mark with the pointer. Both cam lobes will now face upwards.

(4) Remove the distributor cap and accurately mark on the distributor body the rotor button position if not already marked.

(5) Mark the fitted position of the distributor on the base and the cylinder block.

(6) Remove the distributor retaining bolt and clamp and disconnect the vacuum line.

(7) If the engine is installed in the vehicle disconnect the low tension wire from the coil.

(8) Lift the distributor from the engine and again mark the rotor button position in relation to the distributor body.

To Instal

(1) If the engine has been rotated since the distributor was removed rotate the engine in the normal direction of rotation until the cam lobes on number one cylinder face upwards and the 4 deg. mark on the crankshaft pulley is aligned with the pointer.

(2) Insert the distributor into the cylinder block orifice slightly with the vacuum unit facing towards the rear of the engine.

(3) Rotate the rotor button about 35–40 degrees clockwise past the rotor button direction mark on the distributor body to align with the mark made when the distributor was removed.

(4) Fully insert the distributor aligning the scribe lines on the distributor body and the cylinder block.

NOTE: As the drive gears mesh the rotor button will turn anti-clockwise.

(5) Check and ensure that the rotor button is aligned with the installed mark on the distributor body. If necessary lift the distributor slightly and move the rotor button a few degrees to correct the final installed position of the rotor button.

NOTE: Should only a small adjustment be required to align the marks turn the distributor body the required amount and tighten the clamp bolt finger tight.

(6) Instal the distributor clamp plate bolt finger tight and rotate the distributor body clockwise until the contact breaker points are closed, then rotate the distributor body anti-clockwise until the points are just commencing to open and tighten the clamp bolt securely.

(7) Connect the low tension lead to the distributor body.

(8) Instal the distributor cap and connect the high tension leads to the spark plugs, ignition coil, and distributor cap.

AIR CLEANER
To Remove and Instal

(1) Remove the air cleaner top cover after unscrewing the three cover retaining screws.

NOTE: The cover retaining screws are attached to and removed with the top cover.

(2) Bend back the edges of the lock tabs retaining the air cleaner base nuts in position.

(3) Remove the four air cleaner base nuts and the lock tabs.

(4) Remove the nut and bolt retaining the air cleaner rear bracket to the rocker cover.

Ignition Timing Marks on Crankshaft Pulley. Graduations on Pulley are in Two Degree Increments.

(5) Remove the bolt retaining the air cleaner front bracket to the inlet manifold.

(6) Lift the air cleaner from the engine.

Installation is a reversal of the removal procedure using new lock tabs as necessary.

CARBURETTOR AND INLET MANIFOLD
To Remove and Instal

If the engine is removed from the vehicle it is not necessary to carry out the first four operations.

(1) Remove the air cleaner as previously described.

(2) Disconnect the accelerator cable from the accelerator linkage and withdraw the cable retaining link from the accelerator linkage.

(3) Drain the cooling system via the plugs on the radiator lower tank and the left hand side of the cylinder block. When the cooling system has drained instal and tighten the drain plugs.

(4) Disconnect the heater hose and the power brake vacuum hose from the manifold connections.

(5) Remove the fuel line from between the carburettor and the fuel pump.

(6) Disconnect the crankcase ventilation hose from the induction manifold.

(7) Remove the carburettor retaining nuts and lift the carburettor from the manifold.

(8) Remove the inlet manifold to cylinder head retaining bolts/nuts and withdraw the manifold from the cylinder head.

Installation is a reversal of the removal procedure with attention to the following points:

(1) Clean the mating surfaces of the cylinder head and the manifold thoroughly.

(2) Use a new manifold to cylinder head gasket coating both sides of the gasket around the water jacket orifice in the gasket with a suitable type sealer.

(3) Torque the manifold mounting bolts to specifications.

(4) Reconnect the crankcase ventilation hose and the power brake vacuum hose before attempting to start the engine.

ROCKER COVER
To Remove and Instal

(1) Remove the air cleaner as previously described.

(2) Disconnect the spark plug leads from the spark plugs by pulling on the spark plug covers at the ends of the leads.

(3) Unclip the spark plug leads from the side and top of the rocker cover and position the leads to one side.

(4) Slacken the rocker cover bolts in the opposite order to the tightening sequence.

(5) Remove the rocker cover bolts and manoeuvre the rocker cover from the engine.

(6) Wash the rocker cover and clean all traces of the old gasket from the rocker cover and the cylinder head.

Installation is a reversal of the removal procedure using a new gasket and ensuring that the rocker cover bolts are tightened in the correct sequence as per the illustration.

NOTE: After the engine reaches normal operating temperature retighten the rocker cover bolts.

TOOTHED DRIVE BELT AND TENSIONER
To Remove

(1) Remove the three bolts retaining the toothed drive belt cover to the front of the engine and manoeuvre the cover from the engine. Disconnect the battery earth lead.

(2) Rotate the engine in the normal direction of rotation and align the zero mark on the crankshaft pulley with the timing pointer. The crankshaft key should be in the 12 o'clock position.

(3) Ensure that the pointer on the guide plate behind

INDENTED DOT
GUIDE PLATE POINTER
KEY IN 12 O'CLOCK POSITION
SCRIBE MARKS

Aligning Relevant Timing Marks Before Removing or Installing Toothed Drive Belt.

the camshaft gear is aligned with the indented dot in the cylinder head casting just below the camshaft. If the hole in the camshaft gear is above the camshaft rotate the crankshaft one turn and again align the zero mark on the crankshaft pulley with the pointer.

NOTE: Turn the engine in the normal direction of rotation only.

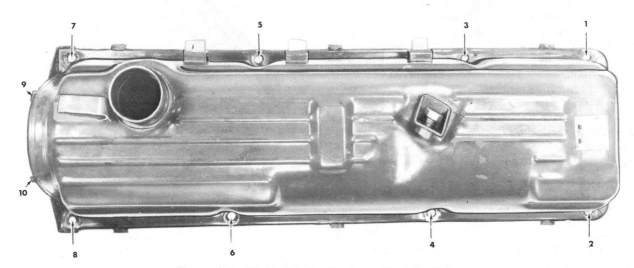

Sequence for Tightening Rocker Cover Retaining Bolts.

Belt Tensioner Mounted to Cylinder Head.

(4) With the timing marks on the crankshaft pulley and the camshaft gear guide plate correctly aligned remove the distributor cap and scribe a line on the end and in the centre of the rotor button.

(5) Mark the distributor body in line with the mark made on the rotor button.

NOTE: Check that alignment marks have not been previously made, before making new marks.

(6) Loosen the mounting bolts and adjusting bolt on the alternator and remove the fan belt.

(7) Loosen the toothed drive belt tensioner retaining bolt using the correct sized allen key.

(8) Loosen the belt tensioner adjusting bolt and push the tensioner away from the belt as far as possible. Tighten the adjusting bolt in this position.

(9) Slide the belt off the camshaft gear and the tensioner, with the belt now removed from the upper gears manoeuvre the belt from behind the crankshaft pulley and remove the belt from the engine.

NOTE: If the belt tensioner only is to be removed it is not necessary to remove the toothed belt from the gears but care must be taken to check that the engine timing marks are not altered when the tensioner is installed and released.

(10) Remove the tensioner retaining bolt and adjusting bolt and remove the tensioner and spring.

To Instal

(1) Instal the tensioner and spring to the engine, fit the end of the spring into the retaining groove of the cover bolt, move the tensioner to the fully off position and

tighten the adjusting bolt to hold the tensioner in this position.

(2) Align the zero mark on the crankshaft pulley with the timing pointer, the crankshaft key should be at 12 o'clock.

(3) Align the rotor button and distributor body marks.

(4) Align the camshaft gear guide plate pointer with the timing indentation mark.

(5) Fit the toothed belt behind the crankshaft pulley and thrust washer.

(6) Position the belt over the tensioner and hold the belt at this position.

(7) Engage the belt with the crankshaft gear and the auxiliary shaft gear with no slack in the belt between the two gears.

(8) With the belt engaged with the crankshaft and auxiliary shaft gears, connect the belt to the camshaft gear ensuring that there is no slack between the auxiliary shaft gear and the camshaft gear.

(9) Loosen the tensioner adjusting bolt and allow the tensioner to tension the belt.

(10) Ensure that the three sets of timing marks are correctly aligned after the belt is tensioned.

(11) Rotate the engine crankshaft twice by hand and realign the zero mark on the crankshaft pulley with the timing pointer.

Recheck to ensure that the three sets of timing marks are still correctly aligned.

(12) With the timing marks correctly aligned tighten the tensioner adjusting bolt and retaining bolt securely.

(13) Further installation is a reversal of the removal procedure ensuring that the fan belt is correctly adjusted.

FRONT CRANKSHAFT OIL SEAL
To Renew

If the engine is removed from the vehicle it is not necessary to carry out the first five operations.

(1) Disconnect the battery earth lead.

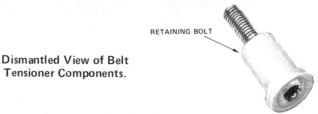

Dismantled View of Belt Tensioner Components.

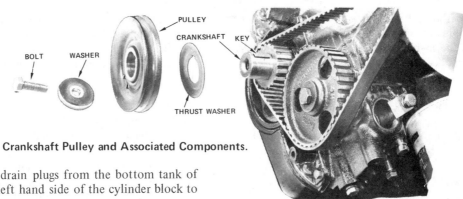

Crankshaft Pulley and Associated Components.

(2) Remove the drain plugs from the bottom tank of the radiator and the left hand side of the cylinder block to drain the cooling system.

(3) When the cooling system has drained instal and securely tighten the drain plugs.

(4) Remove the spark plugs and the radiator hoses.

(5) Remove the radiator retaining bolts and remove the radiator from the engine compartment.

(6) Remove the toothed drive belt cover and the drive belt from the engine as previously explained.

(7) Remove the fan blade retaining bolts and remove the fan blades.

(8) Withdraw the fan pulley from the waterpump and place it aside.

(9) Hold the crankshaft pulley stationary and remove the pulley retaining bolt and washer. As necessary rotate the pulley slightly to realign the timing marks.

(10) Withdraw the pulley from the crankshaft. If necessary use two diametrically opposed screwdrivers to lever off the pulley.

(11) Remove the thrust washer from in front of the crankshaft gear after marking the front of the thrust washer.

(12) Withdraw the crankshaft gear from the front of the crankshaft.

(13) Using a suitable seal removal tool remove the oil seal from the crankshaft cover.

NOTE: Do not damage the seal running surface of the crankshaft.

(14) Coat the outside surface of the new oil seal with a suitable type sealant and lubricate the lip of the seal lightly with engine oil.

(15) Instal the oil seal into the crankshaft cover using a suitable hollow seal installing tool and hammer.

The assembling procedure is a reversal of the dismantling operations with attention to the following points:

(1) Slide the crankshaft gear onto the crankshaft.

(2) Instal the thrust washer according to the mark made and noted on removal (convex side towards the crankshaft gear).

(3) Instal the crankshaft pulley and retaining bolt and washer, tighten the retaining bolt to specifications.

(4) Rotate the engine in the normal direction of rotation and align the zero mark on the crankshaft pulley with the timing pointer, ensure that number one cylinder is on the compression stroke.

(5) Instal the toothed drive belt checking and aligning

the valve timing and ignition timing marks as previously explained.

(6) After installing the cooling system components ensure that the system is filled with coolant.

CAMSHAFT OIL SEAL
To Renew

(1) Carry out the service operations for renewing the crankshaft oil seal up to the removal of the crankshaft pulley and components, it is not necessary to remove these units.

(2) Hold the camshaft gear and remove the camshaft gear retaining bolt and washer.

(3) Withdraw the camshaft gear and the guide plate.

(4) Using a suitable seal removal tool withdraw the oil seal from the front of the camshaft support without damaging the seal running surface of the camshaft.

(5) Coat the outside of a new oil seal with a suitable type sealant and sparingly lubricate the lip of the oil seal with engine oil.

(6) Using a suitable seal installing tool instal the seal squarely into the recess in the camshaft support.

(7) Slide the guide plate and the camshaft gear onto the camshaft and instal the retaining bolt and washer.

(8) Hold the camshaft gear and torque the retaining bolt to specifications.

(9) Instal the toothed belt and cooling system components as described in the crankshaft oil seal and toothed drive belt sections.

CRANKSHAFT REAR OIL SEAL
To Renew

(1) Remove the transmission as described in the transmission section of this manual.

(2) Remove the clutch assembly where fitted as described in the clutch section of this manual.

(3) Mark the relationship of the flywheel or the drive plate to the crankshaft.

(4) Hold the flywheel or drive plate and remove the retaining bolts.

(5) Remove the flywheel or drive plate.

(6) Clean around the outside of the seal and using a suitable seal removal tool withdraw and discard the oil seal.

(7) Coat the outside of a new oil seal with a suitable type sealant and sparingly lubricate the lip of the seal with engine oil.

(8) Using a suitable seal installing tool and hammer,

squarely instal the seal into the rear main bearing recess until the seal abuts the recess in the casting.

(9) Clean the mating surfaces of the flywheel or drive plate and the crankshaft.

(10) Instal the flywheel or drive plate according to the marks made on removal.

(11) Instal the flywheel or drive plate retaining bolts and torque them to specifications.

(12) Instal the clutch assembly where fitted and transmission as described in the appropriate sections.

AUXILIARY SHAFT OIL SEAL
To Renew

(1) Remove the toothed drive belt as previously described.

(2) Hold the auxiliary gear and undo the retaining bolt. Remove the retaining bolt and washer.

(3) Slide the auxiliary shaft gear off the shaft.

(4) Remove the bolts from the seal retaining plate and withdraw the plate and the gasket. Discard the gasket.

(5) Suitably support the seal retaining plate and tap the seal from the plate using a thin drift and small hammer.

(6) Thoroughly wash the seal retaining plate in a suitable cleaning solvent and blow it dry with compressed air.

(7) Coat the outside of a new oil seal with a suitable sealer and sparingly apply engine oil to the seal lip.

(8) Using a suitable seal installing tool and hammer squarely instal the seal into the plate until it abuts the plate recess.

(9) Using a new gasket, coated both sides with a suitable sealant, instal the seal retaining plate and bolts. Tighten the bolts securely.

(10) Place the auxiliary gear onto the shaft, instal the retaining bolt and washer and torque the retaining bolt to specifications.

(11) Instal the toothed drive belt as previously described.

AUXILIARY SHAFT
To Remove and Instal

(1) Remove the toothed drive belt as previously described.

(2) Remove the fuel pump retaining bolts after disconnecting the fuel line from the fuel pump.

(3) Withdraw the fuel pump and discard the gasket.

(4) Withdraw the fuel pump operating rod.

(5) Hold the auxiliary gear and undo the retaining bolt. Remove the retaining bolt and washer.

(6) Slide the auxiliary shaft gear off the shaft.

(7) Remove the bolts from the seal retaining plate and withdraw the plate and gasket. Discard the gasket.

(8) Remove the two set screws from the auxiliary shaft thrust plate and remove the plate.

(9) Withdraw the auxiliary shaft.

Installation is a reversal of the removal procedure with attention to the following points:

(1) Guide the auxiliary shaft into the cylinder block sliding the gear on the auxiliary shaft into mesh with the distributor driven gear.

(2) Instal the thrust plate and the set screws. Tighten the screws securely.

(3) Suitably support the seal retaining plate and drive the seal from the plate using a thin drift and small hammer.

(4) Thoroughly wash the seal retaining plate in a cleaning solvent and blow it dry with compressed air.

(5) Coat the outside of a new oil seal with a suitable sealer and sparingly apply engine oil to the seal lip.

(6) Using a suitable seal installing tool and hammer squarely instal the new oil seal into the plate until it abuts the plate recess.

(7) Using a new gasket, coated both sides with a suitable sealant, instal the seal retaining plate and bolts. Tighten the bolts securely.

(8) Place the auxiliary gear onto the shaft, instal the retaining bolt and washer and torque the retaining bolt to specifications.

(9) Instal the fuel pump operating rod.

(10) Coat both sides of a new fuel pump gasket with a suitable type sealant and instal the fuel pump and the

Drive Gear and Seal Retaining Plate Removed to Show Auxiliary Shaft and Thrust Plate.

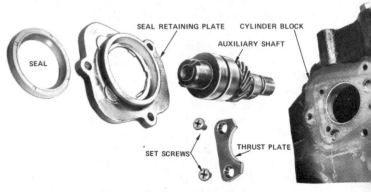

Dismantled View of Auxiliary Shaft and Oil Seal.

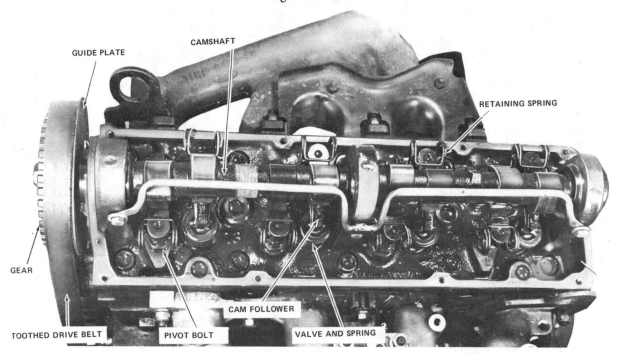

GUIDE PLATE · CAMSHAFT · RETAINING SPRING · GEAR · TOOTHED DRIVE BELT · PIVOT BOLT · CAM FOLLOWER · VALVE AND SPRING

Rocker Cover Removed to Show Camshaft and Valve Arrangement.

retaining bolts. Torque the fuel pump retaining bolts to specifications.

(11) Instal the toothed drive belt as previously described.

4. CYLINDER HEAD AND CAMSHAFT

CYLINDER HEAD
To Remove and Instal

(1) Remove the air cleaner and the rocker cover and disconnect the toothed drive belt as described under the appropriate headings of the MINOR SUB-ASSEMBLIES section.

(2) Drain the coolant from the radiator and cylinder block.

(3) Disconnect the temperature switch wire from the switch below the front of the intake manifold and remove the switch.

(4) Disconnect the accelerator cable from the carburettor linkage and position the cable aside. Withdraw the cable retaining link from the linkage and place it aside.

(5) Disconnect the engine pipe from the exhaust manifold.

(6) Disconnect the heater hose from the intake manifold and remove the top radiator hose.

(7) Disconnect the power brake unit vacuum hose from the inlet manifold.

(8) Remove the fuel line from between the fuel pump and the carburettor.

(9) Disconnect the crankcase ventilation pipe from the inlet manifold.

(10) Remove the vacuum line from between the distributor and the carburettor.

(11) Using a suitable extension and bar slacken the cylinder head bolts in the opposite order of the tightening sequence.

(12) Remove the cylinder head bolts.

(13) Lift the cylinder head from the vehicle and place it on a workbench.

NOTE: Do not rotate the engine with the cylinder head removed unless the toothed drive belt is supported without slack.

(14) Thoroughly clean the mating surfaces of the cylinder block, cylinder head and manifolds removing all traces of the old gasket and any carbon deposits. Clean the tops of all pistons. Take care not to remove metal when cleaning components.

(15) Instal two guide bolts to assist in installing the cylinder head.

(16) Place a new head gasket over the guide bolts onto the cylinder block ensuring that all holes are correctly aligned.

(17) Instal the cylinder head carefully guiding the cylinder head over the guide bolts.

(18) Clean and instal the head studs finger tight. Remove the two guide bolts and instal the remaining two head studs.

(19) Tighten the head studs in three stages referring to specifications and the tightening sequence illustration.

Further installation is a reversal of the removal procedure referring to the appropriate part of the engine section as necessary.

CAMSHAFT
To Remove and Instal

(1) With the cylinder head removed from the engine, remove the carburettor from the manifold and place it aside.

(2) Remove the inlet manifold retaining bolts/nuts and withdraw the manifold from the cylinder head.

(3) Remove the exhaust manifold retaining bolts and withdraw the exhaust manifold from the cylinder head.

(4) With the manifolds removed from the cylinder head suitably position the cylinder head on a workbench or workstand.

(5) Remove the thermostat housing bolts and the thermostat. Withdraw the thermostat and place it aside.

(6) Hold the camshaft gear and remove the camshaft gear retaining bolt and washer.

(7) Slide the camshaft gear and the guide plate off the front of the camshaft.

(8) Remove the oil pipe retaining bolts and withdraw the oil pipe.

(9) Using a pair of long nosed pointed pliers disconnect each side of a cam follower retaining spring from the pivot clip and remove the spring. Remove the remaining seven cam follower retaining springs in the same manner.

(10) With number one cylinder cam followers on the back of the cam loosen the pivot bolt lock nut of the exhaust valve, hold the lock nut, and screw the adjuster fully downwards. Withdraw the cam follower.

Repeat the procedure on number one cylinder inlet valve and remove the cam follower.

NOTE: Keep all cam followers separate and in their correct order of removal.

(11) Rotate the camshaft to bring number two cylinder cam followers to the back of the cam. (When both cam lobes on number two cylinder point upwards).

Remove the two cam followers in the same manner as for number one cylinder.

(12) Repeat the cam followers removal procedure for the remaining two cylinders.

(13) Remove the camshaft thrust plate retaining screws from the rear support and withdraw the thrust plate.

(14) Withdraw the camshaft rearwards from the cylinder head.

(15) Using a suitable seal removal tool remove the seal from the camshaft front support of the cylinder head.

(16) Inspect the seal running surface of the camshaft for wear.

(17) Inspect the camshaft journals and the bearings for wear or scores.

(18) Inspect the cam lobes for wear or pitting.

Renew the camshaft or bearings as necessary.

NOTE: If new bearings are installed align the oil holes with the oil holes in the tunnel supports.

Installation is a reversal of the removal procedure with attention to the following points:

(1) Coat the outside edge of a new oil seal with a suitable sealant and sparingly coat the sealing lip of the seal with oil.

(2) Using a suitable seal installing tool and hammer install the seal until it seats in the recess.

(3) Instal the camshaft from the rear of the cylinder head guiding the front of the camshaft into the seal.

(4) Instal the thrust plate and bolts. Torque the thrust plate bolts to specifications.

(5) Place a dial gauge at the rear of the cylinder head with the plunger bearing onto the camshaft. Push the camshaft forward, zero the scale and push the camshaft rearward and measure the end float on the dial gauge.

(6) Compare the end float obtained to Specifications and if necessary instal a thicker thrust washer. See Specifications.

(7) With the end float correct instal the cam followers and the retaining springs in the reverse manner to that when they were removed.

(8) Rotate the engine until number one cylinder cam followers are on the back of their cams. Refer to Specifications for the valve clearance.

(9) Insert the specified feeler gauge between the cam lobe and the cam follower of number one cylinder exhaust valve. Screw the pivot adjusting screw upwards until the specified clearance is obtained. Tighten the lock nut with the adjusting nut held in this position.

Adjust the inlet valve for number one cylinder to the specified clearance.

(10) Adjust the valve clearance of the remaining valves in the same manner bringing each cam follower to the back of its cam in turn.

NOTE: Tighten the adjusting nut lock nuts securely and then recheck the clearance. The feeler gauge must have a slight drag when inserted and withdrawn.

(11) Instal the oil pipe and the retaining bolts.

(12) Position the guide plate and the camshaft gear onto the camshaft, install the retaining bolt and washer, hold the camshaft gear and torque the bolt to specifications.

(13) Clean the thermostat housing and the cylinder head mating surface. Place the thermostat into position with the coils facing inwards and the arrow towards the carburettor.

(14) Use a new gasket and instal the thermostat cover and bolts. Torque the thermostat housing bolts to specifications.

(15) Use a new gasket and instal the exhaust manifold and bolts. Torque the bolts to specifications.

(16) Coat both sides of a new inlet manifold gasket around the water intake orifice (centre hole) and instal the gasket and manifold.

(17) Instal the bolts/nuts and tighten to specifications.

(18) Instal the carburettor to the manifold and tighten the nuts securely.

(19) Instal the cylinder head to the engine as previously described.

CYLINDER HEAD
To Dismantle

(1) Remove the cylinder head and camshaft as previously described.

(2) Remove the camshaft from the cylinder head as previously described.

(3) Use a suitable valve spring compressor tool to compress the valve springs.

(4) With the valve spring compressed remove the two valve cotters.

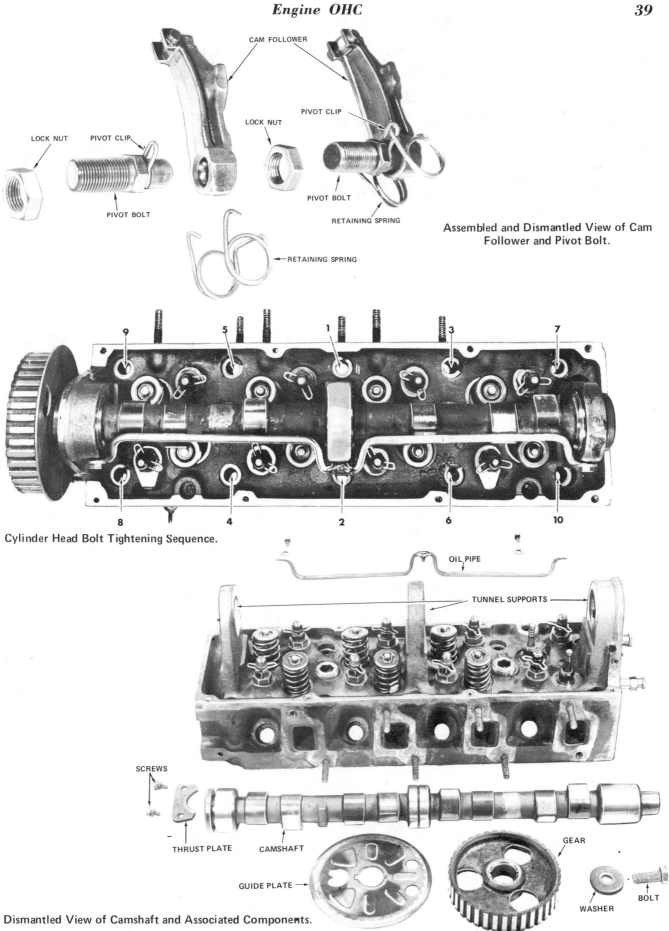

CAM FOLLOWER

PIVOT CLIP

LOCK NUT

LOCK NUT

PIVOT CLIP

PIVOT BOLT

PIVOT BOLT

RETAINING SPRING

RETAINING SPRING

Assembled and Dismantled View of Cam Follower and Pivot Bolt.

Cylinder Head Bolt Tightening Sequence.

OIL PIPE

TUNNEL SUPPORTS

SCREWS

THRUST PLATE

CAMSHAFT

GEAR

GUIDE PLATE

WASHER

BOLT

Dismantled View of Camshaft and Associated Components.

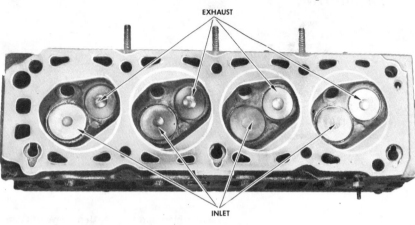

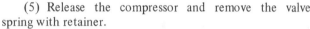

Cylinder Head Showing Valve Arrangement and Water Circulation Holes.

(5) Release the compressor and remove the valve spring with retainer.

(6) Remove the valve and place the valve with the other parts of the valve assembly in a suitable rack or tray to ensure they are installed to their original positions during assembly.

Repeat the removal procedure with the remainder of the valves and then lift the valve stem seals from the tops of the valve guides and discard them.

NOTE: Should difficulty be experienced in separating the valve spring retainer from the collets, apply light pressure to the spring compressor, then sharply tap the edge of the valve spring retainer with the end of a hammer handle.

To Clean and Inspect

(1) Remove all traces of carbon from the combustion chambers and exhaust ports. Clean the manifold mating surfaces of the cylinder head.

(2) Remove the deposits from the water pump passages.

(3) Insert a valve into its mating guide in the cylinder head and check for wear between the valve stem and the guide by moving the valve sideways. Check the wear in different positions by lifting the valve to assimilate an opening valve position.

(4) When a point of maximum movement (wear) is observed support the cylinder head and the end of the valve in this position.

(5) Mount a dial gauge onto the cylinder head with the pointer bearing on the side of the valve head.

(6) Hold the valve against one side of the guide, zero the dial scale and move the valve to the other side of the guide. Note the scale reading and compare the reading (wear) to specifications.

(7) If the wear exceeds specifications the valve guide may have to be reamed to oversize and an oversize valve fitted.

Insert a new valve into the guide and recheck the wear reading. Renew the worn valve or ream the valve guide and fit an oversize valve as necessary.

(8) Repeat the wear checking procedure on the remaining valves.

(9) Inspect the valve seats for damage and wear. If

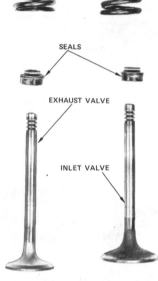

Exploded View of Valve and Spring Components.

necessary the seats should be recut to the specified angle and width, see Specifications.

(10) Inspect the exhaust valves faces for damage and wear. Reface the exhaust valves as necessary after cleaning off all carbon deposits.

(11) Inspect the inlet valves faces for damage and wear. If damage or wear is evident the inlet valve(s) must be renewed as they are ALUMINIZED and must not be faced, ground or lapped. Clean the carbon deposits from serviceable inlet valves.

(12) Lap the exhaust valves into the cylinder head seats with a suitable lapping compound.

(13) Ensure that the lapped mark on the valve face is in the centre of the face. If necessary recut, crown and throat the exhaust valve seat in the cylinder head to centralise the lap marking on the valve face.

NOTE: If the exhaust seat is recut after lapping, lightly reface the exhaust valve face before relapping to check the seat to face position.

(14) When the exhaust valves have been correctly seated sparingly smear the seat face with 'Prussian Blue' (or similar) and insert the valve into the cylinder head evenly. Do not rotate the valve. Withdraw the valve and check the marking on the valve face. The marking must be true and concentric.

(15) Use 'Prussian Blue' (or similar) to check that the mark from the face of the inlet seat is in the centre of the inlet valve face. If necessary recut, crown and throat the

inlet valve seat in the same manner as the exhaust valve seats.

(16) With the valves correctly positioned in their seats remove all traces of 'Prussian Blue' (or similar) and insert the valves into the cylinder head lubricating the stems and faces with engine oil.

(17) Measure the free length of the valve springs and check the tension of the valve springs as follows:

Place the two springs end to end, with a thin plate between them in the jaws of a vice. When the vice is closed approximately 12.7 mm (0.5 in) the original spring should be within five per cent of the length of the new spring when measured from the plate to the vice jaw. Check the remaining springs and renew as necessary.

To Assemble

(1) Instal new seals to the tops of the valve guides guiding the seals over the stems of the valves to prevent damage to the lips of the seals.

(2) Instal the valve springs, retainers and cotters in the reverse manner to that of removal.

(3) Instal the camshaft to the cylinder head as previously described.

(4) Instal the cylinder head and camshaft assembly to the engine as previously described.

TO ADJUST VALVE CLEARANCE

(1) Remove the air cleaner and the rocker cover as described under MINOR SUB-ASSEMBLIES.

(2) Remove the spark plugs and rotate the engine in the normal direction of rotation until number one cylinder is on tdc (that is, with both camshaft lobes on number one cylinder pointing upwards). Refer to Specifications for the valve clearance.

(3) Insert the specified feeler gauge between the bottom of the cam lobe and the top of the cam follower. A slight resistance should be felt on the feeler gauge if the adjustment is correct.

To adjust the clearance slacken the pivot adjusting nut lock nut and screw the adjusting nut in the desired direction. When the adjustment is correct hold the adjusting nut and tighten the lock nut. Recheck the clearance.

Check the clearance on the other valve using the specified feeler gauge.

(4) When both valves have been correctly adjusted on number one cylinder bring the remaining cylinders to tdc in turn and check and adjust the clearance of the valves as necessary.

(5) Instal the spark plugs.

(6) Instal the rocker cover and the air cleaner as previously described.

5. SUMP AND OIL PUMP

SUMP
To Remove and Instal

(1) Remove the engine from the vehicle as previously described.

(2) With the engine mounted on a suitable workstand or work bench clean around the joining surfaces of the sump to cylinder block.

(3) Remove the sump retaining bolts and lift the sump off the cylinder block.

(4) Thoroughly clean all traces of the old gasket from the cylinder block ensuring that no pieces fall into the engine.

(5) Thoroughly clean the sump removing all traces of the old gasket, sludge and impurities from the sump.

(6) Prise out the two tapered sections of the rear main bearing sump seal from the sides of the main bearing cap.

(7) Coat the gasket seating surfaces of the cylinder block with a suitable type sealant.

(8) Instal the two new tapered sections of seal using a blunt screwdriver.

(9) Place the two curved seals in position on the main bearing caps.

(10) Place the two pieces of gasket onto the sump and check that the holes are correctly aligned. As necessary soak the gaskets in warm water to expand them or place them under a strong hot light to shrink them.

(11) Place the sections of the gasket, one at a time, onto the cylinder block sliding the ends of the gasket under the ends of the seals into the seal slots.

(12) Using a suitable type sealant coat the gasket mating surfaces of the sump.

(13) Position the sump over the cylinder block holes and lower the sump into position.

(14) Instal all bolts finger tight before tightening any individual bolt.

(15) Torque the sump retaining bolts to specifications in two stages as follows: Starting at the right hand rear corner (straight side) and proceeding in an anti-clockwise direction tighten all the retaining bolts to 0.2 kg/m. The second stage of tightening commences at the front left hand inner corner, proceeding in an anti-clockwise direction

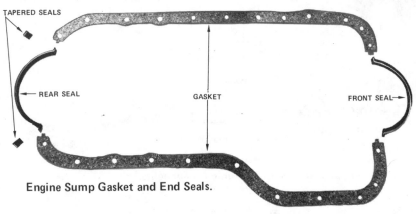

Engine Sump Gasket and End Seals.

tighten all retaining bolts to 0.8 kg/m, then recheck all the retaining bolts continuing in an anti-clockwise direction.

(16) Instal the engine as previously described.

OIL PUMP
To Remove and Instal

(1) Remove the engine from the vehicle and remove the sump as previously described.

(2) Where the oil pump pick-up pipe is retained to the cylinder block by a bolt, remove the retaining bolt and place it aside.

(3) Remove the oil pump retaining bolts and lift the oil pump from the cylinder block.

(4) If the oil pump drive shaft came out with the oil pump, withdraw the drive shaft and using a pair of long nosed pointed pliers insert the drive shaft into the distributor shaft.

Installation is a reversal of the removal procedure with attention to the following points:

(1) Clean the mating surfaces of the cylinder block and the oil pump.

(2) Instal the oil pump onto the drive shaft turning the oil pump as necessary to engage the drive shaft.

(3) Align the mounting holes and loosely instal the retaining bolts.

(4) Where fitted, instal and tighten the pick-up pipe retaining bolt.

(5) Torque the oil pump retaining bolts to specifications.

(6) Instal the sump to the vehicle as previously described.

To Dismantle

(1) With the oil pump removed from the cylinder block thoroughly wash the outside of the pump in a suitable cleaning solvent and blow it dry with compressed air.

(2) Bend back the lock tabs of the pick-up pipe retaining bolts.

(3) Remove the pick-up pipe retaining bolts and withdraw the pick-up pipe from the oil pump. Discard the gasket.

(4) Scribe a line across the cover and down the side of the body to ensure correct assembly.

(5) Remove the oil pump cover retaining bolts and remove the cover.

(6) Suitably mark the relationship of the outer rotor to the inner rotor on the ends next to the cover to ensure correct assembly, do not damage the machined faces of the rotors when marking.

(7) Withdraw both rotors from the oil pump.

(8) With the oil pump supported in a vice, using a small diameter punch and hammer, punch a hole in the centre of the relief valve plug.

(9) Instal a self tapping screw into the relief valve plug and withdraw the plug using a suitable lever or pliers. Discard the plug.

(10) Withdraw the relief valve spring and the relief valve.

(11) Wash all components in cleaning solvent and blow them dry with compressed air.

NOTE: Ensure that the relief valve cylinder in the oil pump body is thoroughly cleaned.

(12) Check the cover for scores and damage, resurface as necessary by rubbing on a sheet of fine emery cloth placed on a flat surface such as a piece of plate glass.

To Assemble

(1) Instal the inner and outer rotors to the oil pump body aligning the marks made on dismantling.

(2) Measure the clearance between the tips of the inner rotor and the shoulders of the outer rotor, if the measurement exceeds specifications renew the rotors.

(3) Measure the clearance between the outer rotor and the oil pump body. If the measurement exceeds specifications repeat using a new matched set of rotors. If the measurement still exceeds specifications renew the oil pump body.

(4) Place a straight edge across the cover face of the oil pump body and measure the clearance between the rotors

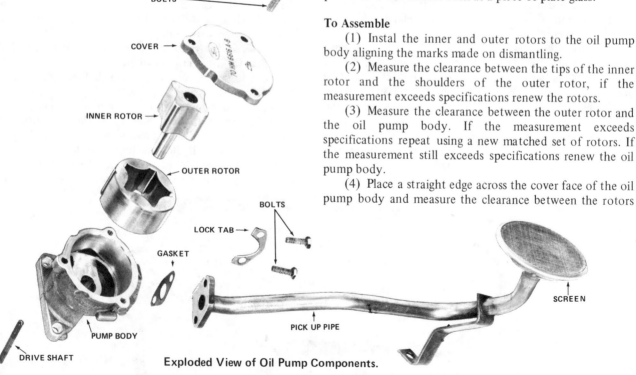

BOLTS

COVER →

INNER ROTOR →

OUTER ROTOR

BOLTS

LOCK TAB →

GASKET

SCREEN

PUMP BODY

PICK UP PIPE

DRIVE SHAFT

Exploded View of Oil Pump Components.

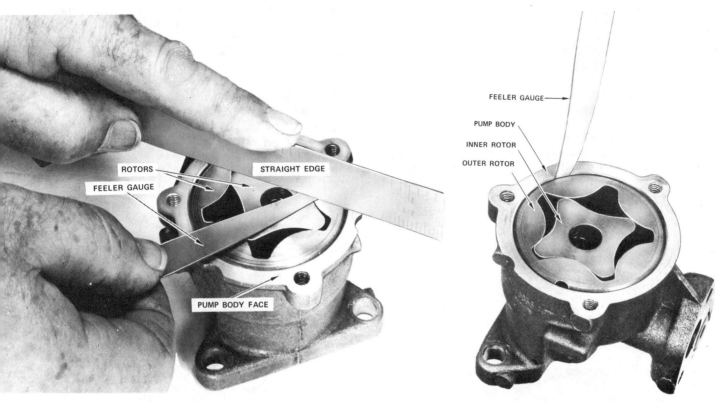

Method of Checking Clearance Between Rotors and Pump Body Face.

Measuring Clearance Between Outer Rotor and Oil Pump Body.

and the straight edge. If the measurement exceeds specifications, repeat the procedure using a new matched pair of rotors. If the measurement still exceeds specifications renew the oil pump body.

(5) With the rotors installed in the oil pump body instal the cover and the retaining bolts. Torque the cover bolts to specifications.

(6) Lubricate a new relief valve and spring with engine oil and instal the new relief valve and spring.

(7) Instal a new relief valve plug with the flat side outwards. The plug is correctly installed when the flat side is flush with the surface.

(8) Instal the pick-up pipe using a new gasket and a new lock tab.

(9) Torque the pick-up pipe bolts to specifications and bend over the lock tab ends.

(10) Instal the oil pump as previously described.

6. PISTONS, CONNECTING RODS AND GUDGEON PINS

TO REMOVE AND DISMANTLE

(1) With the engine removed from the vehicle remove the toothed drive belt, cylinder head, sump and oil pump as previously described.

(2) Rotate the crankshaft until number one piston is on the bottom of its stroke.

(3) Using a suitable ridge removing tool remove the ridge from the top of the cylinder where apparent. Raise the piston to tdc and wipe the top of the piston clean.

(4) Remove the ridge from the remaining cylinders in turn.

(5) If the connecting rods and big end bearing caps are not numbered, then mark the caps in relation to the connecting rods. Also mark the connecting rods and piston assemblies in relation to the cylinders in which they are installed.

(6) Rotate the crankshaft until the first connecting rod and piston to be removed is at the bdc position with the cap nuts accessible.

(7) Remove the big end bearing cap nuts and withdraw the bearing cap and lower bearing shell from the connecting rod.

(8) Using a suitable piece of wood or a hammer handle and being careful not to damage the upper bearing shell in the connecting rod, push the connecting rod and piston assembly through the top of the cylinder bore and remove it from the engine.

(9) Check that the upper bearing shell has remained in the connecting rod, otherwise remove it from the crankpin and position it correctly in the connecting rod.

(10) Instal the bearing cap and lower shell to the connecting rod aligning the numbers, and instal the cap nuts finger tight.

(11) Remove the remaining pistons and connecting rods in the same manner.

(12) Remove the piston rings over the top of the pistons and discard the rings.

(13) Using a piece of broken ring of an appropriate length, clean the carbon deposit from the ring grooves. Avoid damaging the ring lands when scraping.

NOTE: An ideal method of removing carbon deposit from pistons is to immerse the piston in a tank of chemical cleaner. After soaking the carbon can be readily hosed off with water. This method minimises the chance of damage through scraping, particularly with aluminium alloy pistons.

(14) Thoroughly clean the top of the piston, wash the assembly and blow it dry with compressed air.

TO CHECK AND INSPECT

(1) With the pistons and connecting rods removed from the engine refer to the cylinder block section and inspect, measure, hone or rebore and hone the cylinders as necessary.

(2) If the cylinder block was rebored see TO CHECK PISTON CLEARANCE.

(3) If the cylinder block was honed only and the original pistons are to be reused, inspect the pistons as follows.

(a) Inspect the pistons for scores, scuff marks and burning.

(b) Inspect the ring lands for wear or burning.

(c) Check the piston to bore clearance.
Renew the pistons as necessary.

(4) Inspect the big end bearing shells for wear, poor contact and scoring. Renew the bearing shells as necessary.

(5) Inspect the big end crankpins for wear and damage. Measure the crankpins with a micrometer and compare to specifications.

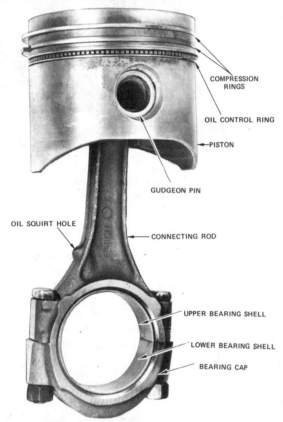

Assembled View of Piston and Connecting Rod

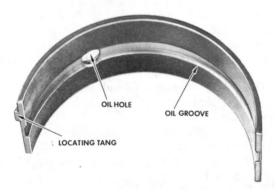

Big End Bearing Shell Showing Locating Tang, and Lubricating Arrangements.

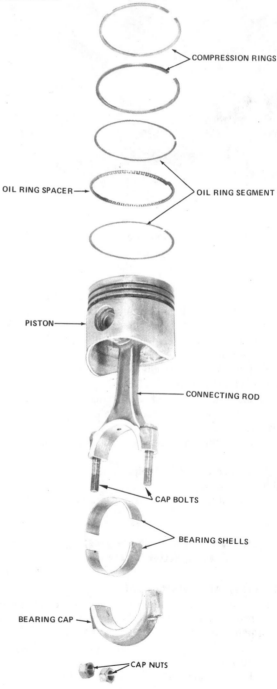

Piston and Connecting Rod Components.

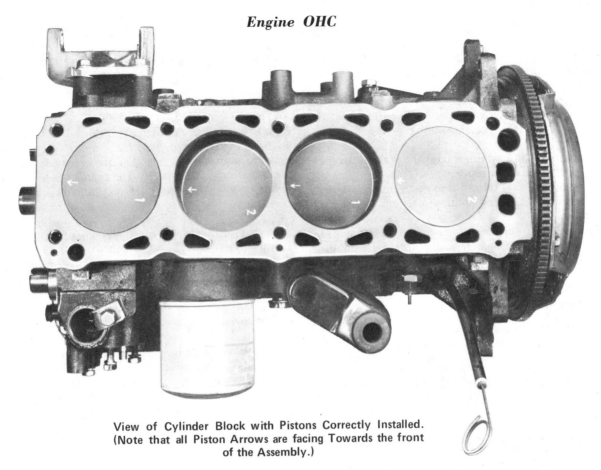

**View of Cylinder Block with Pistons Correctly Installed.
(Note that all Piston Arrows are facing Towards the front
of the Assembly.)**

(6) If the crankshaft is to be removed for grinding see CRANKSHAFT AND BEARINGS sections.

(7) If the bearing shells are being renewed or if the original shells are being reused check the bearing clearance as follows:

(a) Wipe the crankshaft crankpin and the bearing shells with a clean lint free cloth.

(b) Place a piece of Plastigage across the full width of the crankpin.

(c) Insert the piston and connecting rod through the cylinder onto the crankpin, instal the bearing cap and nuts and torque the nuts to specifications.

(d) Remove the nuts and cap and withdraw the piston and connecting rod. Measure the width of the spread of the Plastigage with the packet scale to determine the bearing running clearance.

(e) Repeat the measuring procedure on the remaining crankpins.

NOTE: *Do not rotate the crankshaft with the Plastigage installed or tap the bearing cap with a hammer in an attempt to spread the Plastigage. Torquing the nuts to specifications is sufficient to spread the Plastigage.*

(8) If the bearing clearance exceeds specifications fit the next set of undersize bearings and recheck the clearance.

TO CHECK PISTON CLEARANCE

(1) To check the piston clearance or to select a new piston to maintain the specified piston to bore clearance proceed as follows:

(a) Measure the cylinder bore, across the axis of the crankshaft 70 mm. below the surface of the cylinder block. Note the measurement.

(b) Measure the diameter of the piston at 90 degrees to the centre of the gudgeon pin axis and note the measurement.

(c) The difference between the two measurements is the piston clearance.

(d) Should the clearance exceed specifications select a piston to give the desired piston clearance and then number the cylinder and piston to ensure correct assembly.

(2) To fit a new piston to the connecting rod specialised equipment is necessary to remove and instal the piston and gudgeon pin it is therefore advisable to take the piston and connecting rod assembly with the new pistons to the local Ford dealer or engine reconditioning shop and have the new piston and gudgeon pin installed to the connecting rod and also have the connecting rod alignment checked and rectified as necessary.

TO FIT NEW PISTON RINGS

(1) Select a set of rings to suit the bore size. Standard or oversize as necessary.

(2) Position each ring in turn in the cylinder bore and push the ring down into the relatively unworn section of the bore with an inverted piston.

(3) Withdraw the piston and measure the gap in the ring with a feeler gauge. As necessary adjust the end gap of the ring by filing. See Specifications for ring end gap.

NOTE: *Treat each ring and cylinder bore individually and*

ensure that rings are assembled to the respective piston for the cylinder bore to which they were gapped.

(4) Measure the side clearance of each ring in its respective groove using feeler gauges, see Specifications for clearance limits. If the clearance is excessive renew the piston.

(5) Instal the oil ring spacer onto the piston with the gap towards the rear of the piston.

(6) Instal the lower oil ring chromed segment with the gap of the lower segment positioned 25 mm. from the spacer gap.

(7) Install the upper oil ring chromed segment positioning the gap 25 mm. from the spacer gap in the opposite direction to the lower chromed segment gap.

(8) Using a suitable ring expander instal the lower compression ring and position the ring gap 150 deg. anti-clockwise from the oil ring spacer gap.

NOTE: If the ring is marked top on one side instal the ring with that side towards the top of the piston.

(9) Install the upper compression ring in the same manner as the lower compression ring and position the gap 150 deg. clockwise from the oil ring spacer gap.

TO INSTAL

(1) Lubricate the piston assembly and cylinder walls with clean engine oil.

(2) Ensure that the compression ring gaps are 60 deg. apart and 150 deg. from the oil ring spacer gap.

(3) Rotate number one crankpin until it is at bdc. Wipe the crankpin and smear it with clean engine oil.

(4) Remove the big end bearing cap of number one cylinder and wipe the bearing shell. Smear the bearing shell with clean engine oil.

(5) With the piston rings of number one cylinder compressed by a suitable ring compressor and the piston assembly inserted in the cylinder, use a hammer handle to tap the piston into the cylinder bore guiding the connecting rod onto the crankpin.

NOTE: The piston should be installed in the cylinder with the arrow on the piston crown pointing towards the front of the engine with the squirt hole in the rod to the right hand side.

(6) Wipe the bearing shell in the cap and instal the cap aligning the marks made on removal. Torque the nuts to specifications.

(7) Instal the remaining piston assemblies in a similar manner ensuring that mating pistons and connecting rod caps are installed to their mating cylinders.

NOTE: If a ring jams on the top of the cylinder block when installing remove the assembly, release and retighten the ring compressor and reinstal the assembly. Attempting to force a jammed ring into the cylinder bore may break the ring, damage the ring lands and/or cause scoring of the cylinder walls resulting in unsatisfactory engine operation.

(8) Further installation is a reversal of the removal procedure.

7. CYLINDER BLOCK

TO CHECK CYLINDER BORES

NOTE: To accurately check the cylinder bore wear and condition it is essential that all pistons and connecting rod assemblies be removed from the cylinder block, also that accurate measuring equipment be available to determine the maximum taper and ovality. The cylinder bores should be wiped thoroughly clean with a lint free cloth before checking.

(1) Visually check the cylinder bores for cracks, flaws, scuffing or scoring.

(2) Measure each cylinder bore taper and ovality noting the maximum measurements.

NOTE: Measurements should be taken along the lengthwise and crosswise axis of the cylinder block.

(3) If the wear in any cylinder exceeds the specified limit, rebore and hone all the cylinders to the nearest specified oversize for oversize pistons and rings.

(4) If the engine is completely dismantled remove all plugs and thoroughly clean all galleries and passageways with a suitable solvent.

(5) Blow the engine dry with compressed air and inspect the block for cracks or damage.

DEGLAZING CYLINDER BORES

NOTE: Cylinder bores that are fit for further service with original pistons, but require re-ringing should be deglazed with a hone.

(1) Position plenty of clean rag over the crankshaft under each cylinder bore in turn to prevent particles from entering the crankshaft oilways.

NOTE: When deglazing each cylinder position the crankshaft journal of that cylinder on the bottom of its stroke.

(2) Deglazing of the cylinder walls may be carried out by using a cylinder surfacing hone equipped with 280 grit stones.

(3) Honing should be carried out by moving the hone up and down the cylinder walls fast enough to achieve a cross hatch pattern. When hone marks intersect at 60 deg. the cross hatch angle is most satisfactory for the correct seating of the piston rings.

NOTE: When deglazing it is important that only enough strokes of the hone are made to eliminate the glazed condition of the cylinder. Excessive honing of the cylinder will increase the bore size and thus increase piston to cylinder clearance.

(4) Use a honing lubricant as stipulated by the cylinder hone manufacturer.

(5) After honing it is necessary that the cylinder block be thoroughly cleaned to remove all traces of abrasive.

(6) After the cylinder block has been cleaned and dried, wipe the bores with a lint free cloth, then smear them with engine oil to prevent rusting.

8. CRANKSHAFT AND BEARINGS

TO REMOVE

(1) With the engine removed from the vehicle, remove the toothed drive belt, sump and oil pump as previously described.

(2) Where fitted, remove the clutch assembly as described in the clutch section of this manual.

(3) Mark the relationship of the flywheel or drive plate to the crankshaft.

(4) Hold the flywheel or drive plate and remove the retaining bolts.

(5) Withdraw the flywheel or drive plate from the crankshaft.

(6) Withdraw the crankshaft gear from the front of the crankshaft and mark the front of the gear to ensure correct assembly.

(7) Remove the timing cover bolts and withdraw the timing cover from the front of the cylinder block.

(8) Ensure that the big end bearing caps and connecting rods are numbered in relation to each other to facilitate correct assembly.

(9) Remove the big end bearing cap nuts and lift off the bearing caps. If any bearing shell remained on the crankshaft journal remove the shell and insert it in its correct cap.

(10) Carefully push each connecting rod assembly up the bore as far as possible without exceeding the upper limits of the piston stroke.

(11) Check the crankshaft end float as follows:

Mount a dial gauge onto the front surface of the cylinder block with the plunger bearing onto the end of the crankshaft.

Prise the crankshaft rearward and zero the gauge.

Prise the crankshaft forward and note the reading. If the centre main bearing thrust washers are still serviceable the crankshaft end float will be within specifications.

(12) Ensure that the main bearing caps are marked and numbered in relation to their position in the cylinder block.

(13) Remove the main bearing cap bolts.

(14) Lift the main bearing caps from the crankshaft. If any bearing shell remained on the crankshaft journal, remove the shell and insert it into its correct cap.

To determine the main bearing clearance proceed as follows:

(a) Wipe the crankshaft journal and the bearing shell with a clean lint free cloth.

(b) Place a piece of Plastigage across the full width of the crankshaft journal.

(c) Instal the bearing cap and shell and torque the bolts to specifications evenly.

(d) Remove the bolts and the cap and measure the width of the spread Plastigage with the scale on the packet to determine the bearing running clearance.

(e) Repeat the checking procedure on all journals.

NOTE: Do not rotate the crankshaft with the Plastigage

Centre Main Bearing Cap Removed to Show Crankshaft End-Float Thrust Washers.

installed or tap the bearing cap with a hammer in an attempt to spread the Plastigage, tightening of the bolts is sufficient.

(15) Lift the crankshaft from the cylinder block using care not to dislodge or damage the upper half of the main bearing shells if they are to be used again.

(16) If new bearing shells and/or the centre main bearing thrust washers are to be installed, remove the old parts from the cylinder block.

(17) Remove the rear oil seal from the end of the crankshaft.

TO CHECK AND INSPECT

(1) Visually inspect the crankshaft journals and crankpins for damage or scoring.

(2) If the crankshaft is visually fit for further service, measure the main bearing journals and the big end crankpins.

NOTE: The big end bearing parent bore, the crankpin journal, the main bearing journals and the main bearing journal parent bores can vary in size within standard specifications and are indicated by the letter 'b' or 'r' stamped on the machined surface of the cylinder block on the oil pump side, matched bearings are marked with blue (b) red (r) paint. Blue paint (b) indicates the smaller size and red paint (r) the larger size.

Should the letters 'OS' be stamped on the block after the letters 'b' or 'r' this will indicate that the parent bores are 0.40 mm. oversize and an equivalently marked oversize bearing should be fitted.

(3) Note the measurements and compare them to specifications. If the journals or crankpins are worn have the crankshaft ground to the nearest undersize and renew the bearings.

NOTE: If wear or damage is such that the journals or crankpins cannot be reground to take any one of the range of available undersize bearings, then the crankshaft will have to be renewed.

(4) Check the wearing surfaces of the centre main thrust washers for pitting. If pitting is evident or if the washers were found to be worn excessively when checking the crankshaft end float, then renew the washers.

(5) Clean all traces of the old sump and timing cover gaskets from the cylinder block.

(6) Thoroughly clean the original, new, or reground crankshaft in a suitable cleaning solvent and wipe dry with a clean lint free cloth.

(7) Using a piece of stiff wire ensure that all the oil galleries are clear. As necessary rewash the crankshaft.

TO INSTAL

(1) If the crankshaft is being renewed instal a new spigot bearing into the crankshaft using a suitable tool. Sparingly smear the inside of the bearing with a molybdenum based grease.

(2) Instal new bearing shells where necessary correctly engaging the tangs of the shells in the upper recess of the cylinder block web or connecting rod.

(3) Instal new thrust washers as necessary to the centre main bearing web of the cylinder block.

(4) Smear all the upper bearing shells with engine oil.

(5) Carefully place the crankshaft in position in the cylinder block ensuring that the thrust washers are not dislodged or jammed.

(6) Instal new bearing shells to the caps where necessary correctly engaging the tangs of the shells in the recess of the caps.

(7) Smear the cap bearing shells with engine oil.

(8) Insert the new thrust washers to the centre main bearing cap as necessary.

(9) Instal the main bearing caps to their correct positions in the cylinder block and instal the main bearing bolts finger tight.

(10) Torque the bolts, except for the rear main bearing bolts, to specifications.

(11) Lever the crankshaft rearward and then forward slowly. With the crankshaft held forward torque the rear main bearing bolts to specifications.

(12) Recheck the crankshaft end float as previously described and if necessary fit oversize thrust washers to bring the end float within specifications. Rotate the crankshaft to ensure that it is not binding on the thrust washers or bearings.

(13) Using Plastigage recheck the main bearing clearance to ensure that the correct replacement bearings have been installed.

After checking torque the bolts to specifications.

(14) Draw each connecting rod in turn towards the crankpin and guide the connecting rod onto the crankpin without dislodging the bearing shell.

(15) Instal the big end bearing caps aligning the numbers on the rods and caps correctly.

(16) Torque the big end retaining nuts evenly to specifications. Rotate the crankshaft to ensure that binding is not evident.

(17) Using Plastigage recheck the big end bearing

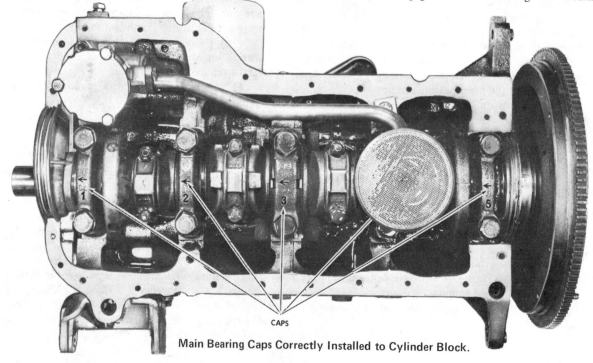

Main Bearing Caps Correctly Installed to Cylinder Block.

clearance to ensure that the correct replacement bearings have been installed.

After checking torque the nuts to specifications.

(18) Coat the outside of a new crankshaft rear oil seal with a suitable type sealant and the lip of the seal with engine oil.

(19) Using a suitable seal installing tool and hammer, instal the new seal into the recess over the rear of the crankshaft.

(20) Instal the flywheel or drive plate according to the marks made on removal. Torque the retaining bolts to specifications.

(21) Using a suitable thin punch and hammer drive the old oil seal from the timing cover with the timing cover suitably supported.

(22) Thoroughly clean the timing cover removing all traces of the old gaskets. Wipe the cover dry with a clean lint free cloth.

(23) Coat the outside of a new seal with a suitable type sealant and the lip of the seal with engine oil.

(24) Support the timing cover, and using a suitable seal installing tool and hammer, instal the new seal squarely into the timing cover.

(25) Coat both sides of a new timing cover gasket with a suitable type sealant and instal the timing cover and gasket.

(26) Tighten the timing cover bolts evenly and securely.

(27) Slide the crankshaft gear onto the front of the crankshaft according to the mark made on removal.

(28) Further installation procedures should be carried out as advised under the appropriate headings and sub-headings for the components being installed.

9. ENGINE MOUNTINGS

FRONT

To Remove and Instal

(1) Raise the front of the vehicle and support on stands placed beneath the lower control arms as close as practicable to the road wheels.

(2) Interpose a block of wood between the engine sump and a jack. Position the jack so that it will raise that side of the engine from which the mounting is being removed.

(3) Take the weight of the engine slightly with the jack.

(4) Remove the engine mounting top and bottom retaining nuts and washers.

(5) Raise the jack sufficiently to enable the engine mounting to be withdrawn from the mounting brackets.

(6) Manoeuvre the engine mounting from between the brackets.

Installation is a reversal of the removal procedure allowing the full weight of the engine assembly to bear on the mounting before tightening the retaining nuts.

REAR

To Remove and Instal

(1) Raise the rear of the vehicle and support it on stands placed beneath the rear axle housing as close as practicable to the road wheels.

(2) Interpose a block of wood between the jack and the transmission and take the weight of the engine and transmission on the jack.

(3) Remove the rear cross-member to side frame bolts.

(4) Remove the centre bolt and withdraw the cross-member from the vehicle.

(5) Remove the retaining bolts and lift the engine mounting from the cross-member.

Installation is a reversal of the removal procedure.

10. ENGINE VENTILATION SYSTEM

DESCRIPTION

With the engine running ventilating air is drawn through the engine by the reduced pressure in the inlet manifold. The volume of air drawn through the engine is dependent on engine loadings (reduced pressure in the manifold) and is controlled by the regulator valve.

Fresh air is drawn in through the oil filler cap into the crankcase then through the oil separator, regulator valve (mounted on the top of the oil separator) and the connecting hose between the regulator valve and the inlet manifold.

The crankcase fumes are drawn into the cylinders and mixed and burnt with the fuel air mixture.

TO CLEAN REGULATOR VALVE

(1) Raise the engine bonnet and fit a fender cover to the left side fender.

(2) Remove the air cleaner from the engine as previously described so as to gain working room.

(3) Disconnect the manifold hose from the regulator valve.

(4) Remove the regulator valve from the oil separator.

(5) Clean the regulator valve in a suitable cleaning solvent and then blow it clean with compressed air.

(6) Instal the regulator valve into the oil separator and reconnect the manifold hose.

(7) Instal the air cleaner as previously described.

(8) Remove the fender cover and close the bonnet.

11. ENGINE FAULT DIAGNOSIS

1. **Engine will not start by normal cranking.**

Possible cause

(a) Dirty or corroded distributor points.
(b) Carburettor flooding.
(c) Moisture on high tension wires and/or inside distributor cap.
(d) Dirt or water in carburettor and fuel system.
(e) Incorrectly set spark plug gaps.
(f) Faulty coil or capacitor.
(g) Faulty low or high tension wires.
(h) Fuel vapor lock.
(i) Faulty fuel pump.
(j) Incorrectly set ignition timing.
(k) Broken or short-circuited low tension lead to distributor points.

Remedy

— Clean or renew and adjust points.
— Check needle valve and float, clean out fuel system.
— Dry out high tension wires and cap.

— Clean out carburettor and fuel system.
— Reset spark plug gaps to specification.
— Test and renew faulty components.
— Test and renew faulty wires.
— Check source of vapor lock and insulate against heat.
— Test and overhaul fuel pump.
— Check and retime ignition.
— Test and renew lead.

2. **Engine will not start — weak or erratic cranking.**

Possible cause

(a) Weak or faulty battery.
(b) Fault in starter lead or solenoid.
(c) Faulty starter.

Remedy

— Recharge or renew battery.
— Test and renew faulty components.
— Test and overhaul starter.

3. **Engine stalls**

Possible cause

(a) Idling speed set too slow.
(b) Idling mixture too lean or rich.
(c) Carburettor flooding or float-level incorrectly set.
(d) Fault in coil or capacitor.
(e) Valve clearance out of adjustment.
(f) Air leak at inlet manifold or carburettor flange.
(g) Carbon tracking or cracked distributor cap.
(h) Weak or faulty battery and/or corroded terminals.

(i) Excessive wear in distributor shaft and bushes or contact breaker cam.
(j) Burned, warped or pitted valves.

Remedy

— Readjust idling speed stop screw.
— Readjust idling mixture screw and idling speed screw.
— Check needle valve or reset float level.
— Test and renew faulty component.
— Adjust valve clearance.
— Tighten securing bolts or renew gaskets.
— Clean or renew cap.
— Recharge or renew battery and/or clean or renew terminals.
— Renew worn components.

— Carry out top overhaul on engine.

4. **Engine missing at idling speed.**

Possible cause

(a) Dirty, defective or incorrectly set spark plugs.
(b) Burned or pitted distributor contact points.
(c) Loose or broken low or high tension wires in ignition system.
(d) Carburettor idling mixture out of adjustment.
(e) Burned or cracked distributor rotor.
(f) Moisture on high tension wires, spark plug or distributor cap.

Remedy

— Clean or renew and set spark plugs.
— Clean or renew and adjust contacts.
— Tighten or renew defective components.

— Adjust idling mixture screw.
— Renew faulty component.
— Dry out high tension system and cap.

5. **Engine misses on acceleration.**

Possible cause

(a) Distributor points dirty or incorrectly adjusted.
(b) Spark plug/s dirty, faulty or gap set too wide.
(c) Dirt or water in carburettor.
(d) Carburettor accelerator pump discharge jet blocked or pump defective.
(e) Coil or capacitor faulty.
(f) Incorrect ignition timing.
(g) Burned, warped or pitted valves.

Remedy

— Clean and readjust points.
— Clean or renew and reset faulty plug/s.
— Clean and blow out carburettor and fuel pump filter.
— Clean out carburettor.

— Renew defective component.
— Check and reset ignition timing.
— Carry out top overhaul on engine.

6. **Engine misses at high speed.**

Possible cause

(a) Distributor points dirty or incorrectly adjusted.
(b) Spark plug/s dirty, faulty or gap set too wide.
(c) Dirt or water in carburettor.
(d) Burned or cracked distributor rotor.
(e) Faulty coil or capacitor.
(f) Dirt in carburettor power jet.
(g) Incorrect ignition timing.
(h) Excessive wear in distributor, shaft or cam.

Remedy

— Clean and readjust points.
— Clean or renew and reset faulty plug/s.
— Clean out carburettor and fuel pump filter.
— Renew faulty component.
— Renew faulty component.
— Clean and blow out carburettor.
— Check and reset ignition timing.
— Renew faulty components.

7. **Engine lacks power.**

Possible cause

(a) Dirty or incorrectly set spark plugs.
(b) Dirt or water in carburettor and fuel system.
(c) Incorrect ignition timing.
(d) Incorrect carburettor float level.
(e) Faulty fuel pump.
(f) Incorrect valve clearance.
(g) Faulty distributor automatic advance.
(h) Restricted muffler or tail pipe.
(i) Faulty coil or capacitor.
(j) Burned or cracked distributor rotor.
(k) Excessive wear in distributor shaft or cam.
(l) Incorrect valve timing.
(m) Burned, warped or pitted valves.
(n) Blown cylinder head gasket.
(o) Loss of compression.

Remedy

— Clean and reset gap to specifications.
— Drain and clean out fuel system and carburettor.
— Check and reset ignition timing.
— Check and reset float level.
— Check and overhaul fuel pump.
— Check and readjust valve clearance.
— Check and rectify or renew.
— Check and clean as necessary.
— Renew faulty component.
— Renew faulty component.
— Renew faulty components.
— Check and reset as necessary.
— Carry out top overhaul on engine.
— Renew gasket.
— Carry out compression test and rectify.

8. **Noisy valve operation.**

Possible cause

(a) Incorrectly adjusted clearance.
(b) Weak or broken valve spring.
(c) Worn valve guide(s).
(d) Worn cam/follower(s).

Remedy

— Check and adjust to specifications.
— Check and renew faulty components.
— Ream and fit oversize valve(s).
— Renew cam follower(s).

9. **Big end bearing noise.**

Possible cause

(a) Lack of adequate oil supply.

(b) Excessive bearing clearance.

(c) Thin oil or crankcase dilution.

(d) Low oil pressure.

(e) Misaligned big end bearings.

Remedy

— Check oil level in sump, condition of oil pump and relief valve. Renew oil filter element.
— Renew bearing shells, check and regrind journals if oval.
— Change to correct oil grade. Check operating conditions and cooling system thermostat.
— Check pressure relief valve and spring, oil filter by-pass valve.
— Align connecting rods and renew bearings if necessary.

10. Apparent main bearing noise.

Possible cause

  (a) Loose flywheel.
  (b) Loose crankshaft pulley.
  (c) Low oil pressure.

  (d) Excessive crankshaft end play.
  (e) Crankshaft journals out of round and excessive bearing to journal clearance.
  (f) Insufficient oil supply.

Remedy

  — Tighten securing bolts to specified torque.
  — Renew or tighten pulley.
  — Check bearing to journal clearance, check condition of oil pump and pressure relief valve. Recondition as necessary.
  — Renew centre main bearing thrust washers.
  — Regrind journals and fit undersize bearings.

  — Replenish oil in sump to correct level.

11. Excessive oil consumption.

Possible cause

  (a) Oil leaks.
  (b) Damaged or worn valve stem oil seals.
  (c) Excessive clearance, valve stem to valve guide.

  (d) Worn or broken rings.
  (e) Rings too tight or stuck in groves.
  (f) Excessive wear in cylinders, pistons and rings.
  (g) Compression rings incorrectly installed, oil rings clogged or broken.

Remedy

  — Check and renew gaskets as necessary.
  — Renew damaged or worn components.
  — Renew valve guides, bushes and valves, or ream and fit oversize valves.
  — Renew rings.
  — Renew rings and clean out ring grooves.
  — Recondition cylinders and renew pistons and rings.
  — Renew rings.

12. Drop in oil pressure.

Possible cause

  (a) Oil level low in sump.
  (b) Thin or diluted oil.

  (c) Oil pump relief valve stuck or spring broken.
  (d) Excessive bearing clearance.

  (e) Excessive wear of oil pump components.
  (f) Air leak in oiling system.

Remedy

  — Check and replenish to full mark.
  — Change to correct oil grade and rectify source of dilution.
  — Free valve or renew broken spring.
  — Renew bearing shells or recondition journals as necessary.
  — Renew or recondition oil pump.
  — Rectify as necessary.

COOLING SYSTEM

SPECIFICATIONS

Water pump:
- Type .... Centrifugal impeller
- Bearing type .... Double row ball bearing and shaft assembly

Thermostat:
- Type .... Wax pellet
- Commences to open ...... 85–89 deg C
- Fully open .... 99–102 deg C

Radiator cap release
- pressure .... 0.91 kg/cm^2

Cooling system capacity with heater:
- 1300 ohv .... 5.8 litres
- 1600 ohv .... 6.3 litres
- 2000 ohc .... 7.1 litres

Fan belt deflection .... 13 mm
Water pump bolt torque .... 0.97 kg/m
Thermostat housing bolt
- torque .... 2.00 kg/m
Fan blade bolt torque ...... 0.97 kg/m

1. DESCRIPTION

The cooling system is the thermo-syphon type with fan and water pump assistance. Two draining points are incorporated in the system, one at the bottom radiator tank and the other at the side of the cylinder block.

The system is also pressurised in order to raise the boiling point of the coolant within the system and so increase the efficiency of the engine.

NOTE: To avoid accidental scalding, use caution when releasing the radiator cap of an engine that is at normal operating temperature.

The fan and water pump are driven by a V-belt from the crankshaft. This belt also drives the generator or alternator whichever is fitted.

The water pump is fitted with a shaft and ball bearing assembly which is pre-lubricated and requires no further lubrication in service.

The water pump seal is a spring loaded carbon thrust washer and rubber bellows assembly.

Temperature in the cooling system is controlled by a thermostat located in the cylinder head water outlet pipe housing.

A by-pass is incorporated in the system to allow limited circulation of the coolant when the thermostat is closed.

2. RADIATOR

TO REMOVE

(1) Drain the cooling system at the tap on the lower radiator tank and from the plug on the side of the cylinder block and remove the radiator filler cap.

(2) Disconnect and remove the upper and lower radiator hoses at the engine and radiator.

(3) Remove the four bolts and washers securing the radiator to the front body panel and lift the radiator out of the vehicle.

NOTE: When a radiator that has been in use for some time is removed from a vehicle for repairs to the engine, it should not be allowed to stand empty for any length of time, it should be immersed in a tank of water or otherwise kept full. Failure to observe this precaution may result in overheating when the engine is put back into service.

This is caused by internal deposits in the radiator drying and flaking and so obstructing the circulation of the coolant in the system.

(4) Securely plug the water outlets in the upper and lower radiator tanks and fill the radiator assembly with clean water.

TO CHECK

(1) With the radiator removed from the vehicle, turn it upside down, apply a hose to the lower tank outlet and reverse flush the unit.

(2) Stand the radiator upright, and, using a jet of water or air pressure to the rear side of the core, remove any dirt or foreign matter that may have collected on the front of the core.

TO INSTAL

(1) Position the radiator assembly in the front panel opening and instal and tighten the four securing bolts and washers.

(2) Connect the upper and lower radiator hoses between the radiator and engine, using a smear of grease between the hoses and pipes.

NOTE: Inspect all hoses before installing for cracking or perishing and renew any hose, that upon inspection, proves to be unserviceable.

(3) Close the cooling system tap and instal the drain plug at the cylinder block.

Fill the system with clean water and instal the pressure cap.

(4) Start the engine and check that the water level in the radiator is approximately within 13 mm. of the bottom of the filler neck.

NOTE: Use care to avoid the risk of scalding when removing the radiator cap if the engine is hot.

3. THERMOSTAT

TO REMOVE AND INSTAL

(1) Remove the pressurised radiator cap and drain the water from the cooling system by opening the tap at the lower radiator tank and by removing the plug at the left hand side of the cylinder block.

NOTE: Use care to avoid scalding when releasing the pressure cap if the engine is hot.

(2) Disconnect and remove the top radiator hose and thermostat housing by releasing the hose clamp at the

View of Thermostat Housing and Thermostat. OHV Models.

radiator and removing the two bolts securing the housing to the cylinder head.

(3) On overhead valve engines withdraw the thermostat from the orifice in the cylinder head.

(4) On overhead cam engines remove the circlip and withdraw the thermostat from the thermostat housing.

NOTE: A visual examination of the thermostat will often determine its serviceability and obviate the necessity for further testing. For instance, a thermostat with its valve open when removed from a cold engine is obviously faulty and should be discarded and a new unit fitted.

Installation is a reversal of the removal procedure.

Fill the cooling system with clean water to approximately 13 mm. below the radiator filler neck. Check for water leaks.

TO CHECK

(1) Check that the thermostat valve is closed when the thermostat is cold.

(2) Suspend and immerse the thermostat, together with a reliable thermometer in a vessel of cold water, ensuring that neither the thermostat or thermometer is touching the sides or bottom of the vessel, and progressively heat the water.

(3) As the water heats, note the temperature readings on the thermometer when the thermostat valve commences to open. Refer to specifications.

A thermostat with opening and closing temperatures not within these specifications should be renewed.

4. WATER PUMP

TO REMOVE AND INSTAL

(1) Drain the cooling system from the two draining points as mentioned previously.

(2) Disconnect the upper and lower radiator hoses and the heater hose (if fitted) and remove the radiator assembly.

(3) Slacken the fan belt adjusting bracket bolt on the top of the generator or alternator and the two bolts attaching the generator or alternator to the mounting bracket on the cylinder block.

(4) Push the generator or alternator towards the cylinder block and remove the fan belt.

(5) Remove the four bolts securing the fan and fan pulley to the water pump and withdraw the fan, spacer and pulley.

(6) Unscrew the three water pump to cylinder block securing bolts and detach the water pump and gasket. Discard the gasket.

Installation is a reversal of the removal procedure.

Use a new gasket between the water pump and the front face of the cylinder block. Adjust the fan belt as described under FAN BELT – TO ADJUST.

TO DISMANTLE

(1) Drain the cooling system and remove the water pump as described previously.

(2) Using a suitable puller, withdraw the pump pulley flange from the forward end of the shaft and bearing assembly.

(3) Remove the bearing retaining clip and press the

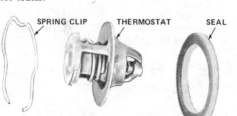

Thermostat and Associated Components. OHC Models.

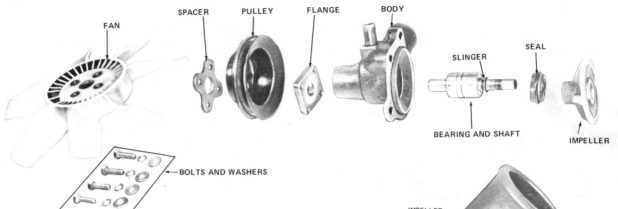

Dismantled View of Water Pump Components. OHC Models.

bearing and shaft assembly together with the seal and impeller out of the pump body.

(4) Press the impeller off the end of the shaft and bearing assembly and withdraw the seal assembly. Remove the water slinger bush from the impeller end of the shaft.

TO CHECK

NOTE: It is generally unnecessary to dismantle the water pump unless it is leaking water past the seal or the ball bearing has become noisy. It is therefore always good policy to instal a new seal assembly, bearing and shaft assembly and impeller.

(1) Check the pump body for cracks or damage.
(2) Check the bearing for looseness in the pump body bore and roughness in rotation.
(3) Check that the water drain hole in the pump body is clear.

NOTE: When cleaning the pump components, do not immerse the shaft and bearing assembly in cleaning solvent, if the assembly is to be used again.

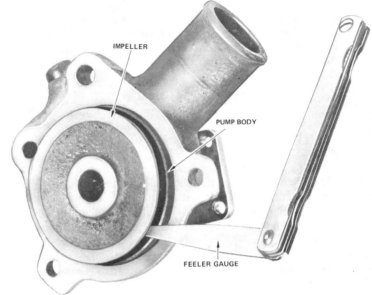

Checking Clearance Between Impeller and Pump Body.

TO ASSEMBLE

(1) Using a small amount of water proof sealing compound applied to the large end of the new seal assembly, press the new assembly into position in the pump body so that the carbon face of the seal will be facing the pump impeller.

(2) Instal the water slinger on the long end of the shaft assembly so that the lip of the slinger is positioned approximately 13 mm. from the end of the bearing outer race.

(3) Apply pressure to the outer race of the bearing and press the bearing and shaft assembly into the pump body from the front, until the groove in the bearing outer race registers with the groove in the inner bore of the pump body and instal the bearing retaining clip.

(4) Support the pump on the front end of the shaft assembly, instal a new impeller with the blades facing the pump body and press it onto the shaft until a clearance of

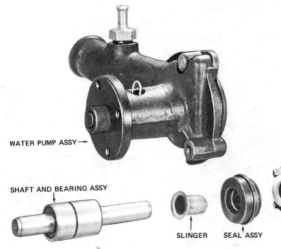

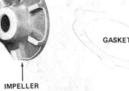

Showing Water Pump Assembly and Internal Components of Pump. OHV models.

0.76 mm. exists between the face of the impeller blades and the corresponding face of the pump body.

(5) Turn the pump over and support it on the impeller end of the shaft.

(6) With the bossed side of the pulley flange facing upwards, press the flange onto the front end of the shaft until the ends of the shaft and flange boss are flush.

NOTE: When pressing the pulley flange onto the shaft as detailed in operation (6), ensure that the assembly is supported directly on the end of the shaft and not on the impeller, otherwise the clearance between the impeller blades and the rear face of the pump body, as given in operation (4) may be decreased, with possible damage to the impeller and seal assembly.

5. FAN BELT

TO RENEW

(1) Loosen the two generator or alternator mounting bracket bolts and nuts.

(2) Loosen the generator or alternator adjusting bracket bolt and push the generator or alternator towards the cylinder block as far as it will go.

(3) Slip the old belt off the pulley and then manoeuvre it off the fan and crankshaft pulleys and remove it from the engine.

(4) Manoeuvre the new belt over the crankshaft and fan pulleys and position it on the generator or alternator pulley.

(5) Adjust the tension on the fan belt and tighten the adjusting bracket bolt

(6) Tighten the two mounting bracket bolts securely.

TO ADJUST

(1) Loosen the two generator or alternator mounting bracket bolts slightly.

(2) Loosen the adjusting bracket bolt, apply pressure at the drive end bracket to pull the generator or alternator away from the cylinder block sufficiently to give the belt enough tension to prevent it slipping on the pulleys.

(3) Hold the generator or alternator in this position and tighten the adjusting bracket and mounting bolts securely.

NOTE: Do not over-tension the fan belt as this could cause rapid wear in the water pump and generator or alternator bearings. The belt will have sufficient tension when it can be flexed approximately 13 mm. with finger and thumb pressure applied between the generator or alternator pulley and water pump pulley.

6. HEATER AND CONTROLS

TO REMOVE AND INSTAL HEATER

(1) Drain the cooling system by removing the plugs from the side of the cylinder block and the bottom tank of the radiator.

(2) Disconnect the electric wires to the heater at the connector.

(3) Disconnect the drain pipe from the heater.

(4) Disconnect the heater hoses from the heater.

(5) Disconnect the temperature control cable from the unit working from inside the vehicle.

(6) Remove the retaining screws and lift the heater unit from the bulkhead and out of the engine compartment.

Installation is a reversal of the removal procedure with attention to the following points:

(1) Use new gaskets as necessary on installation.

(2) Instal all retaining screws finger tight before tightening any individual screw.

(3) Renew unserviceable heater hoses or clips as necessary.

(4) Ensure that the heater drain pipe is securely connected.

(5) Reconnect the temperature control cable and the electrical connector.

(6) Refill the cooling system after installing and tightening the drain plugs.

(7) Start the engine and check for water leaks. Check the operation of the heater and adjust controls as necessary.

(8) Recheck the cooling system level after the engine has reached normal operating temperature.

TO REMOVE AND INSTAL CONTROLS

(1) Remove the radio aperture cover panel or where fitted, the radio.

(2) Remove the knob from the control levers after loosening the retaining screws.

(3) Using a suitable thin punch and small hammer, tap the pin from the centre control lever knob. Withdraw the centre knob.

(4) Working from behind the dash panel push out the bezels from the radio aperture and the heater control.

(5) Disconnect the electrical connections from the control unit.

(6) Disconnect both the upper control cables from the control unit.

(7) Remove the retaining screws and pivot the control unit upwards slightly to gain access to the lower cable retaining clip.

(8) Remove the lower cable outer retaining clip and disconnect the inner cable from the centre lever.

(9) Manoeuvre the control unit from the vehicle.

Installation is a reversal of the removal procedure with attention to the following points:

(1) With the control unit held in position behind the dash panel, move the lower control cable to its right hand side stop and reconnect the inner cable to the lever.

(2) Rotate the air distribution box flap clockwise, hold it in this position and reconnect the outer cable clip to the control unit.

(3) Instal and tighten the control unit retaining screws.

(4) Reconnect the upper left inner cable to the lever and move the lever to the left hand stop (screen) position.

(5) Rotate the flap anti-clockwise at the air distribution box end of the cable, hold the flap in this position and instal the outer cable retaining clip to the control unit.

(6) Connect the upper right inner cable to the lever

and move the control lever to within 3 mm. of the right stop (cool position).

(7) Rotate the temperature control regulator arm fully anti-clockwise, hold it in this position and instal the outer

cable retaining clip to the control unit.

(8) Reconnect the electrical wires to the control unit.

(9) Further installation is a reversal of the removal procedure.

7. COOLING SYSTEM FAULT DIAGNOSIS

1. **Coolant leakage — external.**

Possible cause	*Remedy*
(a) Loose hose clips or faulty hoses.	— Tighten hose clips or renew faulty components.
(b) Leaking radiator core or tanks.	— Repair or renew radiator.
(c) Worn or damaged water pump seal assembly.	— Renew seal assembly.
(d) Worn or damaged water pump bearing assembly.	— Renew water pump bearing and shaft assembly.
(e) Loose or rusted expansion plugs.	— Renew faulty components.
(f) External crack in cylinder block or head.	— Renew faulty components.
(g) Faulty cylinder head gasket or loose holding down bolts.	— Renew gasket and correctly tighten cylinder head bolts.
(h) Leaks at thermostat housing and/or water pump joint gaskets.	— Rectify leaks.

2. **Coolant leakage — internal.**

Possible cause	*Remedy*
(a) Crack in cylinder bore wall.	— Renew cylinder block.
(b) Crack in cylinder head, combustion chambers or valve ports.	— Renew cylinder head.
(c) Cylinder head cracked and leaking into valve rocker compartment.	— Renew cylinder head.
(d) Cracked cylinder block water jacket, leaking into engine tappet compartment.	— Renew cylinder block.
(e) Cylinder head gasket leak due to warped head.	— Reface cylinder head and renew gasket.

3. **Coolant loss by overflow.**

Possible cause	*Remedy*
(a) Over-full system.	— Drain and refill to specifications.
(b) Faulty pressurised radiator cap.	— Renew faulty cap.
(c) Blocked radiator core tubes.	— Clean or renew radiator core.
(d) Coolant foaming due to poor quality anti-freeze or corrosion inhibitor.	— Drain system and renew coolant and additive.

4. **Engine overheating.**

Possible cause	*Remedy*
(a) Obstructed air passage through radiator core from front to rear.	— Blow out obstruction from rear to front of radiator core with compressed air or water pressure.
(b) Incorrect ignition timing.	— Check and reset ignition timing.
(c) Incorrect valve timing.	— Check and reset valve timing.
(d) Low engine oil level.	— Stop engine immediately and replenish oil in sump.
(e) Engine tight after overhaul.	— Check and if satisfactory, stop engine and allow to cool out.
(f) Poor circulation.	— Check and rectify as under item (5).
(g) Loss of coolant due to overflow.	— Check and rectify as under item (3).
(h) Faulty thermostat.	— Renew thermostat.
(i) Restricted muffler or tail pipe, accompanied by loss of power.	— Remove restrictions or renew component/s.
(j) Incorrectly adjusted or dragging brakes.	— Check and rectify by adjustment or renewal of components.

5. **Coolant circulation faulty.**

Possible cause	*Remedy*
(a) Partial blockage of radiator core tubes.	— Clean out or renew radiator core.
(b) Water sludge deposits in engine water jacket.	— Clean and flush engine water jacket and add rust inhibitor to coolant.
(c) Fan belt broken or slipping.	— Renew or adjust fan belt.
(d) Faulty water pump or thermostat.	— Overhaul or renew water pump, renew thermostat.
(e) Collapsing lower radiator hose.	— Check and renew lower radiator hose and check radiator core tubes.
(f) Insufficient coolant in system.	— Replenish coolant.

FUEL SYSTEM
SPECIFICATIONS

FORD CARBURETTOR

Type	Single barrel downdraught

Model applications:

1300 OHV low compression (man. choke)	71—IW—9510—JA
1300 OHV high compression (man. choke)	71—IW—9510—KA
1600 OHV low compression (man. choke)	71—IW—9510—BJA
1600 OHV high compression (man. choke)	71—IW—9510—VA
1600 OHV high compression (auto. choke)	71—IW—9510—ZA
*1600 OHV high compression (man. choke)	
— early productions	71—IW—9510—VA
— late productions	71—IW—9510—VB
*1600 OHV high compression (auto. choke)	
— early production	71—IW—9510—ZA
— late production	71—IW—9510—ZB

*Australian production only.

Venturi diameter:

All models except 71—IW—9510—JA and KA .	28.000 mm
71—IW—9510—JA and KA	25.000 mm

Main discharge jet:

71—IW—9510—JA 71—IW—9510—KA . . . . 71—IW—9510—VB *71—IW—9510—ZB	125 140
71—IW—9510—ZB 71—IW—9510—VA 71—IW—9510—ZA 71—IW—9510—BJA *71—IW—9510—VA *71—IW—9510—ZA	145

*Australian production only.

Float level	27.930 mm
Float travel	6.600 mm

Choke plate pull down clearance:

All models except 71—IW—9510—JA and KA	3.550 mm
71—IW—9510—JA 71—IW—9510—KA	3.30 mm
De-choke setting (auto. choke only)	7.620 mm
Accelerator pump stroke	2.660 mm

Automatic choke models only:

Vacuum piston link hole	Outer
Thermostat spring slot	Centre

Idle speed:

All models except *71—IW—9510—VA and ZA	800 rpm
*71—IW—9510—VA	
*71—IW—9510—ZA	700 rpm

*Australian production only.

Fast idle speed:

With manual choke — BJA — VA — VB	1000 rpm
— JA — KA	1400 — 1600 rpm
All with automatic choke	2050 — 2250 rpm

WEBER CARBURETTOR

Type	Dual barrel downdraught

Model applications:

1600 OHV GT (man. choke) manual trans	71—IF—9510—FB
1600 OHV GT (auto choke) auto trans	71—IF—9510—GB
2000 OHC (auto choke) manual trans	71—HF—9510—DC
2000 OHC (auto choke) auto trans	71—HF—9510—EC
*2000 OHC (auto choke) manual trans —	
— early production	71—HF—9510—EA
— late production	71—HF—9510—EB
*2000 OHC (auto choke) auto trans —	
— early production	71—HF—9510—DA
— late production	71—HF—9510—DB

*Australian production only.

Primary Venturi diameter	26 mm
Secondary Venturi diameter	27 mm

Main discharge jet:

Primary Venturi	140
Secondary Venturi— — 71—IF—9510—FB and GB	135
— 71—HF—9510—EA and DA	125
All other models	140

Air correction jet:

Primary Venturi — — All except 71—IF—9510—FB and GB	170
71—IF—9510—FB — 71—IF—9510—GB	165
Secondary Venturi	160

Emulsion tube type:

Primary	F50
Secondary — — All except 71—IF—9510—FB, GB	F50
— 71—IF—9510—FB — 71—IF—9510—GB	F6

Idling jet:
  Primary Venturi
    – All except 71–HF–
    9510–DA, DB, DC   55
    – 71–HF–9510–DA, DB,
    DC   60
  Secondary Venturi – all
    models   50
Accelerator pump jet:
  All models except 71–IF–
  9510–FB   50
  71–IF–9510–FB ....   50 special
Needle valve ....   2.0 mm
Float level – cover
  vertical:
  *71–HF–9510–DB, EB .. :   37.008 – 37.490 mm
  71–HF–9510–DA, EA ...   38.660 – 39.240 mm
  71–HF–9510–DB, DC,
  EB, EC ....   40.750 – 41.250 mm
  – with plastic float ......   35.000 – 35.500 mm
  71–HF–9510–FB, GB ...   40.750 – 41.250 mm
*Australian production only.
Float drop-cover horizontal:
  71–HF–9510–FB. GB, DC,
  EC, EB, DB ....   50.00 – 51.5 mm
  *71–HF–9510–EA, DA ..   48.77 – 50.6 mm
  71–HF–9510–EB, DB ...   50.50 – 52.00 mm
*Australian production only.
Choke plate pull down:
  71–IF–9510–FB ....   4.450 mm
  71–IF–9510–GB ....   3.500 – 5.500 mm
  71–HF–9510–DC, EB,
  EC ....   4.000 – 6.500 mm
  *71–HF–9510–DA, DB, EA,
  EB ....   4.000 mm
Secondary throttle valve
  adjustment ....   0.051 – 0.076 mm
*Australian production only.
Idling speed:
  All models except
  71–IF–9510–FB ....   700 rpm
  71–IF–9510–FB ....   800 rpm
Fast idling speed setting:
  All models except 71–
  IF-9510–FB and GB .....   1.00 – 1.10 mm
  71–IF–9510–FB ....   0.850 mm
  71–IF–9510–GB ....   0.800 – 0.850 mm
Fast idling speed ....   3000 rpm on high cam

FUEL PUMP

Type ....   Mechanical diaphragm
Delivery pressure:
  1300 and 1600 engine .... $0.250 – 0.350 \text{ kg/cm}^2$
  2000 engine .... $0.260 – 0.350 \text{ kg/cm}^2$
Fuel filter ....   In line nylon mesh type
Fuel tank capacity ....   54.0 litres

AIR CLEANER

Type ....   Replaceable paper element

TORQUE WRENCH SETTINGS

Fuel pump retaining
  bolts ....   2.1 kg/m
Carburettor to manifold nuts:
  OHV engine ....   2.1 kg/m
  OHC engine ....   1.0 kg/m

1. FORD TYPE CARBURETTOR

DESCRIPTION

The Ford carburettor as fitted on the 1300 and 1600 cc engine is a single venturi downdraught submerged jet type.

A power valve brings a further jet into circuit at full load conditions to prevent over lean mixtures at wide open throttle.

This power valve, operated by manifold depression, keeps the additional jet out of circuit at part open throttle and thereby makes it possible to use a smaller main jet thus providing part throttle economy.

Rich mixtures for acceleration are provided by a mechanically operated diaphragm type accelerator pump.

A strangler type semi-automatic choke provides rich mixtures required for starting from cold.

The choke is inter-connected to the throttle to provide a pre-determined throttle opening when the choke valve is closed.

On manual transmission models and all 1300 cc engine models the choke is operated from the fascia, on automatic transmission 1600 cc models a fully automatic choke is incorporated.

Automatic choke control is affected by heated water circulation in conjunction with a thermostatic device and a vacuum piston and lever.

The float chamber is internally vented at speeds above idle by a tube into the carburettor air intake.

An adaptor on the float chamber cover provides venting at idle speeds and when the engine is stopped.

Adjustment for idling is provided by a volume control screw and a throttle stop screw.

Float setting, choke adjustment, fast idle and accelerator pump stroke are adjusted by bending tabs and operating rods to specified dimensions.

TO REMOVE AND INSTAL

(1) Raise the engine bonnet and fit fender covers to both front fenders.

(2) Remove the air cleaner from the carburettor.

(3) Detach the throttle shaft from the throttle lever.

(4) Disconnect the fuel feed pipe and the vacuum advance pipe at the carburettor.

(5) On models fitted with manual choke disconnect the choke control cable.

(6) On models fitted with automatic choke partially drain the cooling system and disconnect the automatic choke hoses.

(7) Remove the two nuts and spring washers securing the carburettor to the inlet manifold and withdraw the carburettor and gasket from the engine. Discard the gasket.

Installation is a reversal of the removal procedure with attention to the following points:

Use a new gasket between the carburettor and the inlet manifold.

Ensure that the choke valve is fully open when the choke control knob is in the full off position on the dash panel.

TO DISMANTLE
Manual Choke Models

(1) Remove the carburettor from the engine as previously described.

(2) Take out the six screws and washers and detach the top cover from the carburettor. Disconnect the choke link from the choke lever during this operation.

(3) Turn the carburettor upside down and withdraw the float lever hinge pin and float. Discard the top cover gasket.

(4) Lift out the needle valve and unscrew the needle valve seat from the top cover. Withdraw the gauze filter and gasket.

(5) Tilt the carburettor main body and remove the accelerator pump discharge weight and ball.

(6) Remove the main jet.

(7) Take out the four securing screws and remove the accelerator pump body and lever assembly, diaphragm and diaphragm spring from the side of the carburettor body.

(8) Detach the accelerator pump push rod and spring assembly from the pump lever and the throttle spindle arm.

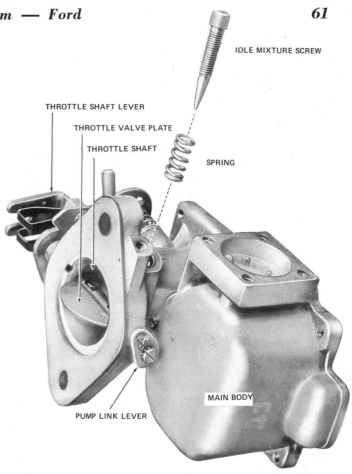

Carburettor Main Body with Idle Mixture Screw and Spring Removed. (Ford carburettor — manual choke.)

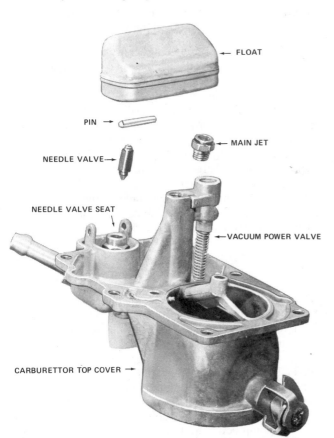

Ford Carburettor Top Cover with Main Jet and Needle Valve and Float Assembly Removed. (Manual Choke.)

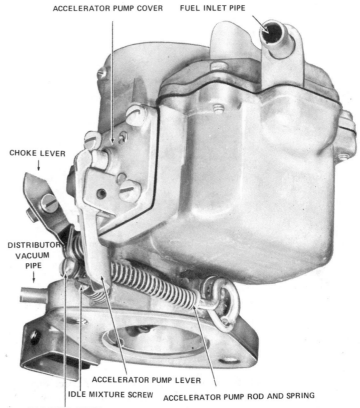

Ford Manual Choke Carburettor.

(9) Remove the idling mixture screw and spring and the throttle stop screw and spring.

NOTE: Further dismantling will be unnecessary unless the throttle valve shaft or the choke valve shaft are to be removed.

(10) Remove the retaining screw and detach the accelerator pump push rod arm from the throttle spindle.

(11) Remove the two peened screws securing the throttle valve to the throttle shaft, lift out the valve plate and withdraw the throttle shaft from the body complete with return spring.

(12) Extract the pins that hold the air cleaner retainer bracket to the carburettor top cover when fitted and remove the retainer bracket.

(13) Remove the two screws securing the choke valve to the choke shaft, lift out the valve plate and withdraw the choke shaft from the top cover complete with the pull down stop and spring.

Automatic Choke Models

(1) Remove the carburettor from the engine as previously described.

(2) Take out the securing screw holding the fast idle cam and choke connecting link to the carburettor main body.

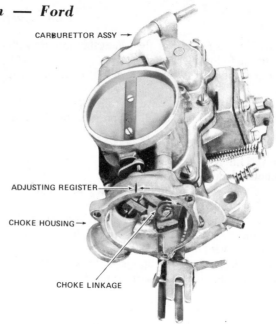

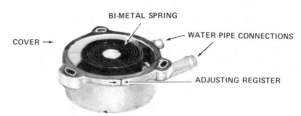

Ford Automatic Choke Carburettor with Choke Cover and Bi-metal Spring Removed.

(3) Take out the six retaining screws from around the carburettor top cover and detach the top cover with gasket.

(4) Turn the carburettor upside down and withdraw the float lever hinge pin and float.

(5) Lift out the needle valve and unscrew the needle valve seat from the top cover. Withdraw the gauze filter and gasket. Remove and discard the top cover gasket.

(6) Tilt the carburettor main body and remove the accelerator pump discharge weight and ball.

(7) Remove the main jet.

(8) Take out the three screws holding the choke unit outer casing to the top cover and remove the outer housing complete with gasket and bi-metal spring.

NOTE: The choke unit inner and outer casings have aligning marks which should be noted on dismantling.

(9) Remove the screw securing the thermostatic spring lever, and withdraw the thermostatic spring lever, the choke piston lever, the choke piston link and the piston from the inner casing.

(10) Take out the two securing screws attaching the choke unit inner casing to the carburettor top cover, slide the inner casing off the choke operating lever shaft complete with teflon bush and gasket.

(11) Take out the four securing screws and remove the accelerator pump body and lever assembly, diaphragm and diaphragm spring from the side of the carburettor body.

(12) Detach the accelerator pump push rod and spring

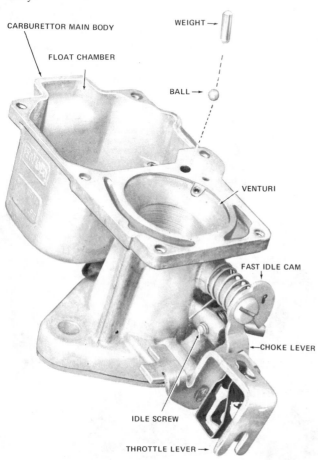

Carburettor Main Body with Accelerator Pump Discharge Weight and Ball Removed. (Ford carburettor — manual choke.)

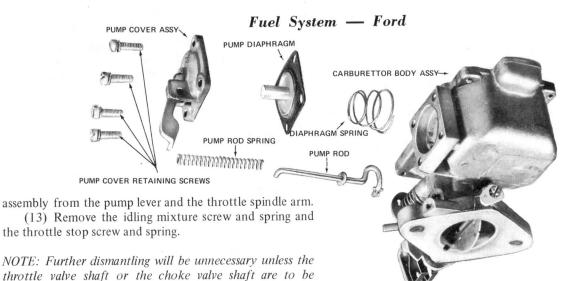

PUMP COVER ASSY.

PUMP DIAPHRAGM

CARBURETTOR BODY ASSY→

DIAPHRAGM SPRING

PUMP ROD SPRING

PUMP ROD

PUMP COVER RETAINING SCREWS

assembly from the pump lever and the throttle spindle arm.

(13) Remove the idling mixture screw and spring and the throttle stop screw and spring.

NOTE: Further dismantling will be unnecessary unless the throttle valve shaft or the choke valve shaft are to be renewed.

(14) Remove the retaining screw and detach the accelerator pump push rod arm from the throttle spindle.

(15) Remove the two peened screws securing the throttle valve to the throttle shaft, lift out the valve plate and withdraw the throttle shaft from the body complete with return spring.

(16) Extract the pins that hold the air cleaner retainer bracket to the carburettor top cover when fitted and remove the retainer bracket.

(17) Remove the two screws securing the choke valve to the choke shaft, lift out the valve plate and withdraw the choke shaft from the top cover complete with the pull down stop and spring.

TO CHECK AND INSPECT

(1) If the carburettor has seen considerable service, check the throttle shaft and bearing bores for wear.

(2) Check the carburettor gasket surfaces for distortion with a suitable straight edge.

(3) Check the fast idle linkage for wear and correct adjustment and that the choke valve is fully closed by the operating arm.

(4) Check the accelerator pump diaphragm for deterioration.

(5) Check the needle valve for wear on its seating surface.

(6) Blow out all jets and passages in the carburettor main body and top cover with compressed air to remove any dirt or foreign matter.

NOTE: Do not use wire probes to clean out jets or air bleeds.

TO ASSEMBLE
Manual Choke Models

(1) Refit the pull down stop and spring to the choke shaft and fit to the carburettor top cover, replace the choke valve plate in position and instal but do not fully tighten the two valve plate retaining screws.

NOTE: The choke valve plate is stamped with a small indent or rectangle, this should be fitted uppermost, adjacent to the choke valve shaft with the indentation side

Accelerator Pump Cover Assembly and Associated Components. (Ford carburettor — manual choke.)

on the top when the choke valve plate is closed.

With the choke valve in the closed position securely tighten the two valve screws.

(2) Replace the air cleaner retainer brackets when fitted and press into position the two retainer pins which secure it to the top cover.

(3) Refit the return spring to the throttle shaft and instal the shaft and spring to the carburettor body, instal the accelerator pump lever to the shaft with the 'O' mark away from the carburettor body, place the throttle valve plate in position but do not tighten the two valve plate securing screws.

NOTE: The throttle valve plate must be fitted with the two indentations adjacent to the throttle valve plate securing screw heads when the valve is in the closed position.

With the throttle valve in the closed position securely .tighten the two valve plate screws.

(4) Refit the idling mixture screw and spring also the throttle stop screw and spring. Do not screw fully home with undue pressure. Screw the mixture screw out 1½ turns as a preliminary adjustment.

(5) Refit the main jet and tighten with a suitable size spanner ensuring that the jet is not overtightened.

(6) Assemble the accelerator pump refitting the diaphragm and plunger to the pump cover, refit the spring with its large diameter over the three locating pegs in the main body, place the diaphragm and cover into position and secure with the four securing screws.

Refit the pump push rod and spring locating the hooked end in the pump operating lever and securing the other end in the throttle shaft lever, secure the lever to the throttle shaft with the securing screw and washer.

(7) Refit the screen gauze and the needle valve seat.

(8) Fit a new gasket to the carburettor top cover.

(9) Instal the needle valve to its seat with the tapered end towards the seating, place the float assembly in position and refit the pivot pin. See the relevant section to adjust the float level.

(10) Refit the accelerator pump discharge ball valve and weight.

(11) Instal the top cover to the carburettor main body connecting the choke link into the pull down stop and fast idle cam. Ensure that the gasket is correctly positioned and refit the six retaining screws and washers. Fit the choke cable retaining bracket and tighten all securing screws.

(12) Instal the carburettor to the engine and connect up as described previously.

(13) Adjust the idling speed, mixture and choke link as described under the appropriate headings.

Automatic Choke Models

(1) Carry out operations 1 to 10 as described for the manual choke carburettors in the preceding section.

(2) Fit a new gasket and teflon bush to the choke unit inner casing, ensuring that the link connecting the choke valve shaft and the choke operating lever shaft is connected.

(3) Slide the choke unit inner casing over the choke operating lever shaft, position on the carburettor top and fit the two securing screws, tightening them evenly.

(4) Refit the piston into the cylinder of the choke unit inner casing, fit the connecting link and piston operating lever, refit the arm connecting the choke operating lever to the bi-metal spring over the two flats provided on the end of the choke operating lever shaft, instal the securing screws and tighten. Ensure that the piston operating lever moves freely on the choke operating lever shaft.

(5) Fit a new gasket to the choke unit outer casing and instal to the inner casing, engaging the tongue of the bi-metal spring in the centre aperture of the arm connecting it to the choke

(6) Align the marks on the choke unit inner and outer casing, refit the three securing screws and tighten evenly.

(7) Instal the top cover to the main carburettor body ensuring that the gasket is correctly positioned before progressively tightening the six securing screws.

(8) Instal the carburettor to the engine and connect up as described previously.

(9) Adjust the idling speed and mixture as described under the appropriate headings.

TO ADJUST IDLING SPEED AND MIXTURE
With Instruments

(1) Connect a vacuum gauge with a suitable 'T' adaptor into the crankcase ventilation tube.

(2) With a tachometer connected to the engine, run the engine until it reaches operating temperature and adjust the throttle stop screw until the correct specified idle speed is obtained.

(3) Adjust the idling mixture screw until the highest vacuum reading on the vacuum gauge is obtained. It may be necessary to readjust the idle speed during this operation.

(4) Stop the engine and detach the vacuum gauge and tachometer.

NOTE: An exhaust gas analyser, if available, can be used to adjust the mixture, or check as a comparison with the vacuum gauge readings. An optimum mixture strength reading is desired on the gas analyser at engine idle.

Without Instruments

NOTE: If instruments are not available to adjust the idling speed and mixture the following method may be used as an alternative.

(1) Start the engine and bring to normal operating temperature by running at approximately 1200 rpm for 15 minutes. After warm up adjust the throttle stop screw to

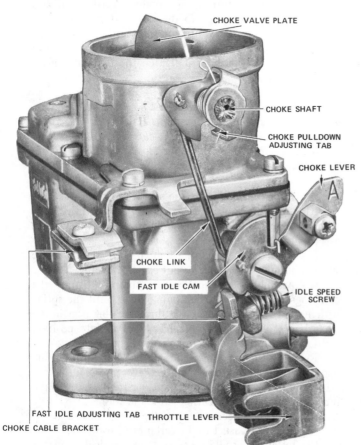

Ford Manual Choke Carburettor Showing Choke and Fast Idle Linkage.

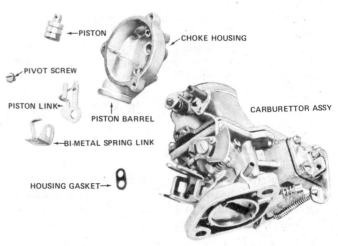

Ford Automatic Choke Carburettor showing Automatic Choke Piston. Linkage and Inner Cover Components.

give an idle speed of approximately 700/800 rpm.

(2) Turn the idling mixture screw in clockwise until the engine slows and begins to falter, then turn the mixture screw anti-clockwise until the engine runs smoothly again, but does not lose speed or hunt.

(3) Re-adjust the throttle stop screw to give the desired idling speed, see Specifications after which it may be necessary to vary the idling mixture by adjusting slightly to maintain smooth idling.

NOTE: Turning the idling mixture screw in a clockwise direction gives a leaner mixture and anti-clockwise a richer mixture.

Correct idle speed and mixture cannot be adjusted or maintained if the carburettor air cleaner element is impregnated with dirt.

TO ADJUST CHOKE PLATE PULL DOWN
Manual Choke

(1) This operation can be done with the carburettor removed or in position on the engine.

(2) Remove the carburettor air cleaner.

(3) Operate the choke lever to which the choke wire is attached until it comes against the abutment stop. The choke should now be in the fully closed position.

(4) Press down the choke valve plate and check the measurement between the bottom edge of the choke valve plate and the side of the carburettor body air intake using the correct size drill shank or gauge rod. This measurement should be as specified, see Specification section.

(5) If adjustment is required, place a drill or gauge rod with a diameter of that specified between the bottom edge of the choke valve plate and the side of the carburettor body air intake. If necessary, bend the metal tab which is located on the end of the choke shaft in the direction required to obtain this measurement.

(6) Instal the carburettor air cleaner.

FAST IDLE ADJUSTMENT
Manual Choke

(1) Remove the carburettor air cleaner.

(2) Connect a tachometer to the engine.

(3) Start and run the engine until its normal operating temperature is reached and an idle speed at 700–800 rpm is maintained.

(4) Hold the choke valve plate in the fully opened vertical position (engine running) and rotate the choke operating lever until it is stopped by the choke linkage.

(5) In this position check the engine rpm on the tachometer.

See Specifications to determine what the correct fast idle rpm should be. Stop the engine and adjust if necessary by bending the tab located against the fast idle cam.

NOTE: It will be necessary to move the accelerator lever linkage to the fully open position to bend the tab in the direction required. Bend the tab up to increase fast idle and down to decrease fast idle.

(6) Instal the carburettor air cleaner.

TO ADJUST CHOKE PLATE PULL DOWN
Automatic Choke

(1) Remove the carburettor air cleaner.

(2) Drain the cooling system at the radiator lower tank.

(3) Loosen the clips holding the water hoses to the automatic choke unit in the carburettor body and remove the hoses.

(4) Unscrew and remove the screws securing the choke unit outer housing and remove the housing complete with gasket and bi-metal spring.

(5) Press down on the vacuum piston, until the vacuum bleed port is revealed. Insert a length of wire 1.01 mm. diameter suitably bent to fit into this port. Allow the piston to rise and trap the wire. Close the choke plate until its progress is stopped through the linkage. Open the throttle valve sufficiently enough for the fast idle tab to clear the cam and measure the distance between the bottom edge of the choke valve plate and the side of the carburettor body air intake by inserting a drill shank or gauge rod of the specified diameter.

(6) If adjustment is required bend the extension of the choke thermostat lever at the vacuum piston linkage end and recheck the choke valve plate for the specified clearance.

(7) After completing the choke pull down adjustment carry out the fast idle adjustment as under the following heading.

FAST IDLE ADJUSTMENT
Automatic Choke

(1) With the choke plate pull down correctly adjusted and held in the full pull down position, check that the throttle lever fast idle tab is in the first tooth on the fast idle cam, if necessary bend the fast idle rod at its existing bend.

(2) Instal the bi-metal spring and choke unit outer housing, locating the spring in the centre slot and aligning the housing marks before finally tightening the retaining screws.

(3) Refit the two choke outer housing water hoses and fill the cooling system with clean water.

(4) Connect a tachometer to the engine and start and run the engine until normal operating temperature is obtained.

(5) Position the throttle lever fast idle tab on the first tooth of the fast idle cam.

(6) In this position check the engine rpm on the tachometer.

See Specifications in the front of this section to determine what the correct fast idle rpm should be for the particular engine and adjust if necessary by bending the tab which contacts the fast idle cam.

(7) Disconnect the tachometer and instal the carburettor air cleaner.

DECHOKE ADJUSTMENT
Automatic Choke Only

(1) Remove the carburettor air cleaner.

(2) Open the throttle to the full open position and hold it against the stop.

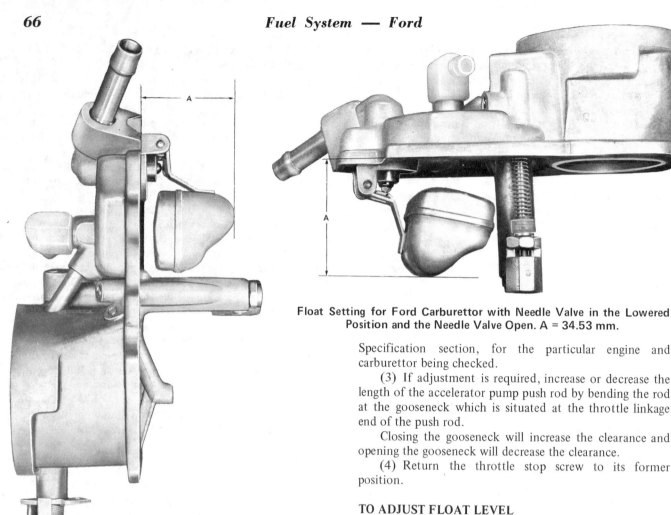

Float Setting for Ford Carburettor with Needle Valve in the
Closed Position. Dimension A = 27.93 mm.

Float Setting for Ford Carburettor with Needle Valve in the Lowered
Position and the Needle Valve Open. A = 34.53 mm.

(3) Check the clearance between the bottom of the choke valve plate and the carburettor body. This measurement should coincide with that given in the Specifications section and can be measured with a drill or gauge rod with a diameter within the specified dimensions.

If necessary bend the projection on the fast idle cam to obtain the correct clearance.

(4) Instal the carburettor air cleaner.

TO ADJUST ACCELERATOR PUMP STROKE
Automatic and Manual Choke

NOTE: The accelerator pump stroke should normally not require adjustment, being set on manufacture for normal operating conditions and temperatures.

(1) Screw back the throttle stop screw so that the throttle valve plate is fully closed, press in the accelerator pump diaphragm plunger and check the clearance between the plunger face and bearing face of the accelerator operating lever.

(2) This clearance can be measured with a drill or gauge rod and should be within the limits as specified in the

Specification section, for the particular engine and carburettor being checked.

(3) If adjustment is required, increase or decrease the length of the accelerator pump push rod by bending the rod at the gooseneck which is situated at the throttle linkage end of the push rod.

Closing the gooseneck will increase the clearance and opening the gooseneck will decrease the clearance.

(4) Return the throttle stop screw to its former position.

TO ADJUST FLOAT LEVEL
Manual Choke

(1) Remove the carburettor air cleaner and the carburettor top cover as described previously.

(2) Check that the float is not punctured or that the float arm is not distorted.

(3) Hold the carburettor top cover at right angles to the work bench so that the float is hanging downwards, the float and needle valve should now be in the closed position.

(4) Measure the distance from the bottom of the float to the gasket surface on the underside of the carburettor top cover.

This measurement should be within the limits as set out in the Specification section under Float level — cover vertical.

(5) If adjustment is required, bend the tab resting on the bearing surface of the needle valve to obtain the desired measurement.

(6) Now hold the carburettor top cover horizontal so that the float is hanging downwards, the float and needle valve should now be in the open position.

(7) Measure the distance from the bottom of the float to the gasket surface on the underside of the carburettor top cover.

This measurement should be within the limits as given in the Specification section under Float drop — cover horizontal.

(8) If adjustment is required, bend the tab resting on the float needle valve housing to obtain the desired measurement.

NOTE: Do not actuate the throttle linkage while the carburettor top cover is removed as the accelerator pump discharge ball and weight may be ejected into the engine where serious damage could result.

Automatic Choke

See to Adjust Float Level as described in the preceding section.

In addition it will be necessary to disconnect the automatic choke before the carburettor top cover is removed, this operation to be carried out as described earlier.

2. WEBER CARBURETTOR

DESCRIPTION

The Weber carburettor is a dual barrel downdraught type with a main and auxiliary venturi in each barrel. The top cover of the carburettor houses the two choke valve plates mounted in the two air intakes, also mounted in the top cover is the needle valve and pivoted float assembly.

A manual or a fully automatic choke is available, the automatic choke is controlled by the water in the engine cooling system. Changes of temperature in the engine cooling system are transferred by means of a bi-metal spring to a mechanical arm controlling the choke valve plates.

The carburettor main body contains the main system, and the progression and idling systems. A mechanically operated diaphragm type accelerator pump is fitted which discharges fuel into the primary barrel while the full load enrichment system discharges into the secondary barrel. The throttle valve in the primary barrel opens before the throttle valve in the secondary barrel to provide smoother operation at high and low engine speeds. A connection is

also provided to supply vacuum to the distributor vacuum advance unit.

TO REMOVE AND INSTAL

(1) Raise the engine bonnet and fit fender covers to both front fenders.

(2) Remove the nuts securing the top cover of the air cleaner and remove the top cover.

(3) Take out the paper air cleaner element.

(4) Prise back the metal tabs on the four securing nuts which attach the air cleaner main body to the carburettor top cover, remove the nuts, lock plates, and the metal and rubber washers if fitted.

(5) Disconnect the two brackets from the air cleaner main body and withdraw the air cleaner from the vehicle.

(6) Remove the gasket where fitted.

(7) Disconnect the fuel feed pipe and the distributor vacuum advance pipe at the carburettor.

(8) Detach the throttle linkage from the throttle lever.

(9) Drain the cooling system and disconnect the coolant hoses at the automatic choke assembly on models so equipped.

(10) Remove the four nuts and spring washers and lift the carburettor from the inlet manifold flange.

Installation is a reversal of the removal procedure with attention to the following points:

Use a new gasket between the carburettor and the inlet manifold.

Run the engine and check for fuel, vacuum and water leaks and carry out necessary carburettor adjustments.

TO DISMANTLE
Manual Choke Models

(1) Remove the carburettor from the engine as previously described.

BELOW: Weber Carburettor in Mounted Position on the Engine Showing Linkage and Coolant Pipe Connections.

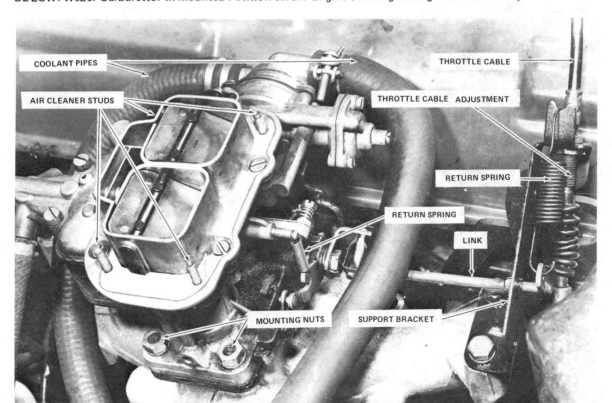

NOTE: *When dismantling keep the primary and secondary components separated.*

(2) Undo the fuel filter retainer from the carburettor top cover and withdraw the gauze filter.

(3) Withdraw the retaining clip and disconnect the choke connecting link from the choke spindle lever.

(4) Unscrew and remove the retaining screws and washers and remove the carburettor top cover and gasket.

(5) Remove the float fulcrum pin and withdraw the float and needle valve from the top cover assembly.

(6) Remove the gasket from the carburettor top cover.

(7) Unscrew and remove the needle valve housing.

(8) Remove the screws to release the spring loaded diaphragm.

(9) Take out the four retaining screws and the operating lever fulcrum pin at the accelerator pump cover plate, detach the cover plate, the diaphragm and the spring.

(10) Unscrew and remove the primary and secondary main jets from the bottom of the float chamber. Do not remove the power valve from the centre of the float chamber.

(11) Unscrew and remove the accelerator pump discharge valve and discharge jet from the top of the main body assembly.

(12) Take out the air correction jets from the top of the main body assembly, turn the assembly upside down and slide out the emulsion tubes.

(13) Unscrew the two idling jet holders at either side of the main body assembly, and remove the idling jets.

NOTE: *Where dual components are used, keep them separate so they can be installed in their original locations*

in relation to the carburettor barrel which they control. This is important as the component numbers differ between the primary and secondary units.

(14) Remove the idling mixture adjusting screw and spring.

Further dismantling will not be necessary unless the throttle shafts and valves require renewal, in which case note the fitted position of all components before removal to ensure their correct position on assembling.

Automatic Choke Models

(1) Carry out operations (1) to (14) as for manual choke carburettors as described in the previous section keeping the primary and secondary components separated.

(2) Remove the split pin and disconnect the choke fast idle link from the throttle stop lever.

(3) Loosen and remove the centre bolt securing the choke unit outer casing and remove the outer casing with the gasket from the choke assembly.

NOTE: *The location of the outer casing should be marked in relation to the thermostat spring housing to facilitate assembly.*

(4) Take out the screws retaining the clamping ring, and withdraw the ring, the thermostat spring housing and the insulating gasket.

(5) Loosen and remove the three screws retaining the diaphragm cover plate and spring and withdraw the cover and the spring from the inner choke casing.

(6) Disconnect the diaphragm shaft at the choke lever

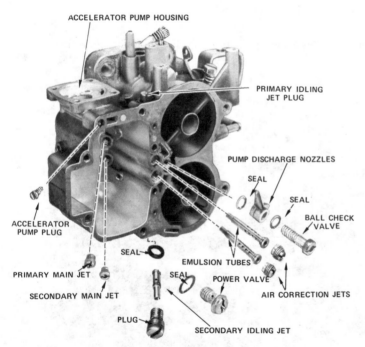

Exploded View of Weber Carburettor Jet Components.

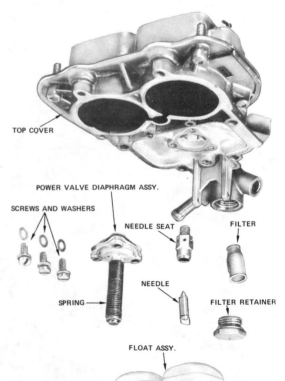

Dismantled View of the Underside of the Top Cover Components. Weber Carburettor.

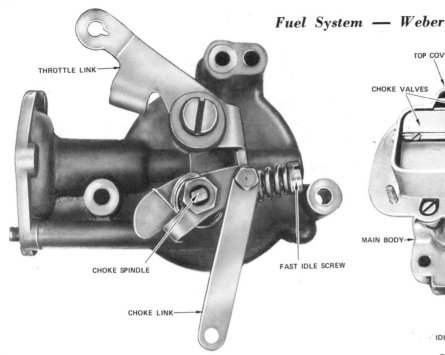

Inner Side of Automatic Choke Housing Showing Linkage Arrangement.

Weber Carburettor with Automatic Choke Showing Main Components.

arm assembly and withdraw the diaphragm from the choke inner casing.

(7) Unscrew and remove the retaining screws securing the inner casing to the carburettor main body, withdraw the casing with the shaft and lever assembly.

Further dismantling will not be necessary unless the throttle shaft and valves require renewal, in which case note the fitted position of all components before removal to ensure their correct position on assembling.

TO CHECK AND INSPECT

(1) If the carburettor has seen considerable service, check the throttle shafts and bearing bores in the main body for wear.

(2) Check the accelerator pump diaphragm for perforation or deterioration, ensure that the diaphragm spring is serviceable.

(3) Blow out all jets and passages in the main body with compressed air to remove any dirt or foreign matter. Do not use wire or probes to clear out jets or air bleeds.

(4) With a steel straight edge check all gasket surfaces on the carburettor main body and top cover for warpage and rectify by filing if necessary.

TO ASSEMBLE
Manual Choke Models

Assembly is a reversal of the dismantling procedure with attention to the following points:

(1) Instal the fuel filter and hexagon headed plug in the top cover.

(2) Instal the idling jets in the idling jet holders and fit one to each side of the float chamber of the main body assembly using new 'O' rings.

NOTE: The idling jet for the primary barrel differs from that of the secondary barrel and must not be interchanged when installing.

(3) Instal the main jets into position at the bottom of the float chamber.

(4) Instal the emulsion tubes into the tube positions and refit the air correction jets to secure the emulsion tubes.

NOTE: Both the air correction jets and the main jets differ between their primary and secondary counterpart and must not be interchanged in position when installing.

(5) Position the accelerator pump operating lever at its pivot in the cover plate and insert the pivot pin. Press home the pivot pin until flush with the casting face.

(6) Instal the accelerator pump spring in the aperture of the main body followed by the diaphragm and the accelerator pump cover plate with a new gasket interposed between the diaphragm and the cover.

(7) Instal the four securing screws and washers through the cover plate and diaphragm holes, and tighten evenly.

(8) Instal the accelerator pump jet, fitting a new gasket and secure the jet with the discharge valve.

(9) Instal the spring loaded diaphragm assembly into the top cover and secure with the retaining screws.

(10) Fit a new gasket washer to the needle valve housing and instal in the top cover.

(11) Instal the float and needle valve and secure the float assembly at the pivot bracket with the fulcrum pin.

NOTE: Check the float setting and adjust if required, see under TO CHECK AND ADJUST FLOAT LEVEL.

(12) If removed, instal the idling mixture control screw and spring, turn the screw in the full limit of its inward travel and then back it out one and a half turns.

(13) Instal the carburettor top cover to the main body assembly with a new gasket positioned correctly between

the two components and instal the retaining screws and tighten securely.

(14) Connect the choke connecting link to the choke spindle lever with the retaining clip.

(15) If removed, instal the throttle stop screw, taking it a half turn after it has contacted the throttle stop lever.

(16) Check and adjust the choke plate pull down. Check also the fast idle setting. These procedures are described under the appropriate headings.

(17) With the secondary throttle valve plate closed, check the clearance between the edge of the valve plate and the side of the barrel at the widest point. Adjust the stop lever to give a clearance of 0.051 – 0.076 mm.

(18) Instal the carburettor on the engine and check and adjust the idling speed and mixture screws as required.

Automatic Choke Models

Assembly is a reversal of the dismantling procedure with attention to the following points:

(1) Carry out operations (1) to (17) excluding operation (14) as described for manual choke carburettors in the preceding section.

(2) Manoeuvre the inner choke casing into position on the carburettor main body and secure in place with the retaining screws.

(3) Connect the fast idle link to the throttle stop lever on the primary throttle shaft and secure with a split pin.

(4) Connect the choke connecting link at the choke spindle lever and secure with the retaining clip.

(5) Instal the diaphragm and shaft assembly into position in the inner casing, so that the choke lever arm seats correctly in the recess provided in the diaphragm shaft.

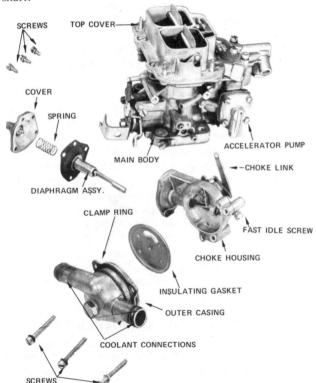

Dismantled View of Automatic Choke Components. Weber Carburettor.

(6) Position the diaphragm spring and cover plate on the diaphragm and secure with the retaining screws.

(7) Instal the insulating gasket and the thermostat spring housing into position on the inner choke casing. Ensure that the spring loop engages the crank pin.

(8) Instal the clamping ring and secure loosely with the retaining screws.

(9) Rotate the thermostat spring housing to position the alignment marks and tighten the clamping ring retaining screws.

(10) Instal the choke assembly outer casing using a new gasket and secure in position with the centre bolt while aligning the marks made when dismantling.

(11) Instal the carburettor on the engine and check and adjust the idling speed and mixture screws as required.

TO ADJUST IDLING SPEED AND MIXTURE
Without Instruments

(1) Start the engine and run it at approximately 1200 rpm for 15 minutes to bring it to normal operating temperature.

(2) Adjust the throttle stop screw to give an idling speed to specifications.

(3) Turn the idling mixture screw in a clockwise direction until the engine slows and begins to falter, then turn the mixture screw anti-clockwise until the engine runs smoothly, but does not lose speed or hunt.

(4) Readjust the throttle stop screw to give the desired idling speed after which it may be necessary to vary the idling mixture adjustment slightly to maintain smooth idling.

NOTE: Turning the idling mixture screw in a clockwise direction gives a leaner mixture and anti-clockwise a richer mixture.

With Instruments

(1) Connect a vacuum gauge with a suitable 'T' adaptor into the crankcase ventilation tube.

(2) With a tachometer connected to the engine, run the engine until it reaches operating temperature and adjust the throttle stop screw until the correct specified idle speed is obtained.

(3) Adjust the idling mixture screw until the highest vacuum reading on the vacuum gauge is obtained. It may be necessary to readjust the idle speed during this operation.

(4) Stop the engine and detach the vacuum gauge and tachometer.

NOTE: An exhaust gas analyser, if available, can be used to adjust the mixture, or check as a comparison with the vacuum gauge readings. An optimum mixture strength reading is desired on the gas analyser at engine idle.

TO CHECK AND ADJUST FLOAT LEVEL

(1) Remove the air cleaner and carburettor top cover as previously described.

(2) Hold the top cover assembly in a vertical position with the float hanging down and the tab on the float arm assembly applying a closing pressure to the needle valve.

(3) With the assembly in this position, measure the

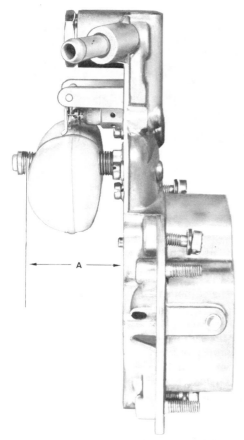

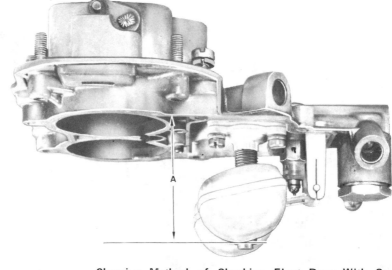

Showing Method of Checking Float Drop With Cover Horizontal. Weber Carburettor. Dimension A = See Specifications.

Showing Method of Checking Float Level with Cover Vertical Needle Valve Closed. Weber Carburettor. Dimension A = See Specifications.

distance between the lower back face of the float (the face furthest from the top cover) and the top cover gasket surface. Refer to Specifications for the correct dimensions.

(4) If adjustment is required, bend the tab resting on the needle valve to obtain the required dimension.

(5) Having set the float level proceed to check the float drop; turn the top cover to the horizontal position with the float hanging down in the open position. Again measure the distance from the lower back face of the float to the gasket surface of the top cover. Refer to Specifications for the correct dimensions.

(6) If adjustment is required bend the tab which abuts the needle valve housing to obtain the correct setting.

(7) Instal the top cover and refit the air cleaner. Check and adjust if necessary, the idling speed and mixture screw.

TO ADJUST CHOKE PLATE PULL DOWN
Manual Choke

(1) Remove the air cleaner. Rotate the choke operating lever on the side of the carburettor main body until it abuts the stop, check that the choke valve plates are fully closed and hold the lever in this position.

(2) Open the choke valve plates against the pressure of the return spring still holding the operating lever in the closed position.

(3) Measure the clearance between the bottom edge of the valve plates and the inside face of the air intake. This should be as specified.

(4) If adjustment is required bend the metal stop of the choke operating lever in the direction required.

Automatic Choke

(1) Remove the air cleaner assembly as previously described.

(2) Drain the cooling system and disconnect the coolant hoses at the automatic choke outer casing.

(3) Loosen and remove the screws retaining the clamping ring and withdraw the clamping ring together with the outer casing, the spring housing and the insulated gasket.

(4) Fully open the carburettor throttle valve plate, and press the choke diaphragm shaft, located in the choke inner casing to the end of its stroke. Close the choke valve plate until it is stopped by the linkage, and check the measurement between the bottom edge of the choke valve plate and the side of the carburettor air intake. See Specifications for the required dimension.

(5) If adjustment is required turn the adjusting screw on the diaphragm cover plate in the required direction until the specified dimension is obtained.

(6) Refit the insulating gasket, the spring housing with the bi-metal spring and the choke outer casing into position and secure in place with the clamping plate and screws.

(7) Before finally tightening the clamping plate retaining screws, align the mating marks on the spring housing and the choke inner casing to ensure correct adjustment of the bi-metal spring.

(8) Connect the coolant hoses at the choke assembly and refill the cooling system.

(9) Check and adjust the idling speed and mixture as described under the relevant heading.

FAST IDLE ADJUSTMENT
Manual Choke

(1) Connect a tachometer to the engine.

(2) Remove the carburettor air cleaner.

(3) Start and run the engine until the normal operating temperature is obtained.

(4) Allow the engine to idle and check that the engine idle is to specifications.

(5) With the engine still running, hold the choke valve

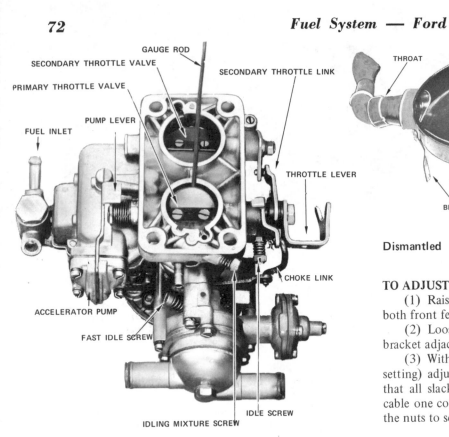

SECONDARY THROTTLE VALVE
GAUGE ROD
SECONDARY THROTTLE LINK
PRIMARY THROTTLE VALVE
PUMP LEVER
FUEL INLET
THROTTLE LEVER
CHOKE LINK
ACCELERATOR PUMP
FAST IDLE SCREW
IDLE SCREW
IDLING MIXTURE SCREW

THROAT
COVER
COVER STUDS
RETAINING NUTS
FILTER
BODY
BRACKETS

Showing Method of Setting the Fast Idle Adjustment with Carburettor Removed Using a Gauge Rod.

plates in the fully open position and turn the choke operating lever until it is stopped by the choke linkage.

(6) Check the engine speed on the tachometer and if necessary adjust the fast idle to specifications by bending the fast idle connecting link.

NOTE: The fast idle speed can be pre-set when the carburettor is removed from the engine by measuring the clearance between the primary throttle valve plate and the inside face of the carburettor bore in which the progression holes are located. This clearance should be as specified.

Adjustment is again effected by bending the fast idle connecting link.

Automatic Choke

(1) With the air cleaner assembly removed and the choke plate pull down correctly adjusted as previously described, connect a tachometer and bring the engine up to normal working temperature.

(2) Make sure the notch on the choke spring housing is correctly aligned with that on the inner choke casing to ascertain the correct adjustment of the bi-metal spring.

(3) Open the throttle and momentarily fully close the choke valve plates. Allow the throttle to close, thus retaining the fast idle cam in the fast idle position with the adjusting screw located on the high cam position, and allow the choke valve plates to return.

(4) Check the reading on the tachometer and adjust the fast idle adjusting screw as required to obtain the correct fast idle speed as given in specifications.

(5) With the adjustment completed, open the throttle to release the fast idle cam.

Dismantled View of Air Cleaner Components. Ford Carburettor Models.

TO ADJUST THROTTLE LINKAGE

(1) Raise the engine bonnet and fit fender covers to both front fenders.

(2) Loosen the locking nuts at the cable flange on the bracket adjacent to the carburettor.

(3) With the throttle in the full off position (slow idle setting) adjust the cable conduit ferrule in the bracket so that all slackness is removed from the cable. Slacken the cable one complete turn of the adjusting nuts and then lock the nuts to secure the cable.

NOTE: Make sure that the choke valves are fully open when adjustment to the throttle linkage is being carried out, the throttle lever must not be held open by the position of the fast idle cam, but should be situated in the slow idle position.

(4) With the aid of an assistant depress the throttle pedal to the full throttle position and check the throttle lever at the carburettor for full throttle.

(5) Lubricate the throttle linkages and adjust the engine idle speed after running the engine until the correct operating temperature is obtained.

3. AIR CLEANER

DESCRIPTION

The air cleaner on all models is the dry paper element type.

The element should be removed and cleaned every 10,000 km. or removed and renewed every 48,000 km., or at shorter intervals according to the conditions under which the vehicle is operating. The initial first replacement when the vehicle is new should be made at 40,000 km.

Care should be taken when removing the element with the air cleaner casing on the vehicle, to avoid the accumulated dust on the outside of the element falling into the throat of the carburettor.

TO REMOVE, SERVICE AND INSTAL
Ford Carburettor Type

(1) Remove the bolt attaching the support bracket to the rocker cover and the two bolts supporting the brackets to the inlet manifold and remove the air cleaner assembly.

(2) Release the screws on the top of the air cleaner and

lift off the air cleaner cover by unclipping the outer edge from the body.

(3) If the paper element is to be cleaned and refitted, tap it lightly on its flat faces on a bench and then blow clean with a low air pressure from the inside out.

(4) Clean out and remove all traces of accumulated dirt and dust from the cleaner main body and top cover.

(5) If the old element is still serviceable, and is to be used again, position it in the cleaner main body, instal the top cover and secure it with the screws.

NOTE: If the air cleaner element is being cleaned or renewed with the air cleaner assembly on the engine, care should be taken to prevent dirt or dust falling down the throat of the carburettor.

(6) If the element is to be renewed, discard the old element. Instal the new element in the main body, and position the cover on the assembly and secure with the top cover screws.

(7) Instal the air cleaner on the engine and instal and tighten the support bracket bolts.

Weber Carburettor Type

(1) Remove the screws in the centre of the air cleaner top cover and lift off the cover.

(2) Lift the element out of the cleaner main body, take care that no dirt or dust falls down the top of the carburettor.

(3) Loosen and remove the retaining bolts to disconnect the brackets securing the air cleaner main body to the manifold.

(4) Release the locking tabs if fitted and unscrew and remove the four nuts with lock plates securing the cleaner body to the carburettor top cover. Lift the main body and gasket off the top of the carburettor.

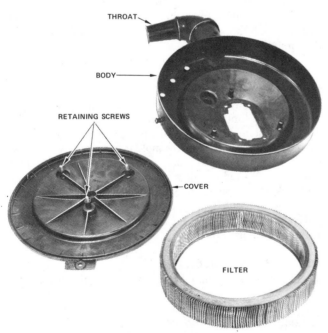

Dismantled View of Air Cleaner Components. Weber Carburettor Models.

(5) Thoroughly clean all dirt and dust out of the cleaner main body. When installing use a new gasket as necessary and position the gasket and cleaner main body on the top of the carburettor.

(6) If lock plates are fitted, instal these followed by the air cleaner main body retaining nuts and tighten securely. Turn up the tabs on the lock plates.

(7) If the old element is still serviceable and is to be used again, tap it lightly on its flat faces on a bench to remove accumulated dirt and dust and then blow clean with a low air pressure from the inside out. Position it in the cleaner main body, instal the top cover and secure with the retaining screws.

(8) If the element is to be renewed, discard the old element and remove and discard the seal rings if fitted in the cleaner body and top cover. Instal a new seal in the main body, position the new element also in the main body, instal a new seal ring in the cover, position the cover on the assembly and secure with the top cover retaining screws.

4. FUEL PUMP

DESCRIPTION

The fuel pump is a mechanically operated diaphragm type actuated by either a rocker arm and link arrangement from an eccentric on the engine camshaft, or a push rod from the auxiliary shaft. The first type will be found on overhead valve engines and the second type on the overhead camshaft engines.

The fuel pump fitted to the overhead camshaft engines is of the non repairable type with the only maintenance in operation being cleaning of the filter and sediment bowl.

The fuel pump fitted to the overhead valve engines can be either a repairable or a non repairable type. All fuel pumps available incorporate a filter bowl and gauze screen to filter the fuel as it enters the pump.

The filter bowl and screen in all cases should be removed and cleaned every 10,000 km.

TO TEST PUMP PRESSURE

If the fuel pump is thought to be defective because of incorrect fuel supply to the carburettor, carry out the following tests prior to removing the pump from the engine.

(1) Instal a 'T' junction in the fuel line at the carburettor connection with a tap between the 'T' junction and carburettor, fit a pressure gauge at or as near to the 'T' junction as possible.

(2) Start the engine and ensure that the fuel system is clear of trapped air, otherwise an incorrect reading will be obtained.

(3) With the engine running at idle speed and the tap between the 'T' junction and the carburettor in the OFF position observe the pressure gauge reading, raise the engine speed to approximately 3000 rpm and again check the pressure reading and compare with Specifications.

(4) Allow the engine to idle with the tap in the ON position then switch off the engine, the reading on the pressure gauge should fall very gradually to nil.

NOTE: If the pressure falls quickly on switching off the

engine, a faulty outlet valve is indicated. A low pressure reading on the pressure gauge with the engine running indicates a defect in the diaphragm assembly in the pump. A high pressure reading indicates incorrect tension of the diaphragm spring.

When diagnosing a problem of low pump pressure do not disregard the possibility of blocked fuel lines and/or filters, or a faulty venting system at the fuel tank.

TO REMOVE AND INSTAL

(1) Raise the engine bonnet and fit fender covers to both front fenders.

(2) Disconnect the fuel lines at the fuel pump.

(3) Take out the two securing bolts and detach the fuel pump and gasket from the engine.

Installation is a reversal of the removal procedure.

Fit a new gasket between the pump and the engine faces.

TO DISMANTLE

The following operation is applicable to the repairable type of fuel pump only, which can be identified by the securing screws attaching the valve housing to the rocker arm body. The non repairable type of fuel pump is of pressed steel construction without securing screws.

(1) Remove the fuel pump from the engine as previously described.

(2) Actuate the rocker arm by hand and expel all fuel out of the pump into a suitable container.

(3) Remove the fuel bowl, gasket and gauze filter, spring the two legs of the fuel bowl retainer outwards and remove the retainer from the pump.

(4) With the corner of a file mark the assembled position of the upper and lower body sections of the pump to facilitate correct assembly.

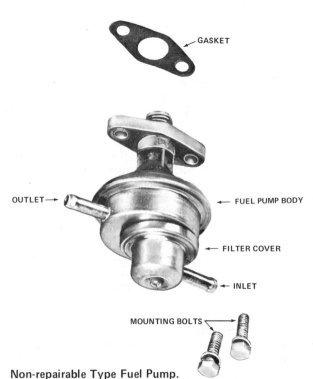

Non-repairable Type Fuel Pump.

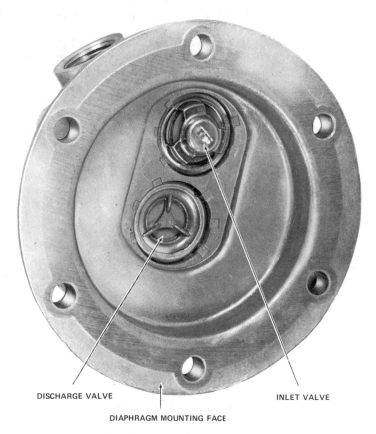

DISCHARGE VALVE　　　　　INLET VALVE

DIAPHRAGM MOUNTING FACE

View of Fuel Pump Valves Mounted in Body. A.C. Repairable Type.

(5) Remove the screws from the pump upper body and separate the two pump body sections.

(6) If necessary from inside the top body section carefully relieve the staking from each valve assembly and remove both valves from the top body. Discard the valve gaskets and note the correct location of the valve assemblies.

(7) Press down on the diaphragm and unhook the stem of the diaphragm from the end of the rocker arm link by turning through 90 deg. in either direction.

(8) Withdraw the diaphragm and lift off the diaphragm spring, take out the seal retainer and withdraw the diaphragm stem oil seal from the pump lower body.

(9) If the rocker arm assembly is to be removed relieve the staking on the pivot pin retainers and with the pump suitably supported on the pivot pin boss, tap on one end of the rocker arm pivot pin with a pin punch to remove it from the opposite end of the pump body. Withdraw the punch and lift out the rocker arm, link spring and link assembly and dismantle.

TO CLEAN AND CHECK

(1) Wash all component parts thoroughly in cleaning solvent.

(2) Check the pump diaphragm and stem oil seal for perforation and/or deterioration.

(3) Check the valve assemblies and mechanical linkage for undue wear.

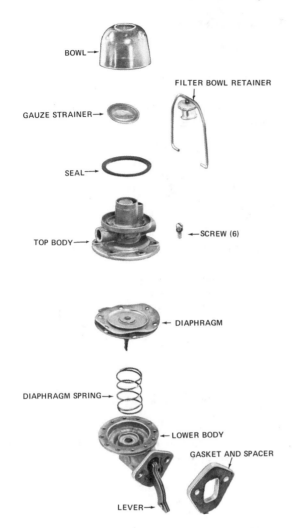

BOWL →

FILTER BOWL RETAINER

GAUZE STRAINER →

SEAL →

TOP BODY → ← SCREW (6)

← DIAPHRAGM

DIAPHRAGM SPRING →

← LOWER BODY

GASKET AND SPACER

LEVER →

Exploded View of Fuel Pump Components. A.C. Repairable Type.

(4) With a suitable flat surface or surface plate check gasket surfaces on both halves of the pump for distortion. Rectify by filing if necessary.

(5) Renew faulty components.

NOTE: If a fuel pump has seen considerable service and is dismantled for repair or inspection it is advisable to fit a repair kit which includes diaphragm, seal, valves and gaskets to ensure a thorough job and further trouble free service.

TO ASSEMBLE

Assembly is a reversal of the dismantling procedure with attention to the following:

Ensure that the valve assemblies are pressed correctly into their respective seats and that each valve is staked at six points around its extremity.

Assemble the mechanical linkage and diaphragm stem with a little oil.

TO CLEAN THE FILTER BOWL AND SCREEN
Non Repairable Type Pump

(1) Raise the engine bonnet and fit fender covers to both front fenders.

(2) Disconnect the fuel line connections from the fuel pump.

(3) Unscrew the centre screw and lift off the filter cap or bowl, the filter and the seal.

(4) Thoroughly clean all components in a suitable cleaning solvent and blow dry with compressed air.

Installation is a reversal of the removal procedure.

Do not omit the rubber 'O' ring situated under the centre screw when refitting the filter cap or bowl.

Run the engine and check for fuel leakage.

Repairable Type Pump

(1) Slacken the clamp nut of the filter bowl retainer and moving the retainer to one side withdraw the filter bowl, the gauze filter and the gasket.

(2) Using a suitable solvent, thoroughly clean the components and blow dry with compressed air.

(3) Installation is a reversal of the removal procedure.

INLINE FUEL FILTER

(1) Loosen the retaining clips and disconnect the fuel lines at the fuel filter, withdraw the filter from the engine.

(2) Using compressed air blow through the filter in the direction opposite to that of the fuel flow, i.e. in the direction opposite to that of the arrow on the filter body.

(3) Refit the filter, noting the direction of the arrow indicating the direction of fuel flow to the carburettor.

5. FUEL TANK

TO REMOVE AND INSTAL

(1) Syphon the contents of the fuel tank into a suitable container.

(2) Raise the rear of the vehicle and support on safety stands.

(3) Disconnect the fuel line and the fuel gauge sender unit wire at the fuel tank.

(4) Loosen and remove the screws securing the filler neck to the guard panel.

(5) Unscrew the tank retaining strap nuts and lower and withdraw the tank from the vehicle.

NOTE: It is extremely important that the fuel tank be steam cleaned or otherwise rendered gas free if repairs are to be carried out on the tank.

Installation is a reversal of the removal procedure.

Check the fuel line connection for leaks after the tank has been refilled with fuel.

6. FUEL SYSTEM FAULT DIAGNOSIS

1. **Engine will not start.**

    Possible cause / *Remedy*

    (a) Lack of fuel in float bowl.
    — Check fuel pump delivery, sticking or clogged needle valve.

    (b) Engine flooded with fuel when cold, by excessive use of choke or accelerator.
    — Hold accelerator flat until engine starts and revise starting procedure.

    (c) Engine flooded when hot, as in (b) above.
    — Hold accelerator pedal flat until engine starts.

2. **Engine stalls at idling speed.**

    Possible cause / *Remedy*

    (a) Incorrect adjustment of idling stop and/or mixture control screws.
    — Check and adjust control screws.

    (b) Carburettor float bowl flooding.
    — Check float level and for sticking needle valve or punctured float. Clean and blow out carburettor.

    (c) Carburettor starving for fuel.
    — Check fuel delivery at needle valve. Clean and blow out carburettor. Check fuel pump.

    (d) Blocked idling tube (jet) or idle air bleed.
    — Clean and blow out carburettor.

    (e) Carburettor to manifold attachment bolts loose.
    — Check and tighten bolts.

    (f) Leaking carburettor flange or intake manifold gaskets.
    — Check and renew faulty gaskets.

    (g) Faulty gasket or loose attachments screws, carburettor main body to top cover assembly.
    — Renew faulty gaskets and tighten securing screws.

3. **Flat spot on acceleration.**

    Possible cause / *Remedy*

    (a) Blocked accelerator pump discharge jet or sticking check valve.
    — Clean and blow out carburettor.

    (b) Punctured accelerator pump diaphragm.
    — Instal new diaphragm.

    (c) Faulty accelerator pump linkage.
    — Check and rectify pump linkage. Check that link is correctly set according to operating conditions.

4. **Engine misfires or cuts out at high speed.**

    Possible cause / *Remedy*

    (a) Obstruction in main or power jet.
    — Dismantle and blow out jets.

    (b) Low fuel level in float chamber or float chamber starving for fuel.
    — Check float level setting, check fuel pump and supply lines.

    (c) Failure of fuel pump to deliver sufficient fuel.
    — Overhaul fuel pump.

    (d) Blockage in carburettor fuel gauze filter.
    — Remove and clean or renew filter gauze.

    (e) Restriction in fuel pump filter bowl.
    — Clean or renew filter.

    (f) Air leak between fuel pump and tank.
    — Rectify air leak.

    (g) Air leak between carburettor top and main body assemblies.
    — Check and renew gasket and tighten securing screws.

    (h) Water in carburettor.
    — Drain and clean fuel system.

5. **Excessive fuel consumption.**

    Possible cause / *Remedy*

    (a) Float level too high.
    — Check and readjust float level.

    (b) Choke butterfly valve partially closed (except GT model).
    — Check and rectify.

    (c) Air cleaner element dirty or requires renewal.
    — Clean element or renew.

    (d) Accelerator pump link requires adjustment or in wrong position.
    — Readjust accelerator pump stroke.

    (e) Fuel pump delivery pressure too high.
    — Check and fit correct diaphragm spring, adjust fuel pressure.

    (f) Faulty fuel pump diaphragm.
    — Overhaul fuel pump and renew as necessary.

    (g) Leaks between fuel pump and fuel tank and fuel pump and carburettor.
    — Check and rectify leaks.

    (h) Fuel leaks at jet plug copper gaskets.
    — Renew jet plug gaskets.

    (i) Economiser jet vacuum leakage.
    — Rectify leakage or renew unit.

    (j) Faulty economiser jets.
    — Check and renew faulty jets.

    (k) Worn or damaged main or economiser jets.
    — Check and renew faulty components.

    (l) Excessive use of choke or accelerator pump.
    — Revise driving habits.

CLUTCH

SPECIFICATIONS

Type . . . .   Diaphragm spring single
dry plate

Operation . . . .   Cable

Type of driven plate
hub . . . .   Spring cushion

Driven plate outside dia-
meter:
1300 and 1600 OHV . . . . .   189 mm
1600 OHV GT
2000 OHC . . . .   215 mm

Cushion springs:
1300 and 1600 OHV   4
1600 OHV GT
2000 OHC   6

Cable adjustment . . . .   3.048 mm at adjuster
abutment

Pedal height . . . .   165.100 mm

Pedal free play . . . .   Nil

TORQUE WRENCH SETTINGS – Maximum

Pressure plate to fly-
wheel . . . .   2.765 kg/m

Propeller shaft to drive
pinion flange . . . .   6.498 kg/m

Centre 'U' joint yoke . . . . . .   4.1 kg/m

Centre bearing carrier . . . . . .   2.3 kg/m

1. DESCRIPTION

The clutch consists of a single dry driven plate assembly splined to slide on the gearbox front driven shaft (input shaft) and a diaphragm spring type pressure plate assembly which is bolted to the engine flywheel.

The driven plate is positioned between the pressure plate and flywheel and this transmits the drive from the engine to the transmission.

Damper springs are interposed between the hub of the driven plate assembly and the plate friction surfaces in order to cushion the drive.

The release mechanism is actuated by the clutch pedal via a cable to the release lever and bearing to the fingers of the pressure plate spring assembly.

Operation of the clutch pedal moves the release bearing and diaphragm centre towards the flywheel, when the outer edge of the diaphragm deflects the clutch is caused to disengage.

Clutch cable adjustment which is the only adjustment necessary to compensate for normal clutch plate wear and cable stretch is adjusted by an adjuster on the clutch outer cable conduit.

2. CLUTCH UNIT

TO REMOVE AND DISMANTLE

(1) Remove the transmission and clutch housing assembly from the vehicle as described in the appropriate section.

(2) Scribe a mark across the clutch pressure plate cover

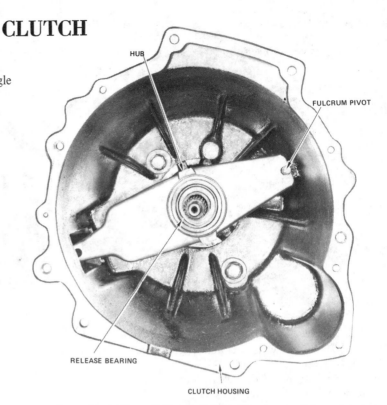

Assembled View of Clutch Release Bearing and Associated
Components.

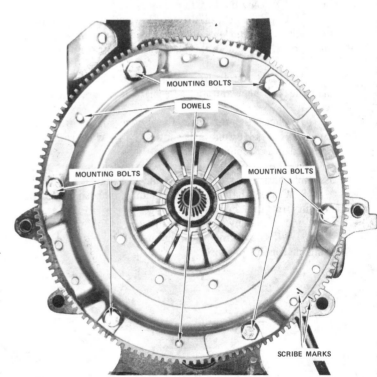

Clutch Driven Plate and Pressure Plate Mounted to
Flywheel.

and the flywheel to facilitate correct installation.

(3) Progressively loosen and remove the clutch pressure plate retaining bolts, working in a diagonal fashion across the assembly.

(4) Remove the clutch pressure plate and driven plate assemblies from the flywheel.

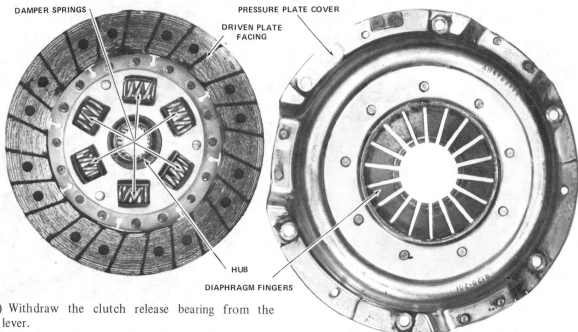

Clutch Driven Plate and Pressure Plate Assemblies.

(5) Withdraw the clutch release bearing from the release lever.

(6) Disconnect the release lever from the fulcrum and remove from the clutch housing.

(7) If necessary press the release bearing from the hub.

TO CHECK AND INSPECT

(1) Check the clutch driven plate facings to ensure that they are not excessively glazed or gummy with saturated oil. If necessary renew the plate complete. Do not fit new facings.

(2) If the clutch driven plate facings are worn, check that the flywheel and pressure plate faces are not badly scored.

(3) Check the runout at the flywheel face with a dial gauge. If excessive runout is shown, the flywheel should be removed and machined.

(4) Check for any defects in the clutch pressure plate assembly and renew or exchange the assembly as necessary.

(5) Check that the transmission input shaft spigot bearing in the crankshaft flange is in a serviceable condition. To renew the bearing proceed as follows:

(a) Withdraw the bearing using the special tool available for this purpose.

(b) Position the new bearing on the installer and gently tap it into place in the crankshaft flange.

NOTE: When cleaning clutch parts do not immerse the clutch release bearing in cleaning solvent. This bearing is lubricated when originally assembled and requires no further lubrication or attention in service.

(6) Check the clutch release bearing for noise or roughness, renew as necessary.

TO ASSEMBLE AND INSTAL

(1) Position the clutch driven plate on the flywheel with the longer side of the plate hub towards the flywheel and the spring retaining plate away from the flywheel.

(2) Place the pressure plate assembly over the driven plate and align the marks made on dismantling. Loosely instal the clutch pressure plate cover securing screws.

(3) With a clutch plate aligning tool or a discarded transmission front drive shaft, align the centre of the driven

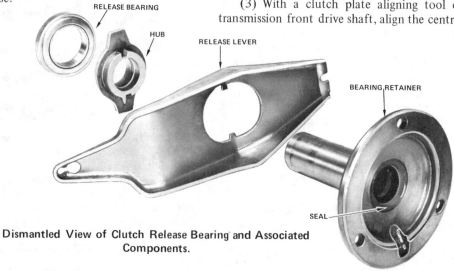

Dismantled View of Clutch Release Bearing and Associated Components.

plate with the spigot bearing in the crankshaft.

(4) Tighten the clutch cover attaching bolts in a diagonal sequence to the correct specified torque. See Specifications.

(5) Withdraw the aligning tool or the discarded transmission front drive shaft.

(6) If necessary instal a new release bearing on the bearing hub so that the thrust face of the bearing is facing away from the lever end of the hub. Lubricate inside the hub with high melting point grease.

(7) Instal the release lever through the aperture in the clutch housing and engage the fulcrum pivot.

(8) Instal the release bearing over the front drive shaft bearing retainer to engage with the lugs on the release lever.

NOTE: It is advisable to secure the release bearing to the release lever with the aid of an elastic band to ensure that the bearing assembly does not move from its correct location when the transmission is being installed.

(9) Instal the transmission and clutch housing assembly as described in the appropriate section of the manual.

3. CLUTCH OPERATING CABLE

TO REMOVE AND INSTAL

(1) Raise the engine bonnet and disconnect the battery earth cable connection.

(2) Raise the front of the vehicle and support on chassis stands.

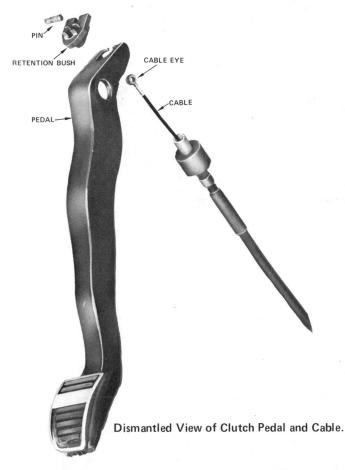

Dismantled View of Clutch Pedal and Cable.

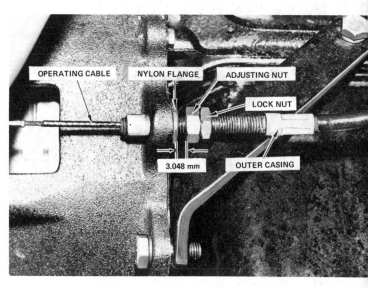

Adjusting Clutch Operating Cable.

(3) Remove the fascia panel and the dash panel assembly as described in the electrical section of this manual.

(4) Remove the rubber plug or the metal disc whichever is applicable from the upper face of the bulkhead.

(5) Slacken the clutch cable at the adjuster on the outer cable conduit.

(6) Slip back the clutch release lever gaiter on the clutch housing and free the ball end of the cable from the lever.

NOTE: Once the cable has been disconnected extreme care must be exercised not to dislodge the release bearing from the release lever as such an occurrence could necessitate the removal of the transmission for the release bearing to be refitted. As a precautionary measure, a block of wood or other such suitable packing can be lodged behind the release lever so as to impose a force against the release bearing.

(7) Using a small screwdriver lever the cable eye and pin from the nylon retension bush in the top of the clutch pedal.

(8) Withdraw the pin from the cable eye and remove the cable assembly from the abutment tube in the dash panel and withdraw the assembly from the vehicle.

Installation is a reversal of the removal procedure. It will be necessary to adjust the cable as described under the following heading.

TO ADJUST

(1) Detach the release lever gaiter on the clutch housing and smear a small amount of molybdenum base grease on the ball end of the release cable. Refit the gaiter.

(2) Slacken the cable locknut and back off the adjusting nut until a clearance of 3.048 mm. exists between the adjusting nut and the nylon flange of the ferrule insert in the clutch housing.

(3) When the required clearance is obtained lock the

two nuts together ensuring that the adjustment is not altered and depress the clutch pedal two or three times to reposition the cable in the nylon ferrule.

4. CLUTCH AND BRAKE PEDAL ASSEMBLY

TO REMOVE AND DISMANTLE

(1) Raise the engine bonnet and disconnect the battery earth cable connection.

(2) The following components must be removed in order to gain access to the pedal bracket assembly, the steering column, the dash fascia panel and the instrument cluster.

(3) Remove the wiring plug from the stop lamp switch and using a small screwdriver, disconnect the clutch cable pin and eye from the clutch pedal assembly.

(4) Loosen and remove the two bolts attaching the pedal bracket to the pedal bracket support.

NOTE: If a dash mounted handbrake is fitted remove the handbrake lever mounting bracket to pedal bracket retaining bolt.

(5) Disconnect the pedal bracket support at the bulkhead and remove the clevis pin to disconnect the master cylinder or booster pushrod from the brake pedal.

(6) Disconnect and remove the brake and clutch pedal return springs.

(7) Remove the bolts attaching the booster bracket where fitted, or the master cylinder to the bulkhead.

(8) Withdraw the brake and clutch pedal bracket assembly through the instrument cluster aperture in the dash panel and remove from the vehicle.

(9) Remove the pivot shaft spring clip and withdraw the clutch pedal and the two clutch pedal bushes and spacer from the pivot shaft.

(10) Remove the hairpin clip retaining the brake pedal and bushing and using a suitable drift, drive the pivot shaft from the bracket assembly.

(11) Withdraw the brake pedal and spacer, the wave washers and the pedal bushes.

(12) Clean all components in a suitable solvent and inspect the nylon flange bushes and pivot shaft for wear, replace as necessary.

Installation is a reversal of the removal procedure with attention to the following points:

(1) Check the pedal stop and stop lamp switch for damage and operation. Replace as necessary. Check the pedal return springs for fatigue or damage.

(2) Lubricate the bushes and the pivot bolt with a suitable grease.

(3) On completion of the installation procedure, check the clutch cable adjustment as described previously.

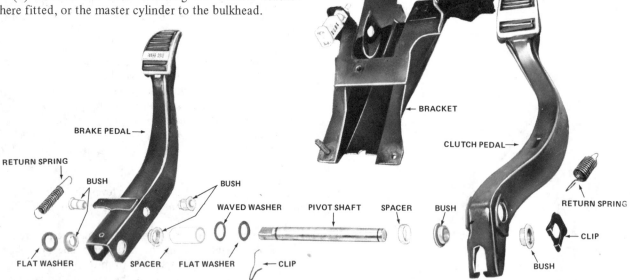

Dismantled View of Brake and Clutch Pedal Assembly.

5. CLUTCH FAULT DIAGNOSIS

1. **Clutch slipping.**

Possible cause	*Remedy*
(a) Clutch cable adjustment.	— Check and adjust to specifications.
(b) Weak or broken diaphragm spring	— Check and renew assembly.
(c) Worn driven plate facings.	— Check and renew driven plate.
(d) Worn or scored flywheel face.	— Renew flywheel and ring gear.

2. **Clutch shudder.**

Possible cause	*Remedy*
(a) Oil or (gummy) driven plate facings.	— Check and renew driven plate.
(b) Scored pressure plate or flywheel.	— Renew pressure plate and cover assembly or flywheel and ring gear.
(c) Loose or damaged engine mountings.	— Check and renew mountings as necessary.
(d) Loose or damaged driven plate hub.	— Check and renew driven plate.
(e) Loose driven plate facings.	— Check driven plate.
(f) Cracked pressure plate face.	— Renew pressure plate and cover assembly.

3. **Clutch grab.**

Possible cause	*Remedy*
(a) Gummy driven plate facings.	— Renew driven plate.
(b) Cracked pressure plate face.	— Renew pressure plate and cover assembly.
(c) Loose or broken engine mountings.	— Check and renew engine mountings as necessary.

4. **Throw out bearing noise.**

Possible cause	*Remedy*
(a) Dry or seized bearing.	— Check and renew bearing.
(b) Incorrect clutch cable adjustment.	— Check and readjust to specifications.
(c) Faulty or broken diaphragm spring.	— Check and renew plate assembly.

MANUAL TRANSMISSION
INTRODUCTION

There are four different transmissions used in these models of Cortinas. With the exception of one, they are very similar in construction, even this one exception is only different in the arrangement of its gear shift linkage components.

In the following section each transmission is treated individually and is referred to as Type 1, 2, 3 or 4. It is essential that the transmission in the operators vehicle is correctly identified as either Type 1, 2, 3 or 4 by identification of the case and housing pictures in each section.

Where fitted, a transmission identification plate will show either A, B, C or D. The transmission type then may be identified by the following scale.

Australian production —		European production—	
Type 1	A	Type 1	B
Type 2	B	Type 2	C
Type 3	C	Type 3	D
Type 4	D		

TYPE 1: TRANSMISSION

SPECIFICATIONS

Type	4 speed synchromesh
Synchromesh	On all forward gears
Ratios:	
Top	1.00:1
Third	1.37:1
Second	1.97:1
First	3.65:1
Reverse	3.66:1
Lubrication:	
Capacity	1.35 litres
Oil grade	SAE 80 EP
Lay gear end float:	
Australian production	0.15 – 0.20 mm
All others	0.15 – 0.45 mm
Lay gear thrust washer thickness	1.55 – 1.60 mm

TORQUE WRENCH SETTINGS

Clutch housing to case bolts	5.5 kg/m
Top cover to case bolts	1.3 kg/m
Extension housing to case bolts	5.0 kg/m
Front bearing retainer bolts	1.3 kg/m

1. GEARBOX

DESCRIPTION

The four speed gearbox has synchromesh on all forward gears and all constant mesh gears are helical cut.

Mainshaft end-thrust is taken at the mainshaft ball bearing, which is secured on the mainshaft and in the gearbox extension by snap rings.

The rear end of the mainshaft is splined to engage the internal splines in the front universal joint yoke sleeve, which in turn runs in a bush and oil seal in the gearbox rear extension housing.

An oil seal is installed in the main drive gear bearing retainer and care is needed when overhauling the assembly to avoid damage to the seal by the front drive shaft splines.

Selection of gears in all models is by means of a floor shift lever which is located at the rear of the extension housing.

The shift lever operates directly on a selector rail which extends from the shift lever into the gearbox casing.

A selector lever, retained on the selector rail by a spring pin, picks up the appropriate selector fork for the actual gear to be selected. In turn the selector fork actuates the synchroniser sleeve for the gear that is required.

A guard plate which is located on a pin in the gearbox side casing, and which engages the selector forks not in use, eliminates the possibility of selecting two gears simultaneously.

The laygear runs on two sets of needle roller bearings,

End float of the laygear is controlled by thrust washers positioned at each end of the laygear.

A comprehensive range of selective snap rings are available when overhauling the gearbox to ensure that end float or backlash on the components concerned is kept to a minimum.

TO REMOVE

(1) Jack up the front and rear of the vehicle and support on chassis stands.

(2) Detach the gear lever gaiter and remove the snap ring which retains the conical spring to the lever.

(3) Bend back the lock tabs, unscrew the plastic dome nut and withdraw the gear lever assembly from the gearbox.

NOTE: Where the vehicle is fitted with a centre console between the front bucket seats, the centre console and the parcel tray above the handbrake lever will have to be removed to enable the gear lever to be removed. Proceed as follows:

(a) Remove the parcel tray retaining screws and the parcel tray.

(b) With the seats fully forward remove the gear lever knob and the lock nut.

(c) Remove the centre console retaining screws and the handbrake lever centre bolt.

(d) Push the seats fully rearwards, lift up the handbrake lever and manoeuvre the console from the vehicle.

(4) Raise the engine bonnet and fit fender covers to both front fenders.

(5) Remove the clamp and detach the exhaust pipe from the exhaust manifold.

(6) Disconnect the battery and remove the oil dipstick.

(7) From within the engine compartment unscrew the upper four gearbox to engine retaining bolts.

(8) Back off the clutch cable adjuster, and from under the vehicle pull away the gaiter and disconnect the clutch cable from the release fork.

(9) Disconnect the starter motor leads, unscrew the retaining bolts, and withdraw the starter motor.

(10) Detach the speedometer cable retaining clip and withdraw the speedometer cable from the gearbox extension housing.

(11) Scribe a mark across the rear propeller shaft flange and the pinion flange to facilitate correct assembly, and disconnect the propeller shaft. Where applicable disconnect and lower the centre support bearing.

(12) Withdraw the propeller shaft from the rear of the gearbox extension housing and fit an old drive shaft yoke in its place, in the housing to prevent lubricant leaking out from the gearbox.

(13) Remove the support stay from between the engine and gearbox and remove the flywheel cover plate.

(14) Position a jack under the engine, to take the combined weight of the engine and gearbox assemblies.

(15) Remove the four bolts that attach the rear engine crossmember to the underbody.

(16) Lower the engine and gearbox on the jack slightly and remove the remaining bolts from around the clutch housing.

(17) Slide the gearbox rearwards, whilst supporting its weight on a suitable trolley jack, and detach it from the engine.

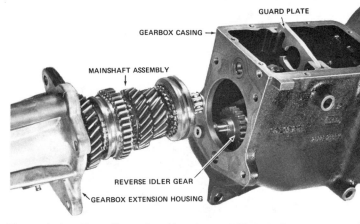

Transmission Rear Extension Housing and Mainshaft Assy Detached from Transmission. Type 1.

NOTE: Care must be taken when removing the gearbox to ensure that the front drive shaft splines are clear of the clutch driven plate before the assembly is lowered. If direct gearbox weight is taken on the clutch driven plate a bent plate could result.

(18) Unscrew the crossmember centre bolt and detach the crossmember from the gearbox.

TO DISMANTLE

(1) Remove the gearbox from the vehicle as previously described. Remove the drain plug and drain off the lubricating oil.

(2) Withdraw the clutch release bearing and lever from the clutch housing. Remove the clutch housing.

(3) Remove the four securing bolts, and detach the front drive shaft bearing retainer and sealing ring from the gearbox.

(4) Unscrew the eight bolts from around the gearbox top cover plate and remove the plate and gasket.

(5) With a suitable drift, drive out the blanking plug from the rear of the extension housing.

(6) Unscrew the selector plunger and spring retaining screw from the gearbox case and withdraw the plunger and spring.

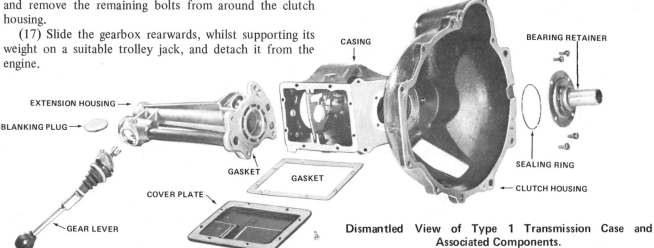

Dismantled View of Type 1 Transmission Case and Associated Components.

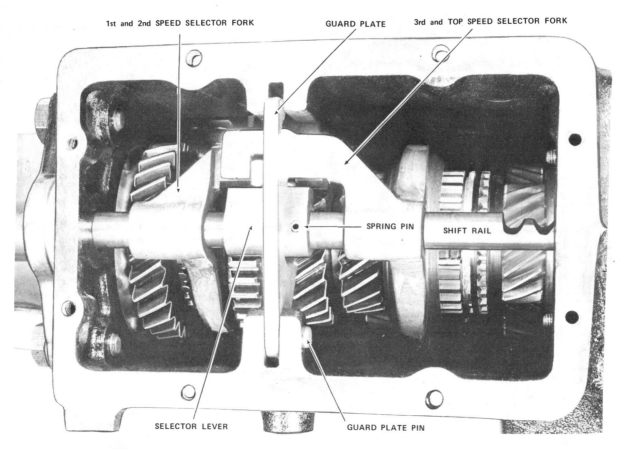

1st and 2nd SPEED SELECTOR FORK   GUARD PLATE   3rd and TOP SPEED SELECTOR FORK

SPRING PIN   SHIFT RAIL

SELECTOR LEVER   GUARD PLATE PIN

Transmission with Top Cover Plate Removed Showing Gear Shift and Selector Mechanism.

(7) With a pin punch and hammer, knock out the spring pin securing the selector lever to the selector rail.

(8) Slide the selector rearwards from the gearbox and extension housing assembly.

(9) Remove the selector forks and the selector lever, noting their relative positions in the assembly.

(10) Take out the four bolts that secure the extension housing to the gearbox casing.

(11) With a soft faced hammer, tap the extension housing rearwards slightly and rotate the housing until the layshaft aligns with the cutaway portion of the extension housing flange.

(12) Drift the layshaft towards the rear of the gearbox sufficiently for it to clear the front casing, insert a dummy layshaft the exact length of the laygear and slightly smaller in diameter than the layshaft, and push the layshaft clear of the box.

(13) During operation (12) support the laygear and when the layshaft is clear of the laygear, lower the laygear to the bottom of the gearcase.

(14) Withdraw the extension housing and mainshaft assembly from the gearcase.

NOTE: *For the above operation it is necessary to slide the third and top synchro sleeve forward a little to provide clearance between the synchro and the laygear.*

(15) Lift away the top speed synchro ring from the front of the mainshaft and with suitable snap ring pliers expand and remove the snap ring at the front of third and top speed synchro hub.

(16) Position the mainshaft and extension housing assembly in a press and press off the third and top speed synchro assembly including third gear.

Ensure that the extension housing and mainshaft assembly is supported to prevent damage from dropping.

(17) Withdraw the plug and the speedometer drive gear from the extension housing.

(18) With a contracting set of snap ring pliers remove the large snap ring securing the mainshaft rear bearing to the extension housing.

(19) Carefully tap the mainshaft assembly from the extension housing using a soft faced hammer.

(20) Remove the snap ring which secures the rear mainshaft bearing to the mainshaft.

(21) Position the mainshaft assembly in a press and press off the speedometer drive gear, circlip, mainshaft bearing, oil slinger and first gear, in that order.

(22) Remove the second gear retaining circlip and withdraw the thrust washer and second gear from the mainshaft. Remove the second gear synchro ring.

(23) Mark the relationship of the 1st and 2nd synchro sleeve to the hub. Slide the sleeve off the hub and remove the shift plates and springs.

NOTE: *The mainshaft and 1st and 2nd synchro hub are renewed together.*

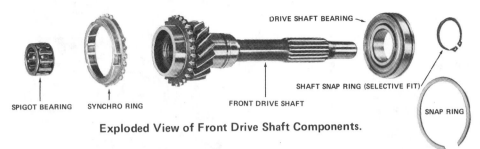

Exploded View of Front Drive Shaft Components.

(24) Remove the needle roller bearing from its bore in the gearbox front drive shaft and with a suitable brass drift carefully tap the drive shaft with bearing through the front of the gear casing.

(25) If necessary, remove the snap ring from in front of the front drive shaft bearing and with a press, remove the bearing from the drive shaft.

NOTE: Do not remove the bearing from the main drive gear unless it is necessary to renew the bearing. As it is necessary to press against the outer race of the bearing, damage may be inevitable.

(26) Lift the laygear assembly and the two thrust washers out of the gear case, being careful not to dislodge the dummy layshaft if the laygear is not to be dismantled.

(27) If necessary, push out the dummy layshaft and remove each set of needle roller bearings with spacers (2 spacers to each bearing).

NOTE: The spacers are placed on each side of the needle rollers with the thicker spacer to the outside.

(28) Using a suitable screw puller, withdraw the reverse gear idler shaft from the gear case and lift out the reverse idler gear.

(29) Withdraw the spring clip and detach the reverse selector relay lever from its pivot pin.

(30) If necessary dismantle the third and top synchro assembly.

Before dismantling the assembly ensure that the synchro sleeve is marked in conjunction with its hub, if no etching marks are visible, mark accordingly. Note the position of the shift plate retaining springs in the assembly so they can be installed in the same position.

Transmission Casing with Reverse Idler Gear and Selector Arm Installed.

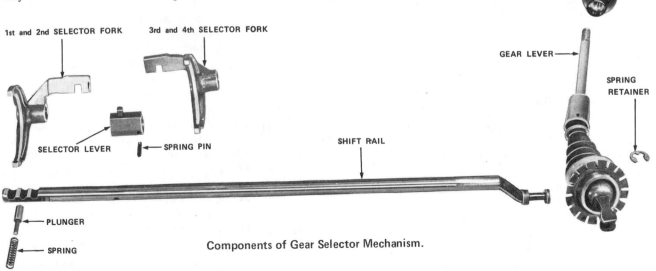

Components of Gear Selector Mechanism.

TO CLEAN AND INSPECT

(1) Clean all components in cleaning solvent and blow dry with compressed air. Ensure that all metal particles are cleaned from the bottom of the gear casing.

(2) Check ball bearings for roughness or excessive side play. Do not rotate the bearings at high speed with compressed air, particularly when the bearings are dry or damage will result.

(3) Check the teeth on all gears for wear, pitting, or burrs on the ends of the teeth.

(4) Check the synchro rings on their corresponding gear cones for wear and the synchronising teeth on the rings for chipping or wear.

(5) Check the needle rollers of the laygear and the front drive shaft for wear or pitting and their corresponding running surfaces, i.e., layshaft, laygear bore and front drive shaft bore.

(6) Check the laygear thrust washers for wear.

(7) Renew all gaskets and oil seals that have been removed.

(8) Check the selector forks, and the selector lever for wear on their operating surfaces.

(9) Check the synchroniser shift plates for wear and the retaining springs for tension loss.

(10) Renew all worn or damaged components as found necessary.

TO ASSEMBLE

NOTE: Oil all gearbox components with clean gear oil before assembly.

(1) Instal the reverse relay lever on the fulcrum pin in the gear casing and secure with a new spring clip.

(2) Push the idler shaft into the gearbox. Fit the reverse idler gear on the shaft and locate the reverse selector relay lever in the groove in the reverse idler gear.

(3) Using a soft faced hammer, drive the reverse idler shaft into position.

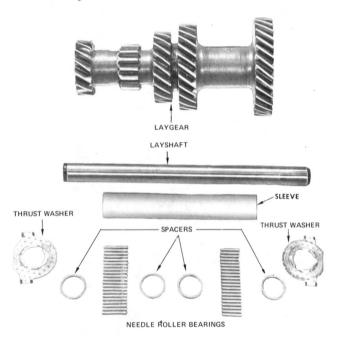

Exploded View of Laygear and Shaft Assembly.

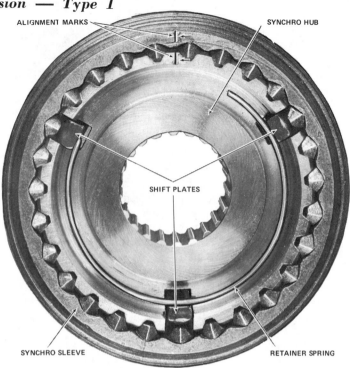

Third and Top Speed Synchro Sleeve and Hub Assembly Showing Alignment Marks.

(4) Place the laygear sleeve and dummy shaft into the bore of the laygear and instal a thin spacer to each end to abut the sleeve shoulders, fill the remaining space with light grease.

NOTE: When installing the set of long needle rollers they are installed to the rear end of the laygear. The thick spacers are installed to the outer ends of the laygear.

(5) Apply a light smear of grease to the needle rollers and instal the long rollers to the rear end of the gear and the short rollers to the front end with the thick spacers to the outside.

(6) Instal the spacers and needle rollers to make up the bearing in the other end of the laygear.

(7) Position the laygear thrust washers at each end of the laygear, ensuring that the convex face of each washer is sitting towards the laygear and that the flat edge of each washer is facing uppermost.
NOTE: A light smear of grease will retain the washer in position as the laygear is installed.

(8) Instal the laygear in the gear case with its large end facing forward and lower it to the bottom of the gear case, taking care not to dislodge either of the thrust washers.

Position a piece of cord or string under each end of the laygear, with each end of the cord or string extending over the top cover opening on each side. Tape the ends of the string to the outside of the gear case.

NOTE: Position the thrust washers so that the lugs are located on each side of the location boss and with the flat of the washer uppermost.

(9) Press the bearing onto the front drive shaft making sure that the bearing is supported on its inner bearing track otherwise damage to the bearing could result.

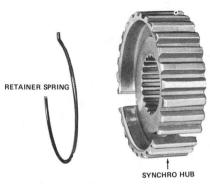

RETAINER SPRING

SYNCHRO HUB

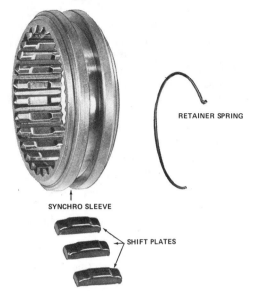

RETAINER SPRING

SYNCHRO SLEEVE

SHIFT PLATES

(10) Fit a snap ring from the range available to secure the bearing to the front drive gear.

NOTE: Choose the thickest snap ring that will fit the groove for the above operation, to ensure that a minimum of clearance is obtained between the race and the snap ring.

(11) Fit a snap ring to the periphery of the front drive shaft bearing.

(12) Instal the front drive shaft to the gearbox and using a soft faced hammer on the outer bearing track carefully tap the assembly into the gearbox until the snap ring on the bearing abuts the case.

NOTE: Ensure that the dog teeth on the front drive shaft gear are not damaged by contact with the laygear when installing the front drive shaft.

(13) Assemble the needle roller bearing to the bore of the front drive shaft.

(14) Fit a new seal to the front drive shaft bearing retainer with the lip of the seal facing the bearing, and fit the retainer to the gearbox as follows:

(a) Fit a new sealing ring to the groove in the retainer.

(b) Cover the splines on the front drive shaft with masking tape and slide the retainer and oil seal over the shaft into position.

(c) Ensure that the oil groove in the retainer aligns with the oil passage in the gearbox casing.

(d) Coat the four retaining bolts with sealer and instal and tighten securely. Remove the masking tape from the splines of the shaft.

(15) Instal the 1st and 2nd synchro sleeve onto the hub so that the mating marks are sligned and on the same side.

(16) Instal a shift plate in each of the three slots in the synchro hub, insert the hooked end of one of the retainer springs in one end of a shift plate and instal the spring over the remaining two shift plates.

(17) Instal a second retainer spring to the other side of the assembly in the same manner with one end of the spring in the same shift plate with the spring running in the opposite direction to the first installed spring.

(18) Slide the second gear and synchro ring onto the mainshaft aligning the grooves in the synchro ring with the three shift plates.

(19) Instal the second gear thrust washer and a new snap ring.

(20) Slide the first gear and synchro ring onto the mainshaft aligning the grooves in the synchro ring with the three shift plates.

(21) Slide the oil slinger onto the mainshaft to abut

Exploded View of Third and Top Speed Synchro Assembly.

the rear face of first gear with the slinger wide face towards the rear of the transmission.

(22) Using a micrometer, measure the width of the rear ball bearing outer track and note the measurement.

(23) Temporarily instal a circlip to the rear ball bearing snap ring groove in the extension housing.

(24) With the snap ring held outwards, measure the distance from the outer edge of the snap ring to the bearing recess of the housing with a suitable depth gauge and note the measurement.

(25) The difference between the two noted measurements is the thickness of the snap ring required. Select a snap ring of the required thickness. Remove the temporarily installed snap ring from the extension housing.

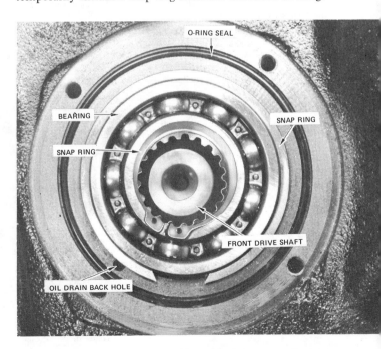

O-RING SEAL

BEARING

SNAP RING

SNAP RING

FRONT DRIVE SHAFT

OIL DRAIN BACK HOLE

Transmission Front Drive Shaft and Bearing. Installed in Transmission with Bearing Retainer Removed.

(26) Position the selected snap ring loosely on the mainshaft adjacent to the oil slinger.

(27) Press the rear bearing into position on the mainshaft and secure with a snap ring from the range available so that the least amount of clearance is obtained between the bearing and snap ring.

NOTE: When pressing the rear bearing on to the mainshaft ensure that the load is taken on the bearing inner track otherwise damage to the bearing could result.

(28) Instal the speedometer drive gear onto the rear of the mainshaft. The speedometer drive gear when correctly fitted should be 51.562 mm. from its rear face to the front face of the rear mainshaft bearing.

(29) With a suitable seal remover extract the seal from the rear of the extension housing.

(30) If the extension housing bush is serviceable fit a new rear oil seal to the extension housing so that the lip of the seal is towards the front of the housing.

NOTE: If the extension housing bush is unserviceable a new bush will have to be fitted before fitting the seal.

(31) Immerse the front end of the extension housing in boiling water to expand the casting and instal the mainshaft assembly to the extension housing with the snap ring in front of the rear bearing.

(32) Instal the speedometer driven gear, and fit a new plug to the extension housing using a suitable sealer.

(33) Assemble the third and top speed synchro assembly, with new shift plates and retaining springs if necessary, in the same manner as outlined previously when assembling the first and second speed synchro assembly.

(34) Assemble the third speed gear with a synchro ring on to the mainshaft with the dog teeth of the gear facing frontwards.

(35) Press the third and top speed synchro assembly on to the mainshaft as far as possible, ensuring that the boss on the synchro hub is facing forward.

NOTE: Before pressing, make sure suitable split rings are

selected for the operation and that no damage is caused through the assembly not being supported properly in the press.

(36) Fit a new snap ring to the front of the mainshaft to retain the third and top synchro assembly.

(37) Position a synchro ring on the front drive shaft gear cone and if necessary instal a new oil seal to the selector rail aperture in the rear face of the gearbox, prior to fitting the mainshaft and extension housing assembly.

(38) Instal a new extension housing gasket using a jointing compound.

(39) Slide the extension housing and mainshaft assembly into position in the gearbox ensuring that the top speed gear synchro ring locates correctly.

NOTE: Slide the third and top speed synchro assembly forward slightly to clear the laygear.

(40) Rotate the extension housing on the mainshaft so that the cut-away portion of the extension housing flange aligns with the layshaft bore in the rear face of the gearcase.

(41) Grasp the ends of the cord or string which were placed under the laygear previously, carefully lift the laygear into mesh with the main drive shaft gear and the mainshaft gears and insert the plain end of the layshaft from the rear of the gear case through the rear thrust washer and lay gear, pushing the dummy shaft out through the front of the gear case. Remove the two pieces of string.

NOTE: Extreme care should be exercised during operation (41) to ensure that the laygear thrust washers do not fall out of position. Ensure that the lug on the rear of the layshaft is positioned horizontally and protruding slightly from the gear case so that it will fit in the recess in the extension housing flange.

(42) Rotate the extension housing until the bolt holes are in alignment and push the extension housing fully home on the gear case.

(43) Use a suitable sealer on the bolts and secure the extension housing to the gear casing. Torque the bolts to specifications.

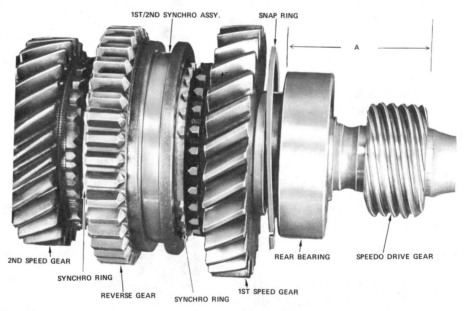

1ST/2ND SYNCHRO ASSY.   SNAP RING   A

2ND SPEED GEAR   SYNCHRO RING   REVERSE GEAR   SYNCHRO RING   1ST SPEED GEAR   REAR BEARING   SPEEDO DRIVE GEAR

Mainshaft Assembly Showing Correct Location for Speedometer Drive Gear in Relation to Rear Bearing. Dimension A=51.562 mm.

(44) Instal the selector forks into their respective synchro sleeves.

(45) Lubricate the selector rail oil seal and insert the rail through the extension housing and the first and second speed selector fork. Instal the selector lever on to the rail and pass the rail through the third and top speed selector fork until the plunger hole in the gear case is aligned with the neutral notch on the rail.

NOTE: During the above operation care must be taken to ensure that the selector rail oil seal is not damaged.

(46) Insert the selector plunger and spring into its bore in the gear case and instal the securing screw with sealer and tighten securely.

(47) With a suitable drift and hammer fit a new spring pin to retain the selector lever to the selector rail.

(48) Drive a new blanking plug coated with sealer into the aperture in the gearbox extension housing behind the selector rail.

(49) Instal the gearbox top cover plate with a new gasket and sealer, ensuring that the breather hole in the plate is facing rearwards.
Tighten the eight cover retaining bolts progressively to the correct torque.

(50) Instal the clutch housing, torque the bolts to specifications and refit the release arm and bearing.

TO INSTAL

(1) Position the crossmember and mounting and fit and tighten the centre bolt to the correct torque to secure the crossmember to the gearbox.

(2) Check that the adapter plate is positioned correctly on the rear of the engine.

(3) With the gearbox assembly secured to a suitable trolley jack instal the gearbox so that the front drive shaft spigot enters the crankshaft pilot bearing. Push the gearbox forward and fully home.

(4) Instal and tighten the four crossmember to underbody securing bolts and the two lower engine to bellhousing bolts.

(5) Remove the engine support jack and trolley jack. Instal the flywheel cover and the engine to gearbox support stay.

(6) Refit the propeller shaft and the centre support bearing.

NOTE: Ensure that the mating marks made when dismantling are aligned when fitting the propeller shaft flange to the differential pinion flange.

(7) Replace the speedometer cable at the gearbox extension housing and retain it with the circlip.

(8) Connect the clutch cable to the clutch release fork and instal the rubber dust excluder in the release fork aperture.

(9) Instal the starter motor and connect up the starter motor cable.

(10) From within the engine compartment instal and tighten the four gearbox to engine securing bolts.

(11) Refit the exhaust pipe to the exhaust manifold.

(12) Adjust the clutch cable as described in the CLUTCH section of this manual.

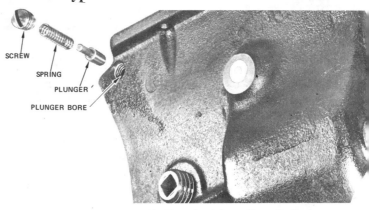

Selector Plunger Assembly Removed from Gear Casing.

(13) Fit the gear shift lever to the extension housing ensuring that the forked end of the lever is engaged correctly with the selector rail. Screw the plastic dome nut home and bend down a lug on the integral locking plate to retain the dome nut. Instal the snap ring to the conical spring after first depressing the spring and instal the gear lever gaiter.

(14) Reconnect the battery and fill the gearbox with the correct grade and quantity of gear oil.

(15) Lower the vehicle to the ground, remove the fender covers and close the engine bonnet.

(16) Start the engine and ensure that all gears can be readily selected. Instal the centre console and parcel tray reversing the removal procedures.

(17) Road test the vehicle and check for oil leaks.

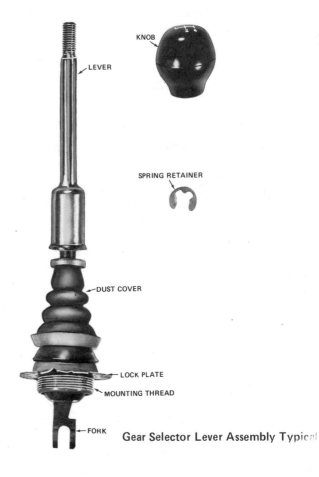

Gear Selector Lever Assembly Typical

TYPE 2. TRANSMISSION

SPECIFICATIONS

Type	. . . .	4 speed synchromesh
Synchromesh	. . . .	On all forward gears
Ratios:		

		Early	Revised
Top	. . . .	1.00:1	1.00:1
Third	. . . .	1.43:1	1.41:1
Second	. . . .	2.01:1	2.40:1
First	. . . .	2.97:1	3.54:1
Reverse	. . . .	3.32:1	3.96:1

Lubrication:		
Capacity	. . . .	0.9 litres
Oil grade	. . . .	SAE 80 EP
Lay gear end float:		
Australian production	. . .	0.15 – 0.20 mm
All others	. . . .	0.15 – 0.45 mm
Lay gear thrust washer		
thickness	. . . .	1.55 – 1.60 mm

TORQUE WRENCH SETTINGS

Clutch housing to case		
bolts	. . . .	5.5 kg/m
Top cover to case		
bolts	. . . .	2.0 kg/m
Extension housing to case		
bolts	. . . .	3.5 kg/m
Front bearing retainer		
bolts	. . . .	2.0 kg/m
Drain and filler		
plugs	. . . .	4.0 kg/m

1. GEARBOX

DESCRIPTION

The four speed gearbox has synchromesh on all forward gears and all constant mesh gears are helical cut. The reverse gear train consists of straight spur type gears.

Mainshaft end thrust is taken at the mainshaft ball bearing which is secured on the mainshaft by a circlip and located in the gearbox extension housing by another circlip.

The rear end of the mainshaft is splined to drive the internal splines in the front universal joint yoke sleeve, which in turn, runs in a bush and oil seal in the gearbox rear extension housing.

The gear case and clutch bellhousing are separate units and are attached to each other by four bolts and spring washers.

The main drive gear spigot is supported at the front end in a caged needle roller bearing pressed into the end of the crankshaft and at the rear end by a ball bearing supported at the front of the transmission case.

An oil seal is installed in the main drive gear bearing retainer and care is needed when overhauling the assembly to avoid damage to the seal by the main drive gear splines.

The laygear in the gearbox operates on two needle roller bearings and laygear end-float is controlled by a thrust washer at each end of the laygear.

Gears are selected by a remote floor change lever. The lever operates on the single selector rail to which is pinned a selector lever. Movement of the gear lever and consequently the selector rail, causes the selector rail to pick up the appropriate selector fork and move it to the required position.

Movement of the first and second selector fork or the third and fourth selector fork causes the appropriate synchroniser sleeve to move as necessary. Movement of the reverse selector relay draws the reverse idler in to mesh with the reverse gear on the mainshaft and the layshaft.

A cam guard pivoted in the gearbox top cover prevents engagement of more than one gear at a time. This cam guard engages with the selector forks not in use and holds them positively out of engagement.

TO REMOVE

(1) With the bonnet opened disconnect the battery and the throttle linkage at the carburettor.

(2) Where the vehicle is fitted with a centre console between the front bucket seats, the centre console and the parcel tray above the handbrake lever will have to be removed as follows:

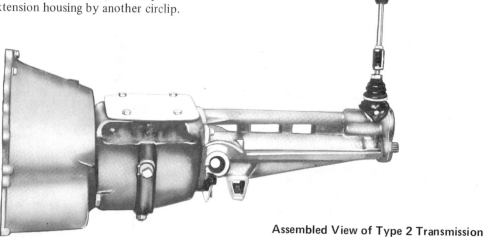

Assembled View of Type 2 Transmission

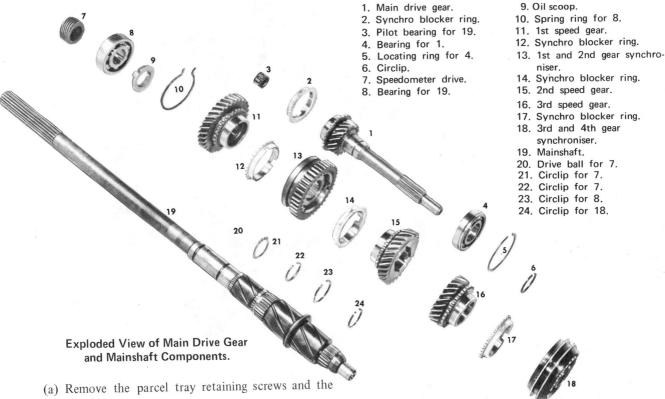

1. Main drive gear.
2. Synchro blocker ring.
3. Pilot bearing for 19.
4. Bearing for 1.
5. Locating ring for 4.
6. Circlip.
7. Speedometer drive.
8. Bearing for 19.
9. Oil scoop.
10. Spring ring for 8.
11. 1st speed gear.
12. Synchro blocker ring.
13. 1st and 2nd gear synchroniser.
14. Synchro blocker ring.
15. 2nd speed gear.
16. 3rd speed gear.
17. Synchro blocker ring.
18. 3rd and 4th gear synchroniser.
19. Mainshaft.
20. Drive ball for 7.
21. Circlip for 7.
22. Circlip for 7.
23. Circlip for 8.
24. Circlip for 18.

Exploded View of Main Drive Gear and Mainshaft Components.

(a) Remove the parcel tray retaining screws and the parcel tray.

(b) With the seats fully forward remove the gear lever knob and lock nut.

(c) Remove the centre console retaining screws and the handbrake lever centre bolt.

(d) Push the seats fully rearwards, lift up the handbrake lever and manoeuvre the console from the vehicle.

Detach the gear lever gaiter and remove the snap ring which retains the conical spring to the lever.

Bend back the lock tabs, unscrew the plastic dome nut and withdraw the gear lever assembly from the gearbox.

(3) Jack up the front and rear of the vehicle and support on stands.

(4) Mark across the edges of the rear universal joint and pinion flanges. Remove the four flange retaining bolts and nuts and disconnect the propeller shaft from the rear axle. Remove the centre bearing support bracket retaining bolts and withdraw the tailshaft from the rear of the gearbox.

(5) Plug the rear of the extension housing to prevent the entry of dirt and the loss of oil.

(6) Wrap the sleeve of the front universal joint with clean cloth.

(7) Remove the circlip and withdraw the speedometer cable from the transmission extension housing.

(8) Disconnect the exhaust pipe from the manifold. Remove the bracket securing the exhaust pipe to the gearbox casing.

(9) Loosen the clutch cable adjusting nut, disconnect the inner cable from the release lever, remove the gaiter and disconnect the cable from the bracket.

(10) Remove the leads and the mounting bolts from the starter motor and remove the starter motor.

(11) Remove the bolts securing the clutch bellhousing to the engine. Make a note of the earth strap secured by one of the top bolts.

(12) Remove the engine to gearbox support stay, and the flywheel cover plate.

(13) Support the rear of the engine with a block of wood and a suitable jack.

(14) Remove the four attachment bolts securing the gearbox crossmember to the body.

(15) Slide the gearbox rearwards; whilst supporting its weight on a suitable trolley jack, and detach it from the engine.

NOTE: Ensure that the gearbox is supported on and secured to the trolley jack so that it cannot become dislodged when it is withdrawn from the vehicle.

(16) Withdraw the gearbox from beneath the vehicle.

TO DISMANTLE

(1) With the gearbox removed from the vehicle drain the oil from the box, remove the crossmember, clutch release lever and bearing, and the clutch bellhousing.

(2) Remove the gear change assembly as described in GEAR CHANGE ASSEMBLY – TO REMOVE.

(3) Undo the four bolts securing the extension housing to the gearbox casing.

(4) Tap the gearbox extension, using a lead or hide mallet, to move it slightly rearwards. Rotate the extension on the mainshaft so that the layshaft aligns with the cut-away in the extension housing flange.

(5) Push the layshaft out to the rear using a dummy

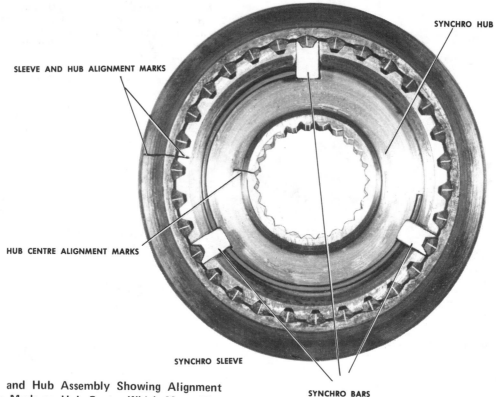

SYNCHRO HUB

SLEEVE AND HUB ALIGNMENT MARKS

HUB CENTRE ALIGNMENT MARKS

SYNCHRO SLEEVE

SYNCHRO BARS

Synchro Sleeve and Hub Assembly Showing Alignment Marks. Note the Mark on Hub Centre Which Must Align with Similar Mark on Shaft.

layshaft slightly shorter than the laygear. The laygear and dummy shaft should be lowered to the bottom of the gearbox.

(6) During operation (5) support the laygear, remove the layshaft, centralise the dummy layshaft in the laygear to lower the laygear to the bottom of the gearcase.

(7) Withdraw the extension housing with the mainshaft assembly.

NOTE: It will be necessary to push the third/top synchroniser sleeve slightly forward to obtain clearance between the synchroniser and laygear.

(8) Remove the spigot bearing from the bore in the main drive gear and lift the top speed synchro ring off the rear of the main drive gear.

Remove the three bolts and spring washers at the front of the gear case and remove the main drive gear bearing retainer (with oil seal) and paper gasket.

(9) Remove the circlip around the main drive gear bearing.

(10) Use a suitable soft drift and tap the main drive gear and bearing assembly out of the gear case.

(11) Remove and discard the circlip in the groove forward of the main drive gear bearing.

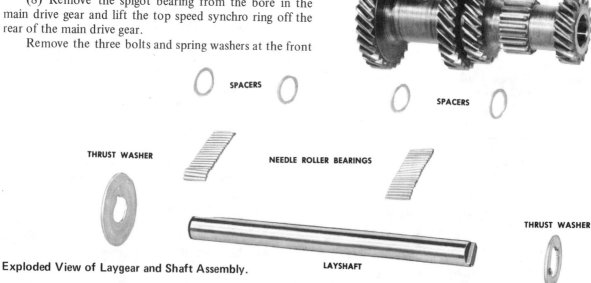

LAYGEAR CLUSTER

SPACERS

SPACERS

THRUST WASHER

NEEDLE ROLLER BEARINGS

THRUST WASHER

LAYSHAFT

Exploded View of Laygear and Shaft Assembly.

(12) Use suitable plates to support the inner race on the gear side and press the bearing off the main drive gear.

(13) Lift the laygear and the two thrust washers (with dummy layshaft) out of the gear case.

(14) Remove the needle rollers, washers and dummy layshaft.

(15) Using a suitable screw puller, withdraw the reverse gear idler shaft from the gear case rear face and lift out the reverse idler gear.

(16) Slide the reverse relay lever from the fulcrum pin on the gearbox casing. Do not remove the pin.

(17) Remove the plug on the extension housing and withdraw the speedometer drive gear.

(18) Remove the circlip securing the mainshaft bearing to the extension housing.

(19) Use a soft hammer and tap the mainshaft assembly out of the extension housing.

(20) Remove the speedometer drive gear circlip and drive gear. Using a magnet remove the speedo drive gear positioning ball from the mainshaft.

(21) Remove the circlip retaining the bearing on the mainshaft.

(22) Support behind the first gear and press the first gear, oil scoop and mainshaft bearing off the mainshaft, discard the bearing.

(23) Remove the circlip securing first and second synchroniser assembly to mainshaft.

(24) Support behind the second gear and press the second gear and first and second synchroniser assembly complete with synchroniser rings off the mainshaft.

NOTE: Ensure that both synchroniser assemblies have mating marks on the sleeve and hub before dismantling. Some gearboxes also have a mating mark on the mainshaft and the hub of both synchromesh assemblies. Realign all marks on assembly or check the fit of the hub splines to the mainshaft splines as necessary.

(25) Dismantle the synchroniser assembly by pulling the sleeve off the hub and withdrawing the synchroniser bars and springs.

(26) Remove the circlip at the forward end of the mainshaft and discard it.

(27) Support around the rear face of the third speed gear and press the mainshaft out of the third/top gear synchroniser assembly and the third gear.

NOTE: Support the mainshaft from below whilst pressing it out to prevent it dropping.

(28) Dismantle the synchroniser assembly by pulling the sleeve off the hub and withdrawing the synchroniser bars and springs.

TO CLEAN AND INSPECT

(1) Clean all the components of the gearbox, taking care to see if there are any metallic particles in the bottom of the gear case.

(2) Inspect all gears for wear or pitting of the teeth or wear on the synchronising teeth.

(3) Check the synchro rings on their corresponding gear cones for wear.

(4) Check the synchro teeth on the gears and the spline ends of the synchro clutch for wear or burring.

(5) Check the mainshaft bearing for looseness in the extension housing.

(6) Check the main drive gear ball bearing for looseness or roughness and the spigot needle roller assembly for wear.

(7) Check the laygear needle rollers and the layshaft and thrust washers for wear or damage.

(8) Check the selector forks for wear, the selector detent ball for wear and the detent spring for breakage or loss of tension.

(9) Renew all worn or damaged components as required.

TO ASSEMBLE

NOTE: Oil all gearbox components with clean gear oil before assembly.

(1) Instal the reverse relay on the fulcrum pin on the gearbox casing.

(2) Push the idler shaft into the gearbox. Fit the reverse idler gear on the shaft and locate the reverse selector relay lever in the groove in the reverse idler gear.

(3) Using a copper mallet, drive the reverse idler shaft into position.

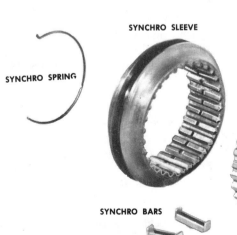
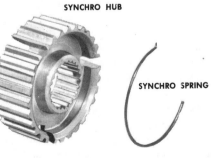

Components of Third and Top Speed Synchro Assembly.

(4) Place the dummy layshaft in the bore of the laygear, instal one of the spacers over one end of the dummy layshaft pushing it into the laygear bore to abut the bore inner shoulder.

(5) Apply light grease to the needle rollers and insert twenty rollers to make one bearing. Instal the outer spacer against the end of the needle rollers.

(6) Instal the spacers and needle rollers to make up the bearing in the other end of the laygear.

(7) If new laygear thrust washers are required to adjust the laygear end-float, select the two thrust washers required and position them in the gearbox so that their convex side fits into the recess in the gear case.

NOTE: A light coat of heavy grease will retain the washers in position as the laygear is placed in position.

(8) Instal the laygear in the gear case with its large end to the front and lower it to the bottom of the gear case, taking care not to dislodge either of the thrust washers. Position a piece of cord or string under each end of the laygear, with each end of the cord or string extending over the top cover opening on each side. Tape the ends of the string to the outside of the gear case.

(9) Position the thrust washers so that the "ears" are located on each side of the location boss and with the flat on the washer uppermost.

(10) Support behind the bearing inner race and press the bearing fully home on to the main drive gear.

(11) Fit the circlip to secure the bearing to the main drive gear.

(12) Position the main drive gear and bearing assembly at the front of the gear case and, using a copper drift, tap on the bearing outer race to drive the bearing into the casing. Tap progressively round the bearing until the circlip groove appears on the outside of the gearbox case.

NOTE: Take care that the dog teeth on the main drive gear are not damaged by contact with the laygear.

(13) Fit the circlip to the periphery of the bearing.

(14) Assemble the spigot bearing to the bore in the end of the main drive gear.

(15) Fit a new oil seal to the main drive gear bearing retainer, with the lip of the seal facing the bearing, and fit the retainer to the gearbox as follows:

(a) Fit a new paper gasket on the gearbox front face.

(b) Cover the main drive gear splines with masking tape and slide on the retainer and oil seal over the main drive gear into assembled position.

(c) Ensure that the oil groove in the retainer aligns with the oil passage in the gearbox casing and also that the paper gasket does not cover this passage.

(d) Coat the three retaining bolts with sealer and instal with spring washers. Tighten securely. Remove masking tape from splines.

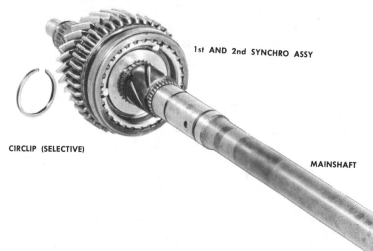

2nd SPEED GEAR

1st AND 2nd SYNCHRO ASSY

CIRCLIP (SELECTIVE)

MAINSHAFT

Mainshaft with Second Speed Gear in Position and First and Second Speed Synchro Pressed into position.

(16) Place the second speed gear on the mainshaft from the rear with the plain face of the gear to the spigot end of the shaft.

(17) Instal the synchro ring on the second speed gear so that the synchro teeth on the ring are adjacent to those on the gear.

(18) If the first and second speed synchroniser assembly has been dismantled, instal the synchro sleeve and reverse gear on to the synchro hub so that the mating marks on each component are in alignment and on the same side.

(19) Instal a synchro bar in each of the three slots in the synchro hub, insert the hooked end of one of the synchro spings in the groove in one end of a synchro bar and locate the spring in the adjacent grooves in the other two synchro blocks. Note the direction of rotation of this spring from the hooked end to the free end.

(20) Instal a second spring in the other ends of the synchro bars on the opposite ends of the assembly, starting with the same bar, but with the direction of rotation opposite to that of the first spring.

(21) Align the mating mark on the centre of the synchro hub with the similar mark on the shaft and instal the first and second synchro assembly so that the end of the hub will abut the plain shoulder on the shaft.

NOTE: If the splines in the synchro hub are a sliding fit on the mainshaft splines, ensure that the hub is not loose enough to rock on the shaft or a replacement assembly must be fitted. If the synchro assembly is correctly installed, the selector fork groove will be to the rear of the reverse gear on the synchro sleeve.

(22) Using a suitable tool press the synchroniser assembly onto the mainshaft as far as possible and secure in position with the circlip which is a selective fit.

(23) Assemble a synchroniser ring to the first speed gear side of the first and second synchroniser assembly on the mainshaft.

(24) Instal the synchro ring on the cone side of the third speed gear and place the gear and ring on the spigot end of the mainshaft so that the plain face of the gear abuts the flange on the mainshaft.

(25) Place the third and top gear synchroniser hub on the spigot end of the shaft so that the mating marks on the end of the hub and on the spline shoulder of the shaft are in alignment and press the hub on to the shaft to abut the shoulder on the shaft at the inner end of the splines.

NOTE: If the synchroniser hub is a slide fit on the shaft ensure that it does not rock on the splines. The long boss of the hub must be to the front.

(26) Instal a new circlip in the groove in the shaft to retain the synchro hub, ensuring that it is a neat fit and correctly seated in the groove. The circlip is a selective fit.

(27) Instal the third and top synchro sleeve on the synchro hub, so that the mating marks on the ends of the splines of both units are in alignment.

(28) Instal a synchro bar in each of the three slots in the synchro hub and install the two synchro springs as detailed in operations (19) and (20) for the first and second speed synchro assembly, giving particular attention to the rotation of one spring in relation to the other and the location of the hooked end of the springs, which must be in the same synchro bar.

(29) Fit the oil scoop on the mainshaft to the rear of the first speed gear (already assembled) so that the larger outer diameter is adjacent to the first speed gear.

(30) Using a micrometer, measure the width of the rear ball bearing outer track and note the measurement.

(31) Temporarily instal a circlip to the rear ball bearing snap ring groove in the extension housing.

(32) With the snap ring held outwards, measure the distance from the outer edge of the snap ring to the bearing recess of the housing with a suitable depth gauge and note the measurement.

(33) The difference between the two noted measurements is the thickness of the snap ring required. Select a snap ring of the required thickness. Remove the temporarily installed snap ring from the extension housing.

Position the selected circlip loosely on the mainshaft adjacent to the oil scoop fitted in operation (29).

(34) Use the special tools, consisting of split rings and press plate base and press the bearing into position in the mainshaft.

(35) Secure the bearing to the mainshaft using the thickest circlip which fits the groove.

(36) Position drive ball in indent on mainshaft and push speedometer drive gear on to mainshaft to just clear circlip groove in mainshaft. Fit new circlip to mainshaft to retain drive gear in position.

(37) Dip the front end of the extension housing in boiling water, instal the mainshaft to the extension housing and secure bearing to housing with circlip.

(38) Instal the speedometer driven gear, and fit a new plug to the extension housing using a suitable sealer.

(39) Locate the top gear synchroniser ring on the main drive gear cone.

(40) Fit a new oil seal to the selector rail aperture in the rear face of the gearcase using suitable stepped drifts.

(41) Instal a new rear extension housing gasket using a jointing compound.

(42) Slide the extension housing and mainshaft assembly into position. Ensure that the top gear synchroniser ring locates correctly.

NOTE: (a) Pull the third/top synchroniser sleeve forward to clear the laygear.
(b) Locate the spigot on the main drive gear carefully as it is possible to dislodge the needle rollers.

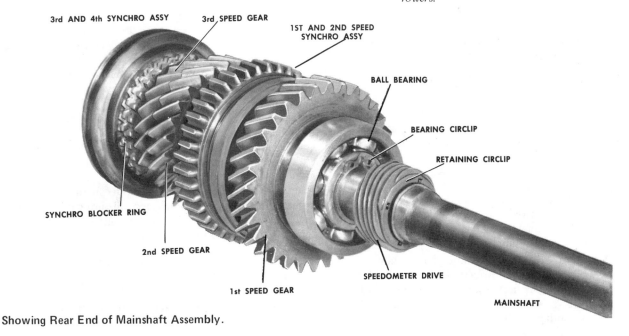

Showing Rear End of Mainshaft Assembly.

(43) Rotate the extension housing on the mainshaft so that the cut-away aligns with the layshaft bore in the rear face of the gear-case.

(44) Grasp the ends of the cord or string placed under the laygear in operation (8), carefully lift the laygear into mesh with the main drive and the mainshaft gears and insert the plain end of the layshaft from the rear of the case through the rear thrust washer and laygear, pushing the dummy shaft out through the front of the gear case. Remove the two pieces of string.

NOTE: Extreme care should be exercised during operation (44) to ensure that the laygear thrust washers do not fall out of position. Ensure that the lug on the rear of the layshaft is positioned so that it will fit in the recess in the extension housing flange.

(45) Rotate the extension housing until the bolt holes are in alignment and push the extension housing fully home on to the gear case.

(46) Use a suitable sealer on the bolts and secure the extension housing to the gear case. Torque the bolts as specified.

(47) Replace the gear change assembly as detailed in GEAR CHANGE ASSEMBLY – TO INSTAL.

TO INSTAL

(1) Position the crossmember on the mounting and fit the centre bolt to secure it to the gearbox. Instal the clutch bellhousing to the gearbox.

(2) Check that the adaptor plate is positioned on the rear of the engine.

(3) With the gearbox assembly secured to a suitable trolley jack instal the gearbox so that the main drive gear spigot enters the crankshaft pilot bearing. Push the gearbox forward and fully home.

(4) Instal the four crossmember to body bolts and spring washers.

(5) Remove the engine support jack and instal the bolts securing the clutch bellhousing to the engine.

NOTE: The two top bolts are plain and one of them secures an earth strap. The remainder are dowel bolts.

(6) Replace the lower dust cover and instal the starter motor.

(7) Fit the clutch cable to the clutch release fork and instal the rubber dust excluder in the release fork aperture.

(8) Connect the exhaust pipe to the manifold and instal the bracket fastening the exhaust pipe to the gearbox casing.

(9) Replace the speedometer cable at the gearbox extension housing and retain it with the circlip.

(10) Refit the drive shaft aligning the mating marks made when dismantling and replace the four bolts and self-locking nuts at the pinion flange.

(11) Position gear lever in the extension housing so that the forked end engages correctly with the selector rail. Screw the plastic dome nut to secure in position and lock by bending down a tab on the integral locking plate. Depress rubber spring and fit circlip.

Where the vehicle is fitted with a centre console replace the console using the reversal to the removal procedure.

(12) Fill the transmission to the correct level with the correct grade of lubricant.

(13) Jack up, remove stands and lower vehicle to ground.

(14) Start the engine and check that all gears can be freely selected.

2. GEAR CHANGE ASSEMBLY

TO REMOVE SELECTOR LEVERS AND SELECTOR FORKS

(1) Remove the gearbox from the vehicle as previously described and mount it suitably supporting under the gearbox and extension housing.

(2) Remove the four bolts securing the top cover to the gearbox and lift off the cover.

(3) Prise off the blanking plug from the rear extension housing.

(4) Remove the plunger screw from the side of the gearbox and withdraw the spring and selector ball.

(5) Drive out the spring pin securing the selector boss to the rail with a suitable punch.

NOTE: If necessary position the synchroniser hub on the mainshaft to enable the spring pin to be punched clear of any mainshaft components.

(6) Withdraw the selector rail to the rear taking care that the selector boss and the C cam do not drop into the gearbox.

(7) Move both selector forks to their furthest positions forward and lift out the forks.

(8) Remove the spring pin securing the third and fourth speed selector fork to the relay arm and remove both selector forks.

TO INSTAL

(1) Replace both selector forks on the relay arm and secure the third and fourth speed selector fork to the arm with a new spring pin.

(2) Position the assembled selector forks on their synchroniser sleeves and move the synchroniser hubs into neutral position so that the selector fork extension arms locate beneath the reverse idler selector arm mounted on the side of the gearbox casing.

(3) Smear the selector rail oil seal in the rear of the gearcase with grease and slide the rail through the extension housing. With the selector boss and the C cam positioned so that the cam locates in the cut-outs in the selector fork extension arms, pass the selector rail through the boss and selector forks until the spring pin holes in the selector rail and boss are in alignment.

NOTE: Ensure that the selector rail oil seal is not damaged during this procedure.

(4) Assemble the selector ball and spring and instal retaining screw using sealer.

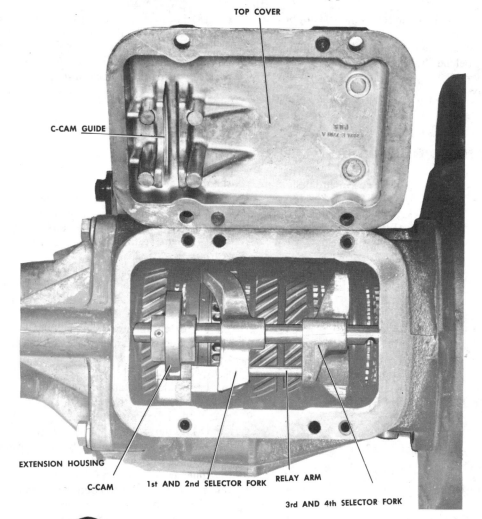

TOP COVER

C-CAM GUIDE

EXTENSION HOUSING

C-CAM

1st AND 2nd SELECTOR FORK

RELAY ARM

3rd AND 4th SELECTOR FORK

Transmission Assembly with Cover Removed to Show Selector and Shift Components.

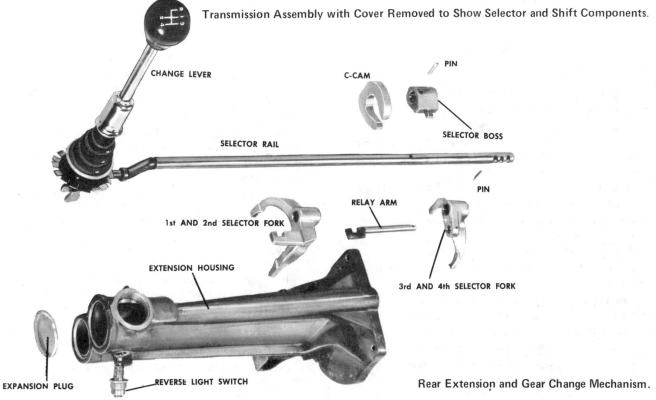

CHANGE LEVER

C-CAM

PIN

SELECTOR BOSS

SELECTOR RAIL

PIN

1st AND 2nd SELECTOR FORK

RELAY ARM

3rd AND 4th SELECTOR FORK

EXTENSION HOUSING

EXPANSION PLUG

REVERSE LIGHT SWITCH

Rear Extension and Gear Change Mechanism.

(5) Instal a new spring pin to retain the selector boss to the selector rail.

(6) Use sealer and tap the blanking plug into the extension housing behind the selector rail.

(7) Use a suitable sealer and instal a new gasket to the top of the gearbox.

(8) Locate the cover on its dowel and secure the cover to the gearcase with the four bolts.

(9) Further assembly is a reversal of the dismantling procedure. Check and top up the oil level in the gearbox as necessary using the correct lubricant.

TYPE 3. TRANSMISSION

SPECIFICATIONS

Type .... 4 speed synchromesh
Synchromesh .... On all forward gears
Ratios:
   Top 1.00:1
   Third 1.41:1
   Second 2.40:1
   First 3.54:1
   Reverse 3.96:1
Lubrication:
   Capacity .... 0.9 litres
   Oil grade .... SAE 80 EP
Lay gear end float .... 0.205 – 0.505 mm
Lay gear thrust washer
   thickness .... 1.55 – 1.60 mm

TORQUE WRENCH SETTINGS

Clutch housing to case
   bolts .... 5.5 kg/m
Top cover to case
   bolts .... 2.1 kg/m
Extension housing to case
   bolts .... 3.5 kg/m
Front bearing retainer
   bolts .... 2.1 kg/m

1. GEARBOX

DESCRIPTION

The four speed gearbox has synchromesh on all forward gears and all constant mesh gears are helical cut.

Mainshaft end thrust is taken at the mainshaft ball bearing which is secured on the mainshaft by a circlip and is located in a bearing carrier sandwiched between the gear case and rear extension housing.

The rear end of the mainshaft is splined to engage the internal splines in the front universal joint yoke sleeve, which in turn, runs in a bush and oil seal in the gearbox rear extension housing.

The gear case and cluth bellhousing are separate units and are attached to each other by four bolts and spring washers.

An oil seal is installed in the main drive gear bearing retainer and care is needed when overhauling the assembly to avoid damage to the seal by the main drive gear splines.

The laygear in the gearbox operates on two needle roller bearings and laygear end-float is controlled by a thrust washer at each end of the laygear.

TO REMOVE

(1) Jack up the front of the vehicle and support it on stands.

(2) Disconnect the battery leads.

(3) Disconnect the solenoid to starter lead at the starter, take out the securing bolts and remove the starter.

(4) Remove the drain plug and drain the oil from the gearbox.

(5) Mark across the edges of the rear universal joint and rear axle pinion flanges, remove the centre bearing support bracket bolts, take out the four bolts at the pinion flange and withdraw the propeller shaft from the rear of the gearbox extension housing.

(6) Plug the rear of the extension housing to prevent tne entry of dirt and wrap the sleeve of the front universal joint with clean cloth.

(7) Undo the retaining bolt and bracket and remove the speedometer drive cable from the speedometer drive gear at the extension housing.

(8) Remove the support stay from beneath the engine and gearbox and remove the flywheel cover plate.

(9) Slacken the clutch cable adjusting nut, disconnect the inner cable from the clutch release lever, remove the gaiter and disconnect the outer cable from the bracket.

(10) Support the engine on the rear end of the sump, remove the bolt and washer from the centre hole in the rear support member.

(11) Remove the four bolts and washers securing the support member to the underbody and withdraw the support member.

(12) Unscrew and remove the gear lever knob, take out the four retaining screws and draw the retainer ring and rubber dust excluder off the gear change lever.

(13) Unscrew the gear lever ball seat cap and withdraw the lever with cap, spring and spring seat, seal and retaining pin. Plug the top of the gear shift cover to prevent entry of dirt.

(14) Unscrew and remove the bolts and spring washers securing the clutch bellhousing to the rear of the engine.

(15) Carefully draw the gearbox rearwards, lower it to clear the floor tunnel and withdraw it from beneath the vehicle.

TO INSTAL

Installation is a reversal of the removal procedure with attention to the following points:

(1) Grease the splines of the input shaft sparingly with a molybdenum based grease.

(2) Lubricate the spigot bearing in the flywheel sparingly with a molybdenum based grease.

(3) With the gearbox installed in the vehicle tighten all bolts securely.

(4) Connect the propeller shaft according to the marks made on removal.

(5) Refill the gearbox with the correct grade and quantity of oil.

(6) Readjust the clutch cable according to the instructions given in the CLUTCH section.

TO DISMANTLE

(1) Remove the gearbox from the vehicle as previously described.

(2) Remove the gear lever housing retaining bolts and lift the housing and gasket off the extension housing. Note the position of the breather bolt.

(3) Remove the clutch release bearing and release lever from the clutch bellhousing.

(4) Remove the four bolts and washers and detach the clutch bellhousing from the front of the gearcase.

(5) Remove the four screws and take off the gearbox top cover and gasket, taking care not to lose the selector shaft detent springs from their positions in the cover plate. Note the exact position of each spring for reassembly.

(6) Remove the three detent balls from their locations in the gearcase gasket face using a magnet.

(7) Cut and remove the wire locking the grub screws securing the three selector forks to the three selector shafts.

(8) Unscrew the third and top gear selector fork grub screw to clear the selector shaft, withdraw the selector shaft rearwards out of the gearbox and remove the spacer tube.

NOTE: Before withdrawing the selector shaft rearwards, remove the spring clip from the 3rd/top selector shaft.

(9) Unscrew the first and second gear selector fork grub screw to clear the selector shaft, withdraw the shaft rearwards out of the gearbox and remove the interlock pin from the forward end of the shaft.

(10) Unscrew the reverse gear selector fork grub screw to clear the selector shaft, withdraw the shaft rearwards and remove it from the gearbox rotating it slightly as necessary.

(11) Remove the selector forks from the locations in the respective gears.

(12) Remove the plug from the side of the gearbox case at the top front and withdraw the two interlock plungers from the cross holes at the forward ends of the selector shaft bores.

(13) Using two diametrically opposed screwdrivers, carefully prise the speedometer driven gear assembly from the extension housing.

(14) Remove the retaining screws and spring washers and remove the rear extension housing from the rear of the gearbox. At this stage, use a feeler gauge to measure and record the laygear end-float.

(15) Tap the layshaft towards the rear of the gearbox sufficiently for it to clear the front of the casing, insert a dummy layshaft, the exact length of the laygear, and push the layshaft out to the rear.

(16) During operation (15) support the laygear, and when the layshaft is clear of the laygear, lower the laygear to the bottom of the gear case.

(17) Mark the mainshaft bearing plate and the rear face of the gear case to facilitate correct assembly, and withdraw the mainshaft assembly out through the rear of the gear case.

(18) Lift the top speed synchro ring off the rear of the main drive gear, (input shaft), and withdraw the needle rollers from the bore in the main drive gear.

NOTE: If the synchro rings are still serviceable, mark them so that they can be installed in their original positions.

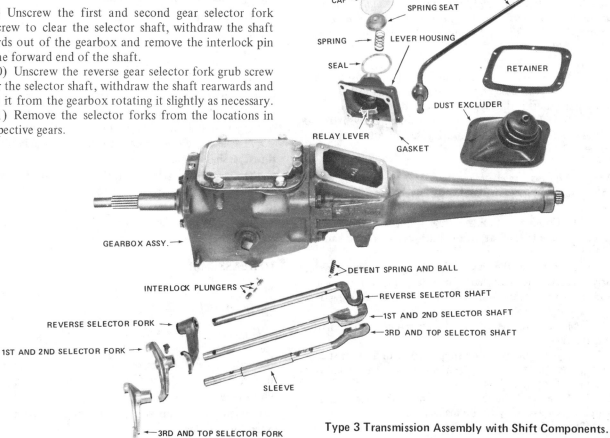

Type 3 Transmission Assembly with Shift Components.

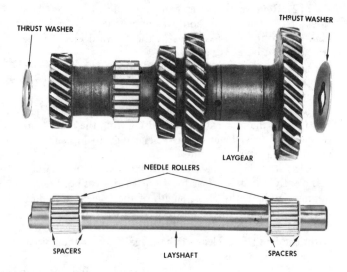

THRUST WASHER   THRUST WASHER

LAYGEAR

NEEDLE ROLLERS

SPACERS   LAYSHAFT   SPACERS

Exploded View of Gearbox Laygear and Shaft Assembly.

(19) Wrap a light layer of masking tape around the splines on the spigot end of the main drive gear to protect the oil seal in the bearing retainer, remove the bolts and spring washers and withdraw the main drive gear bearing retainer and gasket.

(20) Drift the main drive gear out of the gear case towards the front using a soft drift and hammer.

(21) If necessary, remove the circlip retaining the bearing on the main drive gear and press the gear out of the bearing.

NOTE: Do not remove the bearing from the main drive gear unless it is necessary to renew the bearing. As it is necessary to press against the outer track of the bearing, damage may be inevitable.

(22) Lift the laygear assembly and two thrust washers out of the gear case, being careful not to dislodge the dummy layshaft if the laygear is not to be dismantled.

(23) If necessary, push out the dummy layshaft and remove each needle roller bearing set together with the spacers, 2 for each bearing.

NOTE: The spacers are placed one each side of the needle roller bearing sets.

(24) Using a suitable screw puller, withdraw the reverse gear idle shaft from the gear case rear face and lift out the reverse idler gear.

(25) Remove the circlip retaining the speedometer drive gear to the mainshaft. Withdraw the gear rearwards and remove the speedometer drive gear positioning ball from the mainshaft.

(26) Remove the circlip retaining the bearing on the mainshaft.

(27) With the assembly supported behind the first gear in a press, press the first gear, oil scoop and mainshaft bearing off the mainshaft.

(28) Remove the circlip retaining the 1st and 2nd synchroniser assembly to the mainshaft.

(29) With the assembly supported behind 2nd gear in a

press, press the 2nd gear and the 1st and 2nd synchroniser assembly from the mainshaft.

NOTE: Ensure that both synchroniser assemblies have mating marks on the sleeve and hub before dismantling. Some gearboxes also have a mating mark on the mainshaft and the hub of both synchroniser assemblies. Realign all marks on assembly or check the fit of the hub splines to the mainshaft splines as necessary.

(30) Remove the circlip from the forward end of the mainshaft and discard it.

(31) With the assembly supported behind 3rd gear in a press, press the 3rd gear and synchroniser assembly from the mainshaft.

NOTE: Support the mainshaft from below while pressing it out to prevent it dropping.

(32) To dismantle a synchroniser assembly, slide the sleeve off the hub and withdraw the synchroniser bars and springs.

(33) Suitably support the rear bearing plate and press the bearing from the plate.

TO CLEAN AND INSPECT

(1) Clean all the components of the gearbox, taking care to see if there are any metallic particles in the bottom of the gearbox.

(2) Inspect all gears for wear or pitting of the teeth or wear on the synchronising teeth.

(3) Check the synchro rings on their corresponding gear cones for wear.

(4) Check the synchro teeth on the gears and spline ends of the synchroniser hub for wear or burring.

(5) Check the mainshaft ball bearing for looseness in the bearing retaining plate or roughness in operation.

(6) Check the main drive gear ball bearing for looseness or roughness and the spigot needle rollers for wear.

(7) Check the laygear needle rollers and the layshaft and thrust washers for wear or damage.

(8) Check the selector forks for wear, the selector detent balls for wear and the detent springs for breakage or loss of tension.

(9) Renew all worn or damaged components as required.

TO REASSEMBLE

NOTE: Oil all gearbox components with clean gear oil before assembly.

(1) Position the reverse idler gear in the gear case, with the selector fork groove to the rear of the case, insert the idler gear shaft from the rear of the case, through the gear until the edges of the flats on the end of the shaft are flush with the rear face of the gear case and the flats are correctly positioned to line up with the locking recess in the rear extension housing.

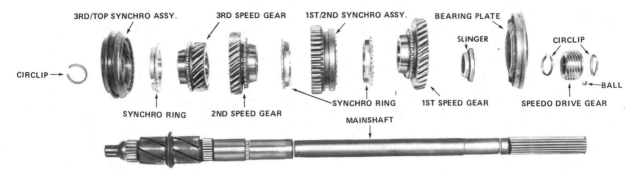

Exploded View of Mainshaft and Gear Synchro Components.

(2) Place the dummy layshaft in the bore of the laygear, instal one of the spacers over one end of the dummy layshaft, pushing it into the laygear bore to abut the bore inner shoulder.

(3) Apply light grease to the needle rollers and insert twenty rollers to make one bearing. Instal the outer spacer against the end of the needle rollers.

(4) Instal spacers and needle rollers to make up the bearing in the other end of the laygear.

(5) If new laygear thrust washers are required to adjust the laygear end-float, select the two thrust washers required and position them in the gearbox with the lug of each washer in the machined groove in the gearcase.

NOTE: A light coat of heavy grease will retain the washers in position as the laygear is placed in position.

(6) Instal the laygear in the gearcase with its large end to the front and lower it to the bottom of the gear case, taking care not to dislodge either of the thrust washers. Position a piece of cord or string under each end of the laygear, with each end of the string extending over the top cover opening on each side. Tape the ends of the string to the outside of the gearcase.

(7) Place the main drive gear (input shaft) ball bearing on the bed of a press, supporting it under the bearing inner race, with the bearing locating snap ring groove in the outer race adjacent to the press bed.

(8) Insert the main drive gear through the bearing and press it in until the bearing inner race abuts the shoulder of the gear.

NOTE: Apply the pressure to the blind end of the spigot bearing bore and not on any other part of the main drive gear.

(9) Instal the circlip in the groove in the main drive gear shaft to secure the bearing. The circlip must be a snug fit in the shaft groove.

(10) Instal the bearing locating snap ring in the groove in the bearing outer race, ensuring that it is a good fit and properly located in the groove.

(11) Instal and new oil seal in the main drive gear bearing retainer so that the lip face of the seal is towards the bearing.

(12) Cover the splines on the main drive gear with a thin layer of masking tape and instal a new gasket on the front face of the gearcase.

NOTE: The masking tape is to prevent the splines damaging the seal when the bearing retainer is installed and the new gasket may be adhered to the front face of the gearcase with a moderate coating of heavy grease.

(13) Instal the main drive gear bearing retainer, with the oil drain slot to the bottom, fit and tighten the three retaining bolts and spring washers. Remove the masking tape from the shaft splines.

(14) Instal the caged set of needle rollers to the end of the main drive gear.

(15) Place the second speed gear on the mainshaft from the rear end with the plain face of the gear to the spigot end of the shaft.

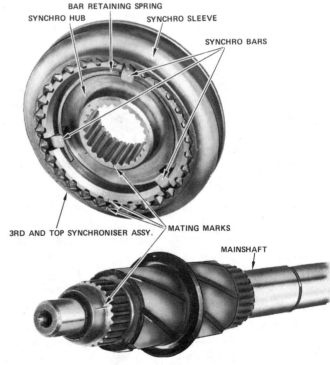

Third and Top Synchro Assembly Showing Mating Marks on Synchro Sleeve Hub and Mainshaft for Correct Assembly.

(16) Instal the synchro ring on the second speed gear so that the synchro teeth on the ring are adjacent to those on the gear.

(17) If the first and second speed synchroniser assembly has been dismantled, instal the synchro sleeve and reverse gear onto the synchro hub so that the mating mark on each component are in alignment and on the same side.

(18) Instal a synchro bar in each of the three slots in the synchro hub, insert the hooked end of one of the synchro springs in the groove in one end of a synchro bar and locate the spring in the adjacent grooves in the other two synchro blocks. Note the direction of rotation of this spring from the hooked end to the free end.

(19) Instal a second spring in the other ends of the synchro bars on the opposite ends of the assembly, starting with the same bar, but with the direction of rotation opposite to that of the first spring.

(20) Align the mating mark on the centre of the synchro hub with the similar mark on the shaft and instal the first and second synchro assembly so that the end of the hub will abut the plain shoulder on the shaft. Instal a new circlip in the shaft groove adjacent to the synchro hub end.

NOTE: If the splines in the synchro hub are a sliding fit on the mainshaft splines, ensure that the hub is not loose enough to rock on the shaft or a replacement assembly must be fitted. If the synchro assembly is correctly installed, the selector fork groove will be to the rear of the reverse gear on the synchro sleeve.

(21) Position the synchro ring on the first speed gear, place the gear and synchro ring with the synchronising end first onto the mainshaft to abut the first and second synchro assembly hub.

(22) Place the oil scoop onto the mainshaft followed by the bearing retaining plate, with a new ball bearing installed. Support the assembly in a press and press on the outer track of the bearing to correctly position the assembly in the mainshaft. Instal a new selective fit circlip.

NOTE: As the bearing is pressed onto the mainshaft ensure that the three grooves in the synchro ring mesh with the three shift plates of the synchroniser assembly.

(23) Place the speedometer drive gear locating ball in the seat on the mainshaft and instal the speedometer drive gear with its plain shoulder to the rear end of the mainshaft.

(24) Instal a new circlip behind the speedometer drive gear.

(25) Instal the synchro ring on the cone side of the third speed gear and place the gear and ring on the spigot end of the mainshaft so that the plain face of the gear abuts the flange on the mainshaft.

(26) Instal the third and top synchro sleeve on the synchro hub, so that mating marks on the ends of the splines of both units are in alignment.

(27) Instal a synchro bar in each of the three slots in the synchro hub as detailed in operations (18) and (19) for the first and second speed synchro assembly, giving particular attention to rotation of one spring in relation to the other and the location of the hooked end of the springs, which must be in the same synchro bar.

(28) Place the third and top gear synchroniser assembly on the spigot end of the shaft so that the mating marks on the end of the hub and on the spline shoulder of the shaft are in alignment and press the hub onto the shaft to abut the shoulder on the shaft at the inner end of the splines.

NOTE: If the synchroniser hub is a slide fit on the shaft ensure that it does not rock on the splines. The long boss of the hub must be to the front.

(29) Instal a new circlip in the groove in the shaft to retain the synchro hub, ensuring that it is a neat fit and correctly seated in the groove. The circlip is a selective fit.

(30) Apply a very light coating of heavy grease on the rear gasket face of the gearcase and instal a new rear extension housing gasket.

(31) Position the top speed synchro ring on the tapered face of the rear of the main drive gear.

(32) Insert the mainshaft assembly through the rear of the gearcase into position, with the spigot end of the mainshaft in the spigot bearing in the main drive gear and the mainshaft ball bearing retainer dowel located at the top in line with the centre of the first and second speed selector shaft hole in the gearcase. In this position the dowel will align with the dowel hole in the face of the extension housing when the housing is installed later.

(33) Grasp the ends of the cord or string placed under the laygear in operation (6), carefully lift the laygear into mesh with the main drive and the mainshaft gears and insert the plain end of the layshaft from the rear of the case through the rear thrust washer and laygear, pushing the dummy layshaft out through the front of the gearcase. Remove the two pieces of string.

NOTE: Extreme care should be exercised during operation (33), to ensure that the laygear thrust washers do not fall out of position.

(34) Align the flat on the rear end of the layshaft to register with the locking recess in the rear extension housing and tap it towards the front until it stands just proud of the front face of the gearcase.

(35) Position the rear extension housing over the rear end of the mainshaft and locate it on the dowel pin in the mainshaft ball bearing retainer, ensure that the flat ends of the layshaft and reverse idler shaft fit into the locking recess in the extension housing and instal and tighten the five retaining bolts and spring washers.

NOTE: When installing bolts in holes which break through into the interior of the gearcase, use a suitable non-hardening sealer to prevent oil seepage along the bolt threads.

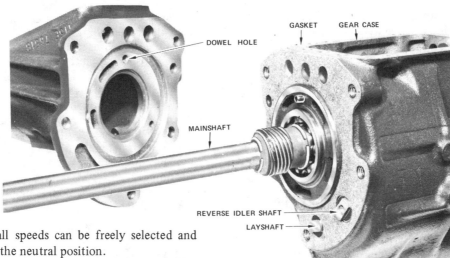

Transmission Mainshaft Assembly with Rear Extension Housing Removed.

(36) Check that all speeds can be freely selected and then place all gears in the neutral position.

(37) If the interlock plungers have been removed from the cross bores in the front wall of the gearcase, place special tool in the bore for the reverse selector shaft so that the cross hole in the tool aligns with the cross bore in the case, insert one interlock plunger in the cross bore from the expansion plug hole in the right hand side of the gearcase, push the plunger through the hole in the tool into the cross bore between the reverse selector shaft and the first and second speed selector shaft bores.

(38) Withdraw the tool and transfer it to the bore for the first and second speed selector shaft. Push the plunger again through the hole in the tool to position it in the cross bore between the first and second speed shaft and third and top speed shaft bores.

(39) Again, transfer the tool back to the reverse selector shaft bore, insert the second plunger, pushing it through the hole in the tool into the cross bore between the reverse selector shaft bore and the first and second speed selector shaft bore. Remove the tool from the reverse selector shaft bore.

NOTE: If a special tool is not available for installing the interlock plungers, one can be made up from a piece of mild steel stock machined to the same diameter as the selector shafts and of a convenient length. Drill a hole through the stock approximately one inch from the end and of a diameter to loosely accommodate one of the interlock plungers. Lightly chamfer each end of the hole.

(40) With all gears in their neutral positions, instal the selector forks, reverse fork in the groove on the rear of the reverse idler gear, and first and second speed fork with off-set to the rear, and insert the reverse selector shaft, plain end first, from the rear of the gearcase through the bore of the reverse fork, into the bore in the front of the gearcase.

(41) Using the same procedure as described in operation (40) instal the first and second speed selector shaft, ensuring that the interlock plunger is located between the two shafts. Before pushing this shaft into the neutral detent position and after turning it through 90 deg, position the

interlock floating pin in the cross hole in the forward end of the shaft.

(42) Insert the third and top speed selector shaft through its bore in the rear of the gearcase, through the spacer sleeve and the selector fork into the neutral detent position ensuring that the second interlock plunger positions correctly between this shaft and the first and second speed selector shaft.

(43) Align the hole in each selector shaft with the hole in its selector fork and instal and tighten the taper nosed screw, locking the screw with soft wire threaded through the hole in the square head of the screw, looped around the shaft and twitching the ends together.

(44) Instal the three detent balls in the holes in the gear case top cover gasket face, apply light pressure on two of the balls to maintain them in neutral detent position while

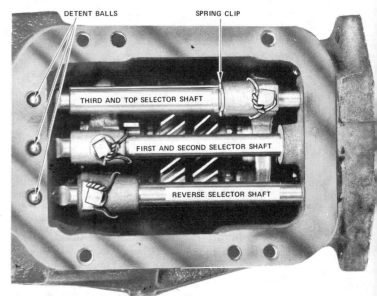

Transmission Top Cover Removed to Show Detent Balls in Position.

trying the other shaft for free selection of its gear/s, ensuring that all gears can be freely selected and will rotate freely.

(45) With third gear selected, use a thin punch to hold the detent ball firmly in the shaft groove and measure the clearance between the spacer sleeve and the selector fork.

NOTE: This clearance is the thickness of the spring clip required.

(46) Select neutral and instal the selected spring clip to the groove on third/top selector shaft.

(47) Instal a new cover gasket on the top of the gear case, position the detent springs on the detent balls and locate the cover on the top of the gearcase. Instal and tighten the four cover retaining bolts and spring washers.

(48) Instal the clutch bellhousing on the front of the gearcase and secure with the four bolts and spring washers.

(49) Using a new gasket, instal the gear lever housing on the rear extension housing and secure with the four bolts and spring washers. Note that the rear left hand bolt is drilled to act as a breather for the gearbox assembly.

(50) Instal the clutch release bearing and lever assembly, and dust excluder in the reverse order of dismantling.

(51) Instal the gearbox assembly into the vehicle as previously described.

TYPE 4. TRANSMISSION

SPECIFICATIONS

Type	4 speed synchromesh
Synchromesh	On all forward gears
Ratio:	
Top	1.000:1
Third	1.412:1
Second	2.214:1
First	3.163:1
Reverse	3.346:1
Lubrication:	
Capacity	1.9 litres
Oil grade	SAE 80 EP

TORQUE WRENCH SETTINGS

Bellhousing to case bolts	5.5 kg/m
Front bearing retainer bolts	2.0 kg/m
Extension housing to case bolts	6.2 kg/m
Selector housing to gearbox bolts	2.0 kg/m
Mainshaft nut	4.1 kg/m
Gearbox operating lever nuts	2.0 kg/m
Linkage lock nuts	3.4 kg/m

1. GEARBOX

DESCRIPTION

The four speed gearbox has synchromesh on all forward gears and all constant mesh gears are helical cut.

Mainshaft end-thrust is taken at the mainshaft ball bearing, which is retained on the mainshaft by a selective fit snap ring.

The rear end of the mainshaft is splined to engage the internal splines in the front universal joint yoke sleeve, which in turn runs in a bush and oil seal in the gearbox rear extension housing.

The clutch bellhousing, gear case, extension housing and selector housing are separate units being retained to each other by bolts.

An oil seal is installed in the main drive gear bearing retainer and care is needed when overhauling the assembly to avoid damage to the seal by the main drive gear splines.

The floor change assembly is mounted directly onto the floor pan tunnel and connected to the gearbox levers by three adjustable rods.

TO REMOVE

(1) Jack up the front and rear of the vehicle and support on chassis stands.

(2) Mark the relationship of each selector rod to each shift lever and selector housing lever using three different colours of quick drying paint.

(3) Remove the spring clips and disconnect and remove the three selector rods. Disconnect the reversing lamp switch wires.

(4) Raise the engine bonnet and fit fender covers to both front fenders.

(5) Remove the clamp and detach the exhaust pipe from the exhaust manifold.

(6) Disconnect the battery.

(7) From within the engine compartment unscrew the upper four gearbox to engine retaining bolts.

(8) Back off the clutch cable adjuster, and from under the vehicle pull away the gaiter and disconnect the clutch cable from the release lever.

(9) Disconnect the starter motor leads, unscrew the retaining bolts, and withdraw the starter motor.

(10) Detach the speedometer cable retaining clip and withdraw the speedometer cable from the gearbox extension housing.

(11) Scribe a mark across the rear propeller shaft flange and the pinion flange to facilitate correct assembly, disconnect the propeller shaft at the centre support bearing, remove the nuts and bolts from the pinion flange.

(12) Withdraw the propeller shaft from the rear of the gearbox extension housing and fit an old drive shaft yoke in its place in the housing to prevent lubricant leaking out of the gearbox.

(13) Remove the support stay from between the engine and gearbox. Remove the flywheel cover plate.

(14) Position a jack under the engine to take the combined weight of the engine and gearbox assemblies.

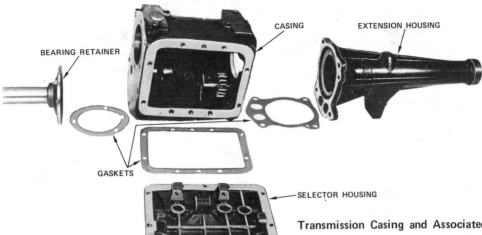

Transmission Casing and Associated Components. Type 4.

(15) Remove the four bolts that attach the rear engine crossmember to the underbody.

(16) Lower the engine and gearbox on the jack slightly and remove the remaining bolts from around the clutch housing.

(17) Slide the gearbox rearwards, whilst supporting its weight on a suitable trolley jack, and detach it from the engine.

NOTE: Care must be taken when removing the gearbox to ensure that the front drive shaft splines are clear of the clutch driven plate before the assembly is lowered. If direct gearbox weight is taken on the clutch driven plate a bent plate could result.

(18) Unscrew the crossmember centre bolt and detach the crossmember from the gearbox.

TO INSTAL

(1) Position the crossmember and mounting and fit and tighten the centre bolt to the correct torque to secure the crossmember to the gearbox.

(2) Check that the adapter plate is positioned correctly on the rear of the engine.

(3) With the gearbox assembly secured to a suitable trolley jack instal the gearbox so that the front drive shaft spigot enters the crankshaft pilot bearing. Push the gearbox forward and fully home.

(4) Instal and tighten the four crossmember to underbody securing bolts and the two lower engine to bellhousing bolts.

(5) Remove the engine support jack and trolley jack and instal the flywheel dust cover to the engine.

(6) Refit the propeller shaft and the centre support bearing bracket bolts.

NOTE: Ensure that the mating marks made when dismantling are aligned when fitting the propeller shaft flange to the differential pinion flange.

(7) Replace the speedometer cable at the gearbox extension housing and retain it with the circlip.

(8) Connect the clutch cable to the clutch release lever

and instal the rubber gaiter to the end of the cable conduit. Adjust the clutch as described in the CLUTCH section of this manual.

(9) Instal the starter motor and connect up the starter motor cables.

(10) From within the engine compartment instal and tighten the four gearbox to engine securing bolts.

(11) Refit the exhaust pipe to the exhaust manifold.

(12) Reconnect the selector rods according to the marks made on removal.

(13) Adjust the selector rods as detailed in the section REMOTE CONTROL AND LINKAGE.

(14) Reconnect the battery and fill the gearbox with the correct grade and quantity of gear oil.

(15) Lower the vehicle to the ground, remove the fender covers and close the engine bonnet.

(16) Start the engine and check that all gears can be readily selected. After road testing check the gearbox for oil leaks.

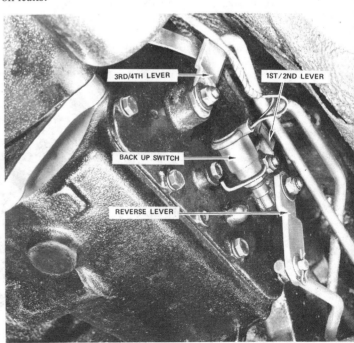

Underbody View Showing Transmission Shift Levers, Rods and Back-Up Switch.

BEARING   INPUT SHAFT   SYNCHRO RING

SNAP RING

SPIGOT BEARING

Dismantled View of Input Shaft Components.

TO DISMANTLE

(1) Remove the gearbox from the vehicle as previously described.

(2) Remove the drain plug and drain the oil. When the oil has drained instal and securely tighten the drain plug.

(3) Remove the clutch release lever and bearing from the bellhousing.

(4) Remove the clutch housing retaining bolts and remove the clutch housing from the gear case.

(5) Remove the eight selector housing bolts and withdraw the selector housing from the gear case.

(6) Withdraw the speedometer driven gear assembly from the extension housing.

(7) Remove the four extension housing retaining bolts and withdraw the extension housing ensuring that the mainshaft splines do not damage the oil seal in the rear of the extension housing.

(8) Drift the layshaft towards the rear of the gearbox sufficiently for it to clear the front casing, insert a dummy layshaft the exact length of the laygear and slightly smaller in diameter than the layshaft and push the layshaft clear of the casing.

(9) During operation (8) support the laygear and when the layshaft is clear of the laygear, lower the laygear to the bottom of the gear case.

(10) Scribe a line across the edge of the bearing plate and the rear of the gear case to assist in assembling.

(11) Withdraw the mainshaft assembly rearwards from the gearbox.

(12) Withdraw top gear synchro ring and the cage of needle rollers from the main drive gear.

(13) Remove the three bolts from the main drive gear retainer.

(14) Remove the main drive gear retainer, support the retainer and tap out the oil seal using a thin drift and hammer. Discard the oil seal and the gasket.

(15) Using a suitable solid drift tap the main drive gear and bearing forwards out of the gear case.

(16) Remove and discard the snap ring retaining the bearing to the main drive gear.

NOTE: Only remove the bearing from the main drive gear if it is to be renewed.

(17) Press the bearing from the main drive gear and discard the bearing.

(18) Remove the assembled lay gear and two thrust washers from the gear case. Remove the spacer and 22 needle rollers from each end of the lay gear.

Slide the dummy lay shaft from the lay gear and remove the two spacers abutting the boss on the inside of the lay gear.

(19) Using a suitable screw puller withdraw the reverse idler gear shaft if necessary. Lift the idler gear from the case.

Below: Transmission with Selector Housing Removed.

MAIN DRIVE GEAR

3RD/TOP SYNCHRO SLEEVE

REVERSE GEAR AND 1ST/2ND SYNCHRO SLEEVE

1ST SPEED GEAR

2ND SPEED GEAR

3RD SPEED GEAR

LAYGEAR

IDLER SHAFT

REVERSE IDLER

(20) Remove the snap ring from in front of the 3rd/top synchro hub and discard the snap ring.

(21) Position the mainshaft assembly in a press with a support placed behind third gear and press the third gear and the third/top synchroniser assembly from the mainshaft.

NOTE: Support the mainshaft to prevent it from dropping.

(22) Place the third gear and the synchroniser assembly aside.

(23) Hold the mainshaft in a vice with soft jaws and bend up the tab of the mainshaft lock nut.

(24) Undo and remove the mainshaft nut.

(25) Withdraw the lock tab and the speedometer drive.

(26) Remove the speedometer drive gear positioning ball and the spacer from the mainshaft.

(27) Support the mainshaft in a press behind 1st gear and press the bearing plate, 1st gear spacer and the first gear from the mainshaft. Press the bearing from the bearing plate.

(28) Remove and discard the 1st and 2nd synchroniser assembly snap ring from the mainshaft.

(29) Support the mainshaft in a press behind 2nd gear and press the 2nd gear and the synchroniser assembly from the mainshaft.

(30) To dismantle a synchroniser assembly proceed as follows:

(a) Ensure that the relationship of the sleeve to the hub is clearly marked.

(b) Withdraw the sleeve from the hub.

(c) Remove the three shift plates and two springs.

(31) As necessary remove the extension housing oil seal using a suitable puller.

(32) If necessary remove the yoke bush from the extension housing using a suitable puller after noting its fitted position.

(33) If it is necessary to dismantle the selector housing see under the heading SELECTOR HOUSING.

TO CLEAN AND INSPECT

(1) Clean all components in cleaning solvent and blow them dry with compressed air. Ensure that all metal particles are cleaned from the bottom of the gear casing.

(2) Inspect ball bearings for roughness or excessive side play. Do not rotate the bearings at high speed with compressed air, particularly when the bearings are dry as damage will result.

(3) Inspect the teeth on all gears for wear, pitting or burrs on the ends of the teeth.

(4) Inspect the synchro rings on their corresponding gear cones for wear and the synchronising teeth on the rings for chipping or wear.

(5) Inspect the needle rollers of the laygear and the front drive shaft for wear or pitting and the corresponding running surfaces of the layshaft, laygear bore and front drive shaft bore.

(6) Inspect the laygear thrust washers for wear.

(7) Renew all gaskets and oil seals that have been removed.

(8) Inspect the shift plates and springs for wear.

(9) Check the tension of the shift plate springs by comparison with new springs.

(10) Slide each synchroniser hub onto the mainshaft in its respective position and check for sideways movement. As necessary, renew the hub and/or mainshaft.

(11) Renew worn or unserviceable components.

TO ASSEMBLE

NOTE: During assembly lubricate all components sparingly with the specified transmission oil and coat all bolt threads exposed to the oil with a suitable type sealant as they are installed.

(1) If the selector housing was dismantled refer to that section and assemble the housing.

(2) If the yoke bush was removed from the extension housing instal a new bush to the position noted before removal.

(3) If the extension housing seal was removed, coat the

Exploded View of Mainshaft Components.

outside sealing edge of a new seal with a suitable type sealant and sparingly lubricate the seal lip with transmission oil.

(4) Using a suitable seal installation tool and hammer, instal the new seal squarely into the housing.

(5) If the synchroniser assemblies were dismantled proceed as follows:

(a) Slide the sleeve onto the hub aligning the mating marks and ensuring that the mating marks are on the same side.

(b) Instal the three shift plates.

(c) Place one shift plate spring into the hub engaging the three shift plates and installing the hooked end of the spring into the shift plate.

(d) Place the other spring into position with the hooked end of the spring in the same shift plate.

NOTE: Both springs must be hooked into opposite ends of the same shift plate and run in the same rotational direction.

(6) Place the second gear onto the mainshaft with the rear face of the gear towards the mainshaft flange.

(7) Place a synchro ring onto the 2nd gear.

(8) Slide the 1st and 2nd synchroniser assembly onto the mainshaft and press the assembly into position by using a hollow tubular drift which fits neatly over the mainshaft to abut the raised section of the hub between the splines and the shift plate spring.

(9) With the 1st and 2nd synchroniser assembly pressed into position on the mainshaft instal a new snap ring to retain the assembly in position.

NOTE: When pressing the mainshaft into the synchroniser assembly guide the synchro ring grooves onto the shift plates.

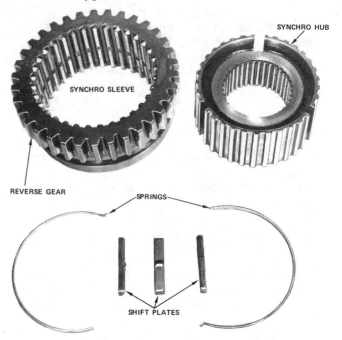

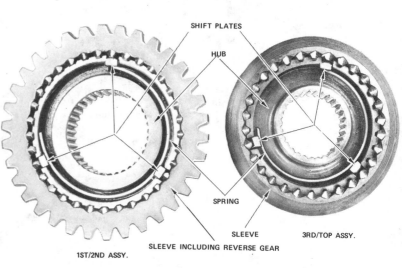

Exploded View of First and Second Speed Synchro Assembly.

(10) Place a synchro ring onto 1st gear and slide the assembly onto the mainshaft aligning the grooves in the synchro ring with the three shift plates.

(11) Instal the 1st gear spacer.

(12) Press the bearing into the bearing plate.

NOTE: The bearing should be a press fit by hand pressure.

(13) Press the bearing and plate onto the mainshaft by pressing on the inner track of the bearing. The dowel hole in the bearing plate must face rearwards.

(14) Slide the spacer onto the mainshaft and insert the speedometer drive gear positioning ball into its hole.

(15) Instal the speedometer drive gear, and new lock washer and nut, support the mainshaft and torque the nut to specifications.

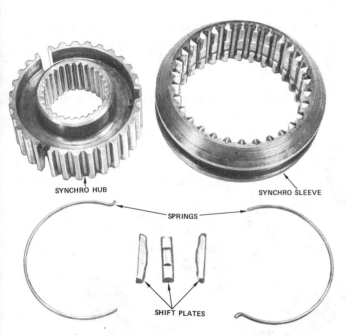

Exploded View of Third and Top Speed Synchro Assembly.

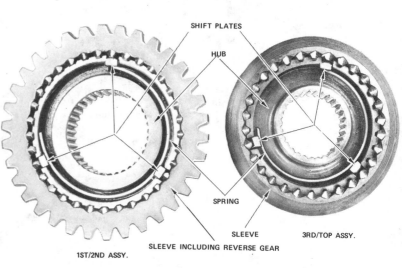

Assembled View of Both Transmission Synchroniser Assemblies.

(16) Bend over the tag of the lock washer to retain the mainshaft nut in position.

(17) Slide the third gear onto the mainshaft with the rear face of the gear towards the mainshaft flange and place a synchro ring onto the gear.

(18) Place the assembled 3rd and top synchroniser assembly onto the front of the mainshaft aligning the marks on the mainshaft and the hub.

NOTE: Some transmissions are not marked between the hub and the mainshaft. In this case select a position on the splines where the hub will be a tight installed fit.

(19) Press the synchroniser assembly onto the mainshaft in the same manner as the 1st and 2nd assembly was installed.

(20) Instal a new circlip onto the mainshaft.

(21) Ensure that there is no sideways movement of the assembly.

(22) Place the reverse idler gear into the gear case with the selector fork groove facing rearwards.

(23) Instal the reverse idler gear shaft using a soft hammer positioning the end of the shaft to align with the extension housing recess.

(24) With the dummy shaft positioned in the laygear, insert a spacer to abut the inside boss of the lay gear, smear 22 needle rollers lightly with grease and insert them around the dummy shaft. Place the second spacer over the ends of the needle rollers and retain it in position with a smear of grease.

Assemble the other set of needle rollers in the same manner to the other end of the lay gear.

(25) Place the two thrust washers in position in the gear case after smearing them lightly with grease. Align the tangs with the grooves in the gear case.

(26) Position the lay gear in the bottom of the gear case ensuring that the thrust washers or outside needle roller spacers are not dislodged.

(27) Place a new bearing onto the main drive gear with the snap ring groove towards the front of the main drive gear.

(28) Support the main drive gear in a press and press the bearing onto the main drive gear by pressing on the inner track of the bearing.

(29) Instal a new snap ring to the outer groove of the bearing. Instal a new snap ring to the main drive gear to retain the bearing in position.

(30) Instal the main drive gear into the gear case guiding the teeth past the lay gear constant mesh teeth.

NOTE: When installing the main drive gear apply gentle pressure to the outer track of the bearing and not the spigot end of the main drive gear.

(31) Instal a new oil seal into the drive gear retainer and position a new gasket onto the front of the gear case aligning the oil drain hole.

(32) Instal the retainer, aligning the oil hole, ensuring that the retainer is guided over the main drive gear splines to prevent damage to the oil seal.

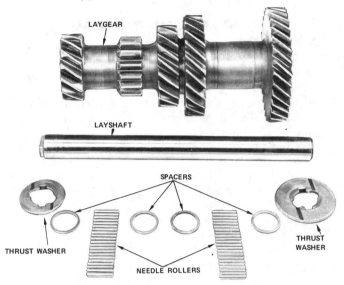

Exploded View of Laygear Components.

(33) Instal the retainer bolts and torque them to specifications.

(34) Instal the cage of needle rollers into the mainshaft gear bore.

(35) Position a new extension housing gasket over the rear of the gear case aligning all holes.

(36) Place a synchro ring onto the cone of the main drive gear.

(37) Manoeuvre the assembled mainshaft in through the rear of the gear case guiding the three grooves in the top gear synchro ring over the ends of the shift plates and aligning the scribe marks on the bearing plate and the rear of the gear case.

(38) Using a piece of strong wire, with a hook in each end, lift the lay gear and instal the lay shaft from the rear displacing the dummy shaft.

NOTE: The rear of the lay shaft must be positioned to align with the extension housing recess.

(39) Tap the lay shaft into the gear case until the front end of the shaft is flush with the front face of the gear case.

(40) Check that the oil passageway in the rear extension housing is clear and instal the extension housing to the gear case ensuring that the oil seal is not damaged by the mainshaft splines.

(41) Instal the extension housing bolts and torque them to specifications.

(42) Instal the speedometer driven gear assembly using a new O-ring.

(43) Using a new gasket instal the selector housing guiding the forms into mesh in the gears.

(44) Instal the selector housing bolts, torque them to specifications and ensure that all gears can be selected and the main drive gear rotated.

(45) Instal the clutch housing and the retaining bolts. Torque the bolts to specifications.

(46) Instal the clutch release lever and bearing.

(47) Instal the gearbox to the vehicle as previously described.

2. SELECTOR HOUSING

TO REMOVE AND INSTAL

(1) Remove the gearbox from the vehicle as previously described.

(2) Remove the reversing lamp switch bracket retaining bolts and withdraw the switch and the bracket from the selector housing.

(3) Remove the eight selector housing retaining bolts and washers.

(4) Carefully lever the selector housing from the gear case using two diametrically opposed screwdrivers.

Installation is a reversal of the removal procedure with attention to the following points:

(1) Clean the mating surfaces of the selector housing and the gear case.

(2) Use a new gasket on installation.

(3) Guide the selector forks into the gear grooves on installation.

(4) Torque the retaining bolts to specifications.

(5) Instal the gearbox as previously described.

TO DISMANTLE

(1) With the selector housing removed from the gear case thoroughly wash the housing and blow it dry with compressed air.

(2) Remove the three self locking nuts and the washers retaining levers to the cams.

(3) Using quick drying paint mark the selector housing underneath each operating lever with the same coloured paint that each operating rod was marked with on removal of the gearbox.

(4) Carefully remove the operating levers without damaging the cam oil seals.

(5) Pivot the 3rd and top selector fork up and out of the cam striker. Slide the selector fork to the end of the shaft to enable the third and top cam to be pushed out.

(6) With a cloth placed over the cams, shafts and forks push the third and top selector cam into the cloth.

NOTE: The cloth will also catch the interlock spring and ball.

(7) Remove the cam, spring and ball from the cloth and place them aside.

(8) Withdraw the interlock pin, the second ball and the interlock sleeve from the housing. Place all the interlock sleeve components together.

(9) Pivot the 1st and 2nd selector fork up and out of the cam striker. Slide the selector fork to the end of the shaft to enable the 1st and 2nd cam to be pushed out.

(10) Mark the 1st and 2nd selector cam and the boss to ensure correct assembly and then push the cam from the housing.

(11) Using a magnet withdraw the two plungers from the reverse selector shaft bosses. One from each boss.

(12) Push the reverse selector cam from the housing.

(13) Place a clean rag over the reverse selector shaft boss adjacent to the 1st and 2nd selector cam and slowly withdraw the reverse selector shaft from the housing.

NOTE: As the shaft is withdrawn through the rear boss the reverse shaft detent ball and spring will pop out. This spring is shorter than the interlock spring.

(14) Remove the detent ball and spring from the rag.

(15) Using a thin punch and hammer tap the retaining pin from the boss at the forward end of the selector fork shaft.

(16) Withdraw the shaft and lift out the two selector forks.

(17) If necessary use a thin punch and hammer tap the selector cam shaft oil seals from the housing.

TO CLEAN AND INSPECT

(1) Thoroughly wash all components and blow them dry with compressed air.

(2) Inspect the interlock balls for wear.

(3) Inspect the selector cam shafts for scoring and the cams for wear where they mate with the interlock balls.

(4) Compare the length of the interlock spring and the reverse selector shaft detent spring to new springs.

(5) Inspect the reverse selector shaft detent ball and the two plungers for wear.

(6) Inspect the selector forks for wear.

(7) Check the fit of the cam strikers in their mating selector forks.

NOTE: Excessive clearance will prevent the selected gear synchro sleeve from fully sliding onto its hub and will cause a jumping out of gear condition.

(8) Renew faulty or worn components.

TO ASSEMBLE

(1) If the oil seals were removed instal new oil seals using a suitable drift and hammer. Instal the oil seals with their lips inwards towards the interior of the gear case.

(2) Slide the selector fork shaft into the rear boss slightly, position the two selector forks in the housing with the grooves for the cam strikers in line with the centre line of the selector cam shaft orifice.

(3) Lift the 1st and 2nd selector fork up slightly and push the selector fork shaft through the fork.

(4) Lift the 3rd and top selector fork up slightly and push the shaft through the fork and align the hole in the shaft with the holes in the bosses.

(5) Instal a new retaining pin and pivot the two selector forks away from the selector cam shaft orifices.

(6) Insert the reverse selector shaft into the rear boss slightly. Place the detent spring into the rear boss through the hole and place the ball on top of the spring.

(7) Using a suitable solid punch push the ball into the boss, compressing the spring. Slide the reverse selector shaft over the ball and withdraw the solid punch. Slide the shaft forward and into the front boss.

(8) With the front of the shaft flush with the front face of the front boss the detent ball will engage with the first slot of the shaft. This is the neutral position. Leave the shaft in this position.

(9) Slide the reverse selector cam into the housing

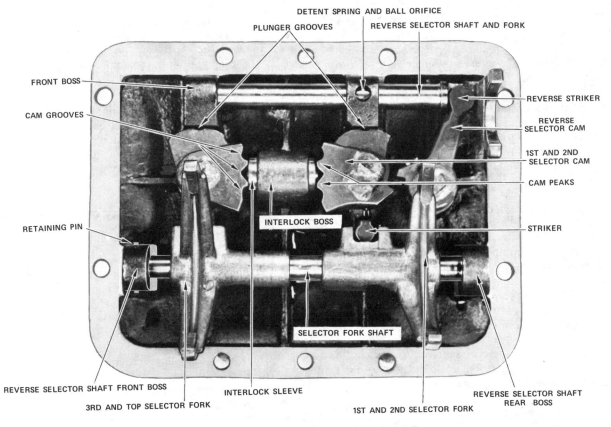

Assembled View of Type 4 Selector Housing and Components.

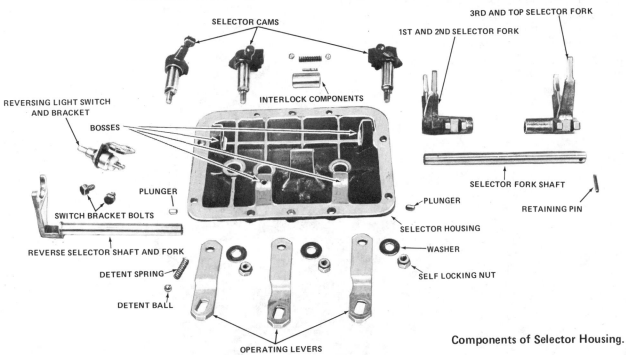

Components of Selector Housing.

aligning the striker with the groove in the reverse selector shaft.

(10) Instal the reverse operating lever washer, and self locking nut.

(11) With the reverse selector shaft still in the neutral position insert the two plungers into the reverse selector shaft bosses.

(12) Slide the 1st and 2nd selector cam into the housing aligning the striker with the groove in the selector fork and sliding the groove in the cam over the reverse shaft plunger in the rear boss.

NOTE: As necessary slide the 1st and 2nd selector fork sideways so that the plunger groove in the cam will slide over the reverse selector shaft plunger in the rear boss.

(13) Instal the 1st and 2nd operating lever, washer and self locking nut.

NOTE: With the end of the reverse selector shaft flush with the front face of the front boss, in neutral position, the centre groove of the 1st and 2nd cam will be in line with the centre line of the interlock orifice.

(14) Slide the interlock sleeve into position and instal the third and top cam in the same manner as the 1st and 2nd cam was installed. Do not instal the operating lever at this stage.

NOTE: At this stage both centre grooves of the cams are in line with the centre line of the interlock.

(15) Move the 3rd and top cam one way so that the peak between two grooves is in line with the interlock centre line. Measure the clearance between the end of the sleeve and the cam peak. Note the measurement.

(16) Move the 3rd and top cam the other way and check the clearance between the end of the sleeve and the peak. Note the measurement.

Return the cam to the centre groove, neutral position, and repeat the measuring procedure on the peaks of the 1st and 2nd cam. Note the measurements.

NOTE: All measurements should be the same and be between 0.013 and 0.190 mm. If necessary instal another interlock sleeve and recheck the clearance. Interlock sleeves are available in six different lengths.

(17) With the clearance between the sleeve and cam peaks correct remove the 3rd and top selector cam and insert a interlock ball into the interlock sleeve.

(18) Slide the interlock pin into the spring and instal the pin and spring in the sleeve.

(19) Place the second interlock ball into the sleeve and compress the spring slightly with the ball.

(20) With the spring compressed and the ball in the sleeve guide the 3rd and top cam into position.

(21) Instal the operating lever, washer and self locking nut.

(22) Torque the self locking nuts to specifications.

(23) Check that all gears can be selected individually and that no two gears can be selected at once.

(24) Instal the selector housing to the gearbox and the gearbox to the vehicle as previously described.

3. FLOOR CHANGE ASSEMBLY AND LINKAGE

TO REMOVE AND INSTAL

(1) Raise the vehicle and support it on stands placed beneath the front and rear of the vehicle. Raise the rear of the vehicle first.

(2) Using three different colours of quick drying paint mark the gear change lever with its mating selector rod.

(3) Disconnect the selector rods from the gear change levers by withdrawing the spring clips.

(4) Remove the gear lever knob and the lock nut.

(5) If a centre console and parcel tray is fitted to the vehicle proceed as follows:

(a) Remove the parcel tray retaining screws and manoeuvre the parcel tray from the vehicle.

(b) Push the seats fully forward and remove the console retaining screws.

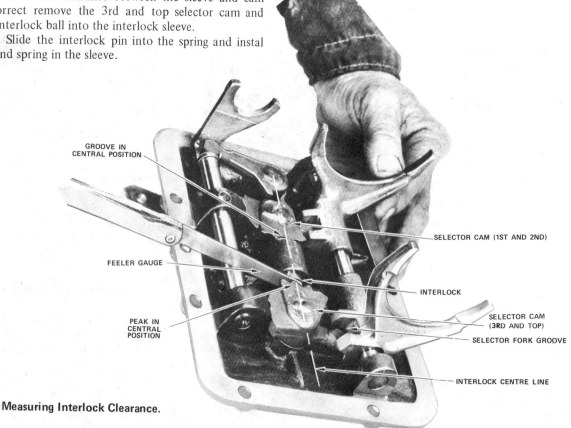

GROOVE IN CENTRAL POSITION

FEELER GAUGE

PEAK IN CENTRAL POSITION

SELECTOR CAM (1ST AND 2ND)

INTERLOCK

SELECTOR CAM (3RD AND TOP)

SELECTOR FORK GROOVE

INTERLOCK CENTRE LINE

Measuring Interlock Clearance.

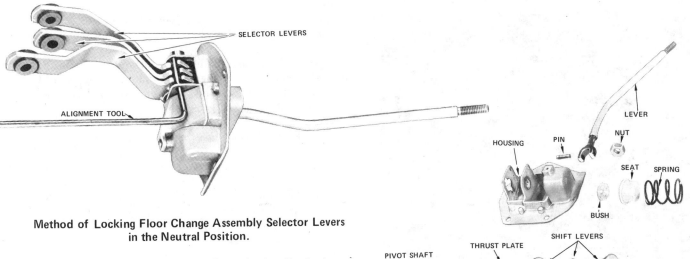

**Method of Locking Floor Change Assembly Selector Levers
in the Neutral Position.**

(c) Remove the centre bolt from the handbrake lever and lift the lever fully upwards.

(d) Push the seats rearwards and manoeuvre the console from the vehicle.

(6) Remove the bolts retaining the remote control to the floor panel and lift the remote control from the vehicle.

(7) Remove the selector rods from the levers.

Installation is a reversal of the removal procedure with attention to the following points:

(1) Instal the selector rods to the levers according to the paint colours.

(2) Instal all the console retaining screws before tightening any individual screw.

(3) Adjust the gear selector rods as described in a following section TO ADJUST SELECTOR RODS if necessary.

TO DISMANTLE

(1) With the floor change assembly removed from the vehicle lift the boot off the assembly and place the boot aside.

(2) Remove the Philips screw retaining the protective cap to the underneath of the assembly. Withdraw the plastic cap.

(3) Using a suitable thin drift and hammer tap the gear lever retaining pin from the selector shaft. Lift the gear lever upwards from the assembly.

(4) Withdraw the plastic bush from the lower end of the gear lever.

(5) Hold the end of the selector shaft against the spring pressure slightly and pivot the three levers rearwards to align the slots in the levers with the slot in the housing.

NOTE: When the slots are correctly aligned the selector shaft will pop out of the levers because it is spring loaded.

(6) Withdraw the selector shaft and spring.

(7) Withdraw the levers and the thrust plate.

(8) Withdraw the selector shaft bush, the reverse block spring and seat.

TO ASSEMBLE

NOTE: Coat all sliding surfaces with grease during assembly.

Exploded View of Floor Change Assembly.

(1) Place the spring seat onto the spring and instal the spring and seat into the housing.

(2) Insert the selector shaft bush into the housing.

NOTE: The thrust surface of the bush must face the levers.

(3) Insert the selector levers, referring to the illustration to observe their installed position, into the housing and align the slots.

(4) Insert the thrust plate between the outer lever and the end flange of the housing.

(5) With the spring inserted in the selector shaft, push the selector shaft through the levers and raise the levers to the upright position when the selector shaft pin is inserted through the thrust washer slot.

(6) Instal the plastic bush onto the lower end of the gear lever.

(7) Place the gear lever in position over the selector shaft in the housing and instal the gear lever retaining pin using a suitable pin punch and hammer.

(8) Place the plastic cap in position beneath the lower end of the gear lever, instal and tighten the retaining screw.

(9) Instal the gear lever boot and then instal the assembly to the vehicle.

(10) Adjust the gear selector rods as follows.

TO ADJUST SELECTOR RODS

(1) Raise the vehicle and support it on stands placed beneath the vehicle, front and rear. Raise the rear of the vehicle first.

(2) Loosen the nuts retaining the pivot pins to the selector rods at the shift control levers.

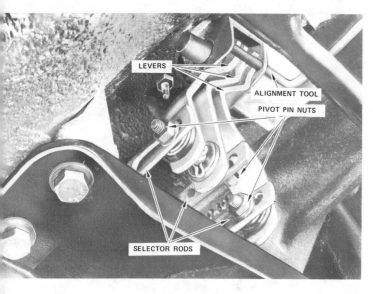

Underbody View Showing Floor Change Assembly with Levers Locked in Neutral.

NOTE: Ensure that the gearbox is in neutral before loosening the nuts.

(3) With the selector housing operating levers in the neutral position insert the short end of an adjustment checking rod through the indents in the levers and the holes in the housing flange.

NOTE: An adjustment checking rod can be made from a piece of rod, 346 mm. long, 5.5 mm. diameter with an 80 deg bend in it 80 mm. from one end.

(4) With the adjusting tool in position, the selector housing operating levers in neutral, ensure that the remote control levers are just touching the adjusting tool.

(5) Tighten the retaining nuts with the levers in this position.

(6) Remove the adjusting tool and torque the selector rod nuts to specifications.

(7) Lower the vehicle to the ground and check that all gears can be selected.

PROPELLER SHAFT

SPECIFICATIONS

Type . . . . One piece or two piece open tubular shaft

Number of universal joints:
  One piece 2
  Two piece 3

Type of universal
  joint . . . . Trunnion and needle roller bearing or constant velocity joint

Flange bolt and nut
  torque . . . . 6.0 kg/m

Centre bearing carrier
  bolts torque . . . . 2.3 kg/m

Centre yoke nut torque . . . . . 4.0 kg/m

Centre universal U-bolt
  nut torque . . . . 2.0 kg/m

1. DESCRIPTION

Three types of propeller shafts are used on these vehicles, namely a one-piece shaft and two types of two-piece shafts.

The one-piece propeller shaft has two trunnion and needle roller type universal joints.

The two-piece propeller shaft is of two types. One type has three trunnion and needle roller type universal joints whereas the second type utilises a constant velocity joint at the centre bearing position with the trunnion and needle roller type universal joint being used at the front and rear ends of the shaft.

Both types of two-piece propeller shafts are supported at the rear of the front section of the shaft by a centre bearing enclosed in a carrier which is bolted to the floor panel of the vehicle.

The front yoke sleeve of the front universal joint has internal splines which slide on mating splines on the rear end of the gearbox mainshaft and is supported on its outer circumference by a bush with an oil seal in the gearbox rear extension.

The universal joint assemblies and propeller shafts on all types are balanced to fine tolerances and the tubular shafts must not be dented or otherwise damaged.

To renew a universal joint, centre bearing or a constant velocity joint the propeller shaft assembly must be removed from the vehicle.

The two-piece propeller shaft has either replaceable or non-replaceable type universal joints. The cups of the replaceable type universal joints have grooves machined in them to accommodate circlips to retain the cups to the trunnions, the non-replaceable type universal joints have the trunnions staked to retain the cups.

2. PROPELLER SHAFT ASSEMBLY

TO REMOVE AND INSTAL (One Piece Propeller Shaft)

(1) Scribe a mark on the propeller shaft and pinion flanges to ensure that the propeller shaft assembly is reassembled in its original position.

(2) Remove the four self locking nuts and withdraw the bolts from the propeller shaft and pinion flanges.

(3) Lower the rear of the propeller shaft and withdraw it from the gearbox.

(4) Plug the gearbox extension housing to prevent any loss of lubricant.

Installation is a reversal of the removal procedure with attention to the following:

When installing the front yoke into the gearbox for engagement with the mainshaft splines ensure that the oil seal or bush in the extension housing is not damaged.

Check the gearbox oil level and top up as necessary.

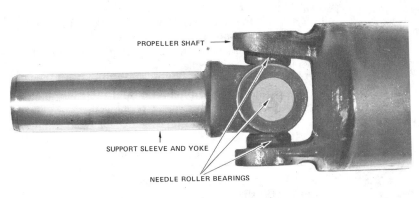

Forward End of Propeller Shaft Showing Universal Joint Yoke and Sleeve.

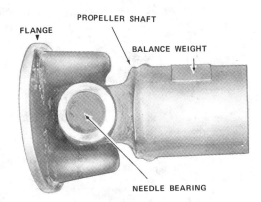

Propeller Shaft Rear Universal Joint.

Tighten the universal joint rear flange nuts progressively to the correct specified torque.

TO REMOVE AND INSTAL (Two Piece Propeller Shaft)

(1) Scribe a mark on the propeller shaft and pinion flanges to ensure that the propeller shaft assembly is reassembled in its original position.

(2) Remove the four bolts and nuts from the propeller shaft and pinion flanges.

(3) Unscrew the two bolts that secure the centre support bearing to the underbody.

(4) Lower the whole propeller shaft and centre support bearing assembly and withdraw it from the gearbox.

(5) Plug the gearbox extension housing to prevent any loss of lubricant.

Installation is a reversal of the removal procedure with attention given to the following:

When inserting the front yoke into the gearbox extension housing for engagement with the mainshaft splines ensure that the oil seal or bushing in the extension housing is not damaged.

Torque the centre support bearing bracket bolts and the universal joint rear flange nuts to their correct respective torques.

Check the gearbox oil level and top up as necessary.

TO DISMANTLE AND ASSEMBLE UNIVERSAL JOINTS (Circlip Retained Type)

NOTE: Each universal joint is serviced as a kit which includes trunnion, seals, circlips and the needle roller bearings and cups.

It is not practicable to dismantle a universal joint unless the components are to be renewed.

Do not hold the sleeve of the front universal joint in the unprotected jaws of a vice, otherwise damage will result.

(1) Remove the propeller shaft assembly from the vehicle as previously described.

(2) Remove the two circlips securing two opposed needle roller bearings in one of the yokes of the universal joint.

(3) Holding the joint in a vice, and using a soft metal drift, tap one of the bearing cups in to drive the other bearing out of the yoke. Lift the bearing out with the fingers to avoid dislodging the needle rollers.

(4) Again using the soft drift, tap the end of the trunnion of the bearing just removed to drive the other bearing out of the yoke, and again remove with the fingers to avoid dislodging the needle rollers.

(5) Manoeuvre the yoke over the end of the trunnion and withdraw the yoke from the shaft assembly.

(6) Repeat this operation on the remaining two bearings of the universal joint to dismantle the assembly completely.

(7) Treat the other universal joint(s) in a similar manner to completely dismantle the propeller shaft.

(8) Check the needle roller bearings and trunnion journals for wear. If wear is apparent renew the trunnion and bearings as a kit. Do not renew individual needle roller bearing assemblies or fit old bearings to a new trunnion. Always use new bearing retaining circlips and bearing seal washers when assembling.

Reassembly is a reversal of the dismantling procedure.

Pack the bearings with a lithium based grease on assembling, ensuring that an air space is left to allow for expansion of the grease at operating temperature.

3. CENTRE SUPPORT BEARING

TO REMOVE

With Staked Type Universal Joints

(1) With the propeller shaft assembly removed from the vehicle mark the centre universal yoke and front universal yoke to ensure correct re-alignment at assembly.

(2) Bend back the lock tab in the centre of the universal joint yoke and slacken the restraining bolt.

Remove the U shaped plate and separate the two halves of the propeller shaft.

(3) Remove the propeller shaft and bearing assembly from the rubber insulator.

(4) Bend back the six tabs and remove the rubber insulator from its carrier.

(5) Using a suitable puller withdraw the bearing and protective caps from the propeller shaft.

With Constant Velocity and Replaceable Type Joints

(1) With the propeller shaft removed from the vehicle separate as follows:

(a) Scribe a line across each end of the centre joint to maintain original balance on reassembly.

(b) On constant velocity joint type, bend back the

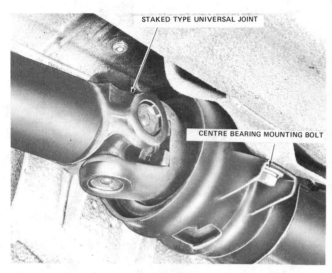

View of Propeller Shaft Centre Bearing. Model Shown has Staked Universal Joints.

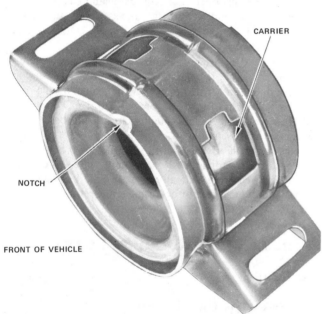

Notch in Centre Support Bearing Carrier must be positioned towards front of Vehicle when Carrier is Installed.

locking tabs and remove the six bolts. On centre universal joint type, remove the four U-bolt self locking nuts and withdraw the two U-bolts.

(c) Carefully prise the two sections apart and separate the two halves of the propeller shaft.

(2) Remove the flange retaining nut or bolt as follows: On constant velocity joint type bend up the retaining bolt, lock tab and remove the bolt, lock tab and washer.

On centre universal joint type remove the retaining nut and washer.

(3) Withdraw the flange from the shaft after marking the flange and shaft mating position.

(4) On centre universal joint type withdraw the splined spacer from the shaft.

(5) Withdraw the centre bearing assembly from the shaft.

(6) Push the bearing assembly from the rubber insert, and lift the two dust covers from the bearing.

(7) Prise up the carrier rubber insert tabs and carefully prise the rubber insert from the carrier.

(8) Inspect the rubber insert for cracks, fatigue or sponginess. Renew as necessary.

TO INSTAL
With Staked Type Universal Joints

(1) Using a tube of suitable size drive the ball bearing and protective caps onto the propeller shaft.

(2) Instal the rubber insulator into the carrier with the boss facing upwards and bend the six tabs on the carrier back over the beaded edge of the rubber insulator.

(3) Slide the rubber insulator and carrier over the bearing assembly.

(4) Instal the securing bolt, into the end of the front propeller shaft using a new lock tab and leaving enough space to allow for the U-shaped plate.

(5) Align the marks made on dismantling on the two universal joint yokes and assemble the propeller shaft.

(6) Assemble the 'U' shaped plate with the pintle side towards the splines under the securing bolt and lock plate, tighten the bolt securely and lock in position.

With Constant Velocity and Replaceable Type Joints

(1) Insert the rubber into the carrier with the boss of the rubber insert facing upwards.

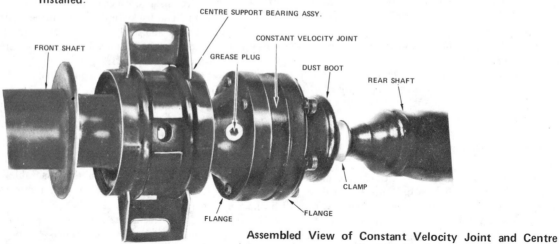

Assembled View of Constant Velocity Joint and Centre Support Bearing.

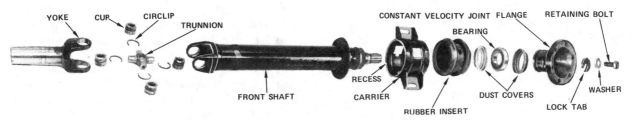

**Front Section of Constant Velocity Type Propeller Shaft
With Centre Support Bearing.**

(2) Lock the rubber insert into the carrier by bending down the six tabs of the carrier.

(3) With the new bearing encased in the two dust covers, slide the bearing assembly into the centre of the carrier rubber insert.

(4) Slide the centre bearing assembly onto the shaft with the notch in the front of the carrier towards the front of the shaft.

(5) On centre universal joint type place the splined spacer onto the shaft.

(6) Slide the flange onto the shaft aligning the marks made on dismantling.

(7) On constant velocity joint type instal the washer, new lock tab and the bolt. Tighten the bolt securely and bend up the lock tab.

On centre universal joint type instal the washer and nut and torque the nut to specifications.

(8) Slide the two halves of the shaft together aligning the scribe line.

(9) On constant velocity joint type instal the six bolts using new lock tabs. Tighten the bolts securely and bend up the lock tabs.

On centre universal joint type instal the two U-bolts and nuts and torque the nuts to specifications.

(10) Instal the propeller shaft to the vehicle as previously described.

4. CONSTANT VELOCITY JOINT

TO RENEW

(1) Remove the propeller shaft from the vehicle as previously described.

(2) Scribe a line from the rear edge of the rear flange, across the constant velocity joint and to the front edge of the front flange.

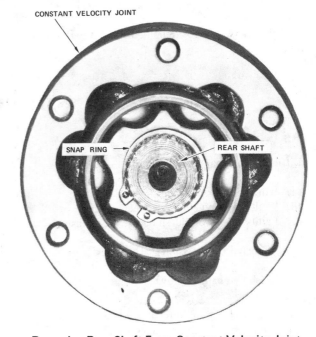

Removing Rear Shaft From Constant Velocity Joint.

NOTE: The rear flange is mounted to the rear section of shaft and the front flange to the front shaft.

(3) Bend up the ends of the lock tabs and remove the six retaining bolts and three lock tabs.

(4) Separate the two sections of shaft and place the front section aside.

(5) Remove the snap ring from the front of the rear shaft.

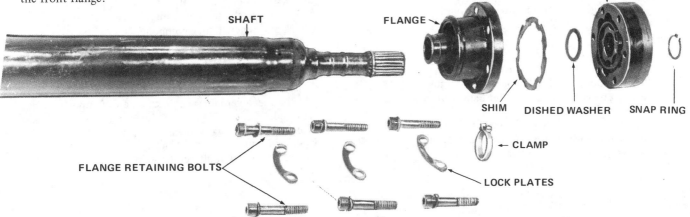

Rear Section of Propeller Shaft with Constant Velocity Joint.

(6) Withdraw the constant velocity joint, shim and dished washer. Discard the joint.

(7) Mark the shaft and the flange to maintain balance on reassembly and withdraw the flange from the shaft after loosening the dust seal clamp.

(8) Remove all traces of the old grease from both flanges, shim and washer.

(9) Pack the new constant velocity joint with a molybdenum based grease.

(10) Slide the flange onto the shaft aligning the marks made on dismantling, position the dust seal clamp and tighten.

(11) Insert two opposite bolts through the flange from the rear.

(12) Position the shim onto the flange over the bolts.

(13) Slide the dished washer over the end of the shaft with the dish rearwards.

(14) Slide the constant velocity joint over the end of the shaft and onto the two bolts.

(15) Instal the snap ring to the front of the shaft. Remove the two bolts.

(16) Assemble the two sections of the shaft together aligning the marks on the flanges.

(17) Use new lock tabs, tighten the bolts securely and bend over each end of the lock tab.

(18) Instal the propeller shaft to the vehicle as previously described.

MANUAL TRANSMISSION FAULT DIAGNOSIS

GEARBOX

1. **Difficult gear change**

Possible cause	*Remedy*
(a) Worn selector mechanism.	— Check and renew faulty components
(b) Faulty gear synchroniser mechanism.	— Overhaul gearbox.
(c) Faulty clutch or clutch release mechanism.	— Check and overhaul clutch and/or adjust release mechanism.
(d) Distorted transmission shaft splines.	— Renew damaged components.

2. **Gear clash on changing down.**

Possible cause	*Remedy*
(a) Faulty clutch or clutch release mechanism.	— Overhaul clutch and/or adjust release mechanism.
(b) Faulty synchro rings and cones.	— Check and overhaul gearbox, renew components as required.
(c) Broken or incorrect positioning of synchro shift plate retaining springs.	— Check and overhaul gearbox, renew components as required.
(d) Lubricating oil too heavy.	— Drain gear case and refill with correct quantity and grade of oil.

3. **Slipping out of gear (1st and 2nd)**

Possible cause	*Remedy*
(a) Weak or broken selector plunger spring.	— Renew plunger spring.
(b) Worn or chipped synchro teeth on 1st and/or second speed.	— Check and overhaul gearbox, renew components as required.
(c) Excessive end float of laygear.	— Check and renew faulty thrust washers.
(d) Worn gearbox front or rear bearings.	— Check and renew worn bearings.
(e) Worn shift or selector mechanism.	— Check and renew faulty components.

4. **Slipping out of gear (3rd and top)**

Possible cause	*Remedy*
(a) Weak or broken selector plunger spring.	— Renew plunger spring.
(b) Worn synchro teeth on third and/or top speeds.	— Check and overhaul gearbox, renew components as required.
(c) Excessive end float of laygear.	— Check and renew worn thrust washers.
(d) Worn gearbox front or rear ball bearings.	— Check and renew worn bearings.
(e) Worn shift or selector mechanism.	— Check and renew faulty components.

5. **Gearbox noise (in neutral)**

Possible cause

(a) Worn front gearbox bearing.

(b) Clipped or pitted constant mesh gears (laygear, front drive gear or 1st, 2nd or 3rd mainshaft gears).

(c) Excessive laygear end float.

(d) Lack of sufficient lubricant.

Remedy

— Overhaul and renew bearing.

— Overhaul and renew components as necessary.

— Check and renew laygear thrust washers.

— Fill gear case with the correct quantity and grade of gear oil.

6. **Gearbox noise (forward gears engaged)**

Possible cause

(a) Worn front and/or rear gearbox ball bearings.

(b) Chipped or pitted constant mesh gears (laygear, front drive gear on 1st, 2nd or 3rd speed mainshaft gears).

(c) Excessive laygear end float.

(d) Chipped reverse idler gear.

(e) Lack of sufficient lubricant.

Remedy

— Overhaul and renew bearings.

— Overhaul and renew components as necessary.

— Check and renew laygear thrust washers.

— Check and renew components as necessary.

— Fill gear case with correct quantity and grade of lubricant.

PROPELLER SHAFT

1. **Shaft vibration.**

Possible cause

(a) Bent propeller shaft(s).

(b) Excessive wear in universal joint trunnion and bearings.

(c) Propeller shaft(s) out of balance.

(d) Excessive wear of front joint sleeve in rear extension housing.

(e) Rear universal joint to pinion flange bolts loose.

(f) Worn centre support bearing.

Remedy

— Renew shaft(s).

— Renew complete universal joint (trunnion and bearings)

— Renew complete propeller shaft(s).

— Renew extension housing bush assembly.

— Renew and tighten loose bolts.

— Renew centre bearing.

2. **Excessive backlash**

Possible cause

(a) Worn universal joint trunnion and bearings.

(b) Worn mainshaft and universal joint sleeve.

Remedy

— Renew joint trunnion and bearings as an assembly.

— Renew worn components.

AUTOMATIC TRANSMISSION

SPECIFICATIONS

Make . . . .   Borg Warner 35
Type . . . .   3 forward speeds and
                                              reverse, epicyclic gear
                                              train with torque con-
                                              verter
Operation . . . .   Automatic-hydraulic
Gear ratios:
  First 2.39:1
  Second 1.45:1
  Third 1.00:1
  Reverse 2.09:1
Converter ratio 1.91:1
Lubricant:
  Type . . . .   Donax T7
  Capacity . . . .   6.4 litres
Front band adjustment . . . . .   0.11 kg/m
Rear band adjustment . . . . . .   1.4 kg/m and back off
                                              one full turn

Shift Speeds — 4.11:1 axle ratio

Upshift speeds — light
  throttle:
    Low to intermed-
    iate . . . .   9—17 km/h
    Intermediate to
    high . . . .   14—22 km/h
Upshift speeds — on kick-
  down:
    Low to intermed-
    iate . . . .   46—62 km/h
    Intermediate to
    high . . . .   82—97 km/h
Downshift speeds — part
  throttle:
    High to intermed-
    iate . . . .   28—40 km/h
Downshift speeds — nil
  throttle:
    Intermediate to
    low . . . .   9—12 km/h
Downshift speeds — on
  kickdown:
    High to intermed-
    iate . . . .   67—85 km/h
    Intermediate to
    low . . . .   32—55 km/h

Shift Speeds — 3.89:1 axle ratio

Upshift speeds — light
  throttle:
    Low to intermed-
    iate . . . .   9—17 km/h
    Intermediate to
    high . . . .   16—24 km/h
Upshift speeds — on kick-
  down:
    Low to intermed-
    iate . . . .   48—62 km/h

Intermediate to
  high . . . .   86—99 km/h
Downshift speeds — part
  throttle:
    High to intermed-
    iate . . . .   37—51 km/h
Downshift speeds — nil
  throttle:
    Intermediate to
    low . . . .   9—14 km/h
Downshift speeds — on
  kickdown:
    High to intermed-
    iate . . . .   75—94 km/h
    Intermediate to
    low . . . .   35—54 km/h

Shift Speeds — 3.70:1 axle ratio

Upshift speeds — light
  throttle:
    Low to intermed-
    iate . . . .   11—17 km/h
    Intermediate to
    high . . . .   16—24 km/h
Upshift speeds — on kick-
  down:
    Low to intermed-
    iate . . . .   50—65 km/h
    Intermediate to
    high . . . .   90—102 km/h
Downshift speeds — part
  throttle:
    High to intermed-
    iate . . . .   38—52 km/h
Downshift speeds — nil
  throttle:
    Intermediate to
    low . . . .   11—16 km/h
Downshift speeds — on
  kickdown:
    High to intermed-
    iate . . . .   78—98 km/h
    Intermediate to
    low . . . .   35—56 km/h

Shift Speeds — 3.45:1 axle ratio

Upshift speeds — light
  throttle:
    Low to intermed-
    iate . . . .   11—19 km/h
    Intermediate to
    high . . . .   17—25 km/h
Upshift speeds — on
  kickdown:
    Low to intermed-
    iate . . . .   52—69 km/h
    Intermediate to
    high . . . .   94—110 km/h
Downshift speeds — part
  throttle:
    High to intermed-
    iate . . . .   35—48 km/h

Downshift speeds – nil
throttle:
Intermediate to
low . . . . 11–16 km/h
Downshift speeds – on
kickdown:
High to intermed-
iate . . . . 83–104 km/h
Intermediate to
low . . . . 38–62 km/h
Stall speed:
1600 . . . . 1750–1950 rpm
2000 . . . . 2050–2250 rpm

TORQUE WRENCH SETTINGS

Oil pan drain plug . . . . 1.4 kg/m
Oil pan bolts . . . . 1.8 kg/m
Valve body bolts . . . . 1.2 kg/m
Front servo bolts . . . . 1.8 kg/m
Rear servo bolts . . . . 3.7 kg/m
Rear band adjuster lock-
nut . . . . 2.5 kg/m
Inhibitor switch lock-
nut . . . . 0.8 kg/m
Torque converter to
drive plate . . . . 4.1 kg/m

1. DESCRIPTION

The automatic transmission combines a torque converter with a fully automatic three speed epicyclic gear train. The torque converter housing and the transmission case are separate casings. The transmission provides three forward ratios and a reverse.

The torque converter provides a means of obtaining smooth application of engine power to the driving wheels and additional engine torque multiplication to first gear and to second gear at low road speeds. The torque converter also provides extreme low speed flexibility in third gear and due to the ability of multiplying engine torque, it gives acceleration from a very low road speed without having to resort to a downshift in the transmission under normal driving conditions.

The hydraulic system consists of one pump and a valve arrangement. The transmission fluid level is checked by a dipstick type indicator located in the oil filler tube.

The gear selection lever is floor mounted and connected to the transmission by adjustable linkage. The selector quadrant, adjacent to the base of the lever is marked P,R,N,D,2,1.

It is necessary for the gear selection lever to be in the N or P position before the engine can be started.

ENGINE TUNING

When tuning or testing the engine the handbrake must be firmly applied and the gear selection lever must be in the P (park) position, otherwise the vehicle could move forward or backward as the engine speed is increased, which could result in severe damage to the vehicle or injury to the operator.

View of Gear Selector Quadrant. Typical.

When adjusting the engine idle speed move the gear selection lever to the P (park) position with the handbrake applied in order that the correct idling speed adjustment may be obtained.

TOWING

For long distance towing the propeller shaft should be disconnected at the rear universal joint and removed from the vehicle. (See propeller shaft in the manual transmission section of the manual). An alternate method is to tow the vehicle suspended from the rear.

The vehicle may be towed up to 30 kilometres not exceeding a speed of 30 km/h provided the reason for towing is not within the transmission, or the rear axle.

It is not practicable to start the engine by either towing or pushing the vehicle. If battery jumper leads are used ensure that the booster battery is connected positive to positive and negative to negative.

2. TRANSMISSION FLUID

Only a recommended type of automatic transmission fluid should be used in the transmission when topping up or changing the fluid in the transmission.

The transmission fluid level in the transmission case should be checked at regular intervals of not greater than 5000 kilometres.

Under normal operating conditions it is not necessary to drain the fluid and remove the oil pan from the transmission unless the unit is to be overhauled. Periodic draining of the transmission is not necessary unless the vehicle is being operated under abnormal driving conditions as follows: hard driving; mountain terrain or towing caravans. Under these conditions drain and remove the oil pan, clean the filters and adjust the rear band every 40,000 kilometres.

TO CHECK AND TOP UP

(1) With the transmission at normal operating temperature and the vehicle on a level floor open the engine bonnet.

(2) Carefully clean around the top of the transmission case filler tube and dipstick to ensure that no dirt or foreign matter can enter the filler tube as the dipstick is withdrawn.

(3) Place the gear selection lever in the P (park) position and firmly apply the handbrake.

(4) Start the engine and allow the engine to idle at idling speed. Ensure that the choke is pushed in.

(5) Withdraw the dipstick from the transmission case filler tube and wipe the dipstick dry on a piece of lint free cloth. Instal the dipstick to get a level indication and again withdraw the dipstick. Observe the reading.

(6) If necessary, add sufficient transmission fluid to the transmission case via the filler tube to bring the level to the 'FULL' (maximum) mark on the dipstick. The difference between the 'LOW' and 'FULL' marks on the dipstick is approximately half of a litre.

NOTE: Do not overfill the transmission or foaming, overheating and unsatisfactory operation of the transmission will result.

(7) Instal the dipstick correctly into the filler tube of the transmission case.

TO DRAIN AND REFILL

(1) With the transmission at normal operating temperature raise the vehicle and support it on stands front and rear.

(2) Unscrew and remove the transmission case oil pan drain plug and drain the transmission fluid into a suitable container.

NOTE: Use care to avoid scalding if the transmission fluid is very hot after a long run.

(3) Instal and tighten the oil pan drain plug to specifications. Lower the vehicle to the ground.

(4) Refill the transmission case with the correct grade of transmission fluid.

Start the engine and firmly apply the handbrake. Move the gear selection lever through each gear position and then back into P (park). Allow a few seconds in each gear position for the transmission fluid to be pumped into the clutches, servos or valves to exhaust any air locks.

(5) With the gear selection lever back in the P (park) position, check the transmission fluid level as described in TO CHECK AND TOP UP and top up as necessary.

NOTE: If the transmission is cold when it is refilled, fill it to the 'LOW' mark on the dipstick, bring the transmission to normal operating temperature and recheck the level of the transmission fluid. Add as necessary.

3. TRANSMISSION CASE OIL PAN

TO REMOVE AND INSTAL

(1) With the transmission at normal operating temperature raise the vehicle and support it on stands front and rear.

(2) Remove the transmission case oil pan drain plug and drain the transmission fluid into a suitable container.

(3) Instal and tighten the drain plug to specifications. Remove the transmission lever stop bracket.

(4) Remove the oil pan to transmission case bolts and remove the oil pan. Discard the gasket. Clean the mounting faces of the oil pan and the transmission case.

NOTE: Two of the oil pan retaining bolts are installed through the torque converter housing. Ensure that these bolts are removed before attempting to remove the oil pan.

(5) Wash the oil pan and the bolts thoroughly in clean white spirits and then blow dry with compressed air.

(6) Place a new oil pan to transmission case gasket on the oil pan and ensure that the gasket is a correct fit.

NOTE: If the gasket is too small, a short soaking in warm water will expand it to size.

(7) With the new gasket on the oil pan hold the oil pan up against the transmission case and instal the retaining bolts finger tight.

(8) Torque the bolts to specifications.

(9) Fill the transmission with the correct grade of transmission fluid, refer to — TO CHECK AND TOP UP and add transmission fluid as necessary.

(10) Lower the vehicle to the ground.

4. FILTER

The filter filters the fluid before it leaves the oil pan. It is retained by screws to the valve body.

Removing and cleaning the filter is not a normal service operation but where the vehicle is being operated under abnormal conditions the filter can be removed for cleaning approximately every 40,000 kilometres.

TO REMOVE AND INSTAL

(1) Remove the oil pan as previously described.

(2) Remove the four screws holding the filter over the front pump suction orifices.

(3) Remove the filter and place it in a wash container with cleaning fluid.

(4) Wash the filter thoroughly and then blow dry with moisture free compressed air.

(5) Inspect the filter for a torn screen or warpage. Renew as necessary.

(6) If the filter is serviceable, then instal when cleaned and securely tighten the retaining screws.

(7) Before installing the oil pan with a new gasket ensure that the oil pipes have not dislodged from the valve body. If necessary use a soft faced hammer to tap them into position.

(8) Instal the oil pan referring to TRANSMISSION CASE OIL PAN.

5. FRONT BAND

This is not a normal service operation as the front band, once it has been initially set is self adjusting. The adjustment is initially set at assembly or at overhaul.

TO ADJUST

(1) Remove the oil pan as described under TRANSMISSION CASE OIL PAN.

(2) Remove the bolt retaining the self adjusting plate and front servo to the transmission case.

(3) Manoeuvre the self adjusting plate from the pipes and place it aside.

(4) Hold the self adjusting spring and undo the adjusting screw a few turns.

(5) Insert a 6.35 mm. band adjusting spacer between the adjusting screw and the front servo piston.

(6) Using a tension wrench torque the adjusting screw to specifications. Remove the tension wrench.

(7) Position the self adjusting spring so that it is one to two threads (1.5 – 2.0 mm.) from the lever.

(8) Remove the band adjusting spacer from between the adjusting screw and the front servo piston.

(9) Manoeuvre the self adjusting plate into position inserting the longer end of the self adjusting spring into the groove of the self adjusting plate. Ensure that the adjusting screw is not altered during the operation.

(10) Instal the retaining bolts and torque to specifications.

(11) Instal the oil pan as described under – TRANSMISSION CASE OIL PAN.

6. REAR BAND

The rear band adjustment is not a normal service operation and may only become necessary as indicated by a harsh shift pattern, a loose adjusting screw lock nut, slippage of a no drive condition in the 1 (low) or R (reverse) ranges, and/or seizure between first and second or at overhaul.

If the vehicle is being operated under abnormal conditions the band adjustment should be checked every 40,000 kilometres.

TO ADJUST

(1) Referring to TRANSMISSION ASSEMBLY, TO REMOVE and TO INSTAL, carry out those operations necessary to lower the transmission and so gain access to the rear band adjusting screw.

(2) Undo the band adjusting screw lock nut a few turns while holding the band adjusting screw.

(3) Using a torque wrench, torque the adjusting screw to specifications and then loosen the adjusting screw according to specifications.

(4) Hold the band adjusting screw in this position and torque the lock nut to specifications.

(5) Raise the transmission and instal and tighten all necessary equipment.

7. TRANSMISSION SELECTOR CABLE

TO ADJUST

(1) Raise the front of the vehicle and support on chassis stands.

(2) Remove the clip and clevis pin securing the selector cable to the operating arm on the transmission.

(3) With the selector lever in '1' position (first or low) and the operating arm fully to the rear, adjust the cable length at the adjuster on the bracket to align the clevis pin holes in the end of the cable and the operating arm. Tighten the nuts.

(4) Lightly smear the clevis pin with grease and instal it in the cable end and operating arm. Fit the clip to retain the clevis pin.

(5) Check that the selector lever moves into all positions indicated on the quadrant and that the engine will only start in 'P' or 'N'.

(6) Remove the stands and lower the vehicle.

8. NEUTRAL SAFETY SWITCH

The neutral safety switch, incorporating the reverse light switch, is attached to the left hand side of the transmission case. The two smaller of the four switch terminals are connected in series with the starter solenoid

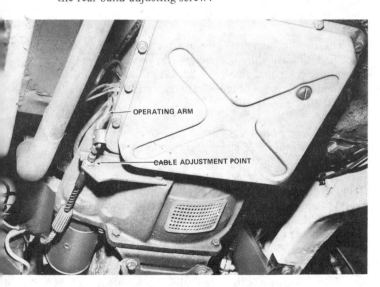

Transmission Selector Cable Adjustment Point. Typical.

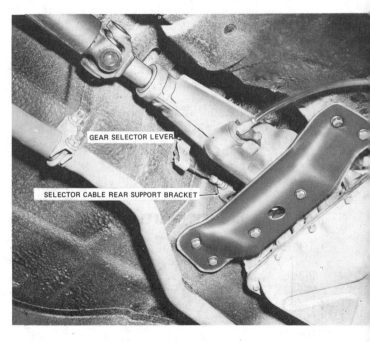

Rear Support Bracket for Transmission Selector Cable. Typical.

switch to ensure that the engine can be started only with the transmission in either the N (neutral) or P (park) positions.

The two larger of the four switch terminals are connected in series with the reverse light, which should only operate when the R (reverse) position is selected on the selector quadrant.

Any adjustment to the transmission linkage should be followed by the neutral safety switch adjustment.

TO ADJUST

(1) With the engine stopped, select D or '1' position on the selector quadrant with the selector lever and apply the handbrake.

(2) Slacken the locknut on the stem of the neutral safety switch sufficiently for the switch to be screwed in or out in relation to the transmission case.

(3) Disconnect the wires to the neutral safety switch smaller terminals and connect a 12 volt test lamp in series with these terminals and the battery and earth, similarly connect a second test lamp across the larger reverse light terminals on the switch.

(4) Screw the safety switch out slowly until the reverse light test lamp lights, then screw it in until the test lamp goes out and note and mark this position.

(5) Continue to screw the switch in until the starter test lamp lights and again note the position of the switch. Screw the switch out to a point midway between the two positions, and tighten the locknut. Check that the starter test lamp is out.

(6) Move the selector lever to the P (park) position. The lamp should be extinguished as the indicator moves to the R (reverse) position on the quadrant and then light again as the indicator registers with the P (park) position on the quadrant. The reverse light test lamp must light only when the R (reverse) position is selected.

(7) If necessary, move the safety switch slightly in or out until the conditions described in operations (4), (5) and (6) prevail and tighten the locknut on the switch mounting.

(8) Move the speed selector lever to the D (drive) and '1' (low) positions in turn. Both test lamps should be extinguished in these positions if the switch is serviceable and correctly adjusted.

If it is impossible to adjust the switch as described, a new neutral safety switch must be installed.

(9) Remove the test lamps and restore the original connections.

9. DOWNSHIFT CABLE

TO REMOVE AND INSTAL

(1) Release the inner cable from the accelerator linkage.

(2) Remove the locknut holding the top of the outer cable to the bracket.

(3) Raise the vehicle and support it securely on chassis stands.

(4) Drain the transmission oil into a suitable container and remove the oil pan.

(5) Loosen the locknut holding the outer cable to the transmission case.

(6) Disconnect the inner cable from the (kickdown) forced downshift cam inside the transmission.

(7) Remove the cable assembly from the transmission by unscrewing the cable in an anti-clockwise direction.

Installation is a reversal of the removal procedure with attention to the following points:

(1) Ensure that the inner cable lug is connected to the (kickdown) forced downshift cam before the oil pan is installed.

(2) See TO DRAIN AND REFILL to ensure correct procedure for adding the transmission fluid.

(3) Adjust the cable by using one of the following procedures.

TO ADJUST

(1) Ensure that the engine and transmission are at normal operating temperature and check the fluid level in the transmission.

(2) With the engine stopped, connect an electric tachometer in parallel with the ignition primary circuit.

(3) Connect a pressure test gauge capable of reading pressures to 21 kg/cm^2 to the pressure take off point on the rear of the transmission case.

(4) Check that the choke valve is fully open and that there is no free play in the accelerator linkage, start the engine and run at approximately 560 rpm.

(5) With the handbrake firmly applied move the gear selector lever to the D (drive) position then adjust the idling speed to exactly 500 rpm.

(6) With the engine idling speed set at 500 rpm the pressure gauge reading should be 3.52 to 4.57 kg/cm^2.

(7) Apply the footbrake in addition to the handbrake, raise the engine speed to 1000 rpm and note the rise in pressure above the actual pressure recorded at 500 rpm.

The pressure rise should be 1.05 to 1.41 kg/cm^2.

NOTE: On 1600 GT models only the pressure reading at 1000 rpm should be 5.62 – 7.03 kg/cm^2. On all models allow the engine speed to return to idling speed as soon as possible and do not exceed 1000 rpm.

(8) If the pressure rise is not within the limits specified, loosen the locknut on the upper end of the downshift cable and screw the adjuster in or out until the specified readings are obtained. Do not forget to tighten the locknut after adjustment.

NOTE: When adjustments are complete crimp the ferrule on the inner cable 0.25 mm off the outer cable end.

(9) Stop the engine when the adjustment is correct, remove the pressure gauge from the transmission case and instal the plug. Remove the tachometer from the engine.

(10) Road test the vehicle and check the shift speeds and kickdown operation.

TO ADJUST – ALTERNATIVE METHOD

The kickdown cable can also be adjusted by the following procedure when renewing the cable.

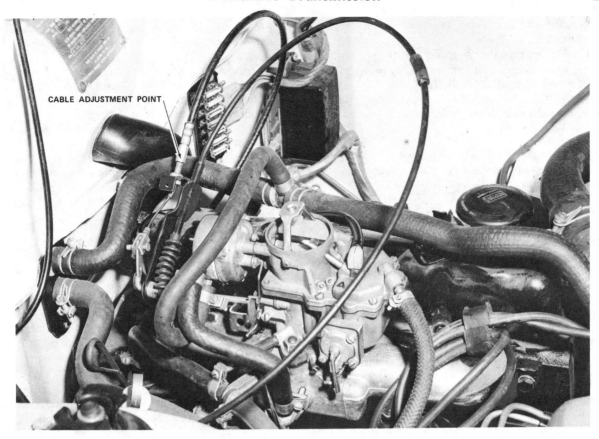

CABLE ADJUSTMENT POINT

Downshift Valve Cable Adjustment. Typical.

(1) Check that the choke is fully open; if necessary, adjust the idling speed and mixture, ensure that there is no lost movement at the throttle linkages.

(2) Drain off the transmission fluid and remove the oil pan as described earlier.

(3) With the accelerator in the released position and the carburettor throttle valve closed, check the position of the kickdown valve cam. The heel of the cam should contact the large diameter of the kickdown valve with no slack in the control cable.

(4) Press the accelerator pedal down to the kickdown position with the carburettor throttle valve fully open, when the kickdown valve should contact the cam on its highest radius directly opposite the cable anchor.

(5) If necessary, adjust the kickdown position of the cam at the adjuster on the kickdown cable.

(6) Recheck the cable adjustment with the carburettor throttle valve in both positions i.e., at idling and at full throttle.

(7) Instal the oil pan, using a new gasket and tighten the securing screws.

(8) Refill the transmission case with the correct grade of transmission fluid to the high mark on the dipstick as described in TRANSMISSION FLUID – TO CHECK AND TOP UP.

(9) Road test the vehicle and check the change speeds and kickdown operation.

(10) If the crimped ferrule was removed from the cable then reposition and crimp 0.25 mm. off the outer cable end.

10. TRANSMISSION ASSEMBLY

TO REMOVE

(1) Disconnect the earth lead at the battery terminal and the leads at the terminals on the starter solenoid switch. Remove the air cleaner assembly.

(2) Disconnect the transmission kickdown control cable at the throttle linkage and release the outer conduit from the bracket.

(3) Raise the vehicle, support it on stands, remove the drain plug and drain off the transmission fluid. Instal the drain plug.

(4) Take out the upper bolts retaining the torque converter housing to the engine.

NOTE: The dipstick tube is retained in position by one of the upper bolts.

(5) Take out the three securing bolts and detach the starter motor.

(6) Remove the clip and bolt attaching the speedometer cable to the transmission and detach the cable.

(7) Working through the aperture for the starter motor rotate the crankshaft as necessary and progressively slacken and remove the drive plate to converter bolts.

(8) Remove the engine to transmission assembly bracing brackets and take out the bolts securing the converter dust cover.

(9) Disconnect the transmission selector cable from

the operating arm and release the outer conduit from the support bracket.

(10) Disconnect the propeller shaft at the rear universal joint flange and the centre bearing from the body, withdraw the propeller shaft from the rear of the transmission and remove the shaft assembly from the vehicle. Plug the rear of the transmission to prevent entry of dirt or loss of fluid.

NOTE: To preserve the original balance of the propeller shaft, mark across the joint and pinion flanges to ensure replacement in the original positions.

(11) With suitable protection on the jack head, support under the gearbox and remove the gearbox supporting crossmember from the car underbody and from the gearbox.

(12) Disconnect the wires at the starter safety switch on the side of the transmission, noting the correct positions of the wires for reassembly.

(13) If installed, disconnect the reversing lamp earth wire from under the appropriate gearbox to extension housing bolt.

(14) Disconnect the exhaust outlet pipe from the manifold.

(15) Lower the transmission by means of the jack and detach the dipstick and tube assembly.

(16) Support the front of the engine with a jack.

(17) Remove the two converter housing to engine securing bolts that remain.

NOTE: Ensure that the transmission is supported on and secured to a suitable jack so that it cannot become dislodged as it is withdrawn from the vehicle. Ensure that the jack cannot damage the transmission oil pan.

(18) Carefully withdraw the assembly rearwards to clear the converter from the drive plate.

NOTE: Use care to ensure that the torque converter does not become dislodged from the front of the transmission.

Attach a suitable retaining strap to the converter housing, bolting it to the housing cover holes so that it retains the converter in position when the transmission is withdrawn from the rear of the engine.

(19) Lower the jack supporting the transmission assembly and withdraw it from beneath the vheicle.

NOTE: On removing the transmission, the converter dust cover, sandwiched between the engine cylinder block and the converter housing, will be freed and fall from the locating dowels.

TO INSTAL

Installation is a reversal of the removal procedure with particular attention to the following points:

(1) Ensure that the converter is fully engaged in the front of the transmission and in the spigot in the rear of the crankshaft.

(2) Ensure that the attachment faces of the torque converter housing and the rear of the engine crankcase are both perfectly clean and free of any burrs.

(3) Ensure that the dust cover is correctly positioned.

(4) Instal the bolts securing the converter to the drive plate and tighten evenly to the specified torque.

(5) Tighten the bolts securing the converter housing to the rear of the engine.

(6) Fill the transmission with the specified grade and quantity of the recommended hydraulic fluid.

(7) Check and if necessary, adjust the selector cable, throttle kickdown cable and neutral safety switch as previously described.

(8) Road test the vehicle and recheck the transmission fluid level as described in TRANSMISSION FLUID – TO CHECK AND TOP UP.

11. AUTOMATIC TRANSMISSION FAULT DIAGNOSIS

The following transmission operating faults can be caused by conditions that may be rectified within the scope of the information given in this section.

1. **No drive in D range.**

Possible cause	Remedy
(a) Low fluid level in transmission.	— Check fluid level and top up.
(b) Incorrectly adjusted selector cable.	— Check and readjust cable as detailed.
(c) Incorrect transmission fluid in unit.	— Drain and refill with recommended grade of fluid (see Specifications).
(d) Incorrectly adjusted downshift valve control cable.	— Check and readjust cable as detailed.

2. **No reverse drive in R quadrant.**

Possible cause	Remedy
(a) Low fluid level in transmission	— Check fluid level and top up.
(b) Incorrectly adjusted selector cable.	— Check and adjust selector cable as detailed.
(c) Reverse band incorrectly adjusted.	— Adjust reverse band as detailed.

3. **Slipping or rough in up-shift.**

Possible cause	Remedy
(a) Incorrectly adjusted throttle linkage.	— Check and adjust linkage as detailed.
(b) Incorrectly adjusted downshift valve control cable.	— Check and adjust cable as detailed.

4. **Slipping in all speeds.**

Possible cause	*Remedy*
(a) Low fluid level in transmission.	— Check fluid level and top up.
(b) Incorrect grade of fluid in unit.	— Drain and refill with recommended grade of fluid (see Specifications).
(c) Incorrectly adjusted selector cable.	— Check and adjust selector cable as detailed.

5. **No transmission kickdown.**

Possible cause	*Remedy*
(a) Incorrectly adjusted carburettor and accelerator linkage.	— Check and adjust linkage as detailed.
(b) Incorrectly adjusted downshift valve control cable.	— Check and adjust cable as detailed.

6. **Engine will not start in P or N positions, or will start in any range.**

Possible cause	*Remedy*
(a) Neutral safety switch incorrectly adjusted.	— Check and adjust switch as detailed.
(b) Neutral safety switch faulty.	— Check and renew switch.
(c) Incorrectly adjusted selector cable.	— Check and adjust selector cable as detailed.

REAR AXLE

SPECIFICATIONS

AUSTRALIAN PRODUCTION

Type	Semi-floating, hypoid final drive
Ratio:	No. of pinion/crown wheel teeth
3.45:1	11/38
3.7:1	10/37
3.89:1	9/35
4.11:1	9/37
Pinion and carrier bearing type	Tapered roller
Carrier bearing pre-load	0.102 mm case spread
Pinion bearing pre-load (including oil seal)	0.173–0.345 kg/m
Crownwheel to pinion backlash	0.127–0.178 mm
Maximum backlash variation between teeth	0.076 mm
Axle oil capacity	1.136 litres
Axle oil type	SAE 90 EP

ENGLISH PRODUCTION

Type	Semi floating hypoid final drive
3.44:1	9/31
3.7:1	10/37
3.89:1	9/35
4.11:1	9/37
Pinion and carrier bearing type	Tapered roller
Pinion bearing pre-load	0.078 – 0.346 kg/m
Crownwheel to pinion backlash	0.102 – 0.228 mm
Axle oil capacity:	
Type 'A' axle	1.0 litre
Type 'B' axle	1.1 litre
Axle oil type	SAE 90 EP

TORQUE WRENCH SETTINGS

Drive pinion retaining nut:	
English production	12 kg/m
Australian production	38.711 kg/m
Differential bearing cap bolts	6.221 kg/m
Rear cover bolts	3.50 kg/m
Crownwheel to differential case bolts:	
English production . . .	8.7 kg/m
Australian production . . .	6.913 kg/m
Axle shaft bearing retainer plate bolts	4.8 kg/m
Rear universal flange to pinion flange bolts	6.5 kg/m
Upper radius arm to rear axle mounting bolt	7 kg/m
Lower radius arm to rear axle mounting bolt	7 kg/m

1. DESCRIPTION

The rear axle is the semi-floating type with hypoid final drive gears.

The crownwheel and differential assembly is carried on two tapered roller bearings and axial adjustment of the assembly controlling the bearing pre-load and crownwheel to pinion backlash is by spacer shims between the bearing outer cups and the housing abutments (Australian production). Vehicles other than Australian production have spacer shims situated between the bearing cones and the differential case.

Shims used to obtain pinion position in relation to the crownwheel centre are situated between the rear pinion bearing outer cup and the housing on Australian produced vehicles and between the pinion head and the rear bearing cone on vehicles other than Australian production.

Pinion bearing pre-load is controlled by a shim placed between the front bearing inner race and a shoulder on the pinion shaft. The pinion is also marked with a figure, e.g. +2, denoting departure of the pinion head thickness from standard.

Axle shaft and bearing assemblies and axle shaft and pinion oil seals can be removed and installed without removing the axle housing from the car.

Removal and installation of the axle assembly is necessary to facilitate the dismantling, assembling and adjusting procedures of the differential.

Two types of axle shaft bearings are used, those being a ball bearing type as fitted to vehicles except Australian production and a roller bearing type fitted to Australian models.

2. AXLE SHAFT AND BEARINGS

TO REMOVE AND INSTAL

(1) Raise the rear of the vehicle and remove the road wheel and brake drum.

NOTE: The rear brake assemblies are fitted with automatic adjusting mechanisms which cannot be backed off by normal means, therefore if difficulty is encountered when removing the brake drum it is advised that the BRAKE SECTION of this manual be consulted for the detailed procedure to back off the adjusting mechanisms.

(2) Using a socket or tube spanner through the holes in the axle shaft flange, remove the four bolts and lock washers securing the bearing retaining plate and the backing plate to the flange on the end of the axle housing.

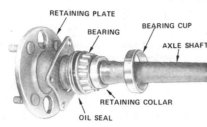

RETAINING PLATE
BEARING
BEARING CUP
AXLE SHAFT
RETAINING COLLAR
OIL SEAL

Rear Axle Shaft and Bearing Assembly. Roller Bearing Type.

(3) Using a suitable puller, withdraw the axle shaft and bearing assembly from the axle tube.

NOTE: On models fitted with roller bearing assemblies, it may be necessary to extract the bearing cup from its seat in the axle tube flange using a slide hammer type puller or suitable tool.

Installation is a reversal of the removal procedure.

TO RENEW BEARING AND/OR OIL SEAL
Ball Bearing Type

(1) Remove the axle shaft, bearing and the oil seal assembly as previously described.

(2) The bearing is of the sealed type and lubricated at assembly. It cannot be cleaned in cleaning solvent.

(3) Rotate the bearing and check for roughness and excessive wear, renew if suspect.

(4) Position the axle shaft assembly on an anvil so that it rests on the bearing retaining collar and, using a cold chisel and hammer, make one or more cuts through the top of the retaining collar.

NOTE: Use care not to damage the axle shaft with the chisel if it is necessary to cut through the retaining collar. Usually several shallow cuts in the collar will be sufficient to expand it so that it may be removed by hand.

(5) Using a suitable press and press plates, support the bearing on the inner race and press the axle shaft out of the bearing. Note the location of the bearing seals.

(6) Withdraw the bearing retaining plate and oil seal from the axle shaft.

(7) Lever the old seal from the retainer plate.

(8) Instal a new seal into the bearing retaining plate and slide the retaining plate down over the axle shaft to abut the flange.

(9) Position the bearing, noting the seal position, on the axle shaft, and press down to abut the inner race against the shoulder on the shaft. Ensure that pressure is applied only on the bearing inner race to avoid damaging the bearing assembly.

(10) Instal a new bearing retaining collar, pressing it on to abut the bearing inner race.

(11) Instal the axle shaft and bearing assembly in the vehicle as detailed under the heading TO REMOVE AND INSTAL.

Roller Bearing Type

NOTE: If the bearing is suspect, the axle shaft end float should be checked before removing the axle shaft from the differential. Maximum end float allowable is 0.6350 mm.

(1) Remove the axle shaft, bearing and the oil seal assembly as previously described.

(2) Thoroughly clean the bearing assembly and blow dry with compressed air. Examine the rollers, tracks and cup for wear, pitting or chips. If the bearing appears to be visually satisfactory, lubricate the roller assembly with light engine oil and fit the bearing cup. Rotate and check for roughness.

(3) If the axle shaft bearing and/or the oil seal or retainer plate requires replacement, proceed as follows.

(4) Position the axle shaft assembly on an anvil so that it rests on the bearing retaining collar and, using a cold chisel and hammer, make one or more cuts through the top of the retaining collar.

NOTE: Use care not to damage the axle shaft with the chisel when cutting the retaining collar. Usually several shallow cuts in the collar will be sufficient to expand it so it may be removed by hand.

(5) Using a suitable press and press plates, support the bearing on the inner cone or track and press the axle shaft out of the bearing. Take care not to damage the oil seal block behind the bearing with the press plates when removing the bearing.

(6) Slide the bearing oil seal and the retaining plate from the axle shaft.

NOTE: Once the bearing assembly has been removed it is advised that a new bearing be installed.

(7) Check the retainer plate for wear and distortion, straighten or replace as necessary.

(8) Clean the bearing recess in the axle housing and check for damage.

(9) Place the shaft bearing retaining plate onto the axle shaft with the flat side away from the axle flange.

(10) Apply grease to the cavity between the sealing lips of the new oil seal and instal it onto the axle shaft so

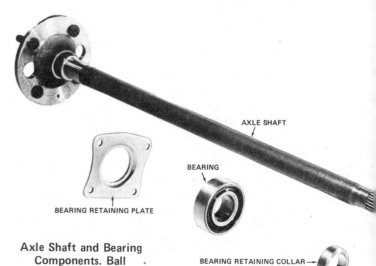

AXLE SHAFT
BEARING
BEARING RETAINING PLATE
BEARING RETAINING COLLAR →

Axle Shaft and Bearing Components. Ball Bearing Type. Typical.

that the lips will face in towards the axle housing.

(11) Position the new bearing on the axle shaft ensuring that the rib-ring is towards the axle flange and retaining plate.

(12) Check that the bearing is positioned squarely on the axle shaft and instal a new retaining collar to abut the bearing inner cone or track.

(13) Press the bearing assembly and the retaining collar on the axle shaft simultaneously using an installing tube and press, to abut the shoulder at the flange.

NOTE: When installing the bearing and retaining collar always apply the fitting pressure through the part of the bearing being fitted, never through the rollers.

(14) The new unit bearing assembly is protectively greased after manufacture and should require no additional lubrication prior to installing, unless it has been cleaned in a cleaning solvent, in which case it should be lubricated with the specified type of differential oil.

3. REAR AXLE ASSEMBLY

TO REMOVE AND INSTAL

(1) Jack up the rear of the vehicle and support on stands under the body just forward of the rear trailing arm front mountings. Remove the road wheels.

(2) With the handbrake in the released position disconnect the rear cable from the equaliser bracket and also from the brackets and guides on the underbody and radius arms.

(3) Mark a line across the rear universal joint flange and the pinion flange to facilitate correct assembly and remove the bolts attaching the joint flange to the pinion flange.

(4) On models so equipped loosen and remove the two bolts attaching the centre bearing support at the underbody and withdraw the propeller shaft assembly from the vehicle.

NOTE: It is advisable to instal a dummy shaft to the rear of the transmission to prevent transmission oil leaking from the extension housing.

(5) Disconnect the brake line hydraulic connection at the flexible brake hose on the rear axle and plug the pipe to prevent loss of fluid.

(6) Detach the differential breather hose from the bracket on the underbody.

(7) Using additional stands to those mentioned in operation (1) support under each lower radius arm directly beneath the coil spring assemblies with the suspension hanging in an unloaded position.

(8) Remove the retaining bolts and detach the upper radius arms from the differential housing.

(9) Loosen and remove the retaining bolts and detach the rear shock absorbers from their lower mountings.

(10) Using a jack to support centrally under the differential housing, disconnect the lower radius arms from the mountings on the axle housing. Lower the jack and withdraw the rear axle assembly from the vehicle.

Installation is a reversal of the removal procedure with attention to the following points:

Raise the rear axle assembly on a jack to the required height under the vehicle and align the lower and upper radius arms with their mountings on the axle assembly. Instal the through bolts but do not tighten.

NOTE: The radius arm mounting bolts must not be fully tightened at this stage, but must be tightened when the full vehicle weight is on the suspension.

Instal the propeller shaft and where fitted the centre bearing assembly, align the mating marks on the propeller shaft and pinion flanges, instal the retaining bolts and tighten to specifications.

Check, top up, or fill the differential as required to the inspection plug level with the correct grade of lubricant, refer to specifications.

Connect the handbrake cables and the hydraulic brake line connections, refer to the BRAKE section for the adjusting and bleeding procedures.

Jack up the rear of the vehicle and remove the stands placed under the body just forward of the rear trailing arm front mountings. Lower the vehicle so that it is supported on the stands placed under the coil spring assemblies at the lower radius arms and tighten the upper and lower radius arm to axle assembly mountings to specifications.

Refit the shock absorbers at their lower mountings and tighten securely.

Instal the road wheels and lower the vehicle to the ground.

4. DIFFERENTIAL AND PINION ASSEMBLY

AUSTRALIAN PRODUCTION
To Dismantle

(1) Remove the rear axle assembly from the vehicle as previously described.

(2) Remove the countersunk screws securing the brake drums to the axle flanges and remove the brake drums.

NOTE: The rear brake assemblies are fitted with automatic adjusting mechanisms which cannot be backed off by normal means, therefore if any difficulty is encountered when removing the brake drums it is advised that the BRAKE section of this manual be consulted for the detailed procedure to back off the adjusting mechanisms.

(2) Using a socket or tube spanner through the holes in the axle shaft flange, remove the four bolts and lock washers securing the axle assembly and backing plate to the flange on the end of the axle housing.

(3) Using a suitable puller, withdraw the axle shaft and bearing assembly from the axle tube.

(4) Take out the securing bolts and remove the differential cover, draining the oil into a suitable container.

(5) Mark the differential carrier bearing caps to facilitate correct installation and remove the cap bolts and caps.

(6) Instal the special housing spreading tool on the

housing face and spread the assembly just sufficiently to enable the crownwheel and differential assembly to be lifted out.

NOTE: In no circumstances must the housing be spread in excess of 0.508 mm.

(7) Mark each differential bearing cup and keep it together with the adjusting shims, so that it can be reinstalled on the same inner cone and roller assembly and on the end of the differential assembly from which it was removed.

NOTE: The remarks outlined in operation (7) apply only to bearings that are fit for further service. If the bearings are to be renewed, keep the shims intact so that they can be reinstalled on the same end of the housing as a starting point for final drive backlash and bearing pre-load adjustment.

(8) Take out the securing bolts and remove the crownwheel from the differential case.

NOTE: If the crownwheel and pinion are to be used again, mark the crownwheel in relation to the differential case flange to facilitate installation.

(9) Drive out the differential shaft retaining pin and remove the differential shaft, withdraw the two differential pinions and concave thrust washers, followed by the two side gears and thrust washers.

(10) Hold the pinion flange and remove the self locking retaining nut and washer.

(11) Using a suitable puller, withdraw the flange from the front end of the pinion shaft.

(12) Using a soft metal drift, tap the pinion and rear bearing inner cone and rollers, together with the bearing pre-load shims out of the axle housing towards the rear.

(13) Using a soft metal drift, drive the front bearing inner cone and roller assembly out towards the front of the housing together with the pinion flange oil seal.

(14) If the pinion bearings are to be renewed, drive the rear bearing cup with pinion positioning shim out towards the rear of the housing bore and the front bearing cup towards the front of the housing bore.

(15) Press the cone and roller assembly of the rear pinion bearing off the pinion.

NOTE: Do not remove the bearing cone from the pinion unless either the pinion or the bearing are to be renewed. It is not always possible to remove the bearing without damage unless special tools are available.

To Clean and Inspect

(1) Wash all parts in cleaning solvent and dry.

(2) Check the crownwheel and pinion teeth for wear, damage or pitting.

NOTE: If the crownwheel or pinion requires renewing, it will be necessary to fit both as the crownwheel and pinion are supplied as a matched set. They are lapped and mated during manufacture.

(3) Check the pinion and the differential carrier bearings for wear and damage. If a bearing is faulty, renew the complete bearing comprising the inner cone and rollers and outer cup.

(4) Check the differential shaft for wear or damage. Check the pinion thrust washers for wear and renew as necessary. These washers are concave in shape.

(5) Check the differential side gears for wear, in the case, the axle shaft splines, or for damage to the teeth. Renew as necessary.

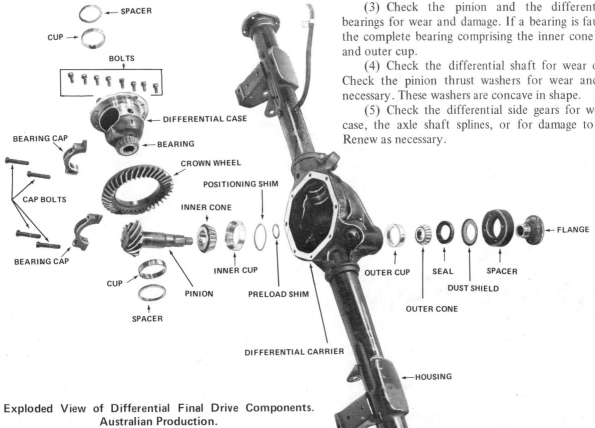

Exploded View of Differential Final Drive Components. Australian Production.

(6) Check the differential side gear thrust washers for wear and renew if necessary, or fit thicker thrust washers if the backlash between the side gears and the differential pinions is excessive.

(7) Use a new differential shaft retaining pin on reassembly.

To Assemble and Adjust Pinion

The position of the pinion in relation to the crownwheel is set in manufacture and any departure from standard in the final lapping of the crownwheel and pinion is marked on the pinion head.

Special tools in the form of a dummy pinion and an arbor are available for determining the thickness of the positioning shim for any final drive gear set. Other marks on the pinion head are the mating set identification number, which corresponds with a similar number etched on the outer circumference of the crownwheel.

A dot or x on the end of one of the pinion teeth, when meshed between a dot or x on the inner end of two crownwheel teeth, provides correct meshing for the gear set.

The specified backlash for the particular gear set is also etched on the outer circumference of the crownwheel.

A +2 etched on the ground face of the pinion head indicates that the head is 0.002 inches (0.05 mm.) thicker than standard and must be installed with a positioning shim 0.002 inches (0.05 mm.) thinner than standard.

Similarly, a −2 etched on the pinion head indicates that a shim 0.002 inches (0.05 mm.) thicker than standard must be used.

Using the Dummy Pinion and Arbor

In order to select a positioning shim of the correct thickness when installing a new pinion and crownwheel set or new pinion bearing proceed as follows:

(1) Instal the pinion bearing outer cups in the housing bore, ensuring that they are completely seated and that the tapers of the cups are opposed with the larger inner diameters to the outside.

(2) Lightly oil the bearing inner cone assemblies, place the rear bearing cone assembly on the dummy pinion, insert the dummy pinion and bearing in the housing bore from the rear, place the front bearing inner cone on the front end of the dummy pinion and instal the pinion flange and nut

and while rotating the dummy pinion to seat the bearings correctly, tighten the pinion nut to 0.173 − 0.288 kg/m.

NOTE: A pinion positioning shim must not be fitted with the rear pinion bearing outer cup at this stage.

(3) Position the arbor of the special tool in place of the crownwheel and differential case, instal the carrier bearing caps and tighten down firmly.

(4) Select a shim that will just slide between the end of the dummy pinion and the under side of the arbor. Shims are available in increments of 0.002 inch (0.05 mm.) from 0.084 to 0.100 inch thickness (2.133 to 2.540 mm.).

(5) If the pinion being fitted has a zero marking indicating that it is exactly standard, the shim selected in operation (4) will be correct thickness.

(6) If the pinion, however, has a +2 marking for example, then the shim selected in operation (4) must be measured with a micrometer and another shim selected, 0.002 inch (0.05 mm.) thinner than the standard shim thickness.

If the pinion has a −2 marking, 0.002 inch (0.05 mm.) must then be added to the standard shim thickness to obtain the correct shim.

It therefore follows that a plus (+) mark on the pinion must be subtracted from and a minus (−) mark added to the standard shim thickness.

(7) When the correct shim thickness has been selected, remove the special arbor, take out and dismantle the dummy pinion and bearings.

(8) Using a suitable press, instal the pinion rear bearing assembly (pinion head bearing) onto the drive pinion. Drift out the rear pinion bearing cup, fit the selected shim in the housing and again drift the cup back into position to abut the shim.

(9) Lubricate the front pinion bearing inner cone and roller assembly and place it in position in the bearing cup in the forward end of the housing bore.

(10) Apply a suitable sealer to the outer circumference of a new pinion oil seal and tap it into position in the front end of the pinion housing bore so that the lipped face of the seal is towards the front pinion bearing.

(11) Lubricate the pinion and rear bearing cone and roller assembly, position the original pinion bearing pre-load shim on the pinion shaft so that the chamfered side of the shim is to the shaft shoulder and insert the shaft in through the housing bore from the rear.

(12) Lubricate the pinion flange and instal it on the front end of the pinion shaft, tapping the assembly together.

(13) Instal the washer and flange nut and tighten the nut gradually to a minimum torque of 38.711 kg/m.

NOTE: During operation (13) rotate the pinion to ensure that the bearings are seated correctly and that they are not excessively pre-loaded.

(14) Using a pre-load gauge on the pinion flange nut, check the torque required to rotate the pinion shaft slowly but continuously. This should be within specifications. If the pre-load is outside these limits remove the pinion

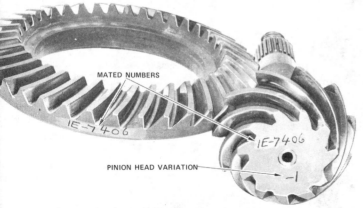

MATED NUMBERS

IE-7406

IE-7406

PINION HEAD VARIATION

−1

Crownwheel and Pinion Showing Mating Numbers and Pinion Head Thickness Variation from Standard.

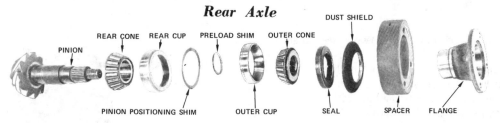

PINION — REAR CONE — REAR CUP — PRELOAD SHIM — OUTER CONE — DUST SHIELD
PINION POSITIONING SHIM — OUTER CUP — SEAL — SPACER — FLANGE

Exploded View of Drive Pinion Components. Australian Production.

flange, withdraw the pinion assembly and increase or decrease the thickness of the bearing pre-load shim. A thinner shim will increase the pre-load and vice versa.

(15) When the pinion bearing pre-load is correct, remove the pinion assembly from the housing bore and place to one side, complete with pre-load shims so that the differential case carrier bearing pre-load can be adjusted.

Alternative Method Without Special Tools

In the event of the arbor and dummy pinion not being available, it will be necessary to use the shims removed from the old pinion, plus or minus, as the case may be, the figure etched on the new pinion head as a starting point for pinion position adjustment. This method of adjustment entails assembling the pinion and adjusting pinion bearing pre-load, fitting crownwheel and differential assembly, adjusting the backlash and taking teeth markings with red lead or engineers' blue. This is a trial and error method, until a satisfactory tooth marking is obtained.

If a new crownwheel and pinion are to be fitted with the old pinion bearings, it is a relatively simple matter to calculate the thickness of the pinion positioning shim. If the shim is kept intact from the old assembly and used again, taking into consideration the markings on both pinions.

Example 1. If both pinion markings are 0 or Zero, the original shim pack will be correct.

If the old pinion marking is 0 or Zero and the new pinion marking is +2, then .002 inch thickness of shims must be subtracted from the original shim pack.

Again, if the new pinion mark is −2, then .002 inch must be added to the original shim thickness to find the correct pinion position.

Example 2. Where the old pinion marking is +2 and the new pinion marking is −2, the position is slightly more complicated. As .002 inch was subtracted from the shim thickness for a zero marked pinion to compensate for the +2 mark on the old pinion head, a .002 inch must now be added to the present shim thickness and a further .002 inch added for the −2 marking on the new pinion head. Thus .004 inch should be added to the shim thickness when replacing the old pinion marked +2 with a new pinion marked −2.

The pinion head positioning shim thickness as calculated in the previous paragraph is an accurate starting point for pinion position adjustment but final assessment will be influenced by the crownwheel and pinion tooth contact markings taken after the crownwheel to pinion backlash adjustment has been made.

To Assemble and Adjust Differential

(1) Lubricate the differential components with hypoid gear oil, and instal the side gears with their thrust washers in the differential case.

(2) Fit thrust washers to both differential pinions and instal in the differential case to mesh with the axle side gears.

(3) Manoeuvre the differential pinions and thrust washers within the differential case to align with the differential pinion shaft holes in the case.

(4) Instal the pinion shaft to align the lock pin hole, and drive in the lock pin to secure the pinion shaft in the differential case.

(5) If the original crownwheel and pinion are still serviceable, place the crownwheel on the differential case according to the marks made on dismantling and against the crownwheel mounting face on the case.

(6) Instal the crownwheel securing bolts and tighten to specifications.

(7) Instal the two carrier bearings on the ends of the differential case using a suitable press.

NOTE: If the original bearings are being refitted they should be installed to the side from which they were removed.

(8) If new carrier bearings are being fitted or if the original bearings are being used, ensure that the cup is fitted to its correct bearing inner cone and rollers. Bearings should only be renewed as complete assemblies and bearing components must not be interchanged.

(9) With the crownwheel and differential case assembled as previously described, place each carrier bearing cup, together with a spacer washer, on its respective cone and roller assembly.

NOTE: The spacers should both be the same thickness but slightly less in total thickness than the original spacers so that slight end float will exist.

(10) Place the assembly in position in the axle housing, lever it carefully against one bearing and rotate the crownwheel so that the bearings will be properly seated.

(11) With the differential held in this position, use a feeler gauge to measure the gap between the bearing spacer and the bearing cup. Take a measurement on each side of the bearing centre line to ensure that the assembly is located squarely and that the measurements will be equal.

(12) Calculate the thickness of the spacers required to give a bearing pre-load of 0.002 inch (0.05 mm.) on each bearing as follows:

If two bearing spacers each 0.260 inch (6.60 mm.) were selected and it was found that 0.012 inch (0.30 mm.) feeler gauge thickness was required to eliminate end float from the assembly then two spacers 0.266 inch (6.756 mm.) in thickness will limit end float to zero. Add a further 0.004 inch (0.101 mm.) overall to provide 0.002 inch (0.05 mm.)

pre-load on each bearing and select two spacers 0.268 inch (6.807 mm.) in thickness.

(13) Instal the spreading tool on the back of the axle housing position a dial gauge on the axle housing so that it is anchored on one carrier bearing bolt with the plunger of the gauge bearing against the opposite side of the housing opening and zero the gauge.

(14) Adjust the spreader tool to give an axle housing spread of approximately 0.304 mm. on the gauge. In no circumstances should the housing be spread in excess of 0.508 mm. Remove the dial gauge from the housing.

(15) Place the differential assembly complete with the bearing cups and the two spacers as selected in operation (12) in position in the housing and release and remove the spreading tool.

(16) Instal the bearing caps and tighten to specifications.

NOTE: Ensure that the bearing cups are fitted to the cone and roller assembly to which they have been mated. This applies to both new or used bearings. Instal the bearing caps according to the marks made on dismantling.

(17) Using a piece of cord wrapped around the differential case adjacent to the rear face of the crownwheel and attached to a spring scale, check the amount of pull required to rotate the assembly. This will be the pre-load on the bearings and should be 1.497 – 2.948 kilogrammes.

(18) If the pre-load is not within the limits specified, use the spreader and remove the assembly, select two spacers either thicker or thinner as required and recheck the pre-load.

(19) When a satisfactory pre-load is obtained, remove the assembly, again using the spreader and place it to one side complete with the bearing cups and spacers for installation and backlash adjustment after the drive pinion has been installed.

To Adjust Backlash

(1) Instal the pinion in the axle housing and recheck the bearing pre-load as previously described.

(2) Using the housing spreading tool, instal the differential case and crownwheel assembly as previously described and remove the spreading tool.

NOTE: The positioning marks on the crownwheel and pinion must be aligned for backlash and drive marking tests as for correct and final assembly.

(3) Set up a dial gauge on the lower centre of the housing cover face so that the gauge plunger will bear on the end of and at right angles to the convex side of a crownwheel tooth.

(4) Hold the pinion flange and rock the crownwheel through the backlash carefully and note the reading on the gauge. Take a check at approximately four positions around the crownwheel. Backlash should be within specification or as shown etched on the crownwheel rim.

(5) If the backlash is incorrect, calculate an average backlash from the four or more readings taken around crownwheel and rectify by adding to the thickness on one

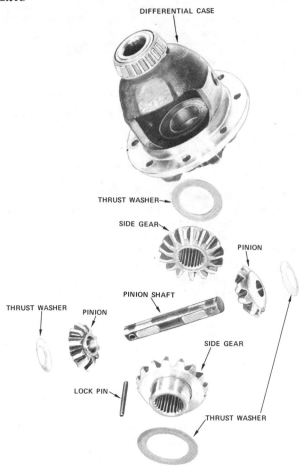

Dismantled View of Differential Case Components.

bearing spacer and reducing the thickness of the other spacer by a similar amount. The overall thickness of the two spacers must remain the same.

NOTE: Changing the overall thickness of the spacers will change the backlash by approximately the same amount. For instance, reducing the thickness of one spacer by 0.05 mm. and increasing the thickness of the other spacer by 0.05 mm. will alter the crownwheel to pinion backlash by approximately 0.05 mm.

(6) When the backlash is adjusted correctly to the specified dimension, check the tooth contact of the crownwheel and pinion by applying a thin coating of red lead and engine oil to both sides of about six or eight of the crownwheel teeth.

(7) Rotate the pinion both ways, placing a bar between the differential case and the axle housing to apply a load to the gear teeth and so obtain a good tooth marking.

If the bearing pre-load and backlash have been correctly set, the area of contact will be as illustrated.

The margin above and below the area of contact should be approximately three quarters the length of the tooth.

(8) When the assembly has been correctly adjusted, instal the rear cover using a new gasket. Instal the axle shaft assemblies preparative to installing the complete axle housing in the vehicle.

DRIVE   OVERDRIVE

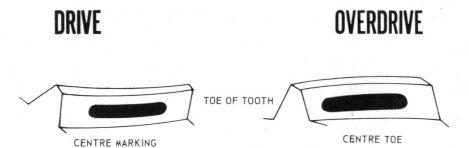

TOE OF TOOTH

CENTRE MARKING   CENTRE TOE

Crownwheel Tooth Marking for Correctly Adjusted Crownwheel and Pinion. Marking will be slightly Closer to Toe of Tooth on Overdrive or Concave Side. Changes in Thickness of Pinion Positioning Shims will Affect Tooth Marking on Overdrive to Greater Extent than on Drive or Convex Side of Tooth. Changes in Backlash have a more Pronounced Effect on Drive Side Markings.

TOE OF TOOTH

TOE LOW   HEEL LOW

Low Profile Marking on Both Sides of Tooth. Rectify by Reducing Thickness of Pinion Positioning Shims and Reset Backlash.

TOE OF TOOTH

HEEL HIGH   TOE HIGH

High Profile Marking on Both Sides of Crownwheel Tooth. Rectify by Increasing of Pinion Positioning Shims and Reset Backlash.

TOE OF TOOTH

TOE CENTRE   TOE SLIGHTLY LOW

Toe Marking on Drive Side and Low Profile Marking on Overdrive Side of Crownwheel Tooth. To Rectify, Increase Backlash. It may be Necessary to Increase Thickness of Pinion Positioning Shims to Maintain Backlash within Specified Limits.

TOE OF TOOTH

HEEL CENTRE   HEEL SLIGHTLY HIGH

Heel Marking on Drive Side and High Profile Marking on Overdrive Side of Crownwheel Tooth. To Rectify, Reduce Backlash. It may be Necessary to Decrease Thickness of Pinion Positioning Shims to Maintain Backlash within Specified Limits.

EUROPEAN PRODUCTION
To Dismantle and Assemble

(1) Remove the rear axle assembly from the vehicle as described under REAR AXLE ASSEMBLY — TO REMOVE AND INSTAL.

(2) Remove the countersunk screws securing the brake drums to the axle flanges and remove the brake drums.

(3) Using a socket or tube spanner through the holes in the axle shaft flange, remove the bolts and lock washers securing the axle assembly and backing plate to the flange on the end of the axle housing.

(4) Using a suitable puller, withdraw the axle shaft and bearing assembly from the axle tube.

(5) Withdraw the backing plate and the hydraulic lines from the axle housing.

NOTE: As extensive knowledge and equipment is required to overhaul and/or repair the differential and pinion assembly, with the cost of the equipment required normally exceeding the repair charges costed by most differential specialists, the differential overhaul is therefore not a worthwhile repair proposition for the average person who has limited knowledge and does not have the required special tools. As an alternative to the services of a repair specialist a new, secondhand or reconditioned unit can be installed.

(6) Assemble the backing plate and axle assemblies to the rear axle assembly and tighten the retaining bolts to specifications.

(7) Relocate the brake hydraulic pipes at their guide clamps on the rear axle housing.

(8) Instal the brake drums and secure in place with the countersunk screws.

Instal the rear axle assembly into the vehicle, refer REAR AXLE ASSEMBLY — TO REMOVE AND INSTAL.

5. DRIVE PINION OIL SEAL

TO RENEW (All Models)
Assembly Fitted to Vehicle

(1) Raise the rear of the vehicle and support on axle stands or raise the vehicle on a hoist.

(2) Mark across the flanges of the pinion and rear universal joint and remove the retaining bolts, remove also if fitted, the bolts attaching the centre bearing support to the underbody and withdraw the propeller shaft from the vehicle.

(3) If available instal a dummy yoke or plug to the transmission extension housing to prevent the loss of transmission lubricant.

(4) Holding the pinion flange against rotation, unscrew and remove the nut and washer securing the flange to the pinion shaft. Mark across the pinion flange and pinion shaft for realignment when assembling.

(5) If necessary, use a suitable puller to withdraw the pinion flange from the splines on the pinion shaft, and remove the pinion flange, drive coupling and slinger.

(6) If available use an extractor to withdraw the old oil seal or alternatively prise the seal out of the end of the housing with a suitable lever.

(7) Clean the bore of the housing of any burrs or old sealing compound.

(8) Apply a coating of suitable sealing compound to the outer circumference of the new seal and lubricate the seal lips with grease.

(9) Carefully drift the seal into position in the housing.

(10) The remainder of the operation is a reversal of the dismantling procedure. Tighten the pinion flange nut to the specified torque after installing the pinion flange to align the marks made when dismantling.

(11) Ensure that the oil level in the rear axle is correct and refill or top up as required using the specified type of lubricant.

6. REAR AXLE FAULT DIAGNOSIS

1. **Rear wheel noise.**

Possible cause	*Remedy*
(a) Wheel loose on axle flange.	— Check condition of axle and tighten or renew components.
(b) Defective brake components (shoes or wheel cylinder).	— Renew faulty components.
(c) Worn or defective axle shaft bearing, lack of lubrication.	— Renew faulty components, lubricate with recommended lubricant.
(d) Bent axle tube or shaft.	— Renew axle housing and/or shaft.
(e) Wheel out of balance or bent.	— Check and rectify wheel balance or renew or true up.

2. **Final drive gear noise.**

Possible cause	*Remedy*
(a) Faulty pinion bearings.	— Renew pinion bearings and readjust gears.
(b) Faulty differential carrier bearings.	— Renew carrier bearings and readjust gears.
(c) Lack of lubrication.	— Check condition of assembly, flush and renew lubricant.
(d) Incorrectly adjusted crownwheel and pinion.	— Check condition of gears and readjust or renew as mated pair.

(e) Incorrectly adjusted bearing preload (pinion or carrier bearings).

— Check condition of assembly, adjust bearing preload or renew faulty components.

(f) Excessive noise or grind under load.

— Overhaul assembly and renew faulty components.

(g) Excessive noise or grind on overdrive.

— Overhaul assembly and renew faulty components.

(h) Excessive noise on coast.

— Faulty final drive gears and adjustment. Renew and readjust.

(i) Bent axle housing.

— Renew housing and faulty components.

3. **Excessive backlash in differential.**

Possible cause

(a) Looseness between axle shaft and differential side gear splines.

(b) Worn differential side gear thrust washers.

(c) Worn differential pinion thrust washers.

(d) Excessive backlash between differential side gears and pinions.

(e) Excessive wear between differential shaft and pinions and/or shaft bore in carrier housing.

Remedy

— Check and renew axle shafts and/or side gears.

— Check and renew differential side gear thrust washers.

— Check and renew differential pinion thrust washers.

— Check condition of gear and pinion teeth and renew, or renew gear and/or pinion thrust washers.

— Check and renew faulty components.

4. **Pinion shaft rotates but will not drive vehicle (No noise).**

Possible cause

(a) Broken axle shaft.

Remedy

— Check and renew axle shaft.

5. **Repeated axle shaft breakage.**

Possible cause

(a) Bent axle housing.

(b) Repeated over loading.

(c) Abnormal clutch operation.

Remedy

— Check and renew housing.

— Revise load capacity.

— Revise driving habits or check condition of clutch.

6. **Loss of rear axle lubricant.**

Possible cause

(a) Faulty final drive pinion or axle shaft oil seals.

(b) Clogged axle housing breather.

(c) Leaking gasket between differential carrier and axle housing.

(d) Incorrect type of lubricant causing excessive foaming.

Remedy

— Check and renew pinion oil seal, replace defective combination axle shaft bearing and seal.

— Remove and wash out breather in cleaning fluid.

— Renew faulty gasket.

— Drain, flush and refill axle housing to correct level with recommended lubricant.

FRONT SUSPENSION

SPECIFICATIONS

Type . . . .   Coil spring independent
                                        short and long arm

Coil spring type ident-
    ification . . . .   Colour

Shock-absorber type . . . . .   Tubular telescopic double
                                        acting

Castor angle . . . .   2 deg 39 min – 3 deg
                                        39 min positive. Maximum
                                        castor variation between
                                        each side must not exceed
                                        30 min

Camber angle . . . .   7 min – 1 deg 7 min
                                        positive

Swivel inclination . . . .   3 deg 5 min – 4 deg
                                        5 min

Toe-in . . . .   4 mm

Toe-out on turns:

Inner wheel at 20 deg—
    outer wheel . . . .   19 deg

Inner wheel at 35 deg –
    outer wheel . . . .   32 deg 18 min

TORQUE WRENCH SETTINGS

*Front hub bearings . . . .   3.7 kg/m

Strut bar retaining
    bolts . . . .   6.9 kg/m

Upper and lower ball
    joint . . . .   9.2 kg/m

Upper control arm pivot
    bolt . . . .   6.2 kg/m

Lower control arm pivot
    bolt . . . .   5.5 kg/m

Tie rod end ball
    joint . . . .   3.0 kg/m

Shock-absorber:
    Upper mounting . . . .   4.8 kg/m
    Lower mounting . . . .   .0.9 kg/m

Brake caliper to stub
    axle support . . . .   6.9 kg/m

*Tighten to 3.7 kg/m while rotating hub and back off 2
flats of the nut.

1. DESCRIPTION

The front suspension is of the long and short arm independent type with coil springs and spherical ball joints.

The outer ends of the suspension control arms are connected together through ball joints and an integral steering knuckle and stub axle assembly.

Coil springs are mounted between the lower arms and the outer ends of the crossmember.

Damping is obtained by double acting tubular type shock absorbers mounted inside the coil springs and anchored to the crossmember at the top and the lower control arm at the bottom.

A strut bar fitted between the forward end of the crossmember and the lower control arm at each front suspension unit controls fore and aft movement of the lower control arm and provides for castor angle adjustment.

All 2000 OHC and 1600 GT model vehicles incorporate a ride stabiliser bar which is attached at each end to the lower control arm on each side through a rubber insulated link, and at the forward end of the sub-frame with two rubber mountings.

A rubber bumper is fitted to the outer ends of the crossmember for the purpose of reducing impact when and if rough roads and/or heavy loads are encountered.

2. FRONT HUB

TO REMOVE AND DISMANTLE

(1) Raise the front of the vehicle, block the rear wheels and support the vehicle on stands.

(2) Remove the road wheel.

(3) Bend back the locking tabs and unscrew the bolts attaching the brake caliper assembly to the stub axle support.

(4) Remove the caliper assembly and support from the underbody of the vehicle using tie wire.

(5) Remove the hub grease cap, take out the split pin and remove the castellated nut retainer, unscrew the hub and bearing retaining nut, remove the keyed washer.

(6) Withdraw the bearing, hub and disc assembly from the stub axle.

(7) Remove the outer bearing cone and roller assembly from the hub.

(8) Carefully tap the inner cone and roller assembly out of the hub inner bearing cup, together with the hub grease retainer.

(9) Using a suitable drift, drive the two bearing cups out of the hub. The inner bearing cup is removed from the

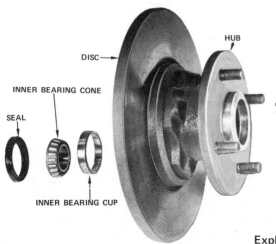
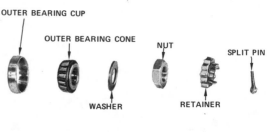

Exploded View of Front Hub and Bearing Components.

inner end of the hub and the outer bearing cup from the outer end of the hub.

TO CLEAN AND INSPECT

(1) Remove all the old grease and wash all parts in a suitable solvent.

(2) Check the bearing rollers and cups for wear, pitting or damage and renew as necessary.

(3) Check the thread on the end of the stub axle and in the retaining nut for deterioration or damage. If the thread on the stub axle is unserviceable the stub axle assembly must be replaced.

TO ASSEMBLE AND INSTAL

(1) Drift the two hub bearing cups into position in the hub so that their tapers are opposed to each other.

(2) Pack the cavity in the hub between the two bearings with a lithium base wheel bearing grease and apply the grease to the inner and outer bearing cone and roller assemblies. Instal the inner bearing cone and roller assembly into position in the hub.

(3) Place a new grease retaining seal on the inner end of the hub and tap it into position.

(4) Instal the hub and disc assembly onto the stub axle and position the outer bearing cone and roller assembly in the outer end of the hub.

(5) Fit the keyed washer and retaining nut to the stub axle and tighten finger tight while rotating the hub to seat the bearings.

(6) Continue to rotate the hub and using a suitable torque wrench, tension the hub retaining nut to 3.7 kilogrammetres torque.

(7) Slacken the retaining nut two flats and check the adjustment by rocking the hub assembly. A slight bearing end-float should be just detectable if bearings are correctly adjusted.

(8) Fit the castellated nut retainer aligning the split pin holes, and instal the new split pin, fit the grease cap to the hub.

(9) If necessary check the run-out on the brake disc as described in the BRAKES section of this manual.

(10) Position the caliper assembly over the disc and secure to the steering knuckle with the retaining bolts. Tighten the retaining bolts to the specified torque setting listed in the specifications and then lock the bolts with the locking tabs.

(11) Instal the road wheel and lower the vehicle.

3. SUSPENSION ASSEMBLY AND CROSSMEMBER

TO REMOVE

(1) Raise the front of the vehicle, block the rear wheels and support the vehicle on chassis stands.

(2) Remove the road wheels.

(3) Disconnect the hydraulic brake pipe (feed pipe) from the three way connector on the rear of the crossmember and plug the open pipe to prevent loss of fluid.

(4) Loosen the two bolts at the clamping plate on the lower steering shaft universal joint coupling and disconnect the universal joint from the upper steering shaft.

(5) Using a suitable jack and a block of wood placed under the engine sump to take the engine weight, disconnect the engine mountings from the suspension crossmember by unscrewing the retaining bolts. Raise the jack sufficiently to relieve the engine weight from the crossmember.

(6) On models fitted with a front stabiliser bar, remove the attaching bolts and disconnect the mounting brackets and rubbers retaining the stabiliser bar at the body sidemember brackets.

(7) With a floor jack raised under the front suspension crossmember to support the weight, remove the four bolts retaining the assembly to the body sidemembers and lower the assembly from the vehicle.

TO INSPECT

(1) Clean and inspect the crossmember for cracking and for general fatigue and damage.

(2) Check the shock absorber upper mountings for cracking and wear.

(3) Check the rubber mountings on the body sidemembers before reassembling.

TO INSTAL

Installation is a reversal of the removal procedure with attention to the following points:

Tighten the crossmember retaining bolts and the engine mounting bolts securely.

Connect the hydraulic pipe at the three way connector and bleed the front braking system as described in the relevant section of this manual.

Tighten the clamping plate retaining bolts at the lower steering shaft universal joint coupling to secure the upper steering shaft, and lock the bolts with the locking plates.

Replace the road wheels and lower the vehicle to the ground.

4. LOWER CONTROL ARM, COIL SPRING AND SHOCK ABSORBER

TO REMOVE

(1) Raise the front of the vehicle and support on chassis stands at the front sidemembers.

(2) Remove the road wheel.

(3) Loosen and remove the shock absorber upper and lower mounting bolts and withdraw the shock absorber from the suspension unit.

(4) Loosen the strut bar lock nut at the forward end of the front mounting bracket.

(5) Remove the two bolts securing the strut bar to the lower control arm.

(6) On vehicles fitted with a stabiliser bar, remove the stabiliser bar link retaining nuts and withdraw the washers, the bushes, the spacer and the link bolt from the lower control arm.

NOTE: *When a stabiliser bar is fitted, the strut bar as mentioned in operation (5) should be disconnected conjointly, when the stabiliser bar connecting link is disconnected.*

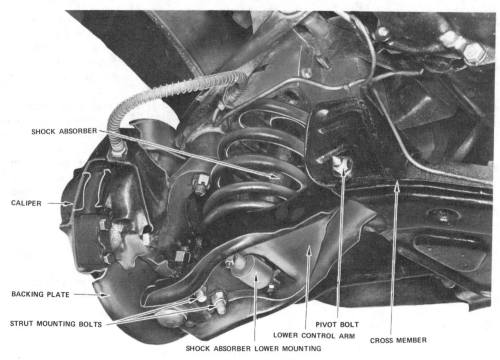

SHOCK ABSORBER

CALIPER

BACKING PLATE

STRUT MOUNTING BOLTS

SHOCK ABSORBER LOWER MOUNTING

PIVOT BOLT
LOWER CONTROL ARM
CROSS MEMBER

Rear Side View of Left Hand Side Front Suspension.

(7) Remove the split pin and loosen the castellated nut of the lower control arm ball joint approximately three turns.

(8) Using a suitable ball joint pressing tool, break the seal of the ball joint stud in the stub axle support.

(9) Remove the split pin and unscrew the castellated nut from the tie-rod end ball joint. Use a suitable ball joint press and disconnect the tie-rod end from the steering arm of the stub axle support.

(10) Raise a jack under the outer end of the lower control arm which is to be removed, and take the full weight of the vehicle.

(11) Unscrew and remove the castellated nut attaching the lower control arm ball joint to the steering knuckle.

(12) Lift the stub axle support and the upper control arm up as far as possible and with a wooden chock placed between the control arm and the spring tower on the outer end of the crossmember, support the hub and disc assembly out of the way.

(13) Slowly lower the jack and remove the coil spring.

(14) Loosen and remove the lower control arm pivot bolt and withdraw the lower arm assembly from the vehicle.

(15) If the lower control arm bush requires replacement it can be removed using a suitable press or, if available, the special tools and a new bush then installed in its place.

NOTE: It will be advantageous to smear a soap solution onto the bushing to aid installation.

TO INSTAL

Installation is a reversal of the removal procedure with attention to the following points:

(1) Lubricate the ends of the lower control arm bushing with glycerine prior to installing the control arm into the vehicle.

(2) Instal the inner end of the control arm to align with the pivot pin holes in the front crossmember, and instal the pivot bolt from the front of the crossmember so that the head of the pivot bolt is facing to the front of the vehicle. Instal the retaining washer and nut to the pivot bolt, but do not tighten at this stage.

(3) Instal the coil spring into the tower in the crossmember and raise the lower control arm by hand to seat against the lower end of the spring.

NOTE: The spring must be installed with the feathered edge uppermost.

(4) Manoeuvre a jack under the end of the control arm and raise the jack to compress the spring and take the weight of the vehicle.

(5) Lower the upper control arm and stub axle support end, guide the lower ball joint stud into position. Fit the ball joint castellated nut and tighten to specifications. Instal a new split pin.

(6) Lower and remove the jack from under the lower control arm.

(7) Instal the shock absorber up through the centre of the coil spring. Fit the upper retaining bolt and nut and tighten to specifications.

(8) Position the bottom shock absorber mounting bracket to the lower control arm and instal the retaining bolts and tighten to specifications.

(9) Position the tie-rod end ball joint to the steering arm, instal the castellated nut and tighten to specifications, insert a new split pin.

(10) Refit the strut bar and the stabiliser bar (where fitted) to the lower control arm and tighten the mounting bolts.

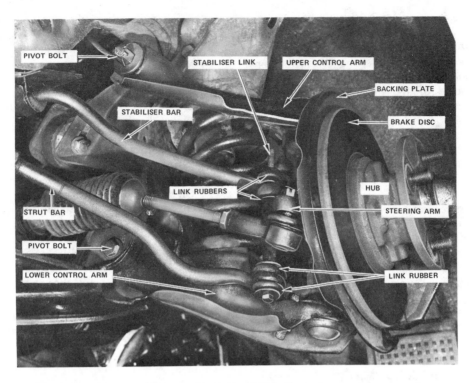

Front Side View of Left Hand Side Front Suspension.

(11) Instal the road wheel and lower the vehicle to the ground.

(12) With the full vehicle weight on the suspension, tighten the lower control arm pivot bolt to the specified torque, see specifications.

NOTE: After working on the front suspension the front wheel alignment should be checked.

5. UPPER CONTROL ARM

TO REMOVE

(1) Remove the front suspension and crossmember assembly as previously described.

(2) Remove the split pin and loosen the castellated nut of the upper ball joint.

(3) Using a suitable ball joint press tool, loosen the ball stud in the stub axle support.

(4) Unscrew the castellated nut and disconnect the upper control arm and upper ball joint from the stub axle support.

(5) Remove the split pin, nut and washer from the upper control arm pivot pin, withdraw the pin and remove the upper control arm from the crossmember.

TO DISMANTLE, INSPECT AND ASSEMBLE

(1) Check the upper control arm for distortion and fatigue, replace if suspect.

(2) If wear is apparent in the ball joint, the entire upper control arm will require replacement as the ball joint is not serviced as a separate item.

(3) If the inner pivot bushes require replacement, they can be pressed out, from the centre of the control arm, using the special tools or a suitable press.

(4) Instal the new bushes into the control arm using the special tools or a suitable press.

(5) Lubricate the bushes with glycerine prior to installing the control arm onto the crossmember.

TO INSTAL

(1) Manoeuvre the upper control arm into position on the suspension crossmember and instal the pivot bolt, flat washer and castellated nut.

(2) Tighten the castellated nut to specifications and fit a new split pin.

(3) Lower the outer end of the upper control arm to locate the ball stud of the ball joint in the stub axle support.

(4) Instal the castellated nut to the ball joint stud and tighten to specifications, fit a new split pin.

(5) Lubricate the upper and lower ball joints with a molybdenum disulphide base grease.

(6) The remainder of the installation procedure is a direct reversal of the removal procedure.

6. BALL JOINTS

TO CHECK ON VEHICLE

(1) Raise the front of the vehicle by placing a jack below the suspension lower control arm and lifting sufficiently to allow the wheel to rotate.

(2) Grasping the top and bottom of the wheel, rock in and out to check for any looseness.

NOTE: If any looseness is obtained, the wheel bearings should first be adjusted before trying to diagnose for further suspension faults. See the relevant section for wheel bearing adjustment.

(3) Repeat operation (2) only this time with a dial gauge positioned directly against the outer wheel rim to measure any horizontal movement in the wheel.

(4) Where looseness still exists, check both the upper and lower ball joints visually while rocking the wheel to pin-point the source of the trouble, and if the total indicator reading on the dial gauge is in excess of 3.50 mm, then the ball joint causing the looseness will require renewal.

(5) Lower the vehicle and if necessary repeat operations (1) to (4) on the other side front suspension to check for ball joint wear.

NOTE: *Any excessive wear found in either the upper or the lower ball joints, will necessitate the replacement of the control arm on which the ball joint is fitted as these components are serviced as an assembly only.*

(6) If the upper ball joint is faulty, refer to UPPER CONTROL ARM — TO REMOVE AND INSTAL.

(7) If the lower ball joint is faulty, refer to LOWER CONTROL ARM, COIL SPRING AND SHOCK ABSORBER — TO REMOVE AND INSTAL.

7. STRUT BAR

TO REMOVE AND INSTAL

(1) Raise the front of the vehicle and support on chassis stands placed at suitable points under the body frame.

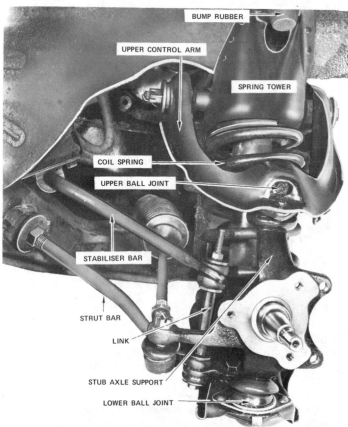

Hub and Backing Plate Removed Showing Layout of Left Hand Side Front Suspension.

(2) Remove the split pin and unscrew the front mounting lock nut and flat washer from the strut bar.

(3) Remove the two nuts and bolts attaching the strut bar to the lower control arm.

NOTE: *On models fitted with stabiliser bar it will be necessary to remove the stabiliser connecting link bolt to disconnect the strut bar from the lower control arm.*

(4) Remove the strut bar from the vehicle.

(5) On early model vehicles — the strut bar mounting rubbers and spacer can be removed with the strut bar.

On later models — the mounting rubbers are held into the crossmember by either screws and tab washers or rivets. Take the necessary steps to either drill out the rivets or unscrew the screws whichever is applicable and remove the mounting rubbers and spacer.

(6) Measure the distance between the front of the strut bar and the adjusting nut, then unscrew the adjusting nut and flat washer and remove from the strut bar.

Installation is a reversal of the removal procedure with attention to the following points:

(1) Check the strut bar for distortion and fatigue.

(2) Renew the mounting rubbers and washers as required.

(3) Screw the adjusting nut and washer onto the forward end of the strut bar until the distance measured in operation (6) is achieved.

(4) Position the new mounting rubbers onto the crossmember with the chamfered side of the mountings uppermost.

(5) On later models, instal the retaining screws and tab nuts and tighten to 0.16—0.20 kg/m, or insert pop-rivets whichever is applicable, to secure the mounting rubbers in place.

(6) Instal the spacer onto the forward end of the strut bar and position the assembly through the front mounting rubbers.

(7) Locate the rear end of the strut bar onto the lower control arm and instal and tighten the retaining bolts to specifications.

(8) Instal the remaining washer and the locknut onto the forward end of the strut bar and tighten securely. Instal a new split pin.

(9) Lower the vehicle to the ground and check the castor and toe-in angles, refer SUSPENSION AND STEERING ANGLES.

8. STABILISER BAR

TO REMOVE AND INSTAL

(1) Raise the front of the vehicle and support on stands under the lower suspension control arms.

(2) Remove the retaining nuts from the top end of the stabiliser bar connecting links at the lower control arms and withdraw the retaining washers and rubbers.

(3) Raise the ends of the stabiliser bar off the connecting links and remove the second rubber, retaining washer and the spacer from the link at each lower control arm.

(4) Take out the bolts and remove the stabiliser bar front bracket clamps, and withdraw the stabiliser bar from the vehicle.

(5) Remove the stabiliser connecting link bolts from each lower control arm and withdraw the additional retaining washers and rubbers.

(6) Withdraw the split rubber front mountings from the stabiliser bar.

Installation is a reversal of the removal procedure with attention to the following points:

Coat the necessary parts of the stabiliser with a suitable rubber lubricant.

Ensure that the rubbers on the connecting links are in a serviceable condition and tighten the link nuts securely.

Ensure that the front mounting rubbers are in a serviceable condition and a good fit in the mounting bracket clamps and on the stabiliser bar, and tighten the clip retaining bolts securely.

9. SUSPENSION AND STEERING ANGLE

TO CHECK AND ADJUST TOE-IN

(1) With the vehicle on a level floor, jack up both front wheels.

(2) Spin each front wheel in turn and, using a piece of chalk, mark a line around the periphery of each tyre as near to the centre as possible.

(3) Lower the front of the vehicle to the floor and bounce the front and rear of the vehicle up and down and let it find its own height. Set the front wheels in the straight-ahead position.

(4) Mark the centre chalk line on both tyres at points approximately 203 mm. above the floor and in front of the front suspension.

(5) Using a suitable telescopic gauge, measure and record the distance between the two marks on the tyre centres.

(6) Maintain the wheels in a straight-ahead position, roll the vehicle forward until the marks are the same distance above the floor, but to the rear of the front suspension.

(7) Again use the telescopic gauge to measure and record the distance between the marks made on the tyres. The distance measured at the front of the wheels must be less than the measurement taken at the rear of the wheels, refer Specifications.

(8) If adjustment of the toe-in is required, loosen both bellows clamp screws and the lock nuts for both tie-rod ends, turn each rod by equal amounts until the toe-in is correct, after each adjustment roll the vehicle forward a short distance to allow the mechanical components to find their neutral position and recheck the toe-in measurement.

(9) When the toe-in measurement is correct, tighten the locknuts and bellows clamp bolts.

NOTE: It is important to make equal adjustments on each tie-rod to maintain the central position of the steering gear and keep the lock angles within specifications.

If an optical or other type of toe-in gauge is used, follow the manufacturer's instructions.

TO CHECK CASTOR AND CAMBER ANGLES

Before any attempt is made to check castor or camber angles or to check and adjust front wheel toe-in, the suspension unit should be thoroughly checked to ascertain that it is in serviceable condition.

The tread of the front tyres should be examined for excessive or uneven wear, as certain conditions of tyre wear are indicative of damaged or worn components in the suspension, steering linkage and/or wheels and bearings. See also WHEELS AND TYRES.

The vehicle should be unladen except for the normal amount of petrol, oil and water, with the tyres inflated to the normal pressure.

(1) Check and adjust the tyre pressures and set the vehicle up with the alignment equipment being used, according to the manufacturer's instructions. Bounce the vehicle up and down several times and let it find its own level.

(2) Check the front wheel alignment (toe-in) and, if necessary, adjust as previously described.

(3) Check the castor, camber and swivel inclination according to the instructions set down for the alignment equipment being used and compare with the Specifications.

(4) If the castor angle is incorrect check the stabiliser bar brackets and rubber bushes. Also check the suspension control arm rubber pivot bush for wear.

(5) If the camber and swivel inclination angles are both incorrect, check the suspension unit upper mounting and lower ball joint for wear or looseness. Check the suspension control arm for distortion or its rubber pivot bush for wear.

(6) If the swivel inclination angle is correct and the camber angle is incorrect, the stub axle is bent and a new stub axle steering knuckle assembly should be installed.

(7) Measure the wheel lock angles of the front wheels using the equipment according to the manufacturer's instructions and referring to the vehicle Specifications for correct settings.

If the toe-in is correctly adjusted and the wheel lock angle on either or both left or right hand turn is incorrect then the tie rods are of unequal length or one or both steering arms may be bent. Check and equalise the tie rod lengths maintaining the correct toe-in setting, recheck the toe-in after setting the wheel lock angle.

In the latter case the steering arm/s must be removed and the steering linkage adjusted.

10. FRONT SUSPENSION FAULT DIAGNOSIS

1. Front end noise.

Possible cause

(a) Loose or worn upper suspension mountings.

(b) Loose or worn lower arm suspension mountings.

(c) Loose or worn suspension mountings.

(d) Noise in shock absorber.
(e) Worn steering linkage.
(f) Maladjusted front hub bearings.

Remedy

— Tighten fulcrum shaft nuts. Check and replace rubber bushes as necessary.
— Check rubber mountings and replace as necessary. Check and tighten bolt at fulcrum shaft.
— Locate points of excessive play. Tighten and replace as necessary.
— Renew shock absorber unit.
— Renew defective components.
— Readjust or renew hub bearings.

2. Poor or erratic road holding ability.

Possible cause

(a) Low or uneven tyre pressure.
(b) Defective shock absorber operation.
(c) Incorrect front end alignment.
(d) Loose or defective front crossmember.
(e) Weak or uneven front coil springs.
(f) Loose or defective front hub bearings.
(g) Maladjusted or defective steering gear or idler.
(h) Defective tyres or front wheel balance.

Remedy

— Inflate tyres to recommended pressures.
— Check and renew faulty unit.
— Check and readjust alignment as necessary.
— Check and tighten or renew member.
— Check and renew springs.
— Adjust or renew hub bearings.
— Adjust or renew faulty components.
— Renew defective tyres and balance front wheels.

3. Heavy steering.

Possible cause

(a) Low or uneven tyre pressure.
(b) Incorrect front end alignment.
(c) Lack of lubricant in steering gear and components.

(d) Worn or damaged front suspension components.

(e) Sagging or broken coil spring/s.
(f) Incorrect adjustment of steering gear.

Remedy

— Check and inflate tyres to recommended pressures.
— Check and adjust alignment.
— Check oil level in steering gear and apply grease gun to all grease nipples.
— Check and renew worn or damaged components and adjust front end alignment.
— Renew coil spring/s.
— Check and adjust steering gear.

4. Front wheel wobble or shimmy.

Possible cause

(a) Tyre and/or wheel unbalance.
(b) Rapid and uneven tyre wear.
(c) Worn or loose hub bearings.
(d) Worn or damaged steering linkage.
(e) Incorrect front end alignment.

(f) Maladjusted or worn steering gear.
(g) Steering gear loose on frame mounting or off centre.

Remedy

— Check and balance tyre and wheel as a unit.
— Check front end alignment (see Wheels and Tyres).
— Check and renew or adjust hub bearings.
— Check, renew faulty components, and adjust.
— Adjust and/or renew suspension components to restore alignment.
— Renew and/or adjust steering gear components.
— Check and tighten mounting and/or centre steering gear.

5. Vehicle pulls to one side.

Possible cause

(a) Low or uneven tyre pressure.
(b) Incorrect or unequal front end alignment – side to side.
(c) High road camber.
(d) Unequal coil spring length.
(e) Weak or broken rear spring.
(f) Front brake dragging.
(g) Steering gear off centre.

Remedy

— Check and inflate tyres to recommended pressures.
— Check and adjust to restore correct alignment.

— Avoid as far as possible.
— Check and renew sagging spring.
— Renew faulty spring.
— Adjust or rectify cause.
— Check and re-centre steering.

REAR SUSPENSION

SPECIFICATIONS

Type .... Live axle with 4 locating arms, 2 coil springs and 2 telescopic shock absorbers

Shock absorber type .... Double action tubular

Spring free height (standard):

Sedan – 1300 ohv	279 mm
– 1600 ohv	279 mm
– 1600 GT ohv	273 mm
– 2000 ohc	273 mm
Wagon – all	290 mm

Spring installed height (standard):

Sedan – 1300 ohv	215.7 mm
– 1600 ohv	215.7 mm
– 1600 GT ohv	217.0 mm
– 2000 ohc	217.0 mm
Wagon – 1300 ohv	215.6 mm
– 1600 ohv	215.6 mm
– 2000 ohc	215.9 mm

NOTE: Heavy duty springs are available as an option.

TORQUE WRENCH SETTINGS

*Upper radius arm nuts	6.9 kg/m
*Lower radius arm nuts	6.9 kg/m
Coil spring lower bolt	4.8 kg/m

*Torque these nuts to specifications only when the vehicle has been lowered to the ground.

1. DESCRIPTION

The rear axle is located by four radius arms and sprung on coil springs with telescopic shock absorbers.

The upper radius arms provide lateral location and also share in controlling axle reaction to drive, braking and acceleration.

The lower radius arms hold the axle square to the vehicle and also share in controlling axle reaction to drive braking and acceleration. They also provide the lower mountings for the coil springs.

Both upper and lower radius arms pivot on rubber bushes at each end.

Upper radius arm rear bushes are carried in lugs on the axle housing. The forward ends of all arms mount to brackets on the vehicle underbody.

Mounts on the axle accommodate the rear of the lower radius arms and the shock absorber bottom attachment.

The upper spring insulator sits on the top of the coil spring and the lower end of the spring is attached to the lower radius arm by a bolt and clamp plate. The bumper stop rubber is pressed over a stud in the recess of the floor panel, directly behind the coil spring and over the axle housing tube on each side.

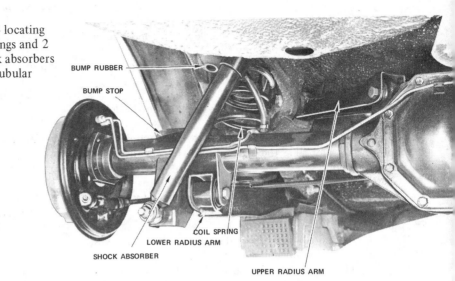

Rear View of Suspension in Assembled Position.

2. SHOCK ABSORBERS

TO REMOVE

(1) Raise the vehicle and support it on stands placed beneath the rear axle housing as close as practicable to the road wheels.

(2) Remove the nut and washer from the lower mounting bolt and slide the bottom of the shock absorber from the bolt.

(3) Remove the top mounting bolt nut, washer and withdraw the bolt.

(4) Remove the shock absorber from the vehicle.

TO TEST

(1) Check the body of the shock absorber for dents or damage and for fluid leakage. The shock absorbers cannot be repaired in service and should be renewed if defective.

(2) Mount the shock absorber upright in a vice by the lower mounting eye.

(3) Grasp the upper half of the shock absorber, pull up to the fully extended position and then slowly push down until the shock absorber is fully compressed.

(4) Repeat operation (3) six to eight times to remove any slack spots caused by air in the system. If slack spots exist and cannot be removed by this method, the shock absorber is evidently defective and should be renewed.

NOTE: As the shock absorber is a double action type the resistance will be the same on the upwards and downwards strokes.

(5) To renew the rubbers, press the sleeve from the centre of the rubber and then prise out the rubber. Grease with soapy water the new rubber bush, push it into the eye and instal the sleeve in the same manner.

TO INSTAL

Installation is a reversal of the removal procedure.

3. SPRINGS

TO REMOVE AND INSTAL

(1) Raise the rear of the vehicle and support it on stands placed beneath the body rear side rails.

NOTE: Do not lower the jack at this stage.

(2) Remove the spring retaining bolt from the lower radius arm.

(3) Remove the lower shock absorber retaining nut and washer and slide the shock absorber from the lower mounting bolt.

(4) Slowly lower the jack.

(5) Remove the spring from the vehicle and withdraw the lower retainer plate and the upper insulator from the spring.

Installation is a reversal of the removal procedure with attention to the following points:

(1) Place the lower retainer into the bottom coil engaging the end of the coil in the tang of the lower retainer plate.

(2) Place the upper insulator onto the top coil of the spring.

(3) Place the coil spring in position and instal the retainer plate and bolt (through the lower radius arm) finger tight.

(4) Raise the jack until the weight of the vehicle is just lifted off the stands.

(5) Torque the spring retaining bolt to specifications.

(6) Slide the shock absorber onto the lower mounting bolt, instal the washer and nut and tighten the nut securely.

(7) Remove the stands and lower the vehicle to the floor.

4. UPPER RADIUS ARMS

TO REMOVE AND INSTAL

(1) Raise the rear of the vehicle and support it on stands placed beneath the body side rails.

NOTE: Leave the jack in the raised position underneath the rear axle housing.

(2) Remove the coil spring as previously described.

(3) Raise the jack until the rear axle housing is approximately in its normal position.

(4) Remove the upper radius arm mounting bolt nuts and washers and withdraw the mounting bolts.

(5) Remove the upper radius arm.

NOTE: The front bush will remain in the suspension arm while the rear bush will remain in the bracket on the rear axle housing.

Check the condition of the bushes. Special tools however are needed to renew the bushes in both the arm and housing bracket.

Installation is a reversal of the removal procedure with attention to the following points:

(1) With the radius arm in position, instal the front mounting bolt, washer and the nut finger tight.

(2) Raise or lower the jack as necessary to align the rear mounting hole, instal the bolt, washer and the nut finger tight.

(3) Instal the coil spring as previously described, lower the vehicle to the ground and torque the upper control arm nuts to specifications.

5. LOWER RADIUS ARMS

TO REMOVE AND INSTAL

(1) Raise the rear of the vehicle and support it on stands placed beneath the rear body side rails.

(2) Remove the coil spring as previously described.

(3) Raise the jack until the rear axle housing is approximately in its normal position.

(4) Disconnect the handbrake cable from the radius arm.

(5) Remove the radius arm mounting bolts, nuts and washers and withdraw the mounting bolts.

(6) Remove the radius arm from the vehicle.

Installation is a reversal of the removal procedure with attention to the following points:

(1) With the radius arm in position instal the front

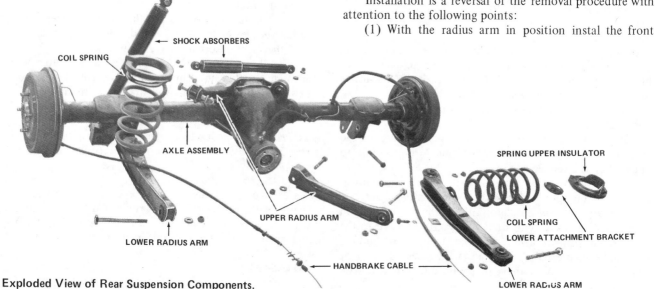

Exploded View of Rear Suspension Components.

mounting bolt, washer and the nut finger tight.

(2) Raise or lower the jack as necessary to align the rear mounting hole, instal the bolt, washer and the nut finger tight.

(3) Instal the coil spring as previously described, and reconnect the handbrake cable to the lower radius arm.

(4) Lower the vehicle to the ground and torque the radius arm nuts to specifications.

6. REAR SUSPENSION FAULT DIAGNOSIS

1. **Noise in suspension.**

   Possible cause
   - (a) Defective shock absorber and/or mounting.
   - (b) Sprung or bent axle housing.
   - (c) Loose or defective radius arm bushes.
   - (d) Loose coil spring lower retaining bolt.

   Remedy
   - — Renew faulty components.
   - — Renew axle housing.
   - — Check, tighten and renew as necessary.
   - — Check, and torque to specifications.

2. **Rear wheels not in alignment with front wheels.**

   Possible cause
   - (a) Spring badly sagging on one side.
   - (b) Sprung or bent axle housing.
   - (c) Distortion of body and subframe.

   Remedy
   - — Renew defective spring.
   - — Renew axle housing.
   - — Check and rectify body alignment.

STEERING

SPECIFICATIONS

Type . . . . Rack and pinion
Overall ratio 18.7:1
Linkage . . . . Direct from rack ends to
                                       tie rods and steering arms
Seals . . . . Convoluted expanding boot
Steering column . . . . Energy absorbing
Steering wheel dia-
meter . . . . 394 x 369 mm (oval)
Steering gear adjust-
ment . . . . Shims
Turns lock to lock 3.7
Maximum turning angle:
  Outer wheel . . . . 38 deg 48 min
  Inner wheel . . . . 35 deg 36 min
Lubricant capacity . . . . 0.142 litres
Lubricant type . . . . SAE 90 Hypoid
Turning circle . . . . 9.55 metres

TORQUE WRENCH SETTINGS

Steering wheel nut . . . . 3.4 kg/m
Steering gear to cross-
member . . . . 2.4 kg/m
Tie rod ball joint to
steering arm . . . . 3.0 kg/m
Flexible coupling to
pinion shaft . . . . 2.1 kg/m
Universal joint to
steering shaft spline . . . . . . 2.1 kg/m
Tie-rod end ball housing . . . . 5.2 kg/m
Tie-rod ball housing
locknut . . . . 6.3 kg/m
Pinion preload cover . . . . 1.1 kg/m
Rock damper cover . . . . 1.1 kg/m
Pinion turning torque . . . . . . 0.06 – 0.17 kg/m

1. DESCRIPTION

The steering gear is mounted in rubber insulators on brackets attached to the front crossmember.

The rack is connected by ball joints to the tie rods on either end, which in turn are connected to the steering arms.

The inner ball joints are protected by rubber bellows clipped on to the rack housing and the tie rods. The outer ball joints are protected by gaiters.

Adjustment by variation of shim thickness is provided, for pinion bearing pre-load and for rack damper end load. All vehicles are equipped with a collapsible type steering column to absorb secondary impact in the event of severe front end collision.

The steering shaft is connected to the pinion on the rack and pinion type steering gear through a flexible coupling.

Wheel lock angles and toe-in are obtained by adjusting the lengths of the tie rods.

Non-adjustable lock stops are incorporated in the steering gear.

No lubrication of the steering gear is required in service.

2. STEERING GEAR ASSEMBLY

TO REMOVE

(1) With the wheels in the straight ahead position, raise the front of the vehicle and support on wheel stands. Alternatively raise the vehicle on a platform type hoist.

(2) Remove the engine oil filter element. (OHV models only).

(3) Remove the split pins, slacken the castellated nuts and using a suitable extractor, press the tie rod ball joints loose in the steering arms.

(4) Remove the castellated nuts.

(5) Remove the nut and bolt securing the flexible coupling to the steering gear pinion splines.

(6) Bend back the lock tabs and remove the bolts securing the steering gear assembly to the crossmember.

(7) Remove the bolts, locking plates and U-clamps and remove the steering gear from the vehicle.

TO DISMANTLE

(1) Slacken the clips securing the bellows to the tie rod and steering gear housing.

(2) Release the lock nuts at the outer tie rod ends and unscrew the ends from the tie rods, noting number of turns required to unscrew them. Unscrew and remove the lock nuts.

(3) Carefully support the steering gear in a vice taking care not to damage it. Position it with one bellows higher than the other.

(4) Remove the top bellows and clips.

(5) Up-end the assembly and drain out the oil into a suitable container while traversing the rack from lock to lock.

(6) Drill out the retaining pin, locking the ball housing and lock nut together, taking care not to drill too deeply.

(7) Using the special ball joint spanners, loosen the ball

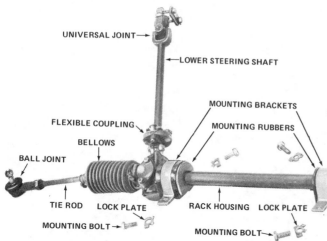

Assembled View of Rack and Pinion Components.

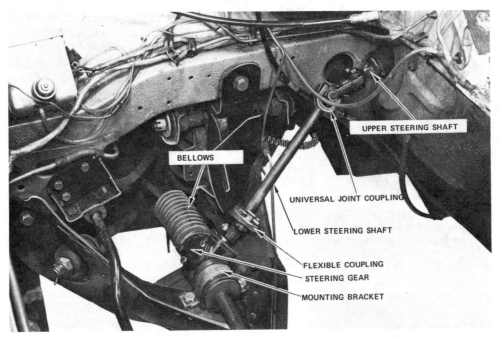

Engine Removed to Show Steering Gear Layout.

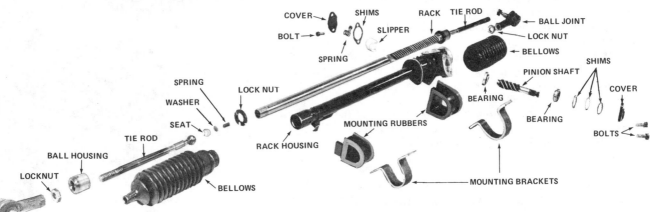

Tie Rod Ball Seat Components.

housing and unscrew the housing from the rack shaft.

(8) Withdraw the tie rod ball and ball housing, the spring and the ball seat from the aperture in the end of the rack.

(9) Carry out the foregoing procedure on the bellows and the tie rod inner ball joint of the other side.

(10) Remove the rack damper cover, the shims and gasket and withdraw the spring and slipper, put the steel shims carefully to one side for possible use on assembly.

(11) Remove the pinion bearing pre-load cover plate and adjusting shims, put the shims to one side for possible use on assembly.

(12) Remove the pinion shaft and the top bearing assembly from the housing.

(13) Withdraw the rack from the pinion end of the steering gear housing.

(14) If necessary remove the lower pinion bearing assembly using a slide hammer or suitable bearing puller.

TO CLEAN AND INSPECT

(1) Wash all parts in cleaning solvent and dry thoroughly, except the tie rod end outer ball joints.

(2) Check all parts for wear or damage. Damage to the rack or pinion teeth will necessitate replacement of the steering gear assembly.

(3) Check the rack support bush and replace as necessary.

(4) Examine the ball at the inner end of the tie rod and the ball housing and replace as necessary.

(5) Check the steering gear mounting rubbers and renew as necessary.

Exploded View of Rack and Pinion Components.

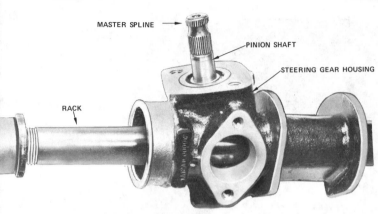

MASTER SPLINE →

PINION SHAFT

STEERING GEAR HOUSING

RACK

Correct Installation of Pinion Shaft with Rack Centrally Situated in Gear Housing and Master Spline on Pinion with Rack Centreline towards Right Hand Side.

(6) Check the tie rod ends for wear and replace as necessary.

(7) Inspect the bellows and gaiters for damage and replace as necessary.

(8) Fit new oil seals and dust seals.

(9) Fit new springs and ball seats.

TO ASSEMBLE

(1) Prise the old pinion oil seal from the pinion cover and fit a new oil seal.

(2) If previously removed, instal a new lower pinion ball bearing into the steering gear housing.

(3) Instal the rack into the steering gear housing and position it so that the teeth are adjacent to the pinion location and, so that it is in the centre of the housing, (measure the protruding length of each end of the housing).

NOTE: Lightly lubricate the parts as assembled with the recommended lubricant.

(4) Assemble the upper ball bearing to the pinion shaft, instal the pinion in the housing and engage it with the rack.

(5) Position the steering gear assembly so that the pinion pre-load can be conveniently checked and pre-load determined.

(6) Instal a shim stack on the pinion bearing with the 2.36 mm. shim at the top to bear against the cover plate.

(7) Instal the pinion cover plate without the gasket and tighten the retaining bolts evenly.

(8) Slacken the cover plate bolts until the cover is only just contacting the shim stack.

(9) Measure and record the gap between the cover plate and the steering gear housing, using feeler gauges at points adjacent to the retainer bolts.

(10) Remove the cover plate and select by either adding to or subtracting from the total shim pack, the thickness of shims required to leave a clearance of 0.28 – 0.33 mm. between the cover plate and the steering gear housing.

NOTE: The shim stack must contain at least two other shims in addition to the 2.36 mm. shim which must be fitted closest to the cover plate.

.(11) Position the selected shim stack onto the pinion upper bearing cap and with the sealing gasket interposed between the cover plate and the steering gear housing, fit the cover plate and tighten the retaining bolts to a torque of 0.9 – 1.1 kg/m.

NOTE: Prior to installing the top cover, pack the pinion shaft oil seal with grease and smear the sealing gasket between the cover plate and the steering gear housing and the retaining bolt threads with a suitable jointing compound.

(12) Instal the damper slipper into the housing to abut the steering rack.

(13) Press the slipper into firm contact with the rack and using a straight edge and feeler gauge, measure the distance between the top of the slipper and the abutment face of the damper cover on the steering gear housing. Record the dimension obtained.

(14) Assemble a shim pack including the sealing gasket of the same total thickness at that dimension recorded in operation (13) plus an additional 0.013 – 0.127 mm. shim to allow for correct spring pressure on the slipper and instal the shim pack and damper cover plate with the spring interposed between the cover and the slipper.

NOTE: The sealing gasket should be smeared with jointing compound and position closest to the damper cover plate when installed.

(15) Fit the damper cover retaining bolts and tighten to a torque of 0.9 – 1.1 kg/m.

(16) Fit a suitable pre-load measuring gauge to the splined end of the pinion shaft and measure the torque required to start the pinion rotating.

Method of Assessing Rack Damper Shim Thickness.

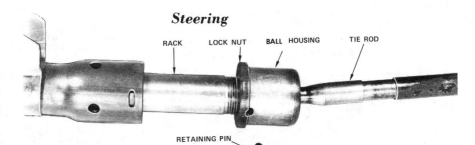

RACK   LOCK NUT   BALL HOUSING   TIE ROD

RETAINING PIN

**Installing Retaining Pin to Tie Rod.
Ball Housing and Lock Nut**

(17) A pre-load reading of 0.058 — 0.137 kg/m is required and any variation from that specified would indicate incorrect shim thickness.

(18) Instal a new spring and ball seat to the aperture in the end of the rack shaft and smear SAE 90 EP oil on the ball, ball housing and ball seat.

(19) Position the tie rod ball end on the ball seat and assemble the lock nut and ball housing over the tie rod. Screw on the ball housing until the movement of the tie rod becomes restricted.

(20) Attach a spring scale to the threaded end of the tie rod about 12 mm. from the end and measure the effort required to move the tie rod from the centre line of the rack shaft, adjust by tightening or loosening the ball housing as necessary until a pull of 2.27 kilograms is registered.

(21) Using the special spanners used for dismantling, tighten the lock nut to the ball housing and recheck the pre-load of the tie rod ball.

(22) After the pre-load is correctly set lock the lock nut and ball housing together in the following manner.

(23) Drill a 3.18 mm. diameter hole on the line of the contact between the ball housing and the lock nut so that half of the hole will be in the ball housing and half in the lock nut.

(24) The hole should be drilled to a depth of 6.35 mm., but this depth must not be exceeded.

NOTE: A new hole must be drilled even though the previous halves of the original hole align.

(25) Insert a retaining pin into the hole drilled, tap into position and peen over the end to secure it in position.

(26) Repeat the same procedure for the other end of the assembly.

(27) Fit a new bellows to one end of the steering gear housing and secure with clips to housing and tie rod.

(28) Up-end the assembly in a soft jawed vice so that the assembled bellows will be at the lower end.

(29) Traverse the rack so the upper tie rod is fully extended.

(30) Pour the correct amount of recommended lubricant into the casing under the tie rod inner ball joint. Move the rack to and fro to assist the oil to flow into the casing.

(31) Fit the upper bellows and secure with clips to housing and tie rod.

(32) Refit the lock nuts and ball joints to the outer ends of the tie rods ensuring that they are screwed on the same number of turns as was required to remove them. Tighten the lock nuts.

TO INSTAL

(1) Check the conditions of the steering gear mounting rubbers and renew if necessary.

(2) Instal the steering gear assembly into position. Position the steering wheel and the steering gear in the straight ahead position.

(3) Align the mating splines on the flexible coupling and the pinion shaft.

(4) Secure the steering gear assembly to its mounting brackets on the crossmember with the U-clamps. With new locking plates under the bolt heads, torque the bolts to specifications. Bend over the locking plate tabs.

(5) Assemble the tie rod ends to the steering arms, fit the castellated nuts and torque to specifications. Fit new split pins.

(6) Torque the flexible coupling to pinion shaft securing bolt to specifications.

(7) Lower the vehicle to the floor.

(8) Check the front wheel toe in and adjust if necessary.

3. STEERING WHEEL

TO REMOVE AND INSTAL

(1) Working from behind the steering wheel, loosen and remove the screws retaining the wheel embellishment and withdraw the embellishment to gain access to the steering wheel retaining nut.

(2) Align the wheels in the straight ahead position.

(3) Loosen and remove the retaining nut and using a suitable puller withdraw the steering wheel.

NOTE: Under no circumstances must the steering wheel be removed by levering up or tapping down with a hammer as damage to the collapsible column could result.

Installation is a reversal of the removal procedure.

4. STEERING COLUMN

TO REMOVE

(1) Open the engine bonnet and fit fender covers to both front fenders.

(2) Disconnect the earth lead at the battery terminal.

(3) Loosen the two bolts at the clamping plate on the steering shaft universal joint to free the upper steering shaft from the universal joint coupling. Mark the position of the steering shaft in relation to its position in the coupling to ensure correct assembly.

(4) Remove the steering wheel, as previously described.

(5) Remove the retaining screw and the annulus ring attaching the two halves of the column shroud and withdraw the shroud assemblies.

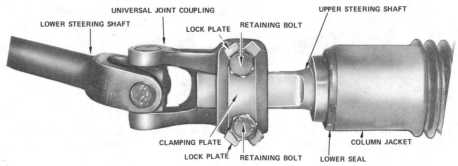

UNIVERSAL JOINT COUPLING
LOWER STEERING SHAFT
LOCK PLATE
RETAINING BOLT
UPPER STEERING SHAFT
CLAMPING PLATE
LOCK PLATE
RETAINING BOLT
LOWER SEAL
COLUMN JACKET

Assembled View of Lower Steering Shaft and Universal Joint Assembly.

NOTE: If a manual choke control is fitted it will be necessary to withdraw the choke control knob to allow for the removal of the column shroud assembly.

(6) With the shroud assemblies removed, disconnect the choke control cable from the bracket on the column jacket. (On models so equipped).

(7) Disconnect the ignition switch and the direction indicator switch wires from the plug connectors under the dash panel. Disconnect the earth wire from the fascia panel screw.

(8) Loosen and remove the direction indicator switch retaining bolts and withdraw the switch assembly from the vehicle.

(9) Remove the indicator cancelling cam and spring from the steering shaft.

(10) Disconnect and remove the brake pedal return spring.

(11) Unscrew the column mounting bolts, and manoeuvre the entire assembly upward and withdraw it from within the vehicle.

TO DISMANTLE AND ASSEMBLE

(1) Place the column assembly on a suitably protected work bench and remove the lower bearing cover.

(2) Using a suitable drift, unstake the lower bearing from the column jacket and remove the bearing.

(3) Remove the upper bearing snap ring and washer from the upper end of the column tube.

(4) Remove the snap ring retaining the upper bearing to the steering shaft and with the ignition switch and lock assembly turned to the on position tap lightly on the steering shaft and withdraw through the lower end of the column jacket.

(5) Remove the upper bearing and rubber insulator from the bearing support housing.

(6) Remove the upper bearing lower snap ring from the steering shaft.

(7) To assemble and instal, fit the upper bearing lower snap ring into the groove provided on the steering shaft.

(8) Instal the steering shaft up through the column jacket and position the upper bearing with insulator fitted, down over the shaft.

(9) With the lower end of the steering shaft suitably supported on a block of wood, use a length of pipe of suitable diameter, that will press evenly on the bearing inner track and lightly tap the bearing into position on the steering shaft.

(10) Instal the snap ring to secure the bearing assembly onto the steering shaft.

(11) Lower the steering shaft and bearing within the column to seat the bearing and insulator in the bearing support housing.

(12) Instal the retaining washer and snap ring to secure the bearing assembly within the bearing support housing.

(13) Invert the column jacket and instal the lower bearing assembly, stake in the places provided to secure in position.

(14) Lubricate the bearing with a suitable grease and instal the lower bearing cover.

(15) Instal the column assembly in the car, guiding the steering shaft lower end into engagement with the universal joint coupling, noting the alignment marks made when removing.

(16) Instal the upper column bracket to dash panel retaining bolts and tighten securely.

(17) With the steering shaft correctly positioned in the universal joint coupling, tighten the bolts of the clamping plate securely and bend up the tabs on the locking plates.

(18) Connect the brake pedal return spring.

(19) Instal the spring and the direction indicator cancelling cam on to the upper steering shaft.

NOTE: The ear on the cam must be adjacent to the cancelling lever of the indicator switch when the road wheels and the steering shaft are positioned for the straight ahead position.

Assembled View of Upper Steering Column Components.

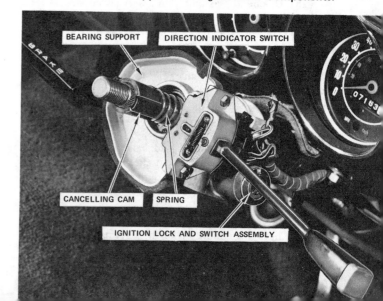

BEARING SUPPORT
DIRECTION INDICATOR SWITCH
CANCELLING CAM
SPRING
IGNITION LOCK AND SWITCH ASSEMBLY

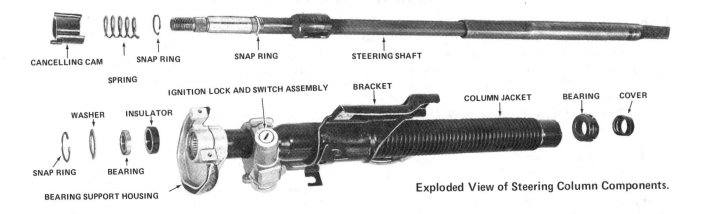

CANCELLING CAM   SNAP RING   SNAP RING   STEERING SHAFT

SPRING

WASHER   INSULATOR   IGNITION LOCK AND SWITCH ASSEMBLY   BRACKET   COLUMN JACKET   BEARING   COVER

SNAP RING   BEARING

BEARING SUPPORT HOUSING

Exploded View of Steering Column Components.

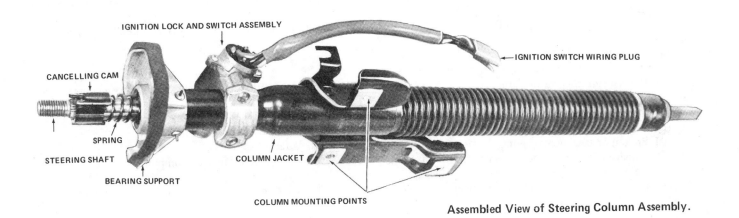

IGNITION LOCK AND SWITCH ASSEMBLY

IGNITION SWITCH WIRING PLUG

CANCELLING CAM

SPRING

STEERING SHAFT

BEARING SUPPORT

COLUMN JACKET

COLUMN MOUNTING POINTS

Assembled View of Steering Column Assembly.

(20) Instal the direction indicator switch assembly onto the column jacket and secure with the retaining screws. Connect the wiring plug to the connection under the dash panel.

(21) Connect the ignition switch wiring plug to the connection under the dash panel.

(22) Connect the earth lead at the dash fascia screw.

(23) Where fitted, connect the choke cable at the bracket on the column jacket.

(24) Refit the column shroud covers and where fitted the choke cable operating knob.

(25) With the road wheels and the steering wheel in a straight ahead position instal the steering wheel to engage with the splines on the shaft and the lug of the cancelling cam.

(26) Retain the steering wheel with the securing nut and tighten securely. Replace the wheel embellishment.

(27) Connect the battery terminal and remove the fender covers.

5. LOWER STEERING SHAFT COUPLINGS

TO REMOVE AND INSTAL

(1) Raise the engine bonnet and fit fender covers to both front fenders.

(2) Loosen and remove the clamp bolt securing the flexible coupling flange to the pinion shaft of the steering gear.

(3) Unscrew the bolts on the clamping plate retaining the universal joint coupling to the upper steering shaft. Mark the location prior to removal.

(4) Withdraw the lower steering shaft assembly from the vehicle.

NOTE: If either the lower flexible coupling or the upper universal joint coupling requires replacement the entire shaft assembly will necessitate replacement, as the individual components cannot be replaced separately.

Installation is a reversal of the removal procedure. Instal the shaft assembly, aligning the master spline of the flexible coupling with that on the pinion shaft.

Locate the universal joint coupling to the upper steering shaft, noting the positioning marks made when removing.

Instal the clamping plate and the retaining bolts with the locking plates and tighten the bolts securely to specifications.

Bend over the locking plates to secure the retaining bolts.

6. STEERING FAULT DIAGNOSIS

1. **Excessive play or loosening in steering gear.**

   Possible cause
   (a) Steering rack and pinion worn.
   (b) Steering linkage ball joints worn or loose.
   (c) Rack housing assembly to sub-frame mounting bolts loose.
   (d) Wear in steering gear to steering shaft coupling points.

   Remedy
   — Overhaul steering gear and renew worn components.
   — Tighten or renew faulty components.
   — Check and tighten mounting bolts.

   — Renew faulty components.

2. **Heavy steering.**

   Possible cause
   (a) Low or uneven tyre pressure.
   (b) Steering gear incorrectly adjusted.
   (c) Lack of lubrication in steering linkage joints.
   (d) Front suspension worn or out of alignment.

   (e) Misalignment between steering gear and column mountings.
   (f) Soft or sagging front spring(s).

   Remedy
   — Check tyres and inflate to recommended pressures.
   — Check and re-adjust steering gear.
   — Check and lubricate steering linkage where applicable.
   — Check front end for wear, renew worn components and re-align front end.
   — Check and align steering gear and column mountings.

   — Renew coil spring(s) and check front end alignment.

3. **Steering pulls to one side.**

   Possible cause
   (a) Uneven tyre wear or pressure.

   (b) Incorrect front end adjustment.
   (c) Dragging brakes.
   (d) Broken or sagging rear spring(s).
   (e) Damaged front suspension or front sub-frame members.
   (f) Faulty or damaged front crossmember.

   Remedy
   — Check condition of tyres and inflate to recommended pressures.
   — Check front end alignment.
   — Check and adjust brake shoes.
   — Renew faulty spring(s).
   — Check and renew damaged components.

   — Check and renew front crossmember.

4. **Front wheel wobble or shimmy.**

   Possible cause
   (a) Looseness in steering gear.
   (b) Uneven tyre wear or incorrect tyre pressures.

   (c) Tyre and/or wheel unbalance.
   (d) Front end damaged or out of alignment.
   (e) Worn or badly adjusted front wheel bearing.
   (f) Front wheel alignment incorrectly adjusted.
   (g) Loose or worn tie rod ends.
   (h) Faulty shock absorbers.

   Remedy
   — Rectify and adjust.
   — Check condition of tyres and inflate to recommended pressures.
   — Check and balance as necessary.
   — Check and rectify front end damage and alignment.
   — Check condition and adjust wheel bearings.
   — Check and adjust front wheel toe-in (alignment).
   — Check and renew faulty components.
   — Check and renew as a pair.

5. **Steering erratic or wandering.**

   Possible cause
   (a) Incorrect or uneven camber and/or castor setting.
   (b) Smooth front tyres.
   (c) Excessive play in steering gear and/or linkage.
   (d) Excessively high or low tyre pressure.
   (e) Loose or incorrectly adjusted front wheel bearings.

   Remedy
   — Check and renew components to rectify.
   — Check and renew tyres as necessary.
   — Check and renew faulty components, readjust.
   — Check and inflate to recommended pressures.
   — Check and adjust front wheel bearings.

BRAKES

SPECIFICATIONS

Type:
Front .... Disc
Rear .... Drum
Operation:
Footbrake .... Hydraulic
Handbrake .... Cables, rear wheels
only

DRUM BRAKES

Drum diameter:
Except Australian
models —
1300—1600 sedan .... 203.20 mm
1300—1600 heavy duty
and GT .... 228.60 mm
2000 OHC .... 228.60 mm
Australian models .... 228.60 mm
Wheel cylinder bore:
Except Australian
models —
1300—1600 — early ...... 20.64 mm
1300—1600 heavy duty
and later .... 19.05 mm
Australian models —
1600 .... 19.05 mm
2000 .... 17.78 mm
Brake shoe adjustment .... Self adjusting
Hand brake adjustment ... Nut at cable flange
Lining thickness — min .... 2.00 mm

DISC BRAKES

Disc diameter .... 247.396 mm
Disc thickness:
Standard .... 12.70 mm
Minimum after machining 11.44 mm
Disc runout — max .... 0.050 mm
Caliper bore .... 54.00 mm

MASTER CYLINDER

Type .... Tandem
Bore diameter:
Except Australian
models —
1300—1600 .... 19.05 mm
1300—1600 heavy duty
and GT .... 20.64 mm
2000 OHC .... 20.64 mm
Australian models —
1600 .... 19.05 mm
2000 .... 20.64 mm

VACUUM SERVO UNIT

Type:
Except Australian
models .... Type 38 or T51/18mmE
Australian models .... Type 38 or 50
Boost ratio 2.2:1

TORQUE WRENCH SETTINGS

Caliper retaining
bolts .... 6.90 kg/m
Brake disc to hub .... 4.70 kg/m
Rear backing plate
retaining bolts .... 2.40 kg/m

1. DESCRIPTION

Disc brakes are fitted to the front wheels and drum brakes to the rear wheels.

The front disc brakes are of the trailing caliper type and require no attention in service apart from periodical inspection for fluid leakage or defects and checking of the disc pads for thickness.

The rear brake assemblies are self adjusting. Adjustment takes place through the operation of the handbrake which, when engaged operates the actuating lever to raise the self adjuster arm and so rotate the ratchet wheel to lengthen the strut. Disengaging the handbrake returns the actuating lever to the released position thus allowing the self adjusting arm to ratchet over the teeth on the ratchet wheel.

The hydraulic system incorporates a bleeder screw on each of the two disc caliper assemblies fitted to the front wheels and one single rear bleeder screw at the O/S/R brake assembly.

The mechanical handbrake comes in either dash mounted control or floor mounted control and operates on the rear brakes only, through cables and an equaliser.

Adjustment is effected on dash mounted models by an adjusting nut and lock nut actuated at the primary cable near the cable equaliser. On floor mounted models adjustment is effected at a body bracket through which the secondary cable passes under the rear right side of the vehicle.

All 2000 OHC and 1300/1600 heavy duty and GT model vehicles are fitted with a suspended vacuum servo unit, mounted between the tandem master cylinder and the foot brake pedal operating in conjunction with the master cylinder to boost the brake pedal effort during application of the brake.

The tandem master cylinder by virtue of its design, provides separate hydraulic circuits for the front and rear brakes, thus ensuring that failure in one circuit will leave the other circuit unaffected and one set of brakes operational.

The master cylinder reservoir is of a single body construction with an internal baffle plate providing separate reservoirs for the primary and secondary hydraulic braking systems.

2. MASTER CYLINDER

TO REMOVE AND INSTAL

(1) Disconnect the brake fluid pipes at the master cylinder and plug the pipes to prevent the entry of dirt.

(2) Remove the two nuts and spring washers attaching the master cylinder to the servo unit or bulkhead, whichever is applicable.

NOTE: Where no servo unit is fitted, disconnect the master cylinder push rod at the brake pedal.

(3) Detach the master cylinder and reservoir assembly. On models fitted with a servo unit hold a finger over the end of the cylinder as it is removed to prevent the piston from coming out as a piston retaining snap ring is not used on these models.

Installation is a reversal of the removal procedure with particular attention to the following points:

It will be necessary to bleed the hydraulic system as described in the appropriate section.

Use care not to spill hydraulic fluid on any lacquered surface.

TO DISMANTLE

(1) With the master cylinder removed from the vehicle, unscrew the reservoir filler cap and drain the fluid from the reservoir.

(2) Remove the two reservoir attaching screws and pivot the reservoir at the front end to gain access to the compensating valve.

NOTE: Do not remove the reservoir, which is retained at the front end by an internal circlip, unless the reservoir requires replacement.

(3) Remove the sealing washer and using an allen key of suitable size, take out the valve retaining plug, and withdraw the primary compensating valve assembly.

(4) On models without a servo unit pull the rubber boot off the open end of the master cylinder, take out the circlip and withdraw the push rod assembly.

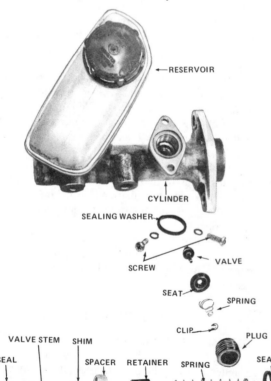

(5) Withdraw the primary piston and spring.

(6) Tap the open end of the cylinder on a block of wood to facilitate the removal of the secondary piston and valve assembly.

NOTE: Alternatively primary and secondary piston assemblies can be expelled from the master cylinder bore by application of air pressure to the secondary compensating valve aperture, all other apertures should be blanked off.

(7) Use a thin bladed screwdriver to prise up the leaf of the spring retainer from the secondary piston and detach the secondary piston.

(8) Compress the valve spring and detach the end of the valve stem from the slot in the retainer and separate the components.

(9) Remove the spring from the valve stem, slide the valve spacer and shim off the valve stem and remove the valve seal.

(10) Remove the seals from both primary and secondary pistons.

TO CLEAN AND INSPECT

(1) Thoroughly clean the master cylinder components and the inside of the master cylinder bore with methylated spirits or brake fluid. Do not use petrol or other mineral spirits.

(2) Check the inside of the master cylinder bore and pistons for wear and/or pitting and renew the assembly if necessary.

(3) Check the rubber components for deterioration, when overhauling a master cylinder all rubber components should be renewed.

(4) Ensure that the breather hole in the reservoir cap is free and remove any sediment that may have accumulated in the bottom of the reservoir.

TO ASSEMBLE

(1) Dip the master cylinder components in clean brake fluid and instal the seals on both pistons.

(2) Instal the valve seal on to the secondary piston compensating valve head with the lip of the seal facing forward.

(3) Place the valve shim on the valve stem so that the convex side of the shim contacts the shoulder of the stem flange.

(4) Slide the valve spacer on the valve stem to abut the shim, with the legs of the spacer over the valve seal.

(5) Position the valve spring on the valve stem assembly, place the spring retainer in the other end of the spring, compress the spring to locate the knob end of the valve stem in the slot in the retainer.

(6) Enter the spigot end of the secondary piston into the spring retainer and using a pair of long nosed pliers

Dismantled View of Brake Master Cylinder Components.

depress the leaf of the spring retainer behind the head of the piston.

NOTE: The retainer leaf should be straight and firmly located behind the piston head.

(7) Lubricate the cylinder bore with clean brake fluid and insert the secondary piston assembly, valve end first, into the cylinder bore taking care not to turn back or damage the seal lips on entry.

(8) Instal the primary piston spring into the cylinder bore followed by the primary piston assembly, taking care not to turn back or damage the seal lips on entry.

(9) On models not fitted with a servo unit instal the rubber dust cover on the push rod, engage the push rod in the end of the primary piston and secure in position with the retainer washer and circlip.

Ensure that the circlip is correctly located in the groove in the cylinder.

Ease the rubber dust cover over the end of the master cylinder body.

(10) Depress the push rod or primary piston slightly to facilitate installation of the primary compensating valve assembly and secure with the retaining plug.

NOTE: Check the operation of the primary compensating valve which should tilt open with the push rod or primary piston in the off position and close when the push rod or primary piston is pushed down the cylinder bore.

(11) Instal a new sealing washer in the recess for the primary compensating valve port and pivot the reservoir into position. Fit and tighten the reservoir securing screws.

(12) Pour a small quantity of clean brake fluid into the reservoirs, instal the reservoir cap and pump the master cylinder push rod until fluid begins to emerge from the outlet ports.

(13) Instal the assembly in the vehicle and bleed the hydraulic system as described in the appropriate section.

3. REAR BRAKE ASSEMBLY

TO REMOVE AND DISMANTLE

(1) Raise the rear of the vehicle and support on stands under the rear axle.

(2) Remove the road wheel and release the handbrake.

(3) Take out the countersunk screw securing the brake drum to the axle flange and remove the drum. Self adjusters are fitted on rear wheel brake assemblies which cannot be released until the brake drum is removed. However, if the brake shoes foul the brake drums, thus preventing its removal, the following steps can be undertaken.

(a) Loosen the handbrake adjustment, and if necessary disconnect the secondary cable at the equaliser.

(b) Withdraw the stop plunger from the backing plate using vice grips or a suitable tool. A new plunger must be installed when assembling.

(c) It should now be possible to remove the brake drum as described in operation (3).

(4) Mark each shoe and return spring for correct assembly, compress the shoe hold down spring, turn the

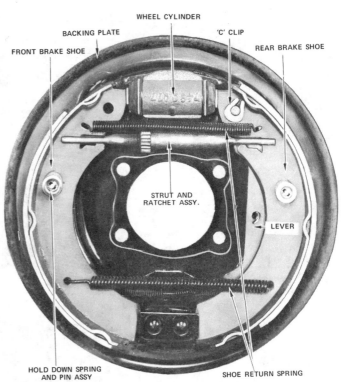

Assembled View of Rear Brake Components.

washer through 90 degrees and remove the spring, the washer and retainer pin. Use the same procedure to remove the hold down spring, washer and retainer pin from the other shoe.

(5) Using suitable brake spring pliers, unhook the shoe return springs, and remove the shoes from the backing plate.

(6) Withdraw the brake shoe strut and ratchet assembly from the backing plate.

NOTE: If both rear brake assemblies are being dismantled it is advisable to mark each strut and ratchet assembly in relation to its corresponding brake assembly to ensure correct installation. The left hand side adjusting ratchet uses a left hand thread while the right hand side has a right hand thread.

(7) Disconnect the handbrake cable from the actuating arm at the rear brake shoe.

(8) Using a screwdriver, prise open the 'C' clip retaining the actuating arm and the self adjusting linkage to the rear brake shoe and remove the assembly together with the pivot pin and the spring.

(9) Disconnect the hydraulic line/s from the wheel cylinder and plug the line/s to prevent the loss of fluid or the ingress of dirt. Remove the two bolts connecting the wheel cylinder to the backing plate and withdraw the wheel cylinder assembly.

TO CLEAN AND INSPECT

(1) Check the brake shoe linings for wear and renew as necessary.

(2) If the linings are still serviceable, check for oil saturation and gumminess.

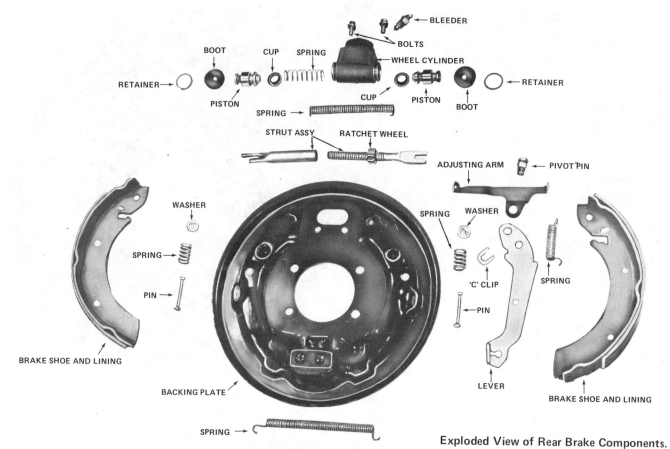

Exploded View of Rear Brake Components.

NOTE: Linings must be renewed as sets with the corresponding linings on the opposite rear wheel.

(3) Check the brake drum for cracks, scoring and out of round, renew or machine as necessary.

(4) Dismantle and wash the wheel cylinder components in methylated spirits and blow dry with compressed air.

(5) Check the wheel cylinder piston and cylinder bore for wear and pitting. Renew the cylinder or lightly hone as necessary.

NOTE: Ensure that the wheel cylinder bleeder valve is dismantled and checked for blocking. Fit new rubber cups and boots to the wheel cylinder pistons as reclaiming of these components is not advisable.

(6) Clean the brake adjusting ratchets and inspect for damage.

(7) Check the tension of the brake shoe return springs by comparison with new springs.

(8) Check the handbrake actuating lever and strut lever for damage or distortion.

(9) Check the backing plate for distortion and ensure that all attaching bolts are securely tightened.

TO ASSEMBLE AND INSTAL

(1) Lubricate the wheel cylinder bore with clean hydraulic brake fluid, dip each piston and cup in the hydraulic fluid and instal the cup on the piston so that the lip edge of the cup will be facing the spigot end of the piston.

(2) Dip each piston and cup assembly in clean hydraulic brake fluid and insert in opposite ends of the wheel cylinder so that the cup lips will be facing each other with the return spring interposed between the two pistons, instal a rubber boot on each end of the cylinder and over the piston to retain the piston assemblies in position in the cylinder.

(3) Fit the spring retainers to secure the rubber boots to the wheel cylinder.

(4) Fit the bleeder screw to the wheel cylinder and tighten.

(5) Instal the wheel cylinder to the backing plate and secure with the two retaining bolts. Fit a suitable clamp to hold the wheel cylinder components in place.

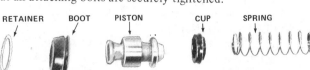

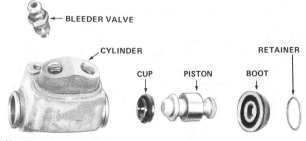

Exploded View of Wheel Cylinder Components.

(6) Ensure that the brake line/s are clean then connect to the wheel cylinder.

(7) Fit the handbrake actuating lever and the self adjuster arm onto the pivot pin and secure the pivot pin through the rear brake shoe with the 'C' clip.

(8) Hook one end of the energising spring to the adjuster arm and hook the other end into the lower hole in the handbrake actuating lever.

(9) Smear a coating of high melting point grease onto the friction surfaces where the brake shoes contact the backing plate.

(10) Refit the handbrake cable into the elbow on the end of the handbrake actuating lever, and if necessary refit the handbrake cable assembly to the equaliser.

(11) Sparingly lubricate the handbrake actuating lever pivot, the adjusting ratchet, the strut and the handbrake cable connection with high melting point grease.

(12) Mount the brake shoes onto the backing plate with the strut adjusting ratchet assembly interposed between the two shoes, and retain the shoes with the hold down springs and pins.

NOTE: If the stop plunger was removed from the backing plate as described in TO REMOVE AND DISMANTLE a new assembly should be installed to the backing plate.

(13) Connect the upper and lower brake shoe return springs to the brake shoes and remove the clamp from the wheel cylinder.

(14) Check that the brake shoes are seating correctly and that they are backed off sufficiently to allow the brake drum to be installed.

(15) Instal the brake drum and secure with the countersunk screw.

(16) Rotate the brake drum to ensure that the brake shoe linings are not dragging.

(17) Fit the road wheel and tighten the retaining nuts in a diagonal sequence.

(18) Adjust the brake shoes and bleed the hydraulic system as described in the appropriate sections.

(19) Lower the vehicle to the ground and road test.

4. FRONT WHEEL DISC BRAKES

BRAKE PADS
To Remove and Instal

The brake pads should be examined for wear every 10,000 kilometres (6000 miles) and should be removed and renewed if upon inspection, they are worn down to a thickness of 4 mm. or less.

(1) Jack up the front of the vehicle, place on stands and remove the road wheel.

(2) Using a suitable pair of pliers close the end of the split pins retaining the brake pads and remove the split pins from the caliper assembly.

(3) Remove the anti squeal shim retaining clips and lift out the brake pads with the two anti squeal shims.

NOTE: Ensure that the brake pedal is not depressed while the brake pads are removed.

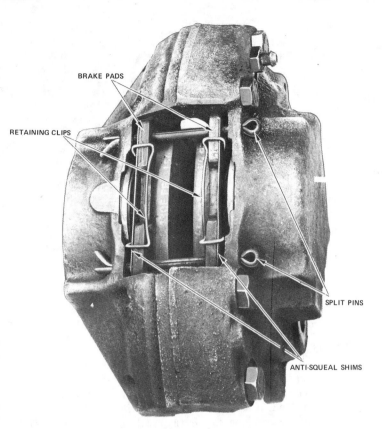

Assembled View of Brake Caliper.

Installation is a reversal of the removal procedure with attention to the following:

When installing the anti squeal shims, position the arrows in the direction of rotation.

CALIPER
To Remove

(1) Remove the brake pads as described in the previous section.

NOTE: If the caliper assembly is being removed for the purpose of overhaul it will be advantageous to depress the brake pedal to bring the pistons out into contact with the disc, thus facilitating the removal of the pistons once the caliper is removed.

(2) Disconnect the brake pipe at the flexible brake hose connection on the caliper shield.

(3) Peen back the locking tabs and remove the two caliper attaching bolts, detach the flexible brake hose and shield and withdraw the caliper assembly from the vehicle.

NOTE: Under no circumstances should the bolts clamping the two halves of the caliper be slackened.

To Dismantle and Assemble

(1) Clean the outside of the caliper with methylated spirits.

(2) Remove the dust cover retaining rings and ease the rubber dust covers out of the groove in piston and off the caliper.

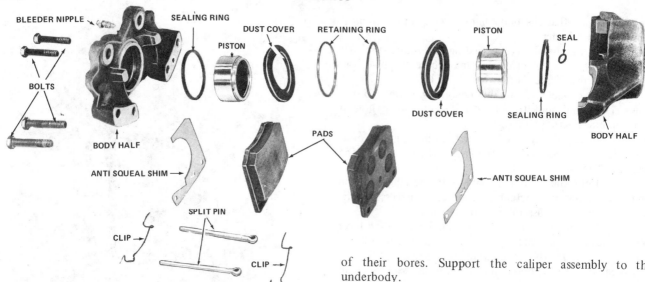

Exploded View of Caliper Components.

(3) Using a low air pressure applied at the hydraulic fluid pipe hole in the caliper, hold against one of the pistons and gently force the other piston out of its bore in the caliper. Withdraw the piston.

(4) Plug the bore of the withdrawn piston with a piece of cloth and force out the other piston in a similar manner.

(5) Remove the sealing rings with a small screwdriver ensuring that the bores or the sealing ring grooves are not damaged.

(6) Clean all components, except the brake pads, in methylated spirits and examine them for wear. Discard the sealing rings and dust covers.

(7) Ensure that new sealing rings are correctly seated in the caliper bore grooves.

(8) Apply brake fluid to the sealing rings, caliper bores and pistons and push the pistons squarely into the bores.

(9) Instal the dust covers, ensuring that the outer lip engages the groove on the caliper, and the inner groove in the piston.

(10) Instal the retaining rings to secure the dust covers in position in the caliper grooves.

To Instal

Installation is a reversal of the removal procedure with attention to the following points:

Torque the caliper attaching bolts to 6.90 kg/m. Bend back the lock tabs to secure the caliper attaching bolts.

After installing the pads, depress the brake pedal to reposition the pistons in the caliper bores.

Top up the master cylinder and bleed the hydraulic system. See the appropriate sections.

BRAKE DISCS
To Remove

(1) Raise the front of the vehicle and remove the wheel cap, road wheel and hub grease cap.

(2) Remove the two securing bolts and locking tabs and remove the caliper from the stub axle bracket, insert a spacer between the pads to prevent the pistons moving out

of their bores. Support the caliper assembly to the underbody.

(3) Remove the split pin, take off the castellated retainer, and unscrew and remove the plain adjusting nut on the end of the stub axle.

(4) Remove the thrust washer and outer hub bearing cone and roller assembly and withdraw the hub and disc assembly from the stub axle.

(5) Mark the hub in relation to the disc, bend back the locking tabs, remove the four securing bolts, and lock plates and separate the hub and brake disc. Discard the four bolts and lock plates.

(6) If necessary, release the lock washers, remove the securing bolts and withdraw the disc shield from the stub axle.

(7) If necessary, remove the hub bearings and seal as described in the FRONT SUSPENSION section of this manual.

To Instal

(1) Clean all parts and inspect for wear, cracks and/or bends, repair or renew as necessary. Ensure that all mating surfaces are perfectly clean.

(2) Mount the disc shield on the stub axle bracket, instal and tighten the securing bolts with lock washers and turn up the lock washer tabs to lock the bolts.

(3) Clean the mating faces of the brake disc and the hub flange, position the disc on the hub flange according to the marks made on removing, and instal four new bolts and locking plates.

(4) Tighten the bolts to a torque of 4.7 kg/m and turn up the tabs on the lock plates to lock the bolts.

(5) If the hub bearings and seals have been removed, assemble, instal and adjust the hub bearings as described in the FRONT SUSPENSION section of this manual.

(6) Check the disc run-out as follows:

(a) Remove the split pin and the castellated nut securing the tie-rod ball joint to the steering arm and using a suitable puller disconnect the two components.

(b) Suitably mount a dial indicator gauge to the steering arm so that the gauge plunger will bear against one side of the disc and as near as possible to the centre of the pad track.

(c) Zero the dial gauge, rotate the hub and disc assembly on the stub axle and check the disc run-out at this point. Run-out should not exceed 0.050 mm. total indicator reading.

(d) If the disc run-out is in excess of the limits specified recheck the hub flange and disc mating surfaces for dirt or burrs, and the hub bearings for correct adjustment. Check the run-out of the hub flange, mount the hub in a lathe and take a cut across the flange face. Do not remove metal in excess of that required to true-up the face of the flange.

If a hub flange is true and the fault is in the disc, fit a new disc and recheck.

(7) Instal the brake caliper assembly and secure with the two retaining bolts and lock tabs as described earlier.

(8) Instal the tie-rod end ball joint at the steering arm and secure with the castellated nut and a new split pin.

(9) Instal the road wheel(s) and tighten the retaining nuts securely.

(10) Lower the front of the vehicle and road test.

5. REAR BRAKE BACKING PLATE

TO REMOVE AND INSTAL

(1) Raise the rear of the vehicle and support on stands placed under the axle housing.

(2) Take off the wheel cap, remove the road wheel, take out the retaining screw and remove the brake drum.

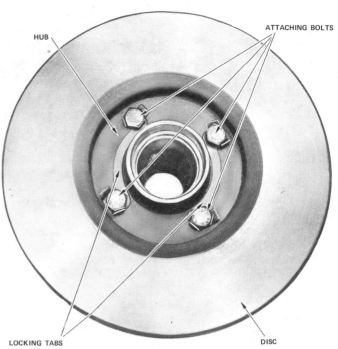

Brake Disc to Hub Attaching Bolts and Locking Tabs.

(3) Using a suitable pair of pointed nose pliers disconnect the handbrake cable from the actuating arm situated on the rear brake shoe.

(4) Disconnect the hydraulic brake pipe/s at the back of the wheel cylinder and plug the pipe and the wheel cylinder to prevent the entry of dirt into the hydraulic system.

(5) Using a tube or socket spanner through one of the holes in the axle shaft flange, remove the four bolts and spring washers securing the axle shaft bearing retainer and brake backing plate to the flange on the end of the axle case tube.

(6) Using a suitable slide hammer type puller attached to the axle shaft flange, withdraw the axle shaft and bearing assembly.

(7) Remove the brake backing plate assembly from the flange on the end of the axle tube and withdraw the brake cable through the backing plate.

Installation is a reversal of the removal procedure with attention to the following points:

Use new gaskets where gaskets are installed.

Adjust the brake shoes and bleed the hydraulic system see appropriate sections for procedures.

6. HANDBRAKE ASSEMBLY

FLOOR MOUNTED TYPE LEVER
To Remove and Instal Lever Assembly

(1) Remove the centre console where fitted and pull back the carpet from around the handbrake lever assembly.

(2) Loosen and remove the retaining screws and withdraw the handbrake lever rubber boot.

(3) With the handbrake in the released position and working beneath the vehicle remove the spring clip, the clevis pin and the wave washer to disconnect the handbrake primary link connection from the handbrake lever arm.

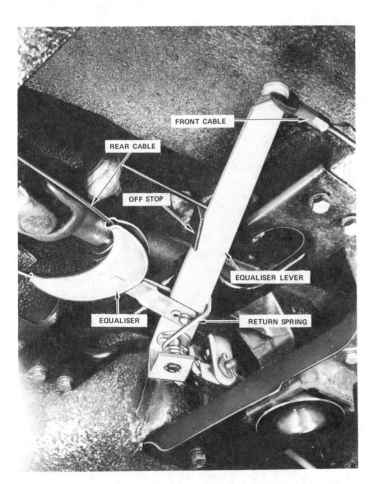

Underbody View Showing Handbrake Equaliser Lever Arrangement for Dash-Mounted Control.

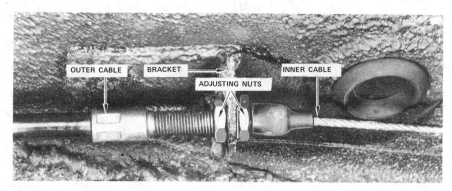

Underbody View Showing Rear Handbrake Cable Adjusting Point.

(4) Unscrew the two bolts attaching the handbrake lever assembly to the floor pan and withdraw the assembly from within the vehicle.

Installation is a reversal of the removal procedure with attention to the following:

Lubricate the cable at the equaliser and the handbrake actuating levers.

Lubricate the cable guides and also the clevis pin at the primary link connection to the handbrake lever. With the handbrake assembly installed it will be necessary to adjust the cable as described in the relevant section.

DASH MOUNTED TYPE LEVER
To Remove and Instal Lever and Front Cable

(1) Raise the rear of the vehicle and place on stands under the axle housing.

(2) Disconnect the front cable from the equaliser lever and loosen the adjusting nuts, withdraw the cable from the bracket under the right hand side floor pan.

(3) From inside the vehicle, unhook the front cable from the handbrake lever through the slot provided in the outer casing.

(4) Remove the bolts attaching the handbrake lever assembly and shroud at the dash panel and bulkhead and remove the assembly complete from the vehicle.

(5) Withdraw the front handbrake cable.

Installation is a reversal of the removal procedure with attention to the following points:

With the handbrake lever assembly installed and the front cable connected, adjust the cable at the adjusting nuts on the bracket under the right hand floor pan, until the slackness is taken up. See BRAKE ADJUSTMENT for the complete adjusting procedures.

Grease the cable fittings at the equaliser lever and at the handbrake lever.

REAR CABLES
To Remove and Instal

(1) Raise the rear of the vehicle and support on stands under the rear axle housing.

(2) Take off the wheel cap, remove the road wheel, take out the countersunk screw and remove the brake drum from both rear wheel assemblies.

(3) Using a pair of suitable pliers disconnect the handbrake cable connection from the actuating lever at both rear brake shoe assemblies.

(4) Loosen the adjusting nuts and disconnect the cable from the bracket under the right hand rear floor pan.

(5) Remove the spring clip and disconnect the cable from the bracket under the left hand rear floor pan.

(6) If not already disconnected, detach the rear cable at the equaliser assembly.

(7) Unclip the cable from the radius arms of the rear suspension and withdraw the assembly from the vehicle.

Installation is a reversal of the removal procedure, with attention to the following points:

Lubricate the equaliser, the cable guides and the handbrake actuating levers.

With the handbrake assembly installed it will be necessary to adjust the cables as described in the relevant section.

7. BRAKE ADJUSTMENT

REAR BRAKE SHOES AND HANDBRAKE

(1) Raise the rear of the vehicle and support on stands under the rear axle housing so that the wheels are clear of the floor.

(2) Rotate the wheels in a forward direction to ensure that the brake shoes are not dragging.

(3) Depress the brake pedal two or three times to centralise the shoes, then apply and release the handbrake continuously until the clicking sound of the brake adjusting ratchets are no longer audible.

(4) Models with floor mounted handbrake control, position the handbrake in the released position, turn the adjusting nuts located on the right hand rear underbody bracket to eliminate all slack from the handbrake cable assembly and give a clearance of 0.500 to 1.000 mm. between the stop plungers and the handbrake actuating levers.

As the adjustment is carried out at the right hand side cable attachment, it will be necessary to relocate the cable position by sliding through the equaliser thus ensuring equal adjustment to both rear brake assemblies.

Models using dash mounted handbrake control, position the handbrake control in the released position, turn the adjusting nuts located at the right hand side underbody bracket for the front cable assembly to give a clearance of 0.50 to 1.5 mm. between the equaliser lever and the stop on the support bracket, thus eliminating all slack from the front cable. Follow the procedure given for models fitted with floor mounted handbrake control to adjust the rear handbrake cable.

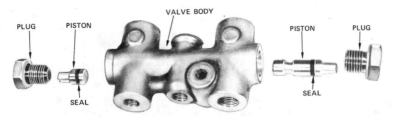

Dismantled View of Brake Pressure Differential Valve and Switch Assembly.

8. HYDRAULIC SYSTEM

TO BLEED

Bleeding the hydraulic system is not a routine maintenance operation and will only be necessary when some portion of the equipment has been disconnected or fluid drained off, thereby allowing air to enter the system.

NOTE: Where pressure differential valve assembly is fitted it will require centralising after the bleeding operations have been completed, see under the appropriate heading for the procedure.

(1) Fill the fluid reservoir with clean hydraulic brake fluid and maintain it at least one-third full throughout the entire bleeding operation.

(2) Attach a rubber bleeder tube to the bleeder valve at the right hand front brake caliper and allow the other end of the tube to be immersed in a small amount of fluid contained in a clean glass jar.

(3) Unscrew the bleed valve one complete turn.

(4) Depress the brake pedal slowly the full extent of its travel and allow it to return without assistance.

(5) Repeat operation (4) until a constant stream of fluid, without any air bubbles, is being discharged into the glass jar, hold the brake pedal down and tighten the bleeder valve.

(6) Carry out the bleeding operation at the other brake assemblies in order of their proximity to the master cylinder.

NOTE: Do not allow the fluid level in the reservoir to fall below the one third full level at any time during the bleeding operation or air will enter the system and a fresh start will have to be made. Always use new fluid for topping up the reservoir.

(7) Remove the bleeder tube and top up the reservoir to the level indicated.

(8) Centralise the pressure differential valve after completing the bleeding operations when fitted, see PRESSURE DIFFERENTIAL VALVE SECTION for procedure.

9. PRESSURE DIFFERENTIAL VALVE

TO REMOVE AND INSTAL

(1) Raise the engine bonnet and fit fender covers to both front fenders.

(2) Disconnect the four brake pipes from the valve and switch assembly and plug the ends to prevent the loss of fluid and ingress of dirt.

(3) Disconnect the wiring plug from the warning light switch.

(4) Remove the retaining bolt and withdraw the differential valve and switch assembly from the vehicle.

Installation is a reversal of the removal procedure.

NOTE: The differential valve assembly is a non-serviceable item and should it prove defective in operation it should be replaced with a new unit.

TO CENTRALISE THE VALVE ASSEMBLY

After a failure in the hydraulic system has been encountered and repaired, the brake warning light will normally continue to be illuminated. In order to deactivate the circuit a pressure differential or unbalanced condition must be attained in the opposite brake system to the one that was repaired or bled last.

With the ignition switch turned to the ON position or the accessories position. Determine the outlet brake pipe at the differential valve which is in the opposite system to the one repaired, and loosen the brake pipe nut.

With the aid of an assistant, depress the brake pedal slowly to centralise the pressure differential valve and extinguish the warning light. Instantly the warning light goes out, tighten the outlet pipe nut.

Recheck the master cylinder reservoir fluid level and top up if necessary.

10. VACUUM SERVO UNIT

DESCRIPTION

The servo unit is of the suspended vacuum type and is installed between the brake pedal and the master cylinder.

The valve and rod assembly of the servo unit and the pedal push rod are on the same axis and in the case of a vacuum failure act as a single push rod without assistance.

TO CHECK OPERATION

(1) Road test the vehicle by driving the vehicle and applying the brakes three or four times to normalise the hydraulic system.

(2) Apply the brakes at approximately 40 km/h, check the stopping ability and that the vehicle brakes evenly.

(3) If on application the vehicle does not stop satisfactorily e.g. the brake pedal is spongy at foot, air is present in the hydraulic system.

Bleed the hydraulic system as described in HYDRAULIC SYSTEM section.

(4) If the vehicle does not brake evenly, i.e. pulling either to the left or right hand side, the brake adjustment is

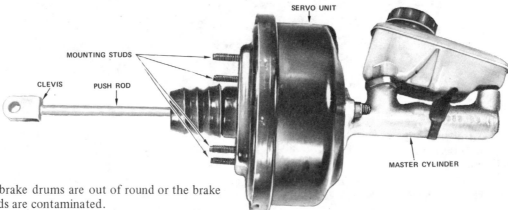

Vacuum Servo Unit and Master Cylinder

incorrect or the brake drums are out of round or the brake linings or disc pads are contaminated.

Adjust the brakes correctly or machine the brake drums or renew the contaminated linings or disc pads and rectify the cause of contamination.

(5) Switch off the engine and place the transmission in neutral and check the servo unit operation.

(6) Pump the brake pedal until the vacuum is deflated. Press the pedal and holding the foot on the pedal, start the engine and check the operation of the vacuum system.

If the pedal falls away under foot then the vacuum system is operative.

Should the pedal fail to fall away when the engine has been started, the vacuum system can be considered inoperative.

(7) Neutralise the transmission and ensure that the brake pedal is fully off, start the engine and run at medium speed then switch off the ignition.

Let the vehicle stand for approximately 1–2 minutes then apply the brake pedal two or three times and check the operation.

If there is no vacuum assistance during the operation then the vacuum system has developed a leak or the one way check valve is defective.

(8) To check the hydraulic system operation, stop the engine, expel the vacuum from the vacuum system, press the pedal and hold the pedal down firmly and check for fall away.

If the pedal gradually falls away under pressure then

the master cylinders or brake lines are leaking. Repair or replace the components where necessary.

TO REMOVE AND INSTAL

NOTE: The servo unit is a non-serviceable item and should it prove defective in operation it should be replaced with a new unit.

(1) Disconnect the brake fluid pipes at the master cylinder and plug the pipes to prevent the entry of dirt.

(2) Disconnect the vacuum pipe from the non-return valve on the servo unit.

(3) Remove the nuts and washers attaching the master cylinder to the servo unit and detach the master cylinder and reservoir assembly.

(4) Take out the spring clip, clevis pin and pin bushes retaining the push rod to the brake pedal.

(5) Remove the nuts attaching the servo unit to the bulkhead and withdraw the assembly from the vehicle.

Installation is a reversal of the removal procedure with particular attention to the following:

It will be necessary to bleed the system as described previously when installation is completed.

Check for fluid and vacuum leaks.

11. BRAKE FAULT DIAGNOSIS

1.   Brake pedal hard.

Possible cause	*Remedy*
(a) Incorrect shoe linings fitted.	— Check and replace linings with recommended type.
(b) Frozen pedal pivot.	— Rectify or renew pivot pin and bush if fitted.
(c) Restricted brake line from master cylinder.	— Check brake line and remove restriction or renew line.
(d) Frozen wheel cylinder or calliper piston/s.	— Check, free up or renew pistons.
(e) Vacuum-servo system inoperative.	— Check servo system and rectify.

2.   Brake drag due to pressure build-up.

Possible cause	*Remedy*
(a) Clogged master cylinder ports.	— Check and clean master cylinder and fluid reservoir.
(b) Frozen wheel cylinder or calliper piston/s.	— Check, free up or renew pistons.
(c) Frozen handbrake linkage.	— Free up or renew linkage.
(d) Broken or stretched brake shoe return springs.	— Renew defective springs.
(e) Frozen handbrake cables.	— Free up or renew cables.
(f) Blocked vent in fluid reservoir cap.	— Check vent and remove obstruction.

3. **Lower spongy brake pedal.**

Possible cause	*Remedy*
(a) Incorrectly adjusted brake shoes.	— Check and adjust brake shoes.
(b) Lack of sufficient fluid in system.	— Check for leaks, replenish fluid to specified level and bleed brake system.
(c) Air in brake hydraulic system.	— Bleed hydraulic system.

4. **Brake locks on application.**

Possible cause	*Remedy*
(a) Gummy linings or disc pads due to oil or fluid contamination.	— Clean and renew linings or disc pads.
(b) Bent or eccentric brake drum/s.	— Check and renew faulty drum/s.
(c) Incorrect linings fitted.	— Check and renew linings in pairs with recommended type.
(d) Broken or stretched brake shoe return spring/s.	— Check and renew faulty spring/s.

5. **Brake pedal pulsates.**

Possible cause	*Remedy*
(a) Bent or eccentric brake drum or disc.	— Check and renew drums or disc as required.
(b) Loose or worn front hub bearings.	— Adjust or renew front hub bearings.
(c) Bent rear axle shaft.	— Check and renew faulty components.

6. **Brake fade at high speed.**

Possible cause	*Remedy*
(a) Incorrect shoe adjustment.	— Check and adjust shoe to drum clearance.
(b) Eccentric or bent brake drum.	— Check and renew faulty component.
(c) Lining/s saturated with hydraulic fluid.	— Renew contaminated lining/s.
(d) Incorrect linings fitted.	— Check and instal recommended linings in sets.

7. **Brakes overheat.**

Possible cause	*Remedy*
(a) Incorrect shoe adjustment.	— Check and adjust shoe to drum clearance.
(b) Broken shoe return spring/s.	— Renew faulty spring/s.
(c) Faulty handbrake cables and/or adjustment.	— Check cables, renew or adjust.
(d) Frozen wheel cylinder pistons.	— Free up or renew faulty components.
(e) Obstructed or damaged hydraulic-hose or line.	— Remove obstruction or renew hydraulic hose or line.
(f) Obstructed master cylinder compensating port.	— Clear compensating port.
(g) Blocked vent in master cylinder reservoir cap.	— Check and remove obstruction in vent.

ELECTRICAL SYSTEM

SPECIFICATIONS

BATTERY

Type	12 volt
Specific gravity:	
Fully charged	1.280 at 20 deg C
Discharged	1.140 at 20 deg C
Polarity	Negative earth

GENERATOR

Make	Lucas
Type	C40
Output maximum	22 amps
Brush length:	
New	18.23 mm
Worn minimum	7.16 mm
Commutator undercut of	
segments	0.30 mm
Field resistance	6 ohms
Ratio — engine to gener-	
ator	1.5:1
Fan belt deflection	13 mm
Torque wrench setting —	
Max:	
Pulley nut	2.35 kg/m
Mounting bracket	3.46 kg/m
Mounting bolts — gener-	
ator	2.49 kg/m

GENERATOR REGULATOR

Type	Lucas RB340
Mechanical adjustments:	
Voltage regulator arm-	
ature to core air gap	1.14 — 1.24 mm
Current regulator arm-	
ature to core air gap	1.14 — 1.24 mm
Cut-out armature to core	
air gap	0.90 — 1.10 mm
Cut-out armature to core	
points just touching	0.40 mm
Cut-out blade deflection .	0.25 mm
Electrical adjustments:	
Cut-out — cut in	
voltage	12.6–13.4 volts
— opening	
voltage	9.25–11.25 volts
Current regulator load	
setting	22 amps
Voltage regulator open	
circuit setting	14.4–15.6 volts at amb-
	ient temp. of 20 deg C
*Voltage setting for	
temperature variation . . .	14.5–15.3 volts at 20
	deg C

*For every 10 deg C rise in ambient temperature reduce the setting by 0.2 volts, for every 10 deg C drop in ambient temperature increase the setting by 0.2 volts.

ALTERNATOR

Make and model:

Lucas	15 AC with 8TR regulator
	15 ACR with 11TR integral regulator
	17 ACR with 11TR integral regulator
Bosch	28 G1 with separate regulator
	35A-K1 with separate regulator

15AC Alternator:

Polarity	Negative earth
Rated output	28 amps at 14 volts and 6000 rpm
Stator windings	3 phase star connected
Field resistance	4.1 – 4.5 ohms at 20 deg C
Brush length – new	13 mm
– worn min ..	5 mm
Brush spring tension	198 – 280 g
Voltage regulator	8TR not adjustable
Regulated voltage	14.1 – 14.5 volts
Pulley nut torque – max ..	3.8 kg/m

15ACR, 17ACR Alternators:

Polarity	Negative earth
Rated output – 15ACR ..	34 amp at 14 volts and 6000 rpm
– 17ACR ...	36 amp at 14 volts and 6000 rpm
Stator windings	3 phase star connected
Stator resistance	0.133 ohms/phase
Field resistance – 15ACR .	4.1 – 4.5 ohms at 20 deg C
Field resistance – 17ACR .	3.9 – 4.4 ohms at 20 deg C
Brush length – new	13 mm
– worn min ..	5 mm
Brush spring tension	198–280 g
Voltage regulator	11TR not adjustable
Regulated voltage	14.0 – 14.4 volts
Pulley nut torque – max ..	3.8 kg/m

28G1, 35A–K1 Alternators:

Polarity	Negative earth
Rated output – 28G1 ...	28 amp
– 35A–K1 .	35 amp
Stator windings	3 phase star connected

Stator resistance	0.23–0.29 ohms/phase at 20 deg C
Field resistance	4.0 – 4.4 ohms
Brush length – new	14 mm
– worn min ..	9 mm
Brush spring tension	300–395 g
Regulated voltage	14.1–14.6 volts
Pulley nut torque – max	
– with key ...	4 kg/m
– without key .	6 kg/m
Regulated voltage	14.1–14.6 volts

STARTER MOTOR

Make and pinion operation:

Lucas	M35G–C inertia
	M35AK inertia
	M35G–HA pre-engaged
	M35J pre-engaged
	M100 pre-engaged
Bosch	U–GF pre-engaged
Number of poles	4

Commutator type:

M35G	Barrel type
M35J–FA	Barrel type
M35J–EA	Face type
M35–AK	Face type
M100	Face type
U–GF	Barrel type

Brush length – min:

Lucas barrel type	9 mm
Bosch barrel type	13 mm
Lucas face type	9.5 mm

Brush spring tension:

M35G–C	420 g
M35G–HA	800 g
M35J–FA	800 g
M35J–EA	480 g
M35–AK	800 g
M100	480 g
U–GF	1275 g
Armature end float	0.1–0.3 mm

Pinion stop clearance:

Lucas – pre-engaged	0.25 – 0.51 mm
Bosch – pre-engaged	0.30 – 0.76 mm

No load current draw – max:

M35J–EA – Lucas	65 amp
U–GF – Bosch	55 amp
All other models	60 amp

DISTRIBUTOR

Control	Vacuum and centrifugal advance

Type and make:

1300 HC – model	71BB – AMA	
– ident. color . .	Red and black	
– make	Motorcraft	
1300 LC – model	71BB – AKA	
– ident. color . .	Red and green	
– make	Motorcraft	
1600 GT – model	71BB – ARA	
– ident. color . .	Purple	
– make	Motorcraft	
1600 HC – model	71BB – AMA	
– ident. color . .	Red and black	
– make	Motorcraft	
1600 LC – model	71BB – ANA	
–ident. color . . .	Red and white	
– make	Motorcraft	
2000 HC – model	71BB – UB	
– ident. color . .	Red	
–make	Motorcraft	
*1600 – model	4R71BB – AA	
– ident. color . .	White	
– make	Lucas	
*2000 – model	71BB – UB	
– ident. color . .	Red	
– make	Autolite	

*Australian produced vehicles

Direction of rotation:

1300	
1600	Anti-clockwise
2000	Clockwise

Drive:

1300	
1600	Skew gear from camshaft
2000	Auxiliary shaft

Firing order:

1300	
1600	1–2–4–3
2000	1–3–4–2

Shaft end float:

Motorcraft	0.38 mm
Lucas	0.13 mm

Breaker point gap:

Motorcraft	0.64 mm
Autolite	0.64 mm
Lucas	0.41 mm

Breaker point spring tension:

Motorcraft	430–530 g
Autolite	430–530 g
Lucas	480–595 g

Dwell angle:

Motorcraft	48–50 deg
Autolite	48–50 deg
Lucas	58–62 deg

Capacitor capacity:

Motorcraft	0.21 – 0.25 mfd
Autolite	0.21 – 0.25 mfd
Lucas	0.18 – 0.25 mfd

Initial advance:

1300	
1600	6 deg btdc
2000	4 deg btdc

SPARK PLUGS AND LEADS

Plug size:

1300	
1600	14 mm
2000	18 mm taper seat

Plug make and type:

1300	
1600	AG22 Autolite
2000	BF32 Autolite

Plug gap	0.64 mm

Plug tightening torque:

OHV engine	3.8 kg/m
OHC engine	2.4 kg/m
High tension leads	Radio suppressed

IGNITION COIL

Type	Ballast resistor
Ballast resistor	1.3 – 1.4 ohms at 24 deg C

1. BATTERY

MAINTENANCE

Maintenance consists mainly of regular inspection and servicing.

(1) Keep the battery and its surroundings clean and dry. Give the top of the battery particular attention to prevent electrical leakage between the cell terminals.

(2) Remove the vent plugs and see that the vent holes are clear.

(3) Check the electrolite level and top up as necessary. The correct level is just over the top of the separators. Do not overfill or acid will escape through the vent holes with detrimental effect to the connections and adjacent parts of the vehicle.

(4) Use only distilled water for topping up.

NOTE: Never use a naked light when examining the battery, as the gases given off by the battery can be dangerously explosive.

(5) If the battery required an excessive amount of topping up, the cause should be sought. If overcharging is suspected, check the regulator setting. If one cell in particular is at fault, check the case for cracks. Never transfer electrolite from one cell to another.

(6) Keep the positive and negative terminals clean and apply a small amount of petroleum jelly to the terminals to prevent corrosion.

TO REMOVE AND INSTAL

(1) Release the terminal screws and carefully remove the cables from the terminal posts.

(2) Remove the battery holding clamp and lift the battery from the vehicle.

Reverse the above operation to instal the battery and smear petroleum jelly on the terminals to prevent corrosion. Do not over tighten the terminal screws and make sure of the correct earth polarity, see specifications.

TO CLEAN BATTERY CASE

(1) Remove the battery from the vehicle as previously described.

(2) Pour hot water over the battery being careful not to pour water through the vent holes of the filler caps.

(3) Wipe the battery case clean and dry.

(4) If there is a crack in the case or around the base of the terminal(s) the faulty components should be renewed.

TO CLEAN BATTERY CARRIER

If the battery electrolite has overflowed and contaminated the surrounding body panels it will be necessary to remove this contamination and repaint the surfaces where necessary. The contamination can be neutralised by using an alkaline solution consisting of two tablespoons of washing soda to a quart of boiling water. Cloudy ammonia can also be used in concentrated form. Both these items are readily available at grocery stores.

After neutralising the contaminated body panels allow them to dry. Clean off the old paint and repaint the surfaces with an anti-rust based paint.

TO TEST

Use a hydrometer to check the specific gravity of the battery electrolite. Refer to specifications for the specific gravity readings of a fully charged and discharged battery.

If the battery is in a low state of charge or 'flat' it should be charged and then each cell tested using suitable cell testing equipment to determine if all the cells are serviceable, a weak or shorted cell will necessitate the battery being renewed.

2. SPARK PLUGS

TO SERVICE

The sparking plugs should be removed for inspection, cleaning and resetting at intervals of 10,000 kms (6000 miles). Sparking plugs removed from an engine in good mechanical condition, operating under normal conditions, should have a light powdery deposit ranging in color from light brown to greyish tan. After considerable service the electrodes will show signs of wear or normal burning.

Sparking plugs showing a thick black oily deposit indicate an engine in poor mechanical condition or possibly that a plug with too low a heat range has been fitted.

Sparking plugs showing a white or yellowish deposit indicate sustained high speed driving or possibly that plugs of too high heat range have been fitted, particularly when these deposits are accompanied by blistering of the porcelain and burning of the electrodes. Check the recommended heat range for the engine (see Specifications) and select the correct heat range if operating conditions are abnormal.

If the heat range is correct, clean the plugs on a sanding machine, and blow clean with compressed air.

Set the electrode gap (see Specifications) by bending the earthing electrode and test the plugs on a reliable tester. *NOTE: Never attempt to set the electrode gap by bending the centre electrode or a cracked insulator will result.*

Clean the sparking plug thread and, using new gaskets, fit the plugs, screwing up finger tight.

Using a torque wrench, tighten the sparking plugs to the recommended torque.

3. HIGH TENSION LEADS

The high tension cables between the sparking plugs and the distributor cap and the centre high tension terminal on the distributor cap and the ignition coil are of special manufacture and have a carbon impregnated core instead of the normal wire core.

This is to eliminate radio interference and care must be exercised when removing the cables from the sparking plugs to ensure that the cables are not damaged by stretching, which will break the core and render the cable unserviceable.

Always remove the cable from a sparking plug by pulling on the cable terminal. Use the same care when connecting the cable to the plug.

If a cable has a broken core it will cause misfiring.

Check the cables for perishing or cracking and renew as required. Never attempt to repair defective cables.

The cables may be carefully cleaned, using a cloth moistened with kerosene, then wiping completely dry.

Also check the distributor cap for cracks or tracking between the high tension terminals on both the inside and outside of the cap. Renew the cap if cracks or tracking is evident.

Check the carbon brush in the centre of the distributor cap for evidence of arcing and renew as necessary.

4. GENERATOR

DESCRIPTION

The generator fitted as standard equipment is a 22 amp 12 volt unit which is controlled by a three bobbin regulator and is driven by a Vee belt from the crankshaft pulley.

The generator is wired and connected negative to earth.

TO TEST IN POSITION

In the event of a fault in the charging circuit, adopt the following procedure to locate the cause of the trouble.

(1) Check that the drive belt is not slipping, and adjust if necessary.

(2) Check that the generator and regulator are connected correctly. The larger generator terminal D must be connected to the regulator terminal D and the smaller generator terminal F to regulator terminal F.

(3) Switch off all lights and accessories, disconnect the cables from the terminals of the generator and connect the two terminals with a short length of wire.

(4) Start the engine and set to run at normal idling speed.

(5) Clip the lead of a moving coil type voltmeter, calibrated 0-30 volts, to one generator terminal and the other lead to a good earthing point on the yoke.

(6) Gradually increase the engine speed, when the voltmeter reading should rise rapidly and without fluctuation. Do not allow the voltmeter reading to reach more than 24 volts and do not race the engine in an attempt to increase the voltage. It is sufficient to run the generator up to about 1000 rpm. If there is no reading

check the brush gear. If there is a low reading of approximately 0.5 to 1 volt, the field winding may be at fault. If there is a reading of 4 to 5 volts, the armature may be at fault.

(7) Examine the commutator and brushes. Hold back each of the brush springs and move the brush by pulling gently on its flexible connector. If the movement is sluggish, remove the brush from its holder and ease the sides by gently polishing on a smooth file. Always replace brushes in their original positions. If the brushes are worn, so that they do not bear on the commutator, new brushes must be fitted and bedded to the commutator.

(8) Test the brush spring tension with a spring scale.

(9) The tension of the springs when new should be to specifications. Fit new springs if the tension is below this figure.

(10) If the commutator is blackened, or dirty, clean it by holding a "com stick" against it while the engine is slowly turned. Re-test the generator; if there is still no reading on the volt-meter there is an internal fault, and the complete unit, if a spare is available, should be replaced. Otherwise the unit must be dismantled for internal examination.

(11) If the generator is in good order, remove the link from between the terminals and restore the original connections, taking care to connect generator terminal D to the regulator terminal D and the generator terminal F to the regulator terminal F.

(12) Remove the lead from the D terminal on the regulator and connect the voltmeter between the cable and a good earth on the vehicle.

(13) Run the engine as before and the reading on the voltmeter should be the same as that taken directly on the generator. No reading on the voltmeter indicates a break in the cable to the generator.

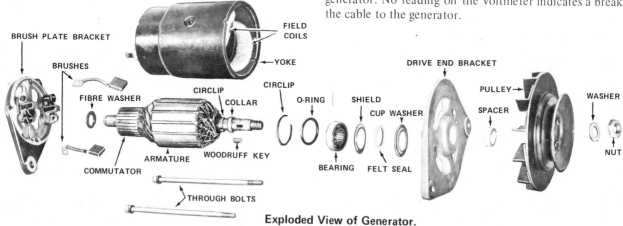

Exploded View of Generator.

(14) Repeat the test on the F terminal of the regulator, connecting the voltmeter between the cable and earth, when the results should be the same.

TO REMOVE AND INSTAL

(1) Disconnect the cables from the D and F terminals on the generator. Note that the heavy cable is connected to the D terminal on the generator.

(2) Slacken the adjusting link and the two pivot bolts on the generator and push the generator in against the cylinder block. Remove the fan belt from the generator pulley.

(3) Remove the two pivot bolts and the adjusting bolt and lift the generator from the engine.

Installation of the generator is a reversal of the removal procedure. Do not overtighten the fan belt, or the generator and water pump bearings will be over-stressed. There should be approximately 13 mm. (0.5 in.) deflection under finger pressure on its longest run between pulleys. Apply a few drops of engine oil to the oil hole for the commutator end bearing of the generator.

TO DISMANTLE

(1) Remove the two through bolts and take off the commutator end bracket. Note the fibre washer on the armature shaft between the end of the commutator and the end bracket.

(2) Withdraw the armature and pulley end bracket as an assembly from the generator body.

(3) Hold the armature in a vice and remove the pulley nut and spring washer. Withdraw the pulley and remove the Woodruff key from the shaft.

(4) Press the armature shaft out of the ball bearing in the pulley end bracket. Note the cup washer and retainer between the bearing and the shoulder of the shaft. If the pulley end bearing is to be renewed, see TO RENEW BEARINGS.

TO CHECK BRUSHES

(1) Check if the brushes are sticking. Clean them with petrol and lightly polish the sides on a smooth file. The brushes must be replaced in their original positions.

(2) Check the brush spring tension. If the tension is below specifications new springs should be fitted.

(3) Renew the brushes if worn to the minimum length and bed the brushes to the commutator.

(4) The brushes can be bedded in the following manner. Wrap a piece of fine sand paper or glass paper around the commutator and fit the brush plate to the armature shaft.

(5) Instal the new brushes into their holders and fit the brush springs into position.

(6) Either glue the ends of the glass paper together or hold them with a suitable tool.

(7) Rotate the brush plate bracket around the commutator while holding the glass paper in place; the brushes will be cut to the shape of the commutator.

NOTE: Make sure the brushes are bedded to the correct rotation of the armature.

TO RECONDITION COMMUTATOR

(1) A commutator in good condition will be smooth and free from pits or burned spots. Clean the commutator with a petrol moistened cloth. If this is ineffective, polish with a strip of fine glass paper while rotating the armature. To remedy a badly worn commutator, mount the armature, with or without the drive end bracket, in a lathe, rotate at high speed and take a light cut with a very sharp tool.

(2) Do not remove more metal than is necessary. Polish the commutator with very fine glass paper. Undercut the insulators between the segments to specifications, a hacksaw blade ground down to the thickness of the insulator will act as a good under-cutting tool.

TO TEST ARMATURE

The testing of the armature winding requires the use of a voltage drop tester and growler. If these are not available the armature should be checked by substitution. No attempts should be made to machine the armature core or to true a distorted armature shaft.

TO TEST FIELD COILS

(1) Measure the resistance of the field coils, without removing them from the generator yoke, by means of an ohmmeter connected between the field terminal and the yoke. A very high reading indicates a faulty connection or an open circuit in the field circuit, whilst a reduced reading indicates an earthed field coil. If an ohmmeter is not available, connect a 12 volt DC supply with an ammeter in series between the field terminal and generator yoke. The ammeter reading should be approximately 2 amperes. No reading on the ammeter indicates an open circuit in the field winding, and a higher reading indicates an earthed field coil.

(2) In either case, unless a replacement generator is available, the field coils must be replaced. To do this carry out the procedure outlined below, using a pole shoe expander and a wheel-operated screwdriver.

(3) Remove the insulation piece which is provided to prevent the junction of the field coils from contact with the yoke.

(4) Mark the yoke and pole shoes in order that they can be fitted in their original positions.

(5) Unsolder the field wires from the terminal post or drill out the terminal post rivet. Note the position of the field wires for reassembly.

(6) Unscrew the two pole shoe retaining screws by means of a wheel-operated screwdriver.

(7) Draw the pole shoes and coils out of the yoke and lift off the coils.

(8) Fit the new field coils over the pole shoes and place them in position inside the yoke. Take care to ensure that the taping of the field coils is not trapped between the pole shoes and the yoke.

(9) Locate the pole shoes and field coils by lightly tightening the fixing screw.

(10) Insert the pole shoe expander, open it to the fullest extent and tighten the screws.

(11) Finally tighten the screws by means of the wheel-operated screwdriver and lock them by staking.

(12) Replace the insulation piece between the field coil connections and the yoke.

(13) Re-solder the field coil connections to the field coil terminal tags and re-rivet the assembly to the yoke.

TO RENEW BEARINGS

The generator is fitted with a ball bearing at the drive end and a porous bronze bush at the commutator end.

Bearings that are worn to such an extent that they will allow side movement of the armature shaft, must be replaced.

To replace the bearing bush at the commutator end, proceed as follows:

(1) The correct method of removing the bush in these cases is to use a lipped expanding type extractor. Where such a tool is not immediately available the bush can be removed by screwing a suitable tap in for a few turns and withdrawing the bush and tap complete. Care should be taken to screw the tap squarely into the bush to avoid damage to the bracket.

(2) Press the new bearing bush into the end bracket using a shouldered, highly polished mandrel of the same diameter as the shaft which is to fit in the bearing. Porous bronze bushes must not be opened out after fitting, or the porosity of the bush may be impaired.

NOTE: Before fitting the new bearing bush, it should be allowed to stand for 24 hours completely immersed in thin engine oil. This will allow the pores of the bush to be filled with lubricant. In cases of extreme urgency, this period may be shortened by heating the oil to 100 deg. C. (212 deg. F.) when the time of immersion may be reduced to 2 hours.

The ball bearing, which is a push fit in the drive end bracket, is replaced as follows:

(3) Drill out the rivets securing the bearing retaining plate to the end bracket.

(4) Push the bearing out of the end bracket and remove the corrugated washer, felt washer and oil retaining washer.

(5) Before fitting the replacement bearing see that it is clean and pack it with high melting point grease.

(6) Place the oil retaining washer, felt washer and corrugated washer in the bearing housing in the drive end bracket.

(7) Locate the bearing in the housing and push it home (hand pressure only is needed).

(8) Fit the bearing retaining plate. Insert the new rivets from the inside of the end bracket and open the rivets by means of a punch to secure the plate rigidly in position.

Under no circumstances is it permissible to use the drive end bracket as a support. This could cause damage to the corrugated washer, and as a result the armature would not maintain its correct position and the brushes may overhang the edge of the commutator.

TO REASSEMBLE

To reassemble the generator reverse the dismantling procedure and note the following points:

(a) Care must be taken when pressing the pulley end bracket on to the armature shaft to avoid damage to the bracket and to the armature windings.

(b) To fit the commutator end bracket, trap the brushes in a slightly raised position with the ends of the brush springs. Fit the bracket to within approximately 13 mm. (0.5 in.) of the end of the yoke and release the brushes with a small screwdriver or similar tool. Ensure that the brush springs seat correctly on the brushes before fitting the two through bolts.

5. GENERATOR REGULATOR

DESCRIPTION

The regulator is a current-voltage control unit employing a cut-out relay and two regulator units, one to control the voltage and the other to control the current in the charging circuit.

Any electrical setting of the unit should be carried out as rapidly as possible to avoid errors due to heating.

The ambient temperature and temperature of the unit windings should be approximately 20 deg c (68 deg F).

Before disturbing any of the electrical settings, be sure that the trouble does not lie outside the regulator unit.

Check that the battery is fully charged and ensure that the generator driving belt is not slipping.

Check that the generator is operating satisfactorily by bridging terminals D and F and connecting a test voltmeter between this link and earth. Run the generator up to 1000 rpm, when a rising voltage should be shown.

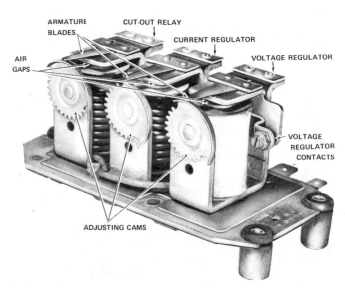

View of Regulator Showing the Cam Adjusters and Control Units.

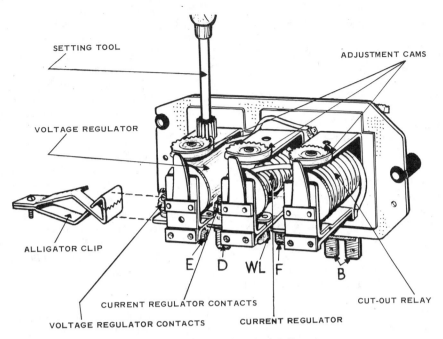

SETTING TOOL

ADJUSTMENT CAMS

VOLTAGE REGULATOR

ALLIGATOR CLIP

E D WL F B

CURRENT REGULATOR CONTACTS

CUT-OUT RELAY

VOLTAGE REGULATOR CONTACTS

CURRENT REGULATOR

Voltage Regulator Electrical Adjustment.

Check the regulator unit earth connections and the continuity of the charging circuit.

If the test ammeter pointer fluctuates beyond the maximum on each side of the mean value with the generator running at a constant speed, the contacts of the voltage and current regulators may require cleaning or the mechanical setting has been upset and the air gap requires adjusting.

TO CHECK AND ADJUST VOLTAGE REGULATOR

Each unit of the control box is correctly adjusted during assembly and it should not be necessary to make further adjustment. If, however, the battery does not keep in a charged condition, or if the generator output does not fall when the battery is fully charged, the settings should be checked and, if necessary, corrected.

It is important before altering the regulator settings to check that the low state of charge of the battery is not due to a battery defect or a slipping drive belt.

The open circuit setting of the voltage regulator unit should be checked with the control box cover in position and at normal operating temperature.

All tests must be made as quickly as possible, to avoid over-heating the regulator windings, in which case a false reading will result.

It is important that only good quality instruments are used in testing and adjusting. These should comprise of 0 to 30 volt moving coil voltmeter and a 40-0-40 scale moving coil ammeter.

NOTE: A generator run at high speed on open circuit will build up a high voltage. When testing and adjusting the voltage regulator, increase the engine speed slowly or a false setting will result.

(1) Disconnect the wire from the regulator terminal B.

(2) Connect the positive lead of the test voltmeter to the regulator terminal D or WL, and the negative lead to the regulator base.

(3) Start the engine and gradually increase the speed until the voltmeter needle flicks and then steadies (approximately 1500 generator rpm). This should occur at a voltmeter reading between 14.4 and 15.6 volts at 20 deg C.

Carefully note the ambient temperature and apply a correction for any temperature variation, refer specifications.

NOTE: If the voltmeter reading is unsteady, this may be caused by dirty contacts, a slipping generator drive belt, incorrect mechanical setting of the regulator unit or a faulty internal connection.

(4) If the voltmeter reading is steady but not within the limits specified, the regulator requires adjustment. Increase the engine speed gradually until the maximum voltmeter reading is obtained. This should not be more than .50 volts above the specified setting. If the voltmeter reading continues to rise, swinging the needle right over, it indicates that either the regulator points are not operating or there is a faulty earth between the regulator and the body.

If the points are not opening, the regulator should be renewed, as it is probable that they are welded together or shorted, or there is an open circuit in the shunt coil.

(5) Adjust the voltage regulator as follows: Stop the engine and remove the regulator cover.

(6) Restart the engine and run at the speed where the voltmeter reading is steady (approximately 1500 generator rpm). Carefully check this reading — it should be to specifications.

(7) Using the adjusting tool Lucas number 54381—742, rotate the voltage regulator adjustment cam until the correct setting is obtained. Turn the tool clockwise to

increase the voltage or anti-clockwise to decrease the voltage.

(8) Check the setting by stopping the engine, re-starting, and running the generator again at the test speed.

(9) Stop the engine, disconnect the voltmeter, reconnect the wire to the B terminal and replace the regulator cover.

TO CHECK AND ADJUST CURRENT REGULATOR

(1) Remove the regulator cover and isolate the voltage regulator unit by bridging the adjustable contacts with an alligator clip.

NOTE: This is necessary to ensure that the generator will develop its maximum rated output, irrespective of the charge condition of the battery.

(2) Disconnect the wire from terminal B of the regulator and connect the test ammeter between this terminal and the disconnected wire.

(3) Connect a lamp load across the battery. This load is necessary to enable the generator to develop its full rated output.

(4) Start the engine, run the engine at approximately 4500 rpm and note the ammeter reading.

This should indicate a current equal to the maximum rated output of the generator ± 1.50 amps.

NOTE: A fluctuating reading may be due to dirty contacts, incorrect mechanical setting, a loose generator drive belt or a faulty internal connection.

(5) If the reading is steady but is outside the specified limits, adjust the current regulator as follows:

Using the special tool, rotate the adjustment cam until the correct setting is obtained. Turn the tool clockwise to increase the current, or anti-clockwise to decrease the current.

(6) Switch off the engine, remove the spring clip from the voltage regulator contacts, remove the ammeter, reconnect the wire to terminal B and replace the regulator cover.

TO CHECK AND ADJUST CUT-OUT ELECTRICAL SETTING

Cut-out Cut-in Voltage

NOTE: When testing and adjusting the voltage regulator, the electrical setting should be completed as quickly as possible to avoid errors due to the coils heating.

(1) Connect the positive lead of the test voltmeter to the regulator terminal D or WL, and the negative lead to the regulator base.

(2) Connect a lamp load across the battery to ensure a drop in the voltmeter reading.

(3) Start the engine and slowly increase the speed. Note the maximum reading obtained on the voltmeter, this should be to specifications of regulated voltage.

NOTE: After registering the maximum reading, the voltmeter needle should drop suddenly, indicating that the cut-out contacts close.

(4) If necessary, adjust the cut-in voltage as follows: Remove the regulator cover, ensure the engine speed is below cut-in speed and using the special tool, rotate the cut-out adjustment cam clockwise to increase the cut-in voltage or anti-clockwise to decrease the cut-in voltage. Re-check the voltage setting.

(5) Repeat the procedure until the correct setting is obtained.

(6) Stop the engine, remove the lamp load, disconnect the voltmeter and replace the regulator cover.

Cut-Out Drop-Off Voltage

(1) Disconnect the wire from the regulator terminal B.

(2) Connect the positive lead of the test voltmeter to terminal B and the negative lead to the regulator base.

(3) Run the engine up to half throttle and then gradually decrease the engine speed, noting the voltage at which the needle flicks back to zero, indicating that the cut-out contacts open. Refer specifications for readings.

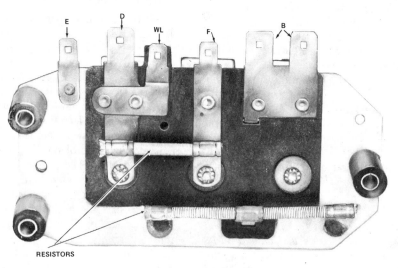

RESISTORS

View of Underside of Regulator.

(4) If the drop-off voltage is outside these limits adjust the cut-out as follows:

(5) Stop the engine and remove the regulator cover.

(6) Carefully bend the cut-out fixed contact bracket to vary the contact gap.

Close the contact gap to increase the drop-off voltage. Open the contact gap to reduce the drop-off voltage.

NOTE: There should be 0.25 – 0.51 mm (0.010 – 0.020") moving contact follow-through or blade deflection when the armature is pressed fully downwards.

(7) Start the engine and re-check as outlined in operation (3).

(8) Stop the engine, disconnect the voltmeter, reconnect the wire to terminal B and replace the regulator cover.

TO CHECK AND ADJUST MECHANICAL SETTINGS

Air gap settings are accurately set during manufacture and should require no further attention.

If, however, the points have been removed for cleaning, it will be necessary to re-set them to obtain the correct armature to core air gap clearance.

After completing any mechanical setting, the regulator must be tested and the electrical settings adjusted as previously outlined.

Current and/or Voltage Regulator Air Gap Adjustments.

(1) Remove the regulator from the car.

(2) Using the special tool, turn the adjustment cam to the position giving minimum lift to the armature spring, i.e., fully anti-clockwise.

(3) Slacken the adjustable point locknut and screw the point a few turns outwards.

(4) Insert the feeler blade (See Specifications for gap setting), between the armature and the top of the core, taking care not to turn up or damage the copper shim. Position the feeler blade over the core as far as the rivet heads will allow and then press the armature firmly downwards.

(5) Whilst holding the armature down, screw the adjustable point inwards until it just touches the fixed point and then secure in this position by tightening the locknut.

(6) Release the armature and check the armature to core air gap. Refer Specifications.

(7) Carry out the electrical setting as previously outlined.

Cut-out Relay Air Gap

The cut-out armature to core air gap should be to Specifications measured by means of a suitable feeler blade inserted as far as the rivet heads will allow.

If an adjustment is necessary, carefully bend the back stop as required. Carry out the electrical settings as previously outlined.

6. ALTERNATOR

DESCRIPTION

The alternator charging unit uses a rotating field and pole shoe assembly and together form a rotor unit. Low amperage current is fed through the slip rings and brushes to the field windings so wear on brushes and slip rings is very slight and maintenance is reduced to a minimum.

The output current is generated in the fixed stator windings and is three phase alternating current (AC).

The stator windings are wound on a laminated soft iron former and are star-connected.

As it is not possible to recharge a storage battery with alternating current, it is necessary to rectify the output of the stator windings to direct current (DC). This is done by the bank of diodes mounted within the alternator end bracket.

The output of the alternator is governed by the control unit and built in characteristics of the alternator.

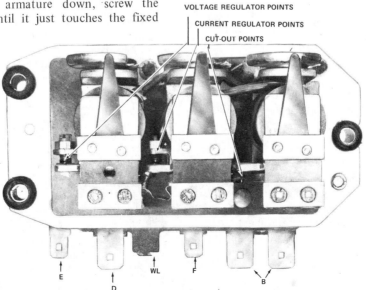

VOLTAGE REGULATOR POINTS
CURRENT REGULATOR POINTS
CUT-OUT POINTS

E   D   WL   F   B

View of Regulator Showing Adjustable Contacts for Armature Air Gap Settings.

An electrical cut-out unit is not necessary with the alternator charging system as the diodes stop a reverse current flow through the alternator.

SERVICE PRECAUTIONS

(1) Make sure the battery is connected the correct way. Refer to Specifications.

(2) Do not short out or ground any terminals common to the charging circuit.

(3) Always disconnect the battery before connecting a battery charger.

(4) If a booster battery is used always connect it in a parallel circuit, i.e. positive to positive (+ to +) and negative to negative (− to −) to maintain a 12 volt supply pressure.

(5) Never disconnect the battery or terminals in the charging circuit while the engine is running.

(6) Regularly check fan belt tension, deflection should be 13 mm (0.5 in).

(7) Keep battery terminals clean and all electrical connections tight.

(8) Disconnect the battery and alternator when arc welding on the vehicle.

(9) Never connect a condenser to the field (F) terminal.

TO REMOVE AND INSTAL THE ALTERNATOR

(1) Fit covers to both fenders and disconnect the battery terminal.

(2) Disconnect the terminal block at the alternator if used by pulling on the terminal block, not the wires, or remove the terminal nuts and lock washers to remove the wiring from the terminals.

(3) Loosen both mounting bolt nuts.

(4) Remove the fan belt from the pulley.

(5) Remove both mounting bolts while supporting the alternator with the hand, do not drop or bump the alternator.

Installation is the reverse of removal with particular attention to the following:

(1) Do not over tighten the mounting bolts as broken mounting lugs could result.

(2) Do not over tension the fan belt.

(3) Apply pressure to the mounting end bracket only, when adjusting the fan belt.

(4) Check the wiring where soldered to the slide on terminals in the terminal block or where soldered to the eye terminals.

TO CLEAN PARTS

(1) Do not immerse units of the alternator in cleaning solvents as damage to the windings will result.

(2) The end brackets and bearings may be washed in kerosene or similar cleaning fluid after they have been completely dismantled from the unit. They should be thoroughly dried after cleaning.

(3) Compressed air can be used to carefully blow out the dust from the stator winding and the field winding on the rotor.

(4) Using a petrol damp rag carefully clean the slip ring assembly and check for any damage or wear. Never machine the slip rings. Any burrs or burn marks can be polished out with very fine sand paper (not emery paper).

(5) Clean the brushes and brush holders using a damp petrol rag and check and remove any burrs from the holders.

TO CHECK AND TEST COMPONENT PARTS

All parts being electrically tested should be resting on a non-conductive pad.

Slip Rings

(1) Visually check the slip ring assembly for damage.

(2) Remove all burrs and burn marks with fine sand paper (not emery paper).

(3) With a 110 volt AC test lamp and prods, test the slip ring unit for an electrical bridge between the slip rings. The test lamp should not light.

NOTE: The above test is carried out with the field leads disconnected.

(4) If the test lamp lights up or burns dimly indicating an electrical bridge, a new slip ring assembly will have to be fitted.

(5) Using the 110 volt AC test lamp and prods check the slip ring to earth insulation by holding one prod on the rotor shaft and touching the other prod to each slip ring in turn.

(6) If the test lamp lights up or burns dimly indicating an electrical short, a new slip ring assembly will have to be fitted.

Field Windings and Rotor Assembly

(1) The insulation to earth test is done with the 110 volt test equipment, connect one of the test prods to one of the field wires and the other test prod to one pole piece of the rotor.

(2) If the test lamp lights or burns dimly and no visual earthing can be seen and rectified, a new rotor assembly will have to be fitted.

(3) To check for bridged or internal shorting of the field coil, connect a pair of test leads to a 12 volt battery with an ammeter connected in series with one lead, connect the test leads one to each field wire and note the ammeter reading; a high reading over 3.5 amps indicates a bridged circuit within the coil. No reading on the ammeter indicates an open circuit exists in the field coil. In both the above cases a new rotor assembly will have to be fitted.

Stator Windings

(1) The insulation to earth test is done with the 110 volt test equipment, connect one test prod to one stator wire and the other test prod to the laminated stator winding frame.

(2) If the lamp lights or burns dimly indicating a short circuit, a new stator winding assembly must be fitted.

(3) To test the continuity of the stator winding connect a pair of test leads to a 12 volt battery, connect in series with one of the leads a 36 watt globe.

(4) Connect the test leads across any two leads of the stator winding, the lamp should light. Repeat the operation to the remaining leads alternately.

(5) If the light fails to light on any one of the tests then the stator winding assembly will have to be renewed.

Diodes

Before the diodes can be tested the wiring has to be unsoldered from the diode leads, using a very hot soldering iron and holding the diode lead with a pair of pointed pliers to dissipate the heat and protect the diode, unsolder each wire in turn after marking and noting their connected positions.

(1) Connect a pair of test leads to a 12 volt battery with a 1.5 watt globe in series with one lead, touch the diode wire with one lead and the heat sink of that diode with the other lead, then reverse the leads.

(2) Repeat the tests to all diodes in turn. The globe should light when the leads are connected in one way only.

(3) If any one or more of the diodes prove faulty, a new rectifier diode pack must be fitted .

NOTE: Never use a hand driven generator type tester to test diodes.

Brush Springs and Brushes

(1) Brush spring tension is tested with a push type spring tension gauge, push the spring and brush into the brush holder with the gauge until the face of the brushes and holder are flush. A serviceable spring should give a reading within specification limits. Replace unserviceable springs.

(2) The brushes should protrude from their holders, without tension on their springs when checking brush length. Fit new brushes when the measurement is less than specified.

Bearings

After cleaning and drying both bearings check both tracks and balls for chips and roughness, if serviceable repack with high melting point grease.

Sealed bearings cannot be washed but should be checked by hand for dryness and roughness.

Fit new bearings when in doubt of the serviceability of the old bearings.

LUCAS 15 AC ALTERNATOR
To Check and Test on Vehicle

The alternator uses a diode pack mounted to the brush end bracket by a nut and washers, the 8TR regulator control unit is mounted separately to the alternator and is not adjustable.

If the ignition warning light stays on after the engine has been started and run at approximately 1000 rpm, carry out the following tests and precautions.

(1) Do not open circuit any parts of the charging circuit while the engine is running.

(2) Do not short out or bridge any wiring or terminals at any time.

(3) Clean battery terminals, tighten all electrical connections, check wiring for shorts to earth and/or bridged circuits, make sure the battery is fully charged. If the battery is low, either charge it or replace it with one fully charged.

(4) Start the engine and allow it to run until normal operating temperature is reached.

(5) Stop the engine when it reaches operating temperature and disconnect the negative battery terminal.

(6) Remove the wiring connector from the alternator by holding the plastic cover and pulling it straight out.

(7) Reconnect the field terminal lead.

(8) Earth the negative (−) alternator terminal with a jumper lead.

(9) Connect a 0—50 amp ammeter to the alternator output terminal and the positive battery terminal.

(10) Connect a 0—20 volt voltmeter between the positive battery terminal and a good earth.

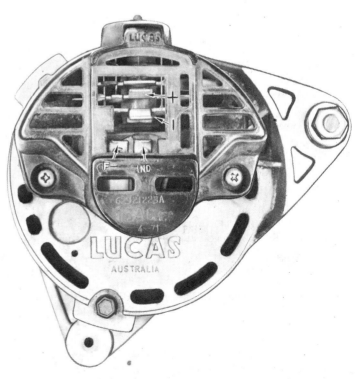

Lucas 15AC Alternator Showing Wiring Terminals.

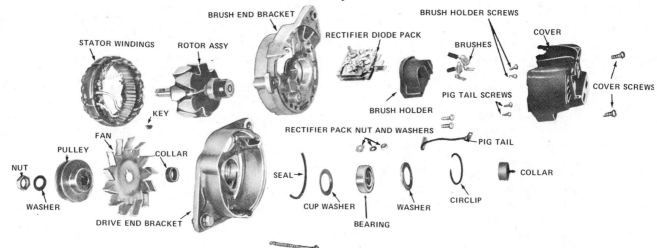

Exploded View of Lucas 15AC Alternator.

(11) Connect a 12 volt 2.2 watt globe between the positive battery terminal and the 'IND' (indicator light) terminal of the alternator with suitable wiring and make sure the globe cannot earth out.

(12) Connect a 35 amp 0–15 ohm variable resistance between the positive battery terminal and a good earth.

IMPORTANT: Only leave this unit connected long enough to complete the test.

(13) Connect a tachometer to the engine.

(14) Reconnect the negative battery terminal.

(15) Restart the engine and bring the engine speed up to 750 rpm and the 2.2 watt globe should go out.

(16) Increase the engine speed to 3000 rpm. Adjust the variable resistance until the voltmeter reads 14.0 volts, the ammeter should now read approximately 28 amps.

(17) If the 2.2 watt globe stays on from a dull glow to bright or fluctuates and the ammeter reading varies greatly, the alternator will have to be removed for repair, see TO REMOVE AND INSTAL THE ALTERNATOR section.

(18) After the test is completed stop the engine and remove the negative battery terminal and the test equipment.

(19) If the test proves the alternator to be serviceable, check the external control unit.

To Dismantle

After the unit is removed from the vehicle proceed to dismantle in the following steps:

(1) Remove the plastic cover by first removing the two mounting screws.

(2) Suitably tag the three stator wires so that they can be soldered back in their correct position.

(3) With a hot soldering iron and holding the diode wire link with a pair of long nosed pliers unsolder the three stator wires.

NOTE: If a very hot soldering iron is used the solder melts immediately and the transfer of heat is reduced to a minimum and so there is less likelihood of damage to the

diodes, *also by holding the wiring with a pair of pliers, the pliers absorb some of the heat, again protecting the diodes.*

(4) Loosen the nuts holding the rectifier unit.

(5) Remove the screws holding the brush holder assembly.

(6) Remove the brush holder and rectifier unit.

(7) Remove the three assembly screws after marking the position of each end bracket and the stator winding relative to each other.

(8) Using the special tool tap out the bearing in the slip ring end bracket.

(9) Remove the bearing, slip ring assembly and rotor as a unit.

(10) Remove the nut, washer, pulley, fan, woodruff key and spacer from the shaft at the drive end bracket.

(11) Press the rotor and shaft from the drive end bracket and bearing.

(12) Remove the bearing retainer clip and remove the bearing and shields from the end bracket.

(13) With a hot soldering iron unsolder the two field wires from the slip ring assembly.

(14) Carefully remove the slip ring assembly from the shaft.

(15) Remove the bearing from the slip ring end of the shaft using a bearing removing tool or by supporting the centre of the bearing in a suitable jig and press it off using a press. Specifications for making the special tool referred to in operation (8).

Select a piece of steel tubing to the following dimensions —

Length . . . . 76 mm (3 in)
Inside diameter . . . . 31.5 mm (1.24 in)
Outside diameter . . . . 33.5 mm (1.32 in)
Cap and plug one end leaving
 a recess of at least . . . . 38 mm (1.5 in)

To Assemble

The reassembling of the alternator is the reverse to dismantling with particular attention to the following points:

(1) Lubricate both ball races with a suitable grease. (Shell Alvania 'RA' or equivalent).

(2) The ball race on the slip ring end of the shaft is fitted with one shielded side next to the slip ring assembly.

(3) When fitting bearings always apply the fitting pressure on the section of the bearing being fitted. Do not apply the pressure through the balls or rollers.

(4) Take care not to damage the slip ring assembly when refitting.

(5) Resolder the field leads to slip rings with a hot soldering iron.

(6) When fitting the bearing and the drive end bracket assembly to the shaft, support the centre of the bearing, refer operation (3).

(7) Make sure the brushes are sitting in their holders.

(8) Fit the fan with blades towards the alternator.

(9) Fit the woodruff key into its keyway.

(10) Tighten the pulley nut to 3.8 kg/m (27 ft/lb).

To Check Voltage Regulator

(1) To test the control unit connect a 0–50 amp ammeter in series with the main alternator lead.

(2) Connect a 0–20 volt voltmeter from the positive battery terminal to a good earth.

(3) Reconnect the negative terminal of the battery.

(4) Start the engine and increase speed until a reading of not more than 5 amps is obtained. It may be necessary to put the parking lights on to give an external light load to the circuit.

(5) The voltmeter reading should now be 14.1 to 14.5 volts.

(6) If the reading is not within these limits the control unit, being non-adjustable, will have to be replaced.

(7) Stop the engine, disconnect the negative battery terminal, remove all test equipment and reconnect the wiring to the correct terminals.

LUCAS 15ACR AND 17ACR ALTERNATORS

These alternators are similar in construction to the 15AC model except that the regulator unit is integral with the alternator. The regulator is mounted on the brush holder and is protected by the end cover.

To Check and Test on Vehicle

If the ignition warning light stays on after the engine has been started and run at approximately 1000 rpm, carry out the following tests and precautions.

(1) Do not open circuit any parts of the charging circuit while the engine is running.

(2) Do not short out or bridge any wiring or terminals at any time.

(3) Clean battery terminals, tighten all electrical connections, check wiring for shorts to earth and/or bridged circuits, make sure the battery is fully charged. If the battery is low, either charge it or replace it with one fully charged.

(4) Start the engine and allow it to run until normal operating temperature is reached.

(5) Stop the engine when it reaches operating temperature and disconnect the negative battery terminal.

(6) Remove the battery live wire from the output

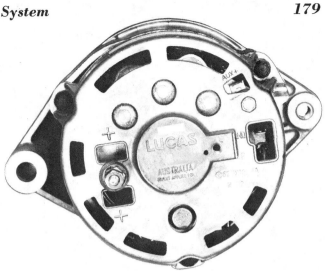

View of Slip Ring End Cover of Lucas 15 ACR, 17 ACR Alternator.

terminal of the alternator and connect a 0–50 amp ammeter in series with the alternator output terminal and the disconnected wire, reconnect the negative battery terminal.

(7) Switch on all lights and allow them to burn for approximately 5 minutes to reduce the charge of the battery and apply a load to the circuit.

(8) Start the engine and increase the speed to 2000 rpm when the ammeter should read approximately 28 amps for the 15ACR unit or 36 amps for the 17ACR unit.

(9) Should the alternator fail to reach the specified output the unit will have to be removed and overhauled or a replacement unit fitted.

To Dismantle and Assemble

The dismantling and assembling procedure is the same as for the 15AC alternator except that the regulator unit is mounted onto the brush holder, to remove the regulator unit remove the mounting screw and the terminal screws from the brush holder and remove the regulator unit.

To Check Voltage Regulator

(1) With a 0–50 amp ammeter connected as for testing the alternator output, connect a 0–20 voltmeter across the battery terminals.

(2) Start the engine and run at 1500–2000 rpm until

Lucas 8TR Alternator Regulator.

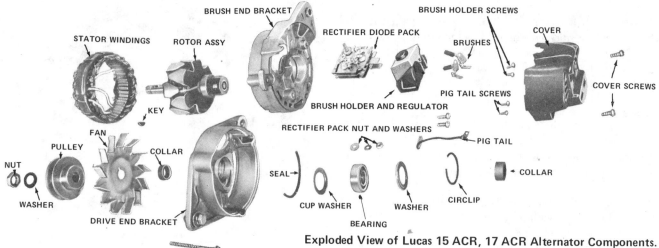

STATOR WINDINGS
ROTOR ASSY
BRUSH END BRACKET
RECTIFIER DIODE PACK
BRUSH HOLDER SCREWS
BRUSHES
COVER
KEY
PIG TAIL SCREWS
COVER SCREWS
BRUSH HOLDER AND REGULATOR
FAN
PULLEY
COLLAR
RECTIFIER PACK NUT AND WASHERS
PIG TAIL
NUT
SEAL
COLLAR
WASHER
CUP WASHER
BEARING
WASHER
CIRCLIP
DRIVE END BRACKET

THROUGH BOLTS

Exploded View of Lucas 15 ACR, 17 ACR Alternator Components.

the indicated charge is just below 10 amps when the voltmeter reading should be 14.1 – 14.5 volts.

(3) Should the above readings not be obtained the alternator will have to be removed and overhauled or a replacement unit fitted.

BOSCH 28G1 AND 35A–K1 ALTERNATORS
To Check and Test on Vehicle

(1) Check the condition and adjustment of the fan belt.

(2) Disconnect the battery negative terminal.

(3) Disconnect the wire from the B+ (BAT) terminal of the alternator.

(4) Connect one lead of a 0–50 amp ammeter to the alternator output terminal B+ (BAT) and the other lead to the lead removed from the output terminal.

(5) Connect the positive lead of a 0–20 test voltmeter

to the alternator output terminal and the voltmeter negative lead to a suitable earth on the alternator frame.

(6) Connect an adjustable carbon rheostat or a lamp bank across the terminals of the battery and ensure that the unit is in the off position.

(7) Disconnect the field wires DF and D+ from the alternator and suitably insulate to prevent them from shorting to earth.

(8) Using a suitable jumper lead, connect the field terminal DF to the alternator output terminal B+ (BAT).

(9) Connect an electric tachometer to the ignition low tension circuit.

(10) Reconnect the battery negative terminal.

(11) Start the engine and gradually increase the speed to approximately 2200 rpm.

(12) Maintain the voltage at 14.0 volts by adjusting the carbon pile or lamp bank.

(13) The reading on the ammeter should equal or exceed the rating of the alternator, refer Specifications.

NOTE: The above test should be carried out quickly. Do not run the engine for any extended period with test equipment connected.

(14) Allow the engine to return to its idling speed, turn off the external load then stop the engine and remove the negative lead from the battery.

(15) Disconnect the instruments and jumper lead from the field terminal.

(16) Reconnect the wires to the B+ (BAT) and DF and D+ terminals of the alternator and the battery lead to the negative post.

A low reading of below 70 per cent of the specified output, accompanied by a humming noise from the alternator is indicative of a short circuited positive diode.

A reading of approximately 5 amps below the rated output indicates a possible shorted diode.

In either case the alternator must be removed for overhaul and/or a replacement alternator fitted.

To Dismantle

(1) Scribe a mark parallel with the rotor shaft across both end brackets and the stator laminations as a reference mark for correct assembly.

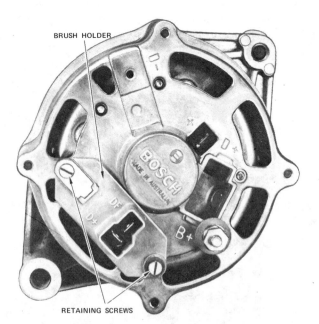

BRUSH HOLDER

RETAINING SCREWS

Bosch Alternator Showing Terminal Connections and Brush Holder Mounting.

(2) Remove the two screws retaining the brush holder to the slip ring end bracket and remove the brush holder.

(3) Remove the four screws securing the alternator components together and prise the drive end bracket and rotor assembly away from the stator and slip ring end bracket.

(4) Remove the waved washer from the bearing recess in the slip ring end bracket.

(5) Hold the rotor shaft in a vice with suitable protection between the shaft and vice jaws, loosen and remove the pulley retaining nut.

(6) Remove the lock washer, spacer where fitted, pulley, second spacer, fan and third stepped spacer from the rotor shaft.

(7) Suitably support the drive end bracket on a press and press the shaft and rotor from the bearing.

(8) Remove the second shouldered spacer from the rotor shaft.

(9) Remove the drive end bearing retaining plate screws and remove the plate, tap or press the bearing out of the drive end bracket.

(10) Using a suitable puller remove the bearing from the slip ring end of the rotor shaft.

(11) Remove the rectifier pack retaining screws and remove the rectifier pack and stator assembly.

(12) Unsolder the stator leads at the diode connections taking care not to overheat the diodes and separate the stator assembly from the diode pack.

NOTE: When soldering or unsoldering stator leads or bridges from the diodes grip the diode lead with a pair of long nosed pliers, this will safeguard the diodes by transferring any excess heat to the jaws of the pliers.

To Assemble

(1) Instal the drive end bearing into the drive end bracket with the shielded side of the bearing to the outside of the alternator, position the retaining plate and instal the screws, tighten evenly and securely.

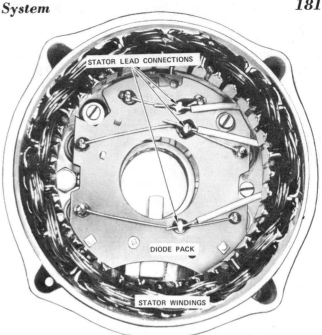

View of the Interior of the Slip Ring End Bracket of the Bosch Alternator Showing the Diode Pack and Stator Lead Connections.

(2) Instal the second stepped spacer removed onto the rotor shaft with the shoulder towards the bearing, check that the shaft stop ring is in the groove of the shaft.

(3) Instal the end bracket onto the rotor shaft, the bearing should not be tight on the shaft but if pressure is required press only on the inner section of the bearing using a suitable sleeve.

(4) Instal the first stepped spacer removed, the larger of the two, onto the rotor shaft with the shoulder towards the bearing.

(5) Instal the fan, plain spacer, pulley, spacer where fitted, lock washer and nut onto the rotor shaft.

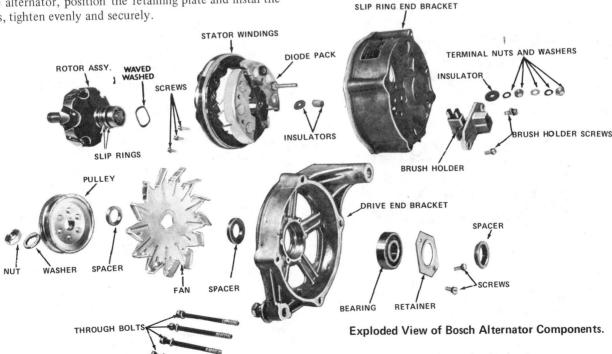

Exploded View of Bosch Alternator Components.

(6) Hold the rotor shaft in a vice with suitable protection between the shaft and vice jaws and tighten the nut to specifications.

(7) Press the slip ring end bearing onto the rotor shaft with the sealed side towards the rotor, only apply the fitting pressure to the centre of the bearing.

(8) Solder the stator leads to the diode connections taking care not to over heat the diodes, use a very hot soldering iron when soldering so that the joint is made quickly.

NOTE: When soldering or unsoldering diode leads or bridges from the diodes, grip the diode lead with a pair of long nosed pliers, this will safeguard the diodes by transferring any excess heat to the jaws of the pliers.

(9) Instal the rectifier pack into the slip ring end bracket and instal the screws and washers as noted on removal, the long screws are installed in the insulated holes and the short screws are fitted in the other two holes, tighten the screws securely.

(10) Position the stator windings onto the slip ring end bracket aligning the marks made before dismantling.

(11) Instal the waved washer in the bearing recess of the slip ring end bracket then instal the rotor assembly into the stator windings and slip ring end bracket aligning the marks made before dismantling.

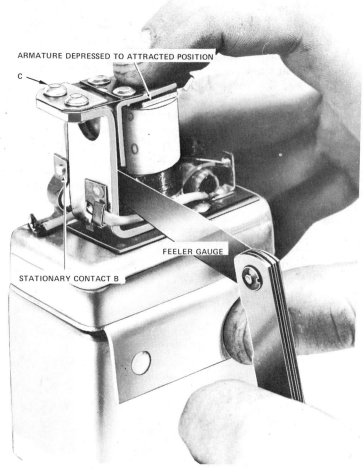

Showing Method of Checking Bosch Regulator Armature to Bracket Air Gap.

(12) Instal the four screws that hold the components together and tighten securely in a diagonal sequence.

(13) Instal the brush holder and brushes to the slip ring end bracket tightening the screws securely.

(14) Check the rotation of the rotor by hand which should spin freely. Instal the alternator on the engine.

To Check Voltage Regulator

(1) Disconnect the earth lead at the negative terminal of the battery and the lead at the alternator output terminal post B+.

(2) Using a 0–50 amp accurate ammeter and a 20 amp capacity variable rheostat connected in series, connect the positive lead of the test set to the lead removed from the alternator B+ terminal post.

(3) Connect the negative lead of the test set to the B+ terminal post on the alternator.

(4) Connect the positive lead of an 0–20 volt voltmeter to the B+ terminal post on the alternator and the voltmeter negative lead to earth on the alternator frame.

(5) Connect an electric tachometer in parallel with the low tension circuit of the distributor according to the manufacturer's instructions.

(6) Reconnect the earth lead to the negative terminal of the battery, start the engine and run at approximately 700 rpm for a quarter of an hour to bring the alternator and regulator to operating temperature.

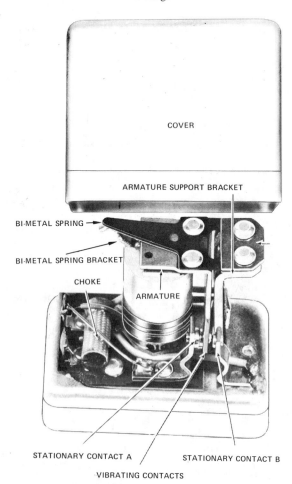

Bosch Regulator with the Cover Removed.

(7) When a stabilised temperature has been reached, adjust the variable rheostat to obtain an ammeter reading of 10 amps. Stop and restart the engine.

NOTE: If a variable rheostat is not available switch on the necessary lamps to obtain the 10 amps load.

(8) If the regulator is correctly set the voltmeter reading should be between 13.7 and 14.4 volts.

(9) Maintain a 10 amp reading on the ammeter by adjusting the variable rheostat, at the same time run the engine up to approximately 2400 rpm and check that the voltmeter reading does not vary from the first reading by minus 0.2 to plus 0.4 volts.

7. STARTER MOTOR

DESCRIPTION

Two makes of starter motor are used on these vehicles namely Lucas and Bosch.

The Lucas models fitted are of two types being inertia or pre-engaged. These starters again are divided into two types depending on their commutator design which is either of barrel or face manufacture.

The only Bosch starter motor fitted is the pre-engaged type with a barrel commutator.

Both makes and all the types of starter motors are controlled by the ignition switch through a solenoid switch.

The inertia type unit has a separately mounted solenoid switch with a heavy cable connecting the switch terminal with the starter terminal.

The pre-engaged type unit has the solenoid mounted on, and incorporated with the starter motor. When the solenoid is energized the plunger engages the pinion with the ring gear through a lever assembly and at the same time closes the electrical circuit to the starter motor.

INERTIA TYPE
To Test in Position

Check the battery condition and state of charge, refer to battery section of this manual.

Clean the battery terminals taking particular care to remove the scale from the positive terminal post and terminal.

Check the earth connections for tightness and cleanliness, do not over tighten terminals.

Switch on the lamps and operate the starter control.

If the lights go dim, but the starter motor is not heard to operate, the indication is given that the current is flowing through the starter motor windings, but that the armature is not rotating for some reason; possibly the pinion is locked in mesh with the geared ring on the flywheel. In this case the motor must be removed from the engine for examination.

Should the lamps retain their full brilliance when the starter switch is operated, check the circuit for continuity from battery to starter motor via the starter switch, and examine the connections at these units. If the switch is found to be faulty, a new switch must be fitted. If the supply voltage is found to be applied to the motor when the switch is operated, an internal fault in the motor is indicated and the unit must be removed from the engine for examination.

Sluggish or slow action of the starter motor is usually caused by a poor connection in the wiring, giving rise to a high resistance in the starter motor circuit. Check as described above.

If the starter motor is heard to operate, but does not crank the engine, indication is given of damage to the drive.

To Remove and Instal

(1) Disconnect the earth lead at the negative terminal on the battery.

(2) Disconnect the lead between the starter solenoid switch and the starter.

(3) Remove the three attaching bolts and remove the starter from the vehicle.

Installation is a reversal of the removal procedure. Take care not to over-tighten the electrical terminal connections.

To Test Brushgear and Commutator
Barrel Type Armature

It is necessary to remove the motor from the engine; first proceed as follows:

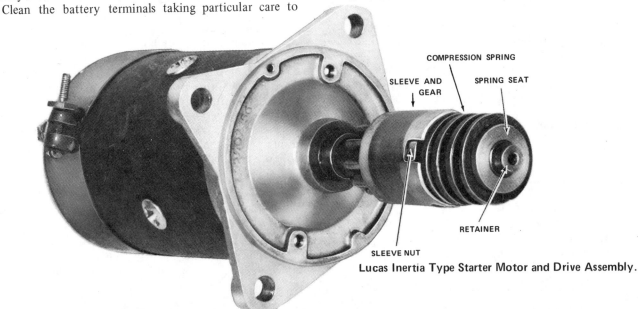

COMPRESSION SPRING

SLEEVE AND GEAR

SPRING SEAT

RETAINER

SLEEVE NUT

Lucas Inertia Type Starter Motor and Drive Assembly.

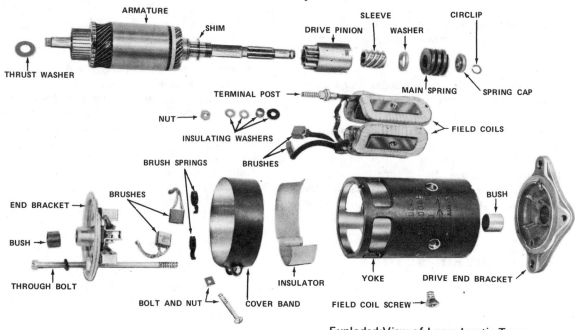

ARMATURE

SHIM

SLEEVE

CIRCLIP

DRIVE PINION

WASHER

THRUST WASHER

MAIN SPRING

SPRING CAP

TERMINAL POST

NUT

FIELD COILS

INSULATING WASHERS

BRUSHES

BRUSH SPRINGS

BRUSHES

END BRACKET

BRUSHES

BUSH

BUSH

THROUGH BOLT

INSULATOR

YOKE

DRIVE END BRACKET

BOLT AND NUT

COVER BAND

FIELD COIL SCREW

Exploded View of Lucas Inertia Type Starter Motor with Barrel Commutator.

(1) Disconnect the cable from the positive battery terminal to avoid any damage by causing short circuits.

(2) Disconnect the heavy cable from the starter motor.

(3) After removing the starter motor from the engine, secure the body in a vice and test by connecting it with heavy gauge cables to a 12 volt battery. One cable must be connected to the starter terminal and the other held against the body or end bracket. Under these light load conditions, the starter should run at a very high speed.

(4) If the operation of the motor is unsatisfactory, remove the cover band and examine the brushes and commutator. Hold back each of the brush springs and move the brush by pulling gently on its flexible connector. If the movement is sluggish, remove the brush from its holder and ease the slides by lightly polishing on a smooth file. Always replace the brushes in their original positions. If the brushes are worn so that they will not bear on the commutator, or if the brush flexible connector is exposed on the running face, they must be replaced.

(5) Check the tension of the brush springs with a spring scale. New springs should be fitted if the tension is below specifications.

(6) If the commutator is blackened or dirty, clean it by holding a petrol-moistened cloth against it while the armature is rotated by hand.

(7) Re-test the starter as described above, if the operation is still unsatisfactory, the unit must be dismantled for detailed inspection and testing.

Face Type Armature

For servicing procedures of starters fitted with this type of armature reference should be made to the appropriate sections under the heading of the LUCAS Pre-engaged Face Type starter motors.

To Dismantle and Assemble
Barrel Type Armature

(1) Remove the cover band, hold back the brush springs and lift the brushes from their holders.

(2) Remove the terminal nuts from the terminal post.

(3) Remove the two through bolts from the commutator end bracket, and withdraw the commutator end bracket from the yoke.

(4) Remove the drive end bracket, complete with armature and drive, from the starter motor yoke. If it is necessary to remove the armature from the drive end bracket it can be done after the drive has been dismantled. Reassembly is a reversal of the dismantling procedure.

Face Type Armature

(1) Remove the terminal nuts and washers from the terminal post.

(2) Remove the two through bolts from the commutator end bracket and ease the end bracket from the yoke.

(3) Note the fitted position of the brushes in the brush holder and remove the two field brushes from the holder.

(4) Remove the two screws holding the brush holder and dust cap to the commutator end bracket.

(5) Remove the earth brushes from the brush holder noting their fitted positions.

(6) Remove the brush holder from the end bracket and remove the brush springs.

(7) Remove the drive end bracket complete with armature and drive from the starter motor yoke. If it is necessary to remove the armature from the drive end bracket it can be done after the drive has been dismantled.

Assembly is a reversal of the dismantling procedure ensuring that the brushes are fitted into their original positions as noted on dismantling.

To Renew Brushes
Barrel Type Armature

If the brushes are worn so that they do not bear on the commutator, or if the flexible connectors are exposed on the running face, they must be replaced.

Two of the brushes are connected to terminal eyelets attached to the brush boxes on the commutator end bracket and two are connected to tappings on the field coils.

The flexible connectors must be removed by unsoldering and the connectors of the new brushes secured in their place by soldering. The brushes are preformed so that bedding to the commutator is unnecessary.

NOTE: The field coil brushes are press welded to the field coil buzz bar extensions, to aid installation of new brushes cut the old brush connectors approximately 6.35 mm. (0.25") from the weld, this section can then be used as a base to solder the new brushes into place.

The earth brushes can be rolled out of their terminals and unsoldered. The new earth brushes can be fitted to the terminals using the old brushes as a guide to the connector length.

Clamp the terminal over the new brush connector at the correct length and solder into position.

After the brush has been soldered into position carefully cut off the excess flexible connector lead with a hack saw.

Face Type Armature

(1) Check the brush holder and insulation of the commutator end bracket, replace burnt or damaged parts.

(2) For further service procedures see under the appropriate heading of the LUCAS Pre-engaged Face Type starter motor.

To Recondition Commutator

A commutator in good condition will be smooth and free from pits and burned spots. Clean the commutator with a petrol-moistened cloth. If this is ineffective carefully polish with a strip of fine glass paper while rotating the armature. To remedy a badly worn commutator, dismantle the starter drive and remove the armature from the end bracket. Mount the armature in a lathe, rotate at a high speed and take a light cut with a very sharp tool. Do not remove any more metal than is necessary. Finally polish with a very fine glass paper. The insulators between the commutator segments must not be undercut.

To Check Armature

(1) Examination of the armature may reveal the cause of failure, e.g., conductors lifted from the commutator due to the starter drive being engaged while the engine is running and causing the armature to be rotated at an excessive speed.

(2) The armature windings can be checked using a 110 volt test light and prod equipment.

(3) Using the test equipment hold one prod on the laminations of the armature and move the other prod around the commutator, the bulb should not light nor should there be any sign of arcing between the windings and the laminations or shaft.

(4) A damaged or shorted armature must be replaced.

(5) No attempt should be made to machine the armature core or to true a distorted armature shaft.

To Test Field Coils
Barrel Type Armature

Test the field coils for continuity by connecting a 12 volt battery with a 12 volt bulb in series between the tapping points of the field coils at which the brushes are connected. Failure of the lamp to light indicates an open circuit in the wiring of the field coils.

Lighting of the lamp does not necessarily mean that the field coils are in order, as it is possible that one of them may be earthed to a pole shoe or to the yoke. This may be checked with a 110 volt test lamp, the test leads being connected to one of the field coil tapping points and to a clean part of the yoke. Should the lamp light, it indicates that the field coils are earthed to the yoke.

In either case, unless a replacement starter motor is available, the field coils must be replaced. To do this, carry out the procedure outlined below, using a pole shoe expander and a wheel-operated screwdriver.

(1) Remove the insulation piece which is provided to prevent the inter-coil connector from contact with the yoke.

(2) Mark the yoke and pole shoes in order that they can be fitted in their original positions.

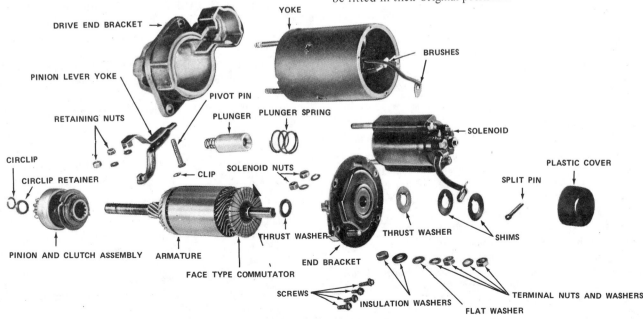

Exploded View of Lucas Pre-engaged Type Starter Motor with Face Type Commutator.

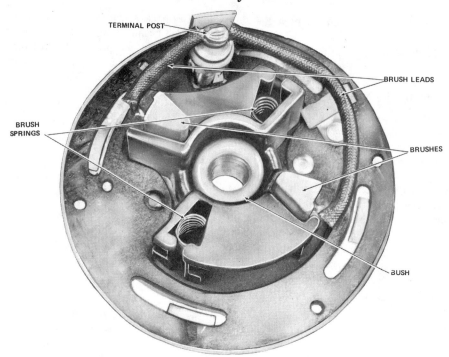

TERMINAL POST

BRUSH LEADS

BRUSH
SPRINGS

BRUSHES

BUSH

Lucas Starter Motor Brush Plate for Face Type Armatures.

(3) Unscrew the four pole shoe retaining screws by means of the wheel-operated screwdriver.

(4) Draw the pole shoes and coils out of the yoke and lift off the coils.

(5) Fit the new field coils over the pole shoes and place them in position inside the yoke. Take care to ensure that the taping of the field coils is not trapped between the pole shoes and the yoke.

(6) Locate the pole shoes and field coils by lightly tightening the fixing screws.

(7) Insert the pole shoe expander, open it to its full extent and tighten the screws.

(8) Finally tighten the screws by means of the wheel-operated screwdriver.

(9) Replace the insulation piece between the field connection and the yoke.

Face Type Armature

For the testing and replacing of the field coils of this type of starter motor reference should be made to Test Field Coils and Renew section of the LUCAS Pre-engaged Face Type starter motor.

To Renew Bearings

Bearings that are worn to such an extent that they will allow excessive side play of the armature shaft must be replaced. To replace the bearing bushes proceed as follows:

(1) Press the bearing bush out of the end bracket.

(2) Press the new bearing bush into the end bracket, using a shouldered, highly polished mandrel of the same diameter as the shaft which is to fit in the bearing. Porous bronze bushes must not be opened out after fitting, or the porosity of the bush will be impaired.

NOTE: Before fitting a new porous bronze bearing bush, it should be completely immersed for 24 hours in clean thin engine oil. In cases of extreme emergency this period may

be shortened by heating the oil to 100 deg. C. (212 deg. F.) when the time of immersion may be reduced to two hours.

PRE-ENGAGED TYPE

To Test in Position

Check the battery condition and state of charge, refer to battery section of this manual.

Clean the battery terminals taking particular care to remove the scale from the positive terminal post and terminal.

Check the earth connections for tightness and cleanliness, do not over-tighten the terminals.

Switch on the head lamps and operate the starter control switch.

If the lights go dim but the starter is not heard to operate it could indicate that a short circuit has developed in the starting system which could be either external or internal.

Check all the external wiring to make sure the fault is not external, if the external circuit proves satisfactory, indicating that the problem is in the starter assembly, the starter will have to be removed and bench checked.

To Remove and Instal

(1) Disconnect the earth lead from the battery.

(2) Remove the battery lead from the solenoid terminal.

(3) Disconnect the switch wire and ignition wire from the solenoid terminals.

(4) Remove the top mounting bolt.

(5) Raise the front of the vehicle and support on stands.

(6) Remove the lower mounting bolts.

(7) Support the starter motor with the hand while removing the third mounting bolt.

(8) Remove the starter from the vehicle.

Installation is a reversal of the removal procedure.

CAUTION: Do not over-tighten the mounting bolts until the starter is sitting flush on its mounting face, otherwise damage to the mounting bracket could result.

Lucas Face Type

To Dismantle

(1) Remove the solenoid mounting nuts and washers.

(2) Remove the solenoid to starter wire terminal nut and washer.

(3) Remove the solenoid.

(4) Remove the split pin from the armature shaft at the brush plate bracket after prising off the plastic cover.

(5) Remove the shims and thrust washer from the shaft.

(6) Remove the brush plate bracket retaining bolts.

(7) Remove the end bracket complete with the brush carrier moulding.

(8) Remove the retaining nuts and washers from the drive end bracket.

(9) Remove the drive end bracket with the armature, clutch assembly and pinion lever yoke.

(10) Remove the pinion lever yoke pivot pin and clip.

(11) Remove the drive end bracket.

(12) Hold the armature in a vice with soft jaws.

(13) With a suitable drift tap the circlip retaining cover from the circlip towards the pinion.

(14) Remove the circlip.

(15) Remove the clutch and pinion assembly.

To Clean and Inspect

Wash the parts in cleaning solvent and thoroughly dry.

CAUTION: DO NOT wash the solenoid, armature, field coils or the clutch and pinion assembly, these items may be wiped over with a damp cloth to clean.

Inspect all parts for wear and damage and replace where necessary.

To Test and Service Armature

(1) Using the 110 volt test prods with a bulb in circuit connect one test prod to the laminations and move the other test prod around the commutator, the bulb should not light nor should there be any indication of arcing between the windings and laminations or shaft.

(2) If the armature proves unserviceable it will have to be replaced.

(3) If the armature is serviceable clean the commutator with a damp petrol rag.

(4) Should the commutator be badly grooved a light skin can be taken off it in a lathe using a sharp tool, after turning, polish the commutator with very fine glass paper. *NOTE: Do not undercut the insulation between the commutator segments.*

To Renew Brushes

(1) Test the insulated brush holders for short circuits using 12 volt test prods with a bulb in series with one lead, connect one prod to the end bracket and the other prod to the brush holders in turn, the bulb should not light on the

insulated holders but will light on the earthed holders.

(2) If the brush holders are shorting, the holders and end bracket will have to be replaced as a unit.

(3) If the brush holders are serviceable cut the old brushes from their terminal post on the brush plate.

(4) Solder the new brush leads to the terminal post using a very hot soldering iron to avoid damage to the insulators.

(5) Cut the old brush leads from the field terminal about 4 mm. (0.187") from the press welded joint, this gives a good base to solder the new brush leads onto.

(6) Solder the new brushes to the field terminal.

(7) Check the brushes in their holders to make sure they do not stick at any point.

(8) Check the brush spring tension by pushing the brush into its holder with a spring tension gauge, refer specifications.

To Test Field Coils and Renew

(1) Using the 110 volt test leads, connect one lead to the yoke of the starter and the other lead to the field terminal, make sure the brushes are not touching to earth, the bulb should not light nor should there be any indication of arcing between the coils and the yoke.

(2) Visually check the field coil insulation for burnt or charred sections.

(3) If the field coils are shorted they will have to be replaced.

(4) Mark the pole shoes and their positions in the yoke.

(5) Remove the pole shoe retaining screws of two opposite pole shoes and remove the pole shoes.

(6) Loosen the other two screws and remove the field coils.

(7) Instal the new field coils.

(8) Instal the two pole shoes and retaining screws.

(9) Check the positioning of the field coils and tighten all the pole shoe screws.

(10) Recheck the field coils for short circuit.

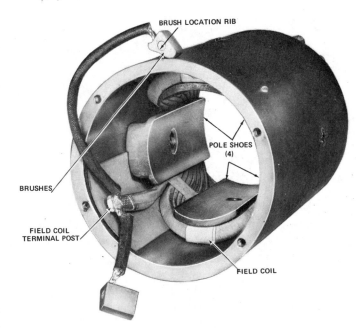

View of Field Coil Arrangement for Lucas Pre-engaged Type Starter Motor.

To Renew Bearings

(1) If the drive end bush and the brush plate bush are worn and allow side movement of the armature they will have to be replaced.

(2) To remove the drive end bush use a suitable mandrel and press it out of the housing.

(3) Replace the drive end bush by pressing it into the housing using a suitable mandril.

(4) To remove the brush plate bush select a suitable tap and screw it into the bush, clamp the end of the tap in a vice and withdraw the bush with the tap.

(5) Press the new bush into place using a suitable mandril.

NOTE: Before fitting a new porous bronze bearing bush it should be completely immersed for 24 hours in clean, thin engine oil. In case of extreme urgency this period may be shortened to 2 hours by heating the oil to 100 deg C.

To Assemble and Adjust

(1) Instal the pinion and clutch assembly onto the armature shaft.

(2) Fit the circlip retaining collar onto the armature shaft and instal the circlip.

(3) Fit the circlip retaining collar over the circlip.

(4) Instal the drive end bracket with the pinion lever yoke onto the armature shaft.

(5) Fit the lever yoke onto the clutch and instal the pivot pin and clip.

(6) Fit the armature with the end bracket, clutch assembly and lever yoke into the yoke of the starter motor.

(7) Instal the drive end retaining nuts and washers and tighten.

(8) Fit the brushes into the brush holders and fit the brush plate bracket to the yoke.

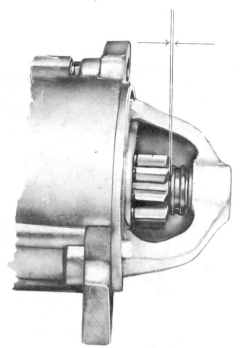

Lucas Starter Motor Showing Pinion to Pinion Stop Clearance.

(9) Instal the brush plate retaining bolts and tighten.

(10) Fit the thrust washer and shims.

(11) Fit the split pin to the shaft and check the end float, refer Specifications.

(12) Adjust the end float with the shims.

(13) Instal the solenoid and tighten the mounting nuts. Do not connect the solenoid to starter lead at this time.

(14) Using a fully charged battery make an 8 volt tapping and energise the solenoid.

(15) With the solenoid energised, measure the gap between the pinion face and the pinion stop, refer Specifications for correct setting.

NOTE: Do not energise the solenoid for more than 2 minutes as the solenoid will overheat.

To Check the Solenoid

(1) With the solenoid mounted as for checking the pinion to stop clearance proceed as follows.

(2) Using a fully charged 12 volt battery make an 8 volt tapping and connect a jumper lead from the tapping to the "STA" terminal of the solenoid.

(3) From the terminal of the 8 volt tapping connect a jumper lead with a bulb in series to the battery terminal of the solenoid.

(4) From this same terminal connect a jumper lead with a switch in series to the small spade terminal of the solenoid.

(5) Fit a stop of 3.2 mm. (0.125") thick between the pinion and drive end bracket to stop the pinion from coming right out.

(6) Close the switch to energise the solenoid, the test lamp should now light indicating that the internal contacts are closing.

(7) Turn off the switch so de-energising the solenoid and remove the temporary stop.

(8) Turn the switch on again to operate the solenoid, hold the pinion in the fully out position by hand.

(9) Turn off the switch, the light should now go out, indicating that the internal contacts are opening.

(10) If either of these tests prove unsatisfactory the solenoid will have to be replaced.

NOTE: Do not energise the solenoid for longer than is necessary to do the test, as the unit will overheat causing possible damage to the internal windings of the solenoid.

Bosch

To Dismantle

(1) Remove the starter motor from the vehicle. See To Remove and Instal.

(2) Disconnect the field coil lead from the solenoid, remove the solenoid mounting screws and the engaging lever fulcrum bolt.

(3) Remove the solenoid by lifting and unhooking the solenoid from the pinion lever.

(4) Remove the two screws from the commutator end cover cap and remove the cap, circlip and thrust washers.

(5) Remove the two through bolts and remove the commutator end cover.

(6) Detach the two field coil brushes from the brush holder assembly and remove the brush holder assembly, remove the thrust washers from the armature shaft noting their fitted position.

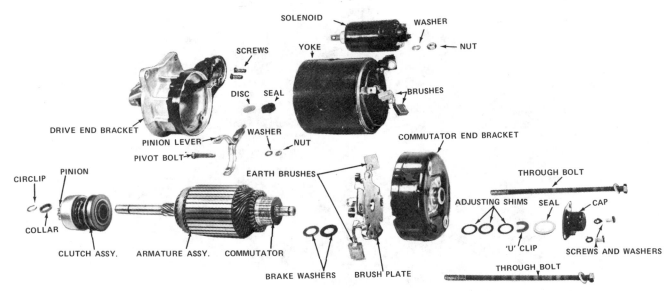

Exploded View of Bosch Starter Motor Components Typical.

(7) Remove the starter yoke.

(8) Remove the pinion lever pivot bolt from the drive end bracket.

(9) Remove the pinion lever and the armature from the drive end bracket.

(10) Using a suitable tool press the bushes from the end brackets and replace them with new bushes. See To Check and Inspect.

(11) To remove the circlip and collar from the armature shaft, tap the collar towards the pinion to gain access to the circlip.

(12) Remove the clutch and pinion assembly from the armature shaft.

(13) If the field coils are to be removed mark the location of each individual pole shoe before removing the field coil screws.

To Check and Inspect

(1) With the starter motor dismantled check the brush holder insulation, using a 110 volt test prod equipment with a globe in series with one lead.

Connect one test prod lead on the brush holder positive side and the other lead on the negative side. If there is any indication of leakage the globe will light or an arcing will occur at the point of shorting, either repair or replace the brush holder if a short circuit is evident.

(2) Check the brushes for adequate length. Brushes should be renewed when their length is below specifications. They should be a free sliding fit in the brush guides.

(3) Check the brush spring tension with a pull scale. Compare with specifications.

(4) Check that the commutator is free from pitting and burning, clean with a petrol moistened cloth, and polish with a strip of fine glass paper.

A badly worn commutator may be cleaned up by mounting in a lathe, spinning at high speed, and a light cut taken with a very sharp tool. After turning recut the insulation between segments to specifications.

(5) Check the armature for short circuit, using a

growler or by using the 110 test volt prods and globe.

(6) Place one of the test prods on the armature core or shaft and move the other prod around the circumference of the commutator. If the test lamp lights at any point, the armature is faulty and should be replaced.

(7) Test the field coils for continuity by connecting the test prods in series with the field windings.

Failure of the lamp to light indicates an open circuit in the wiring of the field coils.

(8) Check the field coil for ground by placing one test prod on the field coil lead and the other lead on the starter yoke. If the globe lights or an arcing occurs between the field coils and earth, remove the field coils and repair or renew.

(9) Check the drive assembly clutch pinion teeth for wear, scoring or chipping. A clutch in good condition should take up the drive in one direction only. It should rotate easily and smoothly in the non-drive direction and the assembly should move smoothly along the armature helical splines.

NOTE: Do not wash the drive assembly or clutch in solvent as this will destroy the clutch lubricant and cause early failure of the unit.

(10) To replace the thrust plate and spring remove the circlip from the sleeve while compressing the spring with the thrust plate.

(11) Check the armature shaft bushes for wear. Check with specifications and replace as necessary. The old bushes must be removed and the new ones pressed into the end brackets using a polished mandrel of the exact diameter of the armature shaft.

NOTE: The new bushes must not be reamed to size, as reaming will impair the porosity of the bushes and cause early failure. New bushes should be allowed to stand immersed in clean light engine oil for 24 hours before fitting. This time period may be shortened to two hours in case of urgency, if the oil is heated to 100 deg C.

SOLENOID

DRIVE END BRACKET

BRUSH PLATE BRACKET

THROUGH BOLT

PINION STOP

ARMATURE END FLOAT
MEASURE HERE

Bosch Starter Motor (Typical).   POLE SHOE SCREW

(12) Check the armature shaft for bend between centres using a dial gauge. Refer Specifications for tolerances. Replace the armature if it is not within the specifications.

To Assemble

(1) Lubricate the drive assembly on the armature shaft splines, armature shaft bushings and solenoid switch moving stud with a light coating of multi-purpose grease.

(2) Assemble the clutch and pinion unit to the shaft, fit the collar with the cup away from the pinion, fit the circlip and stake in position and fit the collar over the circlip.

(3) Assemble the armature, starter clutch and pinion lever to the drive end bracket and instal the lever pivot bolt and tighten.

NOTE: *Make sure the pinion assembly and the lever are correctly meshed.*

(4) Instal the armature and drive end bracket assembly to the yoke and instal the thrust washers on the armature shaft.

(5) Align the brush plate with the through bolts and instal it onto the armature shaft.

(6) Fit the brushes into their correct holders.

(7) Refit the commutator end thrust washers and bracket, instal the through bolts and tighten.

(8) Check the armature end-float, refer to specifications for correct setting. Adjust the end-float by the thickness of the thrust washer.

(9) Hook the solenoid stud to the lever and install the solenoid unit, fit the mounting screws and tighten.

Starter Solenoid to Test and Adjust

The solenoid unit should be tested with the unit mounted on the starter motor and connected in its operating position.

(1) Mount the starter motor securely in a vice, connect the negative terminal of a fully charged 12 volt battery to

the starter motor body using a heavy jumper lead.

(2) Make a 6 volt tapping on the battery and using a suitable jumper lead apply the 6 volt pressure to switch terminal of the solenoid, the solenoid should be activated and the plunger pulled smartly into the solenoid moving the pinion assembly forward on the shaft.

(3) Measure the clearance between the pinion and the pinion stop. Refer Specifications for the correct clearance.

NOTE: *Only hold the solenoid energised long enough to make the measurement as damage to the solenoid could occur from overheating.*

(4) If the pinion to pinion stop clearance is not within specifications, check the plunger eye and pinion lever for wear and renew as necessary, recheck the clearance after installing the new parts.

(5) When the pinion to pinion stop clearance has been checked remove the jumper leads.

Starter Motor to Test

(1) Proceed with the no-load test after checking and adjusting the solenoid and pinion clearance.

(2) Connect an ammeter capable of reading 0–500 amps in series with the positive battery terminal and the solenoid battery terminal using heavy core cable.

(3) Bridge the battery terminal of the solenoid with the switch terminal of the solenoid using a jumper lead with a switch connected in series.

(4) Connect a revolution counter to the armature shaft.

(5) Close the switch in the jumper lead between the battery and the switch terminals and note the rpm and current draw of the starter motor, compare the readings with specifications.

(6) After completing the starter no-load test remove the test instruments and leads.

NOTE: *High amperage reading with low revolutions check for shorted armature, shorted fields, worn bushes, bent armature shaft or poling armature; high amperage draw with no revolutions check for shorted field coils, shorted armature or shorted brushes.*

8. STARTER DRIVE

INERTIA TYPE
Description

The pinion is mounted on a screwed sleeve, which is carried on the armature shaft. The sleeve is so arranged that it can move along the shaft against a compression spring to reduce the shock loading at the moment engagement takes place.

When the starter switch is operated the armature shaft and screwed sleeve rotate. Owing to the inertia of the pinion, the latter is caused to move along the sleeve until the pinion comes into engagement with the flywheel ring gear. The starter will then turn the engine.

As soon as the engine fires and commences to run under its own power the flywheel will be driven faster by the engine than the starter. This will cause the pinion to be screwed back along the sleeve, so drawing the pinion out of mesh with the flywheel teeth. In this manner the drive safeguards the starter against damage due to being driven at high speeds.

A pinion restraining spring is incorporated in the drive. This spring prevents the pinion vibrating into mesh when the engine is running.

Routine Maintenance

If any difficulty is experienced with the starter motor not meshing correctly with the flywheel, it may be that the drive requires cleaning. The pinion should move freely on the screwed sleeve, if there is any dirt or other foreign matter on the sleeve it must be washed off with kerosene.

In the event of the pinion becoming jammed in mesh with the flywheel, it can usually be freed by turning the starter motor armature by means of a spanner applied to the shaft extension at the commutator end. This is accessible by removing the cap, which is a push fit over the boss on the end bracket.

To Dismantle and Assemble

Having removed the armature as detailed earlier, the starter drive can be dismantled as follows:

(1) Hold the armature and drive assembly in a vice by the square on the commutator end of the shaft, compress the drive assembly spring and remove the retaining circlip.

(2) Remove the spring and retaining washer and withdraw the drive as an assembly.

NOTE: If the pinion and barrel or the screwed sleeve are worn or damaged the starter drive must be renewed as an assembly.

Reassembly is a reversal of the foregoing procedure.

PRE-ENGAGED TYPE
Description

The pre-engaged type starter motor drive consists of a pinion, one way over running clutch, a sleeve and a lever and yoke which is connected to the solenoid.

The clutch and pinion are mounted on the common sleeve which is designed to slide on the armature shaft.

When the solenoid is energised the lever and yoke push the pinion into mesh with the ring gear, after which the internal contacts of the solenoid close allowing the current flow to the starter motor armature and field coils.

The turning effort of the armature is transferred to the ring gear by the pinion.

The over running clutch is used to protect the starter motor windings in case the pinion should become jammed in mesh.

A coil spring is mounted on the solenoid plunger to hold the pinion out of mesh when the starter is not being operated.

To Dismantle and Assemble

After the starter has been dismantled and the clutch and pinion assembly removed proceed to dismantle as follows.

(1) Remove the retaining circlip.

(2) Remove the yoke lever collar.

(3) Remove the coil spring.

After wiping all components clean and checking for wear and damage instal them in the reverse order of dismantling.

NOTE: Do not immerse the clutch and pinion in cleaning solvent as the lubricant of the one way clutch will be made ineffective.

9. DISTRIBUTOR

DESCRIPTION

The distributors on the overhead valve engines are driven by a skew gear from the camshaft and rotate in an anti-clockwise direction when looking at the rotor button.

The distributor on the overhead camshaft engine is driven from the auxiliary shaft through a skew gear and rotates in a clockwise direction when looking at the rotor button.

Distributors fitted to both types of engines have both mechanical and vacuum advance controls.

The mechanical advance is by centrifugal weights mounted on the distributor shaft and operates with engine speed against pre-set spring tensions.

The vacuum advance is through a vacuum control unit which is connected directly to the breaker plate, advance is controlled by engine load and a limit slot in the breaker plate.

Overhaul procedure for the Motorcraft, Autolite and Fo Mo Co distributors are the same but reference should be made to Specifications for any variance in assembly and fitting tolerances. The Lucas distributor is different in construction and is covered separately.

TO ADJUST CONTACT BREAKER POINTS

At intervals of approximately 10,000 km the contact breaker points should be removed and inspected.

Points that are badly pitted and burned should be renewed. Points that are still serviceable should be cleaned up to a smooth, square surface on a fine oil stone. Remove all traces of oil from the points by washing in petrol as oil or grease on the points will cause pitting and burning.

(1) With the distributor cap and rotor removed, turn the engine until the heel of the moving contact is on the highest point of a cam lobe. The contact points should now be at the point of maximum opening.

(2) Check the point gap with a feeler gauge, the gauge should be a sliding fit between the points, refer to Specifications for correct setting.

(3) To adjust the gap, loosen the fixed contact lock screw(s), move the fixed contact in the required direction by using a screwdriver in the adjusting slot provided. Tighten the lock screw(s) when the gap setting is correct and recheck with the feeler gauge.

(4) Apply a single drop of light engine oil to the contact pivot pin of Lucas models and to the centre of the cam before installing the rotor button on both models. Using a spring scale check the contact breaker points spring tension at right angles to the contact points, see Specifications for the correct spring tension.

(5) Apply a light smear of high melting point grease to the cam and rubbing block.

(6) Replace the rotor and distributor cap.

(7) Check the timing and dwell angle; refer to these sections in the manual.

TO REMOVE

(1) If it is desired to remove the distributor for overhaul without upsetting the ignition timing do not release the clamp plate pinch bolt on overhead valve engines.

(2) Mark the location of the clamp plate on the crankcase on overhead valve engines or the base of the distributor and the crankcase on the 2000 overhead camshaft engine.

(3) Turn the engine over until the distributor rotor arm is pointing to the cap segment for No. 1 cylinder plug lead and the notch in the crankshaft pulley is in line with the timing mark applicable to the model.

(4) With the cap removed, disconnect the low tension lead at the coil terminal and disconnect the vacuum advance pipe at the distributor.

(5) Remove the bolt securing the distributor or clamp plate to the crankcase and withdraw the distributor, take care not to rotate the distributor shaft and mark the position of the rotor button on the distributor body this will aid in positioning the skew gear when installing the distributor. Do not rotate the crankshaft until the distributor has been replaced.

MOTORCRAFT
To Dismantle

(1) With the distributor cap removed, remove the rotor arm.

(2) Slacken the retaining screw and remove the low tension and capacitor wires from the points.

(3) Unscrew the retaining and adjusting screws, and remove the points.

(4) Remove the vacuum unit pivot post circlip and take out the two screws holding the fixed plate to the distributor body and remove the breaker plate assembly.

(5) Remove the pivot post large circlip and remove the flat washer and wave washer.

(6) Remove the capacitor retaining screws and remove the capacitor.

(7) Turn the upper breaker plate to disengage the holding screw from the keyhole slot in the bottom plate.

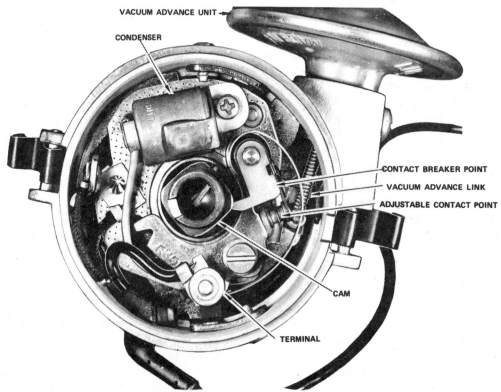

VACUUM ADVANCE UNIT

CONDENSER

CONTACT BREAKER POINT

VACUUM ADVANCE LINK

ADJUSTABLE CONTACT POINT

CAM

TERMINAL

Lucas Distributor with Cap and Rotor Removed to Show Contact Breaker Assembly.

DISTRIBUTOR BASE TO CYLINDER BLOCK MARKS

ROTOR AND DISTRIBUTOR BODY SCRIBE MARKS

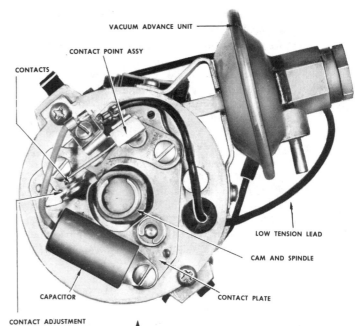

VACUUM ADVANCE UNIT

CONTACT POINT ASSY

CONTACTS

LOW TENSION LEAD

CAM AND SPINDLE

CONTACT PLATE

CAPACITOR

CONTACT ADJUSTMENT

Showing Contact Breaker Adjusting Point, FoMoCo, Motorcraft and Autolite Distributors.

◀ Distributor Rotor Set in Firing Position For No. 1 Cylinder.

DISTRIBUTOR BODY

WEIGHT SPRING

WEIGHTS

ADVANCE SLOT

ADVANCE SLOT MARKING

RETAINING CLIP

10L

CAM
RETAINING CLIP

15L

RETAINING CLIP

ADVANCE SLOT

ADVANCE SLOT MARKING

STOP

CAM

WEIGHT SPRING

View of Centrifugal Advance Mechanism Showing Advance Slots, FoMoCo, Motorcraft and Autolite Distributors as fitted to 1300-1600 OHV Engines.

NOTE: Do not lose the earthing spring between the upper and lower breaker plates.

(8) Remove the insulation and retaining grommet for the low tension lead from the bottom plate.

(9) Remove the governor centrifugal weights retaining 'E' clips from the pivot posts and remove the weights.

(10) Note the position of the advance springs in relation to the spring posts and unclip the springs.

(11) Remove the two Phillips head screws and spring washers securing the vacuum unit to the distributor body and remove the vacuum unit.

(12) Remove the felt pad in the top of the cam spindle. Expand and remove the spindle retaining clip.

(13) Before removing the cam spindle, make a note of the position of the cam slot for maximum vacuum advance.

(14) If the shaft and bushes are worn, remove the gear retaining pin using a suitable drift and remove the gear, thrust washer and wave washer.

(15) Remove the distributor shaft with the mechanical advance mounting plate attached.

(16) Remove the thrust washers from under the mechanical advance mounting plate.

(17) Remove the nut and gasket on the end of the vacuum unit and withdraw the vacuum spring, stop and shims.

To Clean and Inspect

(1) Wash the distributor parts in cleaning solvent and dry thoroughly.

NOTE: Do not immerse the capacitor, vacuum advance unit, rotor arm or distributor cap in solvent, these items may be wiped clean with a damp cloth and then dried.

(2) Check all parts for wear and damage and renew as necessary.

(3) Clean the contact points on an oil stone and rewash and dry thoroughly, if the contact points are badly pitted replace with a new set.

NOTE: Before installing the points apply a small amount of high melting point grease to the moving point rubbing block.

(4) Check the rotor electrode and the distributor cap carbon brush for burning and looseness.

To Assemble

Reassembling the distributor is a direct reversal of the dismantling procedure, with particular attention to the following.

If a new shaft and/or gear has to be fitted proceed as follows.

(1) Fit the top thrust washers to the shaft and instal the shaft in the housing.

(2) Fit a new thrust washer and wave washer to the bottom end of the shaft.

(3) Using a piece of shim stock or a shim washer 0.38 mm. (0.015 in.) thick cut a slot the width of the diameter of the shaft.

(4) Instal the gear on to the shaft and fit the made up shim spacer with the thrust washer and wave washer.

(5) Use a suitable clamp to push the gear along the shaft until the wave washer is compressed with no slack. Do not over-tighten the clamp.

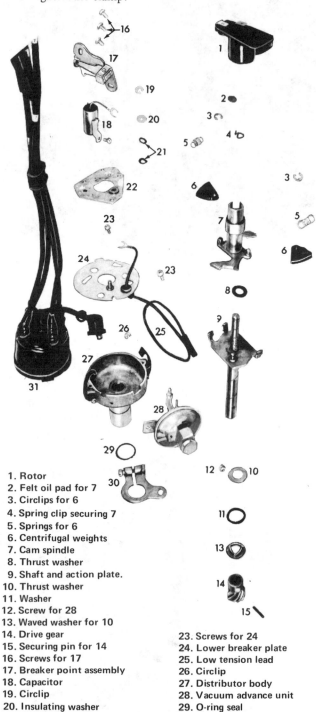

1. Rotor
2. Felt oil pad for 7
3. Circlips for 6
4. Spring clip securing 7
5. Springs for 6
6. Centrifugal weights
7. Cam spindle
8. Thrust washer
9. Shaft and action plate.
10. Thrust washer
11. Washer
12. Screw for 28
13. Waved washer for 10
14. Drive gear
15. Securing pin for 14
16. Screws for 17
17. Breaker point assembly
18. Capacitor
19. Circlip
20. Insulating washer
21. Washers
22. Contact breaker plate
23. Screws for 24
24. Lower breaker plate
25. Low tension lead
26. Circlip
27. Distributor body
28. Vacuum advance unit
29. O-ring seal
30. Clamp plate
31. Cap and high tension leads

Exploded View of Distributor Components, 1300–1600 OHV Engines.

(6) If a new gear is being installed, position the pilot hole on the gear at 90 degrees to the rotor slot with the governor weights at rest position.

(7) Mount the distributor body and shaft in "V" blocks and carefully drill a 3.175 mm. (0.125 in.) diameter hole through the gear and shaft, using the hole in the gear as a pilot hole.

NOTE: When using the original gear with a new shaft drill the retaining pin hole at 90 deg. to the original hole.

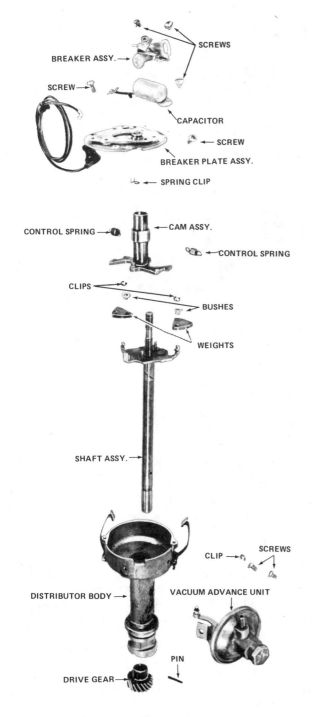

Exploded View of Distributor Components, 2000 OHC Engine.

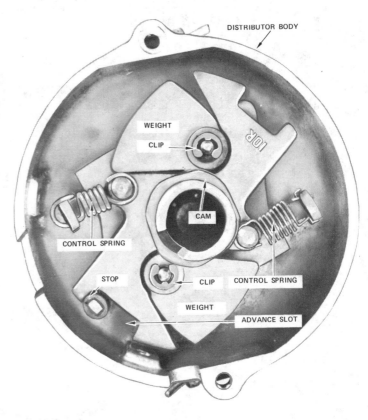

View of Centrifugal Advance Mechanism Showing Advance Slots, Motorcraft and Autolite Distributors, 2000 OHC Engines.

(8) Instal a new retaining pin, release the clamp and remove the made up shim, the distributor shaft should now have its correct pre-load.

(9) Lubricate each component as necessary with thin engine oil and fit all components in their original positions in the centrifugal weight assemblies.

(10) Ensure that the advance stop is located in the correct slot for the particular engine when installing the cam spindle.

(11) Apply high melting point grease to the centrifugal weight pivot posts and rubbing points, to the cam spindle fitting the recess in the shaft before installing the cam assembly, also apply a smear of high melting point grease to the cam lobes.

(12) When refitting the centrifugal weight springs to their posts ensure that the primary spring with larger coil diameter and the secondary spring are fitted to their correct posts as noted on dismantling.

NOTE: Ensure that the earth spring between the upper and lower breaker plates is replaced.

(13) When setting the contact point gap make sure the rubbing block is on the highest point of the cam lobe, check the gap on all lobes of the cam and even the gap if possible, if variation between lobes exceeds more than 0.05 mm. (0.002 in.), replace the cam assembly.

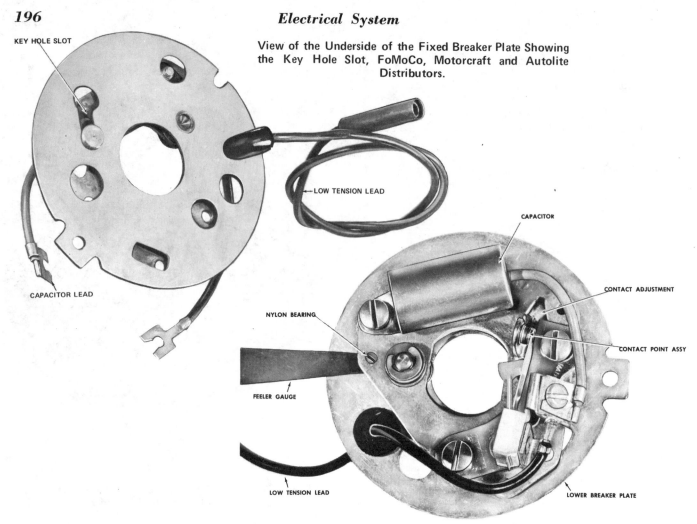

View of the Underside of the Fixed Breaker Plate Showing the Key Hole Slot, FoMoCo, Motorcraft and Autolite Distributors.

KEY HOLE SLOT

LOW TENSION LEAD

CAPACITOR LEAD

CAPACITOR

CONTACT ADJUSTMENT

CONTACT POINT ASSY

NYLON BEARING

FEELER GAUGE

LOW TENSION LEAD

LOWER BREAKER PLATE

Checking Breaker Plate Clearance Beneath the Nylon Bearing, 1300-1600 OHV Engines.

To Instal

(1) If the engine has been disturbed turn the engine over until the timing mark (applicable to the model) is in line with the notch or mark on the crankshaft pulley with No. 1 piston on compression stroke.

(2) Hold the distributor at its mounting hole with the vacuum control unit towards the rear of the engine.

(3) Move the rotor arm to align with the mark made when the distributor was removed.

(4) Insert the distributor to mesh the gears. The rotor should rotate slightly when the gears mesh.

(5) If necessary re-position the clamp by loosening the pinch bolt and without turning the distributor so that the centre of the slotted hole in the clamp plate is in line with the hole in the cylinder block.

(6) Fit the retaining bolt and tighten.

LUCAS
To Dismantle

NOTE: It is extremely important that before dismantling the distributor, a careful note is made of the relative positions of the various components to ensure correct replacement on assembly.

Components of the centrifugal weight assembly need not be dismantled unless they are to be renewed.

(1) With the distributor cap removed, detach the rotor arm.

(2) Remove the nut and washer from the contact breaker arm spring anchor. Withdraw in the following order; the insulator sleeve, capacitor lead, low tension lead, contact breaker arm spring, at the same time sliding the contact breaker arm off its pivot pin and remove the large insulating washer from the pivot pin and the small one from the anchor pin.

(3) Remove the single screw with spring and flat washers and lift off the fixed contact. Slide out the low tension terminal and lead. Remove the vacuum diaphragm connecting link and remove the vacuum advance unit.

(4) Remove the capacitor and contact breaker base plate noting that one of the screws securing the base plate to the distributor body also secures the earth lead.

(5) Remove the screw from the centre of the spindle and lift off the cam.

(6) Lift off the centrifugal weights as two assemblies. These assemblies need not be dismantled further unless the components are to be renewed.

(7) Mark the position of the driving gear in relation to the shaft, drive out the pin retaining the driving gear and

remove the gear and thrust washer. Remove the shaft from the distributor body.

To Clean and Inspect

(1) Wash the distributor parts in cleaning solvent and dry thoroughly.

NOTE: Do not immerse the capacitor, vacuum advance unit, rotor arm or distributor cap in solvent, these items may be wiped clean with a damp cloth and then dried.

(2) Check and test the capacitor on a capacitor tester.

(3) Clean the contact points on an oil stone and rewash and dry thoroughly, if the contact points are badly pitted replace with a new set.

(4) Check the low tension and earth wires for possible fractures.

(5) Check the distributor shaft or bush for wear and renew as necessary. Excessive wear will necessitate shaft and bush replacement.

(6) Check the cams for wear or roughness. Variations in lift between any two cams in excess of 0.05 mm. (0.002 in) will necessitate renewing the cam and shaft assembly.

(7) Inspect the governor weights for binding with the pivot pin.

(8) Check the distributor cap for cracks, carbon tracks, burned or corroded terminals.

(9) Check centre carbon for wear and protrusion. Carbon protrusion should be sufficient to bear on the rotor button.

(10) Inspect rotor for damage or deterioration.

(11) Check the vacuum advance unit for a leaking diaphragm. To do this, push in on the diaphragm connecting link, place a finger over the suction pipe and release the connecting link. The vacuum on the finger should hold for at least 30 seconds.

(12) Check the rubber O-ring seal and renew as necessary.

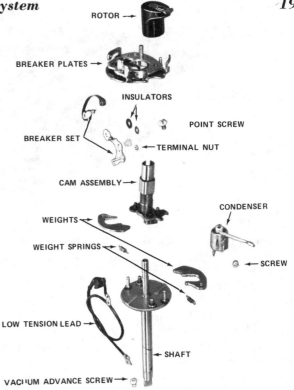

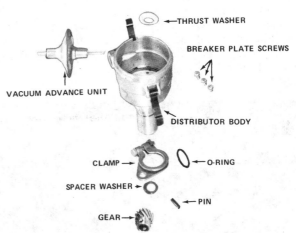

Exploded View of Lucas Distributor Components.

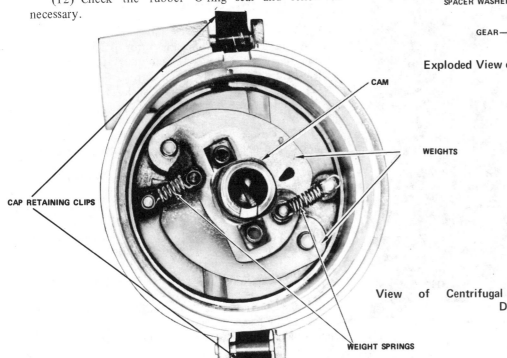

View of Centrifugal Advance Mechanism, Lucas Distributor.

DEGREE GRADUATIONS

NOTCH IN PULLEY

Ignition Timing Marks Degrees Shown are Before Top Dead Centre, OHV Engines.

To Assemble

Assembling the distributor is a direct reversal of the dismantling procedure, with particular attention to the following points:

(1) Check the rotor electrode and the distributor cap carbon brush for burning and looseness. Check that the contact breaker points are clean and serviceable. They must be flat and free from burning and pitting.

(2) Check all parts for wear and renew as necessary. If a new bush is to be fitted use a shouldered mandril to instal the bush. The new bush should be allowed to stand in thin engine oil for 24 hours prior to fitting and should not be reamed to size.

(3) Lubricate each component as necessary with thin engine oil and fit all components in their original position.

(4) After installing the drive gear check the shaft end float and adjust with shims to specifications.

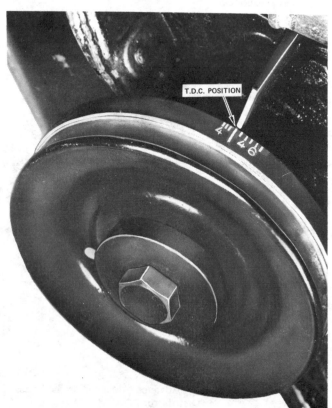

T.D.C. POSITION

Ignition Timing Marks on Crankshaft Pulley. 2000 OHC Engine.

(5) Engage the cam driving pins in their original positions in the centrifugal weight assemblies.

(6) Adjust the contact breaker point gap. See Specifications for the correct gap and under the heading TO ADJUST CONTACT BREAKER POINTS for procedure.

To Instal

(1) If the engine has been disturbed turn the engine over until the timing mark (applicable to the model) is in line with the notch or mark on the crankshaft pulley with No. 1 piston on compression stroke.

(2) Hold the distributor at its mounting hole with the vacuum control unit towards the rear of the engine, but at an angle of 45 deg from the engine centre line.

(3) Move the rotor arm to align with the mark made when the distributor was removed.

(4) Insert the distributor to mesh the gears. The rotor should rotate slightly when the gears mesh.

(5) If necessary re-position the clamp by loosening the pinch bolt and without turning the distributor so that the centre of the slotted hole in the clamp plate is in line with the hole in the cylinder block.

(6) Fit the retaining bolt and tighten.

TO ADJUST IGNITION TIMING
Static Method

(1) With the distributor installed on the engine (as described in To Instal) and the rotor pointing to the position of the segment connected to No. 1 spark plug slacken the distributor body clamp bolt.

(2) Turn the distributor body slightly, as necessary, until the contact breaker points are just opening.

NOTE: If excessive movement is necessary to set the points indications are that the distributor is installed one tooth out, in which case remove the distributor and move the gear one tooth in the direction required and re-instal the distributor.

(3) Tighten the distributor body clamp bolt.

(4) Replace the distributor cap and reconnect the spark plug leads bearing in mind the firing order of the engine and the rotation of the rotor.

(5) Reconnect the high tension and low tension leads to the coil.

(6) Road test the vehicle and make fine adjustment by slackening the screw securing the clamp plate to the cylinder block and advancing or retarding as necessary.

TO ADJUST IGNITION TIMING
Stroboscope Method

(1) Connect the leads of the timing light in accordance with the manufacturer's instructions.

(2) Mark the timing marks on the crankshaft pulley and the front cover with chalk or white paint.

(3) Disconnect the vacuum pipe to the distributor, start the engine and allow it to idle.

(4) Aim the timing light at the timing pointer and check that the mark on the crankshaft pulley aligns with the appropriate mark on the front cover or timing pointer according to the model. See Specifications.

(5) If the marks do not align, slacken the distributor body clamp bolt and turn the distributor body as necessary to obtain alignment.

(6) Check the operation of the mechanical advance by slowly increasing the engine rpm, the mark on the crankshaft pulley should move towards the advance end of the indicator mark on the timing cover case or pulley. Any sudden movement of the mark will indicate sticking centrifugal weights or weak springs.

(7) Reconnect the distributor vacuum pipe.

(8) Road test the vehicle and make fine adjustment by slackening the screw securing the clamp plate to the cylinder block and advancing or retarding as necessary.

TO CHECK AND ADJUST CONTACT DWELL

(1) Connect the dwell meter and tachometer according to manufacturer's instructions.

(2) Start the engine and allow it to idle at the specified rpm, adjust as necessary.

(3) Check the dwell angle reading which should be to specifications, to adjust, stop the engine remove the distributor cap and slightly open or close the points as necessary to obtain the correct dwell angle.

(4) After the correct dwell is obtained at idle slowly increase the engine to 3000 rpm, noting any variation in the dwell angle, a variation of more than 3 deg. indicates a worn shaft or bushings or distributor body.

10. SWITCHES AND CONTROLS

COMBINATION SWITCH
Description

The combination switch includes the headlamp dipper switch and in countries where required by law the headlamp high beam flasher switch, the turn signal switch and the horn operating switch.

The switch unit is mounted on the exterior of the steering jacket and is accessible after removing the upper covers of steering jacket.

To Remove and Instal

(1) Remove the upper steering column shroud covers as detailed in the STEERING section.

(2) Disconnect the wiring plug terminal from the switch.

(3) Remove the switch retaining screws and remove the switch assembly.

Installation is a reversal of the removal procedure.

IGNITION SWITCH
Description

The ignition switch is mounted on the steering column and is operated through the steering lock assembly, the switch may be removed from the lock assembly leaving the lock in place on the column.

To Remove and Instal

(1) Remove the upper steering column shroud covers as detailed in the STEERING section.

(2) Disconnect the battery earth lead.

(3) Disconnect the switch wiring connector at the dash panel or unsolder the wires at the switch terminals noting the fitted position of each wire should a connector not be fitted.

(4) Remove the two switch retaining screws and remove the switch from the base of the steering lock assembly.

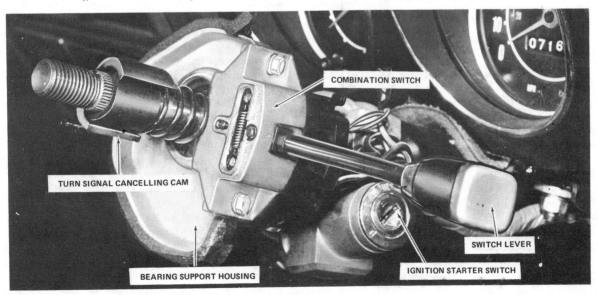

Steering Column with the Steering Wheel and Covers Removed Showing the Mounted Position of the Combination Switch.

Rear View of Combination Meter.

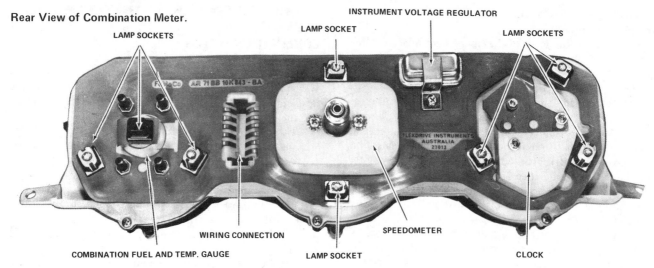

(5) To remove the locking barrel unscrew the escutcheon nut and remove the barrel after inserting the key.

Installation is a reversal of the removal procedure ensuring that the switch keyways are aligned.

HEADLAMP SWITCH
To Remove and Instal

(1) Disconnect the battery earth lead.

(2) Pull the switch knob from the switch lever.

(3) Unscrew the escutcheon nut and remove the switch towards the rear of the panel.

(4) Ease the wiring from its clips and remove the switch.

Installation is a reversal of the removal procedure.

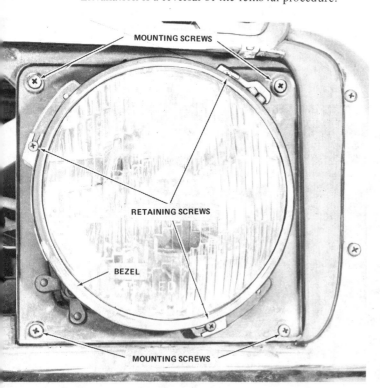

Headlamp Unit Showing Lamp Bezel Retaining Screws and Lamp Mounting Screws.

WIPER SWITCH
To Remove and Instal

(1) Disconnect the battery earth lead.

(2) Pull the heater control knobs off the levers.

(3) Remove the heater and radio escutcheon retaining screws and remove the escutcheon.

(4) Pull the knob off the wiper switch lever and remove the escutcheon nut.

(5) Remove the switch towards the rear of the dash panel, disconnect the wiring connector and remove the switch.

Installation is a reversal of the removal procedure.

INSTRUMENT CLUSTER
To Remove and Instal

(1) Disconnect the battery earth lead.

(2) Pull the choke control knob off the choke lever and remove the steering column shroud cover, see STEERING section.

(3) Remove the instrument fascia retaining screws and remove the panel.

(4) Remove the instrument cluster retaining screws and ease the cluster forward sufficiently to undo the speedo cable and multi-plug connector at the rear of the cluster and remove the cluster.

Installation is a reversal of the removal procedures.

STOP LAMP SWITCH
To Remove and Instal

(1) Pull off the choke control knob and remove the upper steering column shroud covers as detailed in the STEERING section.

(2) Remove the instrument fascia panel to gain access to the switch.

(3) Remove the wiring from the switch.

(4) Loosen and remove the switch locknut and remove the switch.

Installation is a reversal of the removal procedure with attention to the following adjusting points:

With the switch installed and the brake pedal in the released position screw the switch in until the stop lamps go out then turn the switch a further turn.

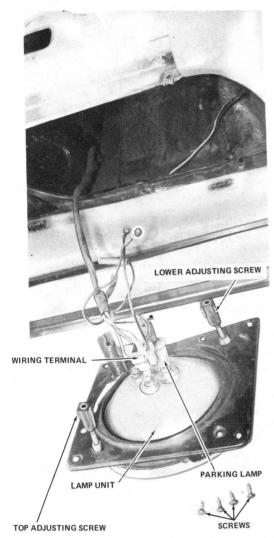

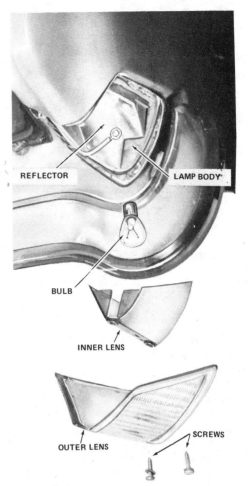

Left Hand Front Turn Signal Lamp with Lens and Bulb Removed.

Headlamp Removed Showing Adjusting Screws and Wiring Connections.

Lock the lock nut and check that the stop lamp lights when the brake pedal is moved the distance of its free travel and goes out when the pedal is released, carry out minor adjustments to obtain this result.

11. LAMP UNITS

HEADLAMPS
To Remove and Instal

(1) Remove the radiator grill retaining screws and remove the grill.

(2) Remove the bezel retaining screws and remove the bezel.

(3) On sealed beam units remove the terminal plug assembly from the rear of the lamp unit and remove the lamp unit.

On lamps fitted with a bulb, turn the bulb holder to release it from the lens and reflector assembly, remove the reflector and lens and remove the bulb from its holder.

Installation is a reversal of the removal procedure. The headlamp focus or adjustment should be checked after installing new components.

To Adjust Headlamps

(1) Make sure the tyres are inflated to their correct pressures.

(2) Position the vehicle in relation to the testing and adjusting equipment being used, i.e. headlamp tester or aiming board, paying particular attention to the equipment instructions.

(3) Turn on the headlamp switch, ensuring that the dipper switch is on the high beam. This is important for correct beam adjustment.

(4) To raise or lower the headlamp beam the top adjusting screw is used.

(5) To move the beam to the left or right the lower adjusting screws are used.

(6) When using a headlamp aiming board cover the lamp not being adjusted with a suitable cloth so that only one beam is projected onto the board.

NOTE: Reference should be made to the local regulations governing headlamp focus and the lamps should be focused accordingly.

FRONT TURN SIGNAL LAMP
To Renew Bulb

(1) Remove the lens retaining screws and remove the lens.

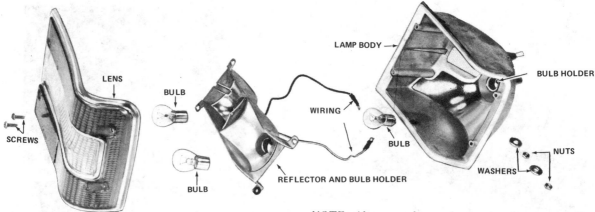

Dismantled View of Rear Combination Lamp.

(2) Press in on the bulb and turn slightly anti-clockwise and remove the bulb.

Installation is a reversal of the removal procedure.

NOTE: Always replace a damaged or burnt out bulb with a bulb of the same voltage and wattage as that which has been removed.

To Remove and Instal Lamp Unit

(1) Working from inside the wheel arch remove the lamp retaining nut and washer.

(2) Disconnect the wiring at the connector and push the lamp unit forward out of its mounted position.

Installation is a reversal of the removal procedure ensuring that adequate sealing compound is placed between the lamp body and fender opening.

REAR COMBINATION LAMP
To Renew Bulb

(1) Remove the lens retaining screws and remove the lens.

(2) Press in on the bulb and turn slightly in an anti-clockwise direction and remove the bulb.

Installation is a reversal of the removal procedure.

NOTE: Always replace a damaged or burnt out bulb with a bulb of the same voltage and wattage as that which has been removed.

To Remove and Instal Lamp Unit

(1) Working inside the luggage compartment disconnect the wiring to the lamp unit.

(2) Remove the nuts and washers and remove the lamp assembly.

Installation is a reversal of the removal procedure ensuring that the seal between the lamp body and panel will not allow water entry to the luggage compartment.

LICENCE PLATE LAMP
To Renew Bulb

(1) Remove the lamp retaining screws and remove the lamp from the bumper bar.

(2) Remove the lens retaining screws and remove the lens.

(3) Remove the bulb from the holder.

(4) To remove the lamp unit from the vehicle disconnect the wiring and feed it through the grommets as the lamp is removed.

Installation is a reversal of the removal procedure.

NOTE: Always replace a damaged or burnt out bulb with a bulb of the same voltage and wattage as that which has been removed.

12. ELECTRICAL FAULT DIAGNOSIS

BATTERY AND GENERATOR SYSTEM

1. **Battery undercharged.**

Possible cause	*Remedy*
(a) Loose or broken generator drive belt.	— Adjust or renew belt.
(b) Faulty or incorrectly adjusted generator regulator.	— Renew or adjust regulator unit.
(c) Faulty battery.	— Renew or repair battery.
(d) Faulty generator.	— Overhaul or renew generator.
(e) Fault in charging circuit wiring.	— Check and repair or renew wiring harness.
(f) Faulty connections in charging circuit.	— Check and renew or repair component/s.

2. **Battery overcharged.**

Possible cause	*Remedy*
(a) Faulty or incorrectly adjusted generator regulator.	— Renew or adjust regulator.
(b) Faulty battery.	— Renew or repair battery.
(c) Faulty generator.	— Overhaul or renew generator.
(d) Faulty charging circuit wiring or connections.	— Check and renew or repair faulty components.

3. **Charge indicator light remains on.**

Possible cause	*Remedy*
(a) Loose or broken generator drive belt.	— Adjust or renew drive belt.
(b) Faulty or incorrectly adjusted regulator unit.	— Check and renew or adjust regulator unit.
(c) Faulty generator.	— Check and overhaul generator.
(d) Low regulator voltage setting.	— Check and adjust voltage setting on regulator unit.
(e) Short to earth in warning light circuit.	— Check and repair.
(f) Warning light off when ignition switched on but comes on when engine started.	— Check fuse holder and fuse, replace fuse.

4. **Charge indicator light does not operate.**

Possible cause	*Remedy*
(a) Light bulb blown.	— Check and renew faulty bulb.
(b) Open circuit in wiring or bulb socket.	— Check and rectify open circuit.
(c) Fuse blown.	— Locate cause and renew fuse.

5. **Noise in drive belt or generator.**

Possible cause	*Remedy*
(a) Drive belt frayed or out of alignment with pulleys.	— Renew drive belt and/or align pulleys.
(b) Loose generator mounting bolts or worn bearings.	— Tighten mounting bolts and/or renew bearings.
(c) Loose generator pulley.	— Tighten pulley retaining nut.
(d) Faulty generator.	— Overhaul or renew generator.

BATTERY AND ALTERNATOR SYSTEM

1. **Battery undercharged.**

Possible cause	*Remedy*
(a) Loose or broken alternator drive belt.	— Adjust or renew drive belt.
(b) Defective alternator regulator unit.	— Renew regulator unit.
(c) Faulty battery.	— Renew or repair battery.
(d) Faulty alternator.	— Overhaul or replace unit.
(e) Defect in charging circuit wiring.	— Check and repair or replace wiring harness.
(f) Faulty connections in charging unit.	— Check and renew or repair faulty components.

2. **Battery overcharged.**

Possible cause	*Remedy*
(a) Defective alternator regulator unit.	— Renew regulator.
(b) Faulty battery.	— Renew or repair.
(c) Faulty alternator.	— Overhaul or renew unit.
(d) Faulty charging circuit wiring or connections.	— Check and repair or renew defective components.

3. **Indicator light remains on.**

Possible cause	*Remedy*
(a) Loose or broken drive belt.	— Adjust or renew drive belt.
(b) Faulty alternator/regulator.	— Check and replace faulty unit.
(c) Short to earth in warning light circuit.	— Locate and repair.

4. **Indicator light does not operate.**

Possible cause	*Remedy*
(a) Light bulb blown.	— Check and renew faulty bulb.
(b) Open circuit in wiring or bulb socket.	— Check and rectify open circuit.

5. **Noise in drive belt or alternator.**

Possible cause	*Remedy*
(a) Drive belt frayed or out of alignment with pulleys.	— Renew drive belt and/or align pulleys.
(b) Loose alternator mounting bolts or worn bearings.	— Tighten mounting bolts and/or renew bearings.
(c) Loose alternator pulley.	— Tighten pulley retaining nut.
(d) Faulty alternator.	— Overhaul faulty unit.
(e) Faulty diode or heat sink.	— Overhaul alternator test diodes.

BATTERY AND STARTING SYSTEM

1. Starter lacks power to crank engine.

Possible cause	*Remedy*
(a) Battery undercharged.	— Check charging system and rectify as necessary.
(b) Battery faulty, will not hold charge.	— Check and repair or renew battery.
(c) Battery terminals loose or corroded.	— Clean and tighten terminals.
(d) Faulty starter motor.	— Check and overhaul starter motor.
(e) Faulty starter solenoid switch or contacts.	— Check and renew solenoid as necessary.

2. Starter will not attempt to crank engine.

Possible cause	*Remedy*
(a) Open circuit in starting system.	— Check for: dirty or loose terminals, dirty commutator, faulty solenoid, faulty switch.
(b) Discharged battery.	— Check for fault or short circuit in system.
(c) Battery fully charged but will not crank engine.	— Check for: locked drive and ring gear, internal starter fault or seized engine.

HEADLAMP SYSTEM

1. Lamps fail to light.

Possible cause	*Remedy*
(a) Burnt out sealed beam unit/s, or bulb/s where fitted.	— Check and renew faulty unit/s, or bulb/s.
(b) Open circuit in wiring or connections.	— Check and rectify.
(c) Faulty light switch.	— Check and renew switch.
(d) Blown fuse.	— Eliminate cause and renew fuse.

2. Lamps flare with engine speed increase.

Possible cause	*Remedy*
(a) Faulty battery.	— Check and renew or repair battery.
(b) Battery in low state of charge.	— Recharge battery and check charging system.
(c) High resistance or faulty connections between generator and battery.	— Check circuit and rectify condition.
(d) Poor earth connection between battery and engine or generator.	— Check battery earth lead and strap between engine and body.
(e) Voltage regulator setting too high or unit inoperative.	— Check and adjust voltage regulator setting on generator system or renew regulator on alternator system.

TURN INDICATOR LIGHT SYSTEM

1. Indicator warning lamp does not burn and no audible clicking from the flasher unit, when turn is selected on switch lever.

Possible cause	*Remedy*
(a) Fuse blown.	— Rectify fault and renew fuse.
(b) Bulb blown on one or both sides.	— Check system and renew bulbs.
(c) Faulty flasher unit.	— Renew flasher unit. Do not attempt repair.
(d) Faulty turn indicator switch.	— Renew or repair switch.
(e) Fault in wiring circuit.	— Check and repair fault.

2. Indicator warning lamp does not flash but audible clicking from flasher unit, when turn is selected on switch lever.

Possible cause	*Remedy*
(a) Warning lamp bulb blown.	— Check and renew bulb.
(b) Front bulb blown on opposite side to turn selected.	— Check and renew bulb.

3. **Both warning lamps flash weakly and at greater than normal speed when turn is selected on switch lever.**

    Possible cause
    (a) Front bulb blown on turn side.
    (b) Rear bulb blown on turn side.
    (c) Faulty flasher unit.

    Remedy
    — Check and renew bulb.
    — Check and renew bulb.
    — Check and renew flasher unit.

4. **Both indicator warning lamps burn constantly when turn is selected on switch lever.**

    Possible cause
    (a) Front and rear bulbs blown on turn side.
    (b) Faulty flasher unit.

    Remedy
    — Check and renew bulbs.
    — Check and renew flasher unit.

IGNITION SYSTEM

1. **Engine will not start.**

    Possible cause
    (a) Fault in ignition primary circuit wiring.
    (b) Faulty ignition switch.
    (c) Fault in coil primary winding.
    (d) Burnt or dirty contact breaker points.
    (e) Fused or broken low tension wire from breaker arm to low tension terminal.
    (f) Faulty capacitor or capacitor lead.
    (g) Fault in coil high tension circuit.
    (h) Cracks in distributor cap.
    (i) Cracks in distributor rotor.
    (j) Faulty high tension leads.
    (k) Faulty or incorrectly adjusted spark plugs.
    (l) Damp distributor cap, leads or plugs.

    Remedy
    — Check circuit and repair as necessary.
    — Renew ignition switch.
    — Renew coil.
    — Clean or renew and adjust points.
    — Renew low tension terminal block and wire.

    — Check and renew capacitor.
    — Test and renew coil as necessary.
    — Renew distributor cap.
    — Renew distributor rotor.
    — Check and renew leads.
    — Renew or clean and adjust spark plugs.
    — Dry out internal and external of distributor cap and rotor arm, dry plug leads and plugs.

2. **Engine starts but misfires under load.**

    Possible cause
    (a) Faulty, dirty or incorrectly adjusted spark plugs.
    (b) Dirty or incorrectly adjusted contact points.
    (c) Uneven wear on distributor cam.
    (d) Condensation moisture in distributor cap.
    (e) Cracked spark plug insulator/s.
    (f) Faulty ignition coil.

    Remedy
    — Renew and/or clean and adjust spark plugs.
    — Clean, adjust or renew points.
    — Check and overhaul distributor.
    — Check and dry out and examine cap for cracks.
    — Renew faulty spark plug/s.
    — Check and renew coil.

3. **Engine runs but lacks power.**

    Possible cause
    (a) Ignition timing incorrectly set or contact points require adjusting.
    (b) Centrifugal advance mechanism seized or excessively worn.
    (c) Vacuum advance unit inoperative.
    (d) Vacuum unit operates, but ineffective.

    Remedy
    — Check and readjust timing and/or contact points.
    — Overhaul distributor.

    — Check for broken vacuum pipe or faulty unit.
    — Advance unit link disconnected or broken.

Wiring Diagram for Right Hand Drive Models with Automatic and Manual Transmission.

KEY

1. *Inertia starter circuit.
2. *Pre-engaged starter circuit.
3. Distributor.
4. Ignition coil.
5. Series resistance.
6. *Alternator and regulator assembly.
6A. *Generator and regulator charging circuit.
7. Wiper motor.
8. Windscreen washer motor.
9. Heater.
10. Fuse panel.
11. Oil warning lamp sender unit.
12. Engine temperature sender unit.
13. Headlamp relay.
14. Fuel gauge sender unit.
15. Stop lamp switch.
16. Reverse lamp switch manual transmission models.
17. Inhibitor switch automatic transmission models.
18. Horns.
19. Wiring connector.
20. Wiring connector.
21. Quadrant lamp automatic transmission models.
22. Instrument panel printed circuit and connector.
23. Hazard indicator lamp.
24. Hazard lamp switch.
25. Wiper switch.
26. Heater switch.
27. Cigar lighter.
28. Glove box lamp.
29. Glove box lamp switch.
30. Combination and turn signal switch.
31. Ignition switch.
32. Headlamp switch.
33. Rear window heater warning lamp.
34. Rear window heater switch.
35. Rear window heater relay.
36. Rear window heater unit.
37. Electrical flasher unit.
38. Radio.
39, 40. L.H. side two-door or four-door courtesy lamp switches.
41, 42. R.H. side two-door or four-door courtesy lamp switches.
43. *Rear compartment lamp and switch, station sedan models.
44. *Rear door courtesy lamp switch, station sedan models.
45. *Courtesy lamp, models without sunshine roof.
46. *Courtesy lamp switch, models without sunshine roof.
47. *L.H. pillar courtesy lamp, models with sunshine roof.
48. *L.H. pillar courtesy lamp switch, models with sunshine roof.
49. *R.H. pillar courtesy lamp, models with sunshine roof.
50. *R.H. pillar courtesy lamp switch, models with sunshine roof.
51. R.H. rear turn signal lamp.
52. R.H. reverse lamp.
53. R.H. stop lamp.
54. R.H. tail lamp.
55. Licence plate lamp.
56. L.H. tail lamp.
57. L.H. stop lamp.
58. L.H. reverse lamp.
59. L.H. rear turn signal lamp.
60. R.H. front turn signal lamp.
61. R.H. headlamp.
62. R.H. parking lamp.
63. L.H. parking lamp.
64. L.H. headlamp.
65. L.H. front turn signal lamp.
*See inserts for wiring circuitry.

COLOR CODE

B—Black.
W—White.
R—Red.
BL—Blue.
Y—Yellow.
G—Green.
V—Violet.
P—Purple.
PK—Pink.
GRY—Grey.
BRN—Brown.
BY—Black/yellow trace.
BW—Black/white trace.
BV—Black/violet trace.
BP—Black/purple trace.
BG—Black/green trace
BR—Black/red trace
B BRN—Black/brown trace.
B R Y—Black/red and yellow trace.
B BL—Black/blue trace.
B WG—Black/white and green trace.
RW—Red/white trace.
RY—Red/yellow trace.
RB—Red/black trace.
R BL—Red/blue trace.
BL G—Blue/green trace.
BL W—Blue/white trace.
BL R—Blue/red trace.
GW—Green/white trace.
G W B—Green/white and black trace.
GRY B—Grey/black trace.
GRY R—Grey/red trace.
GRY W—Grey/white trace.
GRY G—Grey/green trace.
GRY Y—Grey/yellow trace.
BRN Y—Brown/yellow trace.

Wiring Diagram Inserts of Charging, Starting and Interior Lighting Circuitry for Right Hand Drive Models with Automatic and Manual Transmission.

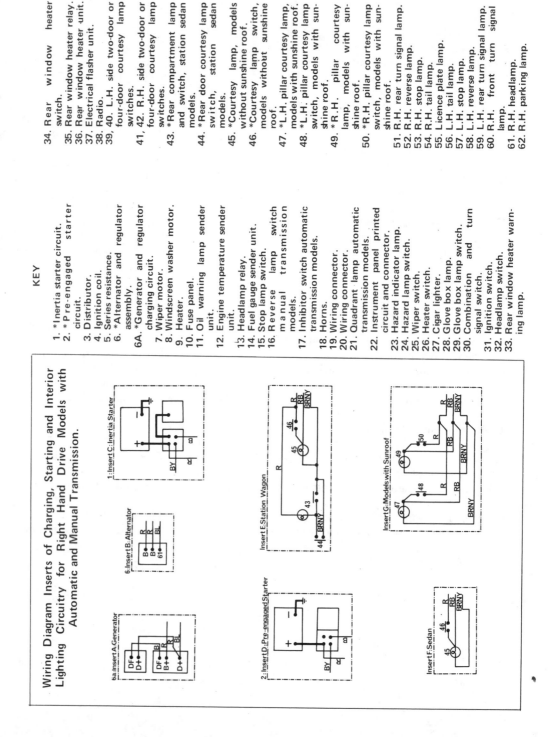

6a.Insert A.Generator

6.Insert B.Alternator

1.:Insert C.Inertia Starter

2.Insert D.Pre-engaged Starter

Insert E.Station Wagon

Insert F.Sedan

Insert G.Models with Sunroof

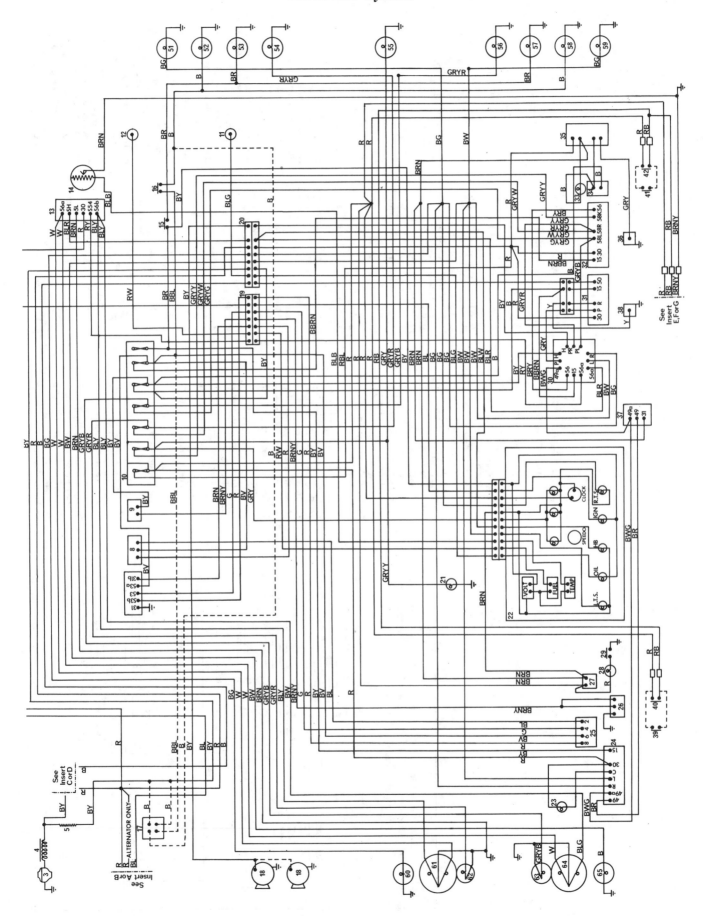

Wiring Diagram for Left Hand Drive Models with Automatic and Manual Transmission.

KEY

1. Distributor.
2. Ignition coil.
3. *Inertia starter circuit.
4. *Pre-engaged starter circuit.
5. Wiper motor.
6. Heater motor.
7. Series resistance.
8. *Generator charging circuit.
9. *Alternator charging circuit.
10. Dual brake warning lamp switch.
11. Fuse panel.
12. Rear window heater relay.
13. Rear window heater unit.
14. Fuel gauge sender unit.
15. Stop lamp switch.
16. Reverse lamp switch, manual transmission models.
17. Engine bay illumination lamp.
18. Inhibitor switch, automatic transmission models.
19, 20. Horns.
21. Wiring connector.
22. Oil pressure warning switch.
23. Engine temperature warning switch.
24. Wiring connector.
25. Headlamp relay.
26. Instrument panel printed circuit and connector.
27. Quadrant lamp, automatic transmission models.
28. Hazard indicator warning lamp.
29. Dual brake warning lamp test switch.
30. Dual brake warning lamp.
31. Cigar lighter.
32. Heater switch.

33. Windscreen washer foot switch.
34. Windscreen wiper switch.
35. Hazard relay.
36. Turn signal relay unit.
37. Combination and turn signal switch.
38. Wiring connector.
39. Ignition switch.
40. Headlamp switch.
41. Rear window heater warning lamp.
42. Rear window heater switch.
43. Radio.
44. Glove box lamp and switch.
45. *Left and right door pillar lamps and switch circuits, vehicles with sunshine roof.
46. *Luggage compartment lamp.
47. *Interior lamp and switch circuits, vehicles without sunshine roof.
48. R.H. rear turn signal lamp.
49. R.H. stop lamp.
50. R.H. tail lamp.
51. R.H. reverse lamp.
52. Licence plate lamp.
53. L.H. reverse lamp.
54. L.H. tail lamp.
55. L.H. stop lamp.
56. L.H. rear turn signal lamp.
57. R.H. front turn signal lamp.
58. R.H. headlamp.
59. R.H. parking lamp.
60. R.H. driving lamp when fitted.
61. L.H. driving lamp when fitted.
62. L.H. parking lamp.
63. L.H. headlamp.

64. L.H. front turn signal lamp.

*See inserts for wiring circuitry.

COLOR CODE

B–Black.
W–White.
R–Red.
BL–Blue.
Y–Yellow.
G–Green.
V–Violet.
P–Purple.
PK–Pink.
GRY–Grey.
BRN–Brown.
BY–Black/yellow trace.
BW–Black/white trace.
BV–Black/violet trace.
BP–Black/purple trace.
BG–Black/green trace
BR–Black/red trace
B BRN–Black/brown trace.
B R Y–Black/red and yellow trace.
B BL–Black/blue trace.
B WG–Black/white and green trace.
RW–Red/white trace.
RY–Red/yellow trace.
RB–Red/black trace.
R BL–Red/blue trace.
BL G–Blue/green trace.
BL W–Blue/white trace.
BL R–Blue/red trace.
GW–Green/white trace.
G W B–Green/white and black trace.
GRY B–Grey/black trace.
GRY R–Grey/red trace.
GRY W–Grey/white trace.
GRY G–Grey/green trace.
GRY Y–Grey/yellow trace.
BRN Y–Brown/yellow trace.

Wiring Diagram Inserts of Charging, Starting and Interior Lighting Circuitry for Left Hand Drive Models with Automatic and Manual Transmission.

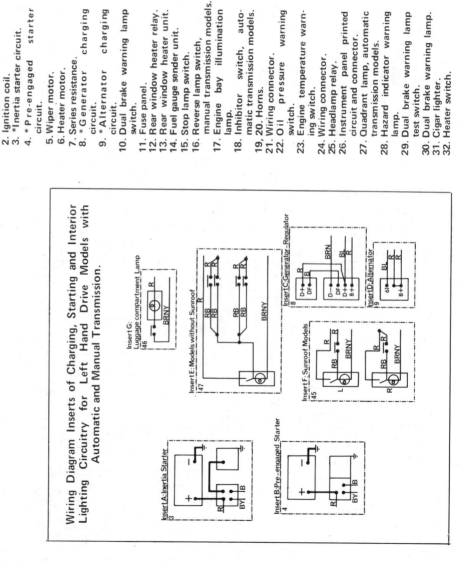

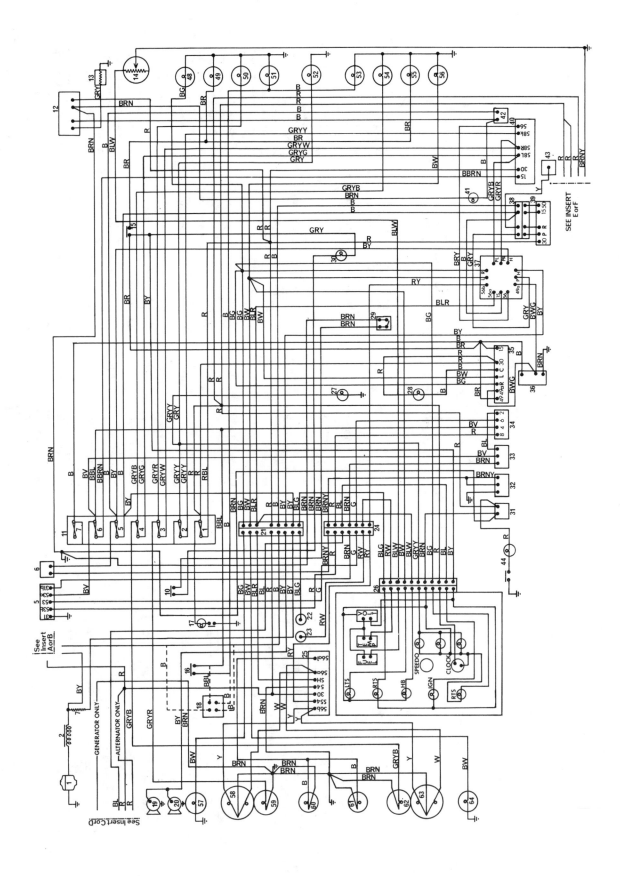

Wiring Diagram for Australian Produced Models with Automatic and Manual Transmission.

KEY

1. Distributor.
2. Ignition coil.
3. Series resistance.
4. *Lucas starter circuit.
5. *Bosch starter circuit.
6. Wiper motor.
7. Heater motor.
8. Fuse panel.
9. Fuel gauge sender unit.
10. Alternator regulator.
11. Alternator.
12. Engine compartment lamp.
13. Engine compartment lamp switch.
14. Inhibitor switch, automatic transmission models.
15. Reverse lamp switch, manual transmission models.
16. Dual brake warning lamp switch.
17. Wiring connector.
18. Stop lamp switch.
19, 20. Horns.
21. Oil pressure warning lamp switch.
22. Engine temperature sender unit.
23. Headlamp relay.
24. Wiring connector.
25. Instrument panel printed circuit and connector.
26. Quadrant lamp, automatic transmission models.
27. Hazard indicator warning lamp.

28. Dual brake warning lamp test switch.
29. Dual brake warning lamp.
30. Cigar lighter.
31. Glove box lamp and switch when fitted.
32. Heater switch.
33. Windscreen washer foot switch.
34. Windscreen wiper switch.
35. Hazard relay.
36. Turn signal relay unit.
37. Combination and turn signal switch.
38. Wiring connector.
39. Ignition switch.
40. Radio.
41. Headlamp switch.
42. * Luggage compartment lamp.
43. *Interior lamp and door switches.
44. R.H. rear turn signal lamp.
45. R.H. stop and tail lamp.
46. R.H. reverse lamp.
47. Licence plate lamp.
48. L.H. reverse lamp.
49. L.H. stop and tail lamp.
50. L.H. rear turn signal lamp.
51. R.H. front turn signal lamp.
52. R.H. headlamp.
53. R.H. parking lamp.
54. L.H. parking lamp.
55. L.H. headlamp.
56. L.H. front turn signal lamp.

*See inserts for wiring circuitry.

COLOR CODE

B—Black.
W—White.
R—Red.
BL—Blue.
Y—Yellow.
G—Green.
V—Violet.
P—Purple.
PK—Pink.
GRY—Grey.
BRN—Brown.
BY—Black/yellow trace.
BW—Black/white trace.
BV—Black/violet trace.
BP—Black/purple trace.
BG—Black/green trace
BR—Black/red trace
B BRN—Black/brown trace.
B R Y—Black/red and yellow trace.
B BL—Black/blue trace.
B WG—Black/white and green trace.
RW—Red/white trace.
RY—Red/yellow trace.
RB—Red/black trace.
R BL—Red/blue trace.
BL G—Blue/green trace.
BL W—Blue/white trace.
BL R—Blue/red trace.
GW—Green/white trace.
G W B—Green/white and black trace,
GRY B—Grey/black trace
GRY R—Grey/red trace.
GRY W—Grey/white trace.
GRY G—Grey/green trace.
GRY Y—Grey/yellow trace.
BRN Y—Brown/yellow trace.

Wiring Diagram Inserts of Starting and Interior Lighting Circuitry for Australian Produced Models with Automatic and Manual Transmission.

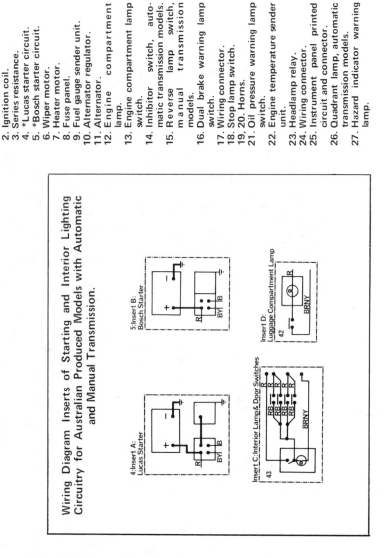

4:Insert A:
Lucas Starter

5:Insert B:
Bosch Starter

Insert C:Interior Lamp & Door Switches

Insert D:
Luggage Compartment Lamp

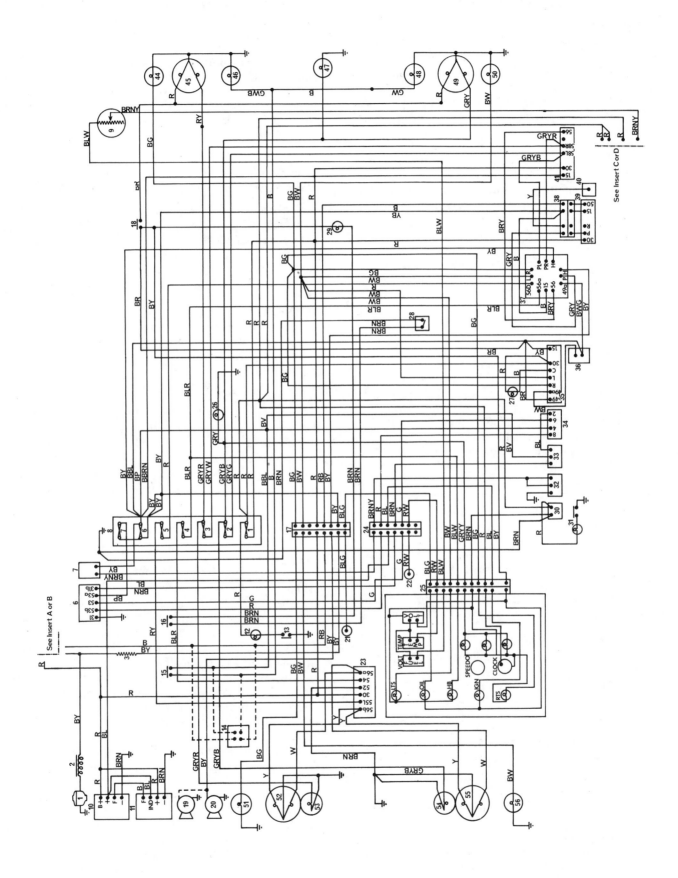

BODY

1. WINDSCREEN

TO REMOVE

(1) Cover the bonnet and scuttle panel with a suitable protective cloth to avoid damage to the paint work.

(2) Remove the windscreen wiper arms and blades from the front of the windscreen.

(3) Push the weatherstrip lip under the top and sides of the windscreen aperture flange. Use a suitable lipping tool for this operation.

(4) Applying firm pressure from inside the car, push the windscreen and weatherstrip assembly forward and out of the windscreen aperture.

(5) Prise out the joint cover clip and pull the finish strip out of the weatherstrip. Remove the weatherstrip from the glass.

TO INSTAL

(1) Clean all old sealing compound from the glass and the body flange grooves in the weatherstrip and from the flange of the body aperture. Check the weatherstrip for deterioration.

(2) Place the weatherstrip correctly on the windscreen glass.

(3) Using a suitable pressure gun and sealing compound, apply the compound to the weatherstrip rubber to body groove.

(4) Insert a length of strong cord in the weatherstrip rubber to body groove, starting at the lower centre of the assembly and continuing around the periphery of the windscreen glass to meet and cross the start of the cord, and tape both ends to the glass on the inside.

(5) With the aid of a second operator, position the windscreen and weatherstrip assembly centrally in the windscreen aperture, applying firm pressure to the outside of the glass. Ensure that the ends of the cord are not trapped between the weatherstrip and the body flange.

(6) From inside the vehicle, carefully pull each end of the cord from the lower centre of the glass assembly, across the bottom of the lower corners of the body aperture to seat the lip of the rubber over the body aperture flange.

(7) Using a suitable pressure gun with swan-necked nozzle and sealing compound, apply the compound to the rubber to glass groove.

(8) Replace the finish strip in its groove in the weatherstrip with the use of the lipping tool. Replace the joint cover clip.

(9) Clean off any excess sealing compound with a cloth soaked in petrol and wipe the assembly clean.

(10) Replace the windscreen wiper arms and blades.

2. REAR WINDOW

TO REMOVE

(1) Remove the rear seat cushion retaining screws and manoeuvre the cushion from the vehicle.

(2) Remove the rear seat squab retaining screws from the bottom corners.

(3) Working from inside the boot remove the retaining screws from the top of the rear seat squab.

(4) Manoeuvre the squab from the vehicle.

(5) Remove the rear parcel shelf retainers.

(6) Working from inside the boot, bend up the lock tabs.

(7) From inside the cabin, lift up and manoeuvre the parcel shelf from the vehicle.

(8) Place protective covering over the luggage compartment lid.

(9) Working from inside the vehicle, using a suitable lipping tool carefully prise the top edge of the weatherstrip from the body flange while applying pressure to the top of the window.

NOTE: Apply pressure to the top of the window in an outwards direction having a second operator outside the vehicle supporting the window.

(10) Remove the window and weatherstrip assembly from the body opening and place the assembly on a suitably padded workstand.

(11) Remove the moulding joining clips and carefully pull each moulding strip in turn from the weatherstrip.

(12) Remove the weatherstrip from the window.

TO INSTAL

(1) Clean all the old sealer from the body flange, the window glass and the grooves of the weatherstrip.

(2) Inspect the weatherstrip for cracks, deterioration or perishing.

(3) Inspect the body flange for distortion and repair as necessary.

(4) Using a suitable type sealant injector gun, run a continuous bead of sealant around the window groove of the weatherstrip and also around the flat surface of the body flange opening.

(5) Smear the bead of sealant on the flange out evenly and if necessary apply more sealant to completely cover the flange surface.

(6) Instal the weatherstrip onto the window and wipe off any excess sealant.

(7) Insert each moulding strip in turn into the weatherstrip.

(8) With the moulding strips in position instal the moulding joining clips.

(9) Insert a length of strong cord in the weatherstrip to body groove, starting at the lower centre of the assembly and continuing around the periphery of the window to meet and cross the start of the cord, and tape both ends to the window glass on the inside.

(10) With the aid of a second operator, position the windscreen and weatherstrip assembly centrally in the body opening, applying firm pressure to the outside of the window. Ensure that the ends of the cord are not trapped between the weatherstrip and the body flange.

(11) From inside the vehicle, carefully pull each end of the cord from the lower centre of the assembly, across the bottom of the lower corners of the body opening to seat the lip of the weatherstrip over the body aperture flange.

(12) Using the sealant injector gun complete the sealing between the weatherstrip and the body.

(13) Wipe off all excess sealant and clean the window and surrounding body panels using a suitable type solvent after removing the protective covering from the luggage compartment lid.

3. REAR FIXED WINDOW AND/OR TAILGATE WINDOW

TO REMOVE

(1) Working from inside the vehicle, using a suitable lipping tool carefully prise the edge of the weatherstrip from the body/tailgate flange while applying pressure to the top of the window.

NOTE: Apply pressure to the top of the window in an outwards direction having a second operator outside the vehicle supporting the window.

(2) Remove the window and weatherstrip assembly from the body/tailgate opening and place the assembly on a suitably padded workstand.

(3) Remove the moulding joining clips and carefully pull each moulding strip, in turn from the weatherstrip.

(4) Remove the weatherstrip from the window.

TO INSTAL

Installation is a reversal of the removal procedure with attention to the following points:

(1) Clean all the old sealer from the body/tailgate flange, the window and the grooves of the weatherstrip.

(2) Inspect the weatherstrip for cracks, deterioration or perishing.

(3) Inspect the body/tailgate flange for distortion and repair as necessary.

(4) Using a suitable type sealant injector gun, run a continuous bead of sealant around the window groove of the weatherstrip and also around the flat surface of the body/tailgate flange opening.

(5) Smear the bead of sealant on the flange out evenly and if necessary apply more sealant to completely cover the flange surface.

(6) Instal the weatherstrip onto the window and wipe off any excess sealant.

(7) Insert each moulding strip in turn into the weatherstrip.

(8) With the moulding strips in position instal the moulding joining clips.

(9) Insert a length of strong cord in the weatherstrip to body/tailgate flange groove. Start at the lower centre of the assembly and continue around the outside of the window to meet and cross the start of the cord.

NOTE: Tape both ends of the cord to the inside of the window.

(10) With the aid of a second operator, position the window and weatherstrip assembly centrally in the body/tailgate opening, applying firm pressure to the outside of the window. Ensure that the ends of the cord are not trapped between the weatherstrip and the body flange.

(11) From inside the vehicle, carefully pull each end of the cord from the lower centre of the window across the bottom, up the sides, and across the top to seat the lip of the weatherstrip over the body/tailgate flange.

(12) Using the sealant injector gun, complete the sealing between the weatherstrip and the body.

(13) Wipe off all excess sealant and clean the window and surrounding body panels with a suitable type solvent.

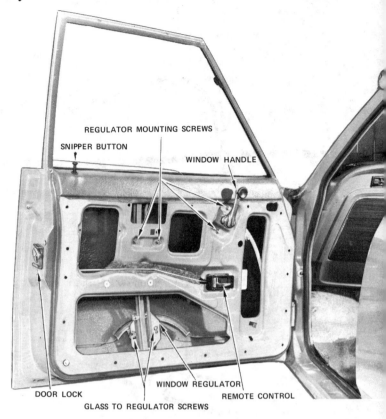

Front Door with Trim Panel Removed.

4. FRONT DOOR

TRIM PANEL
To Remove and Instal

(1) Carefully prise the insert from the window regulator handle. Remove the retaining screw and lift off the handle and escutcheon washer.

(2) Remove the door pull or arm rest retaining screws and remove the unit from the door.

(3) Remove the snipper rod button where necessary.

(4) Slide the remote control housing bezel forwards and out of the trim panel.

(5) Using a wide thin bladed lever inserted between the trim panel and the door near a retaining clip, lever the clip out of its retaining hole taking care not to damage the door paint work.

(6) Lever each clip free in turn and remove the door trim panel.

(7) Carefully remove the plastic sealing sheet from the inner door panel and place it aside.

Installation is a reversal of the removal procedure with attention to the following points:

(1) Ensure that the plastic sealing sheet is correctly repositioned and the edges reglued as necessary.

(2) Position the trim panel on the inside of the door, align the clips with the holes in the door panel and progressively engage the clips in the holes. At the same time maintaining the trim panel correctly in relation to the door panel.

(3) Position the escutcheon washer on the window regulator handle, place the handle and washer on the

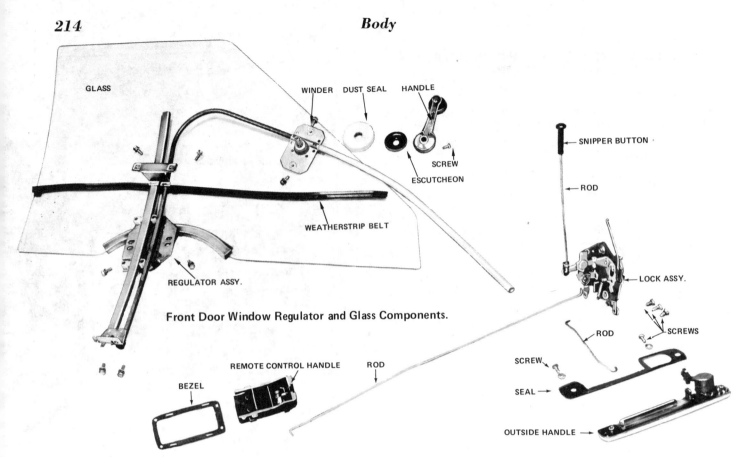

Front Door Window Regulator and Glass Components.

Front Door Lock and Handle Components.

window regulator stem with the handle pointing in the same direction as the handle on the opposite door when both windows are in the same position.

(4) Instal the snipper rod button if it was removed.

(5) Place the door pull or arm rest in position, instal and tighten the retaining screws.

(6) Instal the insert to the window regulator handle.

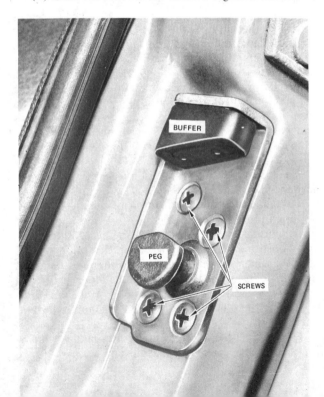

DOOR GLASS
To Remove and Instal

(1) Lower the door glass and remove the trim panel as previously described.

(2) Carefully prise the outer and inner weatherstrip belts from the opening in the top of the door.

(3) Raise the door glass slightly as necessary to gain access to the door glass retaining screws.

(4) Remove the door glass retaining screws, pivot the glass rear edge upwards and manoeuvre the door glass through the top of the door.

Installation is a reversal of the removal procedure.

NOTE: Do not drop the door glass into the door as the glass could be scratched, chipped or broken.

WINDOW REGULATOR
To Remove and Instal

(1) Lower the door glass and remove the trim panel as previously described.

(2) Remove the door glass to regulator retaining screws.

(3) Raise the door glass fully by hand and wedge it in the raised position.

(4) Remove the two screws from the window regulator stem plate.

(5) Remove the window regulator retaining screws and manoeuvre the assembly through the work aperture in the bottom of the door.

Door Striker Plate Showing Mounting Screws Locking Peg and Buffer.

(6) If necessary remove the dust shield from the window regulator stem.

Installation is a reversal of the removal procedure with attention to the following points:

(1) When installing the door glass to regulator retaining screws, instal them finger tight only.

(2) Raise the door glass to the fully raised position and tighten the door glass retaining screws securely.

(3) Check that the door glass slides freely up and down in the run channels.

(4) If necessary slacken the door glass retaining screws and move the door glass fore or aft as required. Retighten the screws.

REMOTE CONTROL
To Remove and Instal

(1) Remove the trim panel as previously described.

(2) Slide the remote control forwards slightly and then lift it out of the inner door panel far enough to gain access to the remote control rod.

(3) Support the remote control rod and disengage the remote control from the rod.

(4) Remove the remote control from the door.

Installation is a reversal of the removal procedure.

OUTSIDE HANDLE
To Remove and Instal

(1) With the door glass in the fully raised position, remove the trim panel as previously described.

(2) Using a long thin screwdriver, prise the two rods from the door lock which connects the outside handle to the lock.

(3) Remove the bolts retaining the handle to the door and withdraw the handle and rods from the door.

(4) Note the fitted position of the lock cylinder rod and the door lock opening rod to the outside handle before unclipping the rods from the handle.

Installation is a reversal of the removal procedure ensuring that all rods are engaged fully during installation.

DOOR LOCK
To Remove and Instal

(1) Remove the remote control and the outside handle as previously described.

(2) Remove the door lock retaining screws and the snipper button. Remove the door lock with the remote control rod and snipper button rod attached through the upper work aperture of the inner door panel.

(3) Note the fitted positions of the rods to the door lock before disconnecting them.

Installation is a reversal of the removal procedure.

LOCK STRIKER
To Renew and Adjust

(1) Remove the four retaining screws and detach the striker plate.

(2) Fit the new striker plate to the door pillar and fit the retaining screws.

(3) Tighten the retaining screws to just hold the striker in position.

(4) Press the door outside lever and gently close the door.

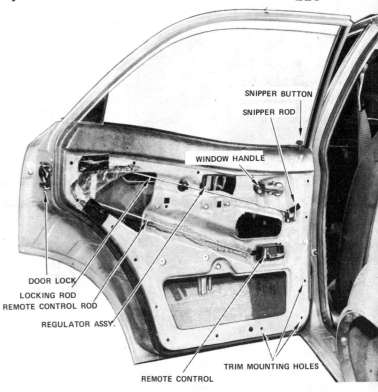

Rear Door with Trim Panel Removed.

(5) Release the lever and move the door in or out as necessary to align the door flush with the body.

(6) Depress the lever and gently open the door and check that the striker plate is vertical.

(7) Tighten the retaining screws and recheck the door closing and positioning.

NOTE: Ensure that the safety catches engage fully when the door is shut.

5. REAR DOOR

TRIM PANEL
To Remove and Instal

(1) Carefully prise the insert from the window regulator handle. Remove the retaining screw and lift off the handle and the escutcheon washer.

(2) Remove the door pull or arm rest retaining screws and remove the unit from the door.

(3) Remove the snipper rod button where necessary.

(4) Slide the remote control housing bezel forwards and out of the trim panel.

(5) Using a wide thin bladed lever inserted between the trim panel and the door near a retaining clip lever the clip out of its retaining hole taking care not to damage the door paint work.

(6) Lever each clip free in turn and remove the trim panel from the door.

(7) Carefully remove the plastic sealing sheet from the inner door panel and place it aside.

Installation is a reversal of the removal procedure with attention to the following points:

(1) Ensure that the plastic sealing sheet is correctly repositioned and the edges reglued as necessary.

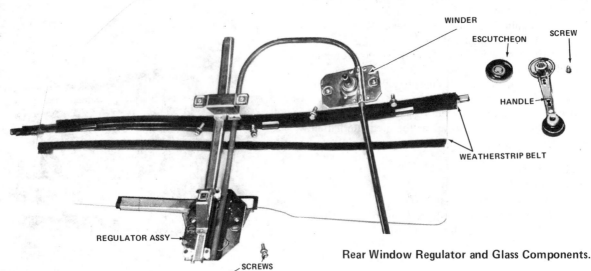

Rear Window Regulator and Glass Components.

(2) Position the trim panel on the inside of the door, align the clips around the edge of the trim panel with the holes in the door panel and progressively engage the clips in the holes. At the same time maintaining the trim panel correctly in relation to the door panel.

(3) Position the escutcheon washer on the window regulator handle, place the handle and washer on the window regulator stem with the handle pointing in the same direction as the handle on the opposite door when both windows are in the same position.

(4) Instal the snipper rod button if it was removed.

(5) Place the door pull or arm rest in position, instal and tighten the retaining screws.

(6) Tighten the retaining screw and instal the insert to the window regulator handle.

DOOR GLASS
To Remove and Instal
(1) With the door glass fully lowered remove the trim panel as previously described.

(2) Carefully prise the outer and inner weatherstrip belts from the opening in the top of the door. Raise the door glass.

(3) Remove the door glass rear run channel retaining screws and manoeuvre the channel assembly from the door.

(4) Support the rear of the glass during the next operation.

(5) Lower the door glass to gain access to the door glass retaining screws.

(6) Remove the door glass retaining screws, move the door glass rearwards, slightly out of the front glass run channel and push the door glass upwards and out of the door opening. Place the door glass aside.

Installation is a reversal of the removal procedure with attention to the following points:

(1) Manoeuvre the door glass into the front run channel, after it has been inserted into the door and instal

the door glass to regulator retaining screws. Tighten the screws securely.

(2) Guide the rear run channel into position in the door engaging the run channel with the door glass.

(3) Instal and securely tighten the rear run channel retaining screws.

(4) Instal the inner and outer weatherstrip belts without damaging the paint work.

(5) Instal the trim panel as previously described.

WINDOW REGULATOR
To Remove and Instal
(1) Remove the trim panel as previously described.

(2) Lower the door glass and remove the door glass to regulator retaining screws.

(3) Raise the door glass fully by hand and wedge it in the raised position.

(4) Remove the two screws from the window regulator stem plate.

(5) Remove the window regulator retaining screws and manoeuvre the assembly through the work aperture in the bottom of the door.

Installation is a reversal of the removal procedure with attention to the following points:

(1) When installing the door glass to regulator retaining screws, instal them finger tight only.

(2) Raise the door glass to the fully raised position and tighten the door glass retaining screws securely.

(3) Check that the door glass slides freely up and down in the run channels.

(4) If necessary slacken the door glass retaining screws and move the door glass fore or aft as required. Retighten the screws.

REMOTE CONTROL
To Remove and Instal
(1) Remove the trim panel as previously described.

(2) Slide the remote control forwards slightly and then lift it out of the inner door panel far enough to gain access to the remote control rod.

BEZEL — REMOTE CONTROL HANDLE — ROD — LOCK ASSY. — SCREWS — SCREWS — SEAL — OUTSIDE HANDLE

Rear Door Lock and Handle Components.

(3) Support the remote control rod and disengage the remote control from the rod.

(4) Remove the remote control from the door.

Installation is a reversal of the removal procedure.

OUTSIDE HANDLE

To Remove and Instal

(1) With the door glass in the fully raised position, remove the trim panel as previously described.

(2) Using a long thin screwdriver, prise the rod from the door lock which connects the outside handle to the door lock.

(3) Remove the bolts retaining the handle to the door and withdraw the handle and rod from the door.

(4) Disengage the rod from the handle.

Installation is a reversal of the removal procedure.

DOOR LOCK

To Remove and Instal

(1) Remove the remote control and the outside handle as previously described.

(2) Remove the rear glass run channel retaining screws and manoeuvre the channel from the door.

(3) Remove the door lock retaining screws and snipper button, remove the door lock with the remote control and snipper button rods attached.

(4) Note the fitted positions of the rods to the door lock before disconnecting them.

Installation is a reversal of the removal procedure ensuring that the rear glass run channel is engaged with the door glass before installing the channel retaining screws.

LOCK STRIKER

To Renew and Adjust

(1) Remove the four retaining screws and detach the striker plate.

(2) Fit the new striker plate to its mounting position and instal the retaining screws.

(3) Tighten the retaining screws to just hold the striker in position.

(4) Press the door outside lever and gently close the door.

(5) Release the lever and move the door in or out as necessary to align the door flush with the body.

(6) Depress the lever and gently open the door and check that the striker plate is vertical.

(7) Tighten the retaining screws and recheck the door closing and positioning.

NOTE: Ensure that the safety catches engage fully when the door is shut.

6. ENGINE BONNET

TO REMOVE

(1) Release the catch, raise the bonnet and support it with the bonnet stay.

(2) Using a soft lead pencil, mark around the outside edge of each hinge plate on the bonnet hinge panel.

(3) Place protective covers on the body and front fenders to prevent damage to the paint work by the corners of the bonnet.

(4) Remove the two bolts and washers securing each hinge plate to the hinge panel and, with the help of a second operator, lift the bonnet clear of the vehicle.

TO INSTAL AND ALIGN

(1) With the aid of a second operator, place the bonnet in position on the vehicle and support it at the front on the bonnet stay.

(2) Instal the two bolts and washers securing each hinge plate to the hinge-panel, position hinge plates according to the marks made on removal and tighten the bolts securely.

(3) Close the bonnet on the safety catch and check its alignment in relation to each front fender along the sides and along the rear edge of the bonnet to the body.

(4) If adjustment is required, open the bonnet and loosen the bolts securing the hinge plates to the bonnet just sufficiently to enable the bonnet to be moved slightly sideways or fore and aft.

(5) Loosen the bolts securing the bonnet lock plate to upper grille member, loosen the locknuts and screw down the rubber covered bump bolts, one each end of the grille upper panel.

(6) Close the bonnet past the safety catch, but do not completely close it on the final lock.

(7) Move the bonnet sideways or fore and aft until the space between the bonnet and each front fender is uniform, and the space between the rear edge of the bonnet and the corresponding edge of the body is also uniform.

(8) Carefully raise the bonnet and tighten the bolts securing the hinge plates to the bonnet and the bonnet lock plate to the upper grille member.

(9) Close the bonnet completely on the final catch and recheck the alignment.

(10) Check the up and down clearance across the rear of the bonnet in the closed position.

(11) If adjustment is necessary, open the bonnet, loosen the bolts securing the lower hinge plates to the body just sufficiently to allow up and down movement of the bonnet and hinge assembly.

(12) With the bonnet closed, carefully move the rear of the bonnet up or down until the desired clearance is obtained between the underside of the bonnet rear edge and the body.

(13) Carefully open the bonnet and securely tighten the lower hinge plate bolts. Close the bonnet and recheck the adjustments.

7. LUGGAGE COMPARTMENT LID

TO REMOVE

(1) Raise the compartment lid and mark around the hinge plates on the underside of the lid with a soft pencil.

(2) With the aid of a second operator to support the lid, take out the two bolts securing each hinge plate to the lid, and remove the compartment lid from the vehicle.

TO INSTAL

(1) With the aid of a second operator, place the compartment lid in position on the hinges according to the marks made on removal and instal the two bolts and washers to secure each hinge plate to the lid.

(2) Close the lid and check the vertical and lateral alignment of the lid in relation to the body.

(3) If adjustment is necessary, slacken the hinge securing bolts and move the lid until the clearance at the front and sides is equal. Tighten the hinge plate bolts securely.

(4) If vertical adjustment at the rear of the lid is necessary, slacken the bolts securing the lock striker to the rear body panel and move it up and down as required. Tighten the bolts securely.

8. TAILGATE

TAILGATE ASSEMBLY
To Remove and Instal

(1) Open the tailgate and mark around the outside edge of the hinges on the tailgate with a soft lead pencil.

(2) With the aid of a second operator support the tailgate and remove the hinge retaining bolts.

(3) Lift the tailgate off the hinges and place it aside.

Installation is a reversal of the removal procedure with attention to the following points:

(1) Position the tailgate on the hinges according to the soft lead pencil marks.

(2) Tighten the retaining bolts securely.

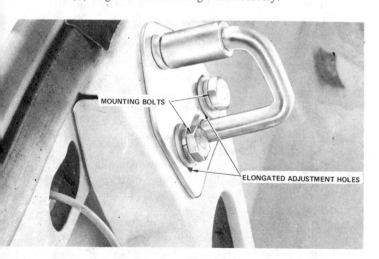

Luggage Compartment Lid Striker.

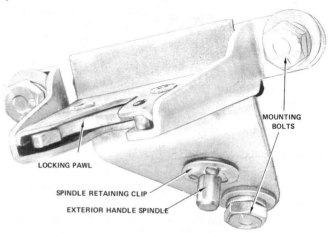

Luggage Compartment Lid Lock.

TORSION BAR AND HINGE ASSEMBLY
To Remove and Instal

(1) Remove the tailgate as previously described.

(2) Using a soft lead pencil mark around the outside edges of the hinge to ensure correct reassembly.

(3) Remove the retaining bolts and lift the assembly from the tailgate.

Installation is a reversal of the removal procedure aligning the pencil marks on installation.

LOCK AND HANDLE ASSEMBLY
To Dismantle

(1) Remove the trim panel.

(2) Undo and remove the lock cylinder hexagonal retaining nut.

(3) Remove the lock cylinder.

(4) Remove the lock retaining bolts.

(5) Remove the lock and operating rod assembly.

(6) Remove the handle retaining nuts and remove the handle and gasket.

To Assemble

(1) Place the gasket and handle onto the tailgate outer panel, instal and securely tighten the retaining nuts.

(2) Place the lock and operating rod assembly into the tailgate and loosely instal the retaining bolts.

(3) Guide the lock cylinder into the tailgate outer panel locating the operating rod assembly on the cylinder keyways.

(4) Instal and tighten the hexagonal retaining nut.

(5) Hold the operating rod against the cylinder keyways and tighten the lock retaining bolts.

(6) Instal the trim panel.

STRIKER PLATE
To Renew

(1) Open the tailgate and using a soft lead pencil mark around the outside edges of the striker plate to floor.

(2) Remove the retaining screws and lift off the striker plate.

(3) Place the new striker plate in position according to the pencil marks.

(4) Instal and tighten the retaining screws ensuring that the pencil marks are correctly aligned.

WHEELS AND TYRES

SPECIFICATIONS

AUSTRALIAN PRODUCTION

Model	Tyre Size	Wheel Size	Inflation Pressure PSI	
	Standard	*Standard*	*Front-Rear*	
1600 Sedan	560 4 ply	13x4½ JJ	26	26
2000 Sedan	A78L 4 ply	13x5½ JJ	26	26
1600 Wagon	B78L 4 ply	13x4½ JJ	26	30
2000 Wagon	B78L 4 ply	13x5½ JJ	26	30

EUROPEAN PRODUCTION

Model	Tyre Size	Wheel Size		
1300 Sedan	560 4 ply	13x4½ J	23	24
1600 Sedan	560 4 ply	13x4½ J	23	24
1600 GT	165SR radial	13x4½ J	23	23
2000 GT	165SR radial	13x4½ J	23	23
1300 Wagon	600 4 ply	13x4½ J	21	23
1600 Wagon	600 4 ply	13x4½ J	21	23
2000 Wagon	175 radial	13x4½ J	21	24

NOTE: All quoted tyre inflation pressures are for normal load running with up to three persons.

For sustained high speed and for fully laden driving the inflation pressures must be increased by approximately 3 psi.

1. WHEEL AND TYRE ASSEMBLY

TO REMOVE

(1) Apply the handbrake.
(2) Detach the hub cap from the wheel to be removed.
(3) Unscrew the wheel nuts approximately three-quarters of a turn.
(4) Jack up the vehicle.
(5) Remove the wheel nuts and withdraw the wheel from the vehicle.

TO INSTAL

Installation is a reversal of the removal procedure with attention to the following points:

Tighten the wheel nuts in a diagonal sequence, but do not overtighten.

TO MAINTAIN

Proper tyre and wheel maintenance is essential for economical and safe operation.

(1) Check and adjust tyre pressures when the tyres are in a cold condition. Frequent loss of pressure should be investigated and the leakage rectified.

NOTE: Never adjust tyre pressures when the tyres are warm otherwise pressures will be incorrect when the tyres cool down.

(2) Inspect tyres regularly for damage and abnormal wear. Any abnormal wear may be due to one or more of the faults shown in the illustrations or listed in the Fault Diagnosis section. Attention should be given to penetrations or cuts in the tyre which will allow the entry of moisture into the carcass resulting in premature failure.

(3) Ensure that tyres are kept free of oil or grease.

(4) Inspect the wheel studs and nuts for thread damage and the stud holes in the wheels for elongation.

(5) Check the wheels for radial and lateral run-out and for damage to the flanges and bead seats.

(6) Tighten wheel retaining nuts securely.

(7) Periodically rotate wheels and tyres according to the illustration sequence.

(8) Maintain correct wheel balance.

2. TUBED TYRES

TO REMOVE

(1) Jack up the vehicle and remove the wheel.

(2) Remove the valve cap and valve core.

(3) Separate the inside bead from the inside wheel flange and using tyre levers, with rounded edges, lever the bead of the tyre over the inside edge of the flange.

NOTE: Exercise extreme care during operation (3) to ensure that the levers do not damage the tube by forcing it against the rim.

(4) Push the valve of the inner tube into the tyre interior and withdraw the inner tube out between the inner bead of the tyre and the inner flange of the wheel.

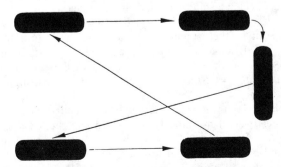

Diagram for Correct Wheel Rotation to Prolong Tyre Life and Minimise Tyre Wear.

(5) Separate the outside bead of the tyre from the outside flange at the wheel and using tyre levers with rounded edges, lever the bead of the tyre over the inside flange of the wheel separating the two components.

TO INSTAL

(1) Remove any loose or excessive scale or rust from the wheel flanges and finally clean with a wire brush or emery paper.

(2) Position the inside flange of the wheel partially inside one of the tyre beads and using tyre levers in good condition lever the remainder of the tyre bead over the flange onto the wheel.

NOTE: During operation (2) ensure that the position of the tyre bead opposite the side where the levers are applied is seating in the wellbase of the wheel rim.

(3) Place the inner tube inside the tyre and insert the valve through the hole in the wheel.

Screw a valve core removing tool on the end of the valve to prevent the valve slipping back into the interior of the tyre when the other tyre bead is being placed on the wheel.

(4) Fit the second bead of the tyre over the wheel inner flange, using the tyre levers or a rubber mallet, and ensuring that the side of the bead adjacent to the tube valve goes over the wheel flange last.

NOTE: In the event of a tyre being marked with a balance dot, place the dot adjacent to the valve stem to maintain correct tyre balance.

(5) Stand the wheel and tyre upright, fit the valve core and inflate the tube until the tyre beads commence to position themselves on the wheel bead seats.

(6) Bounce the tyre on the floor several times to position the tyre beads against the wheel flanges. Inflate the tyre and tube to the recommended pressure and finally check the valve core for leakage and instal the valve cap.

3. TUBELESS TYRES

TO TEST FOR LEAKS

(1) With the wheel removed from the vehicle, inflate the tyre to the recommended pressure, immerse the tyre and wheel in a water tank and check for leaks.

(2) Place the assembly in the tank so that the valve is uppermost, then submerge the valve and check for bubbles.

(3) Release and allow the assembly to float, ensuring the channel between the rim flange and the tyre is filled with water, carefully check for air bubbles emitting from this area.

(4) Turn the wheel assembly over and submerge the wheel rivets if not already submerged and check for leaks.

(5) Submerge the assembly and fill the channel between the flange and the tyre, allow to float and check for leaks. If leaking, wipe area dry and mark the position of the leak with chalk.

TO REPAIR LEAKS

(1) Repair of a small fracture not exceeding 2.38 mm (0.093 in) in the tyre may be repaired by applying sealing cement or dough with a suitable applicator.

(2) Minor repairs to the rim seat can be effected by deflating the tyre and holding the bead away from the seat and cleaning off the affected area.

(3) To repair fractures not exceeding 6.35 mm (0.250 in) in diameter remove the tyre from the wheel and repair the fracture by inserting a rubber plug coated in cement into the hole with the needle provided in the repair kit. Withdraw the needle, after ensuring it has fully penetrated the tyre, and cut the rubber leaving approximately 6.35 mm (0.250 in) protruding above the tread.

NOTE: Should the fracture be in excess of 6.35 mm (0.250 in) the repair should be carried out by an authorised tyre dealer.

(4) If the valve stem is leaking, deflate the tyre and remove from the wheel. Remove the valve from the wheel and inspect for splitting, crushing or dirt between the wheel and the valve. Clean area or replace if necessary.

When fitting a new valve, wet the valve stem and valve hole with soap and insert from the inside of the wheel. Using Schrader tool No. 553 pull the valve through until correctly seated on rim. Do not use pliers or similar hand tools to fit valve.

TO REMOVE

(1) Remove the wheel from the vehicle, remove the valve cap and core.

(2) Separate both inside and outside beads from the wheel flanges so that the beads are in the base of the rim.

(3) Using tyre levers with rounded edges, lever the beads of the tyre, one at a time, off the inner flange of the wheel.

Prior to removal use a soap solution on the beads and wheel flange, and see that the beads, diametrically opposite the point of leverage, are seating on the bottom of the wellbase.

TO INSTAL

(1) Remove loose or excessive scale or rust from the wheel, taking care not to damage paint. Repaint the wheel if necessary.

(2) Remove any dents from the rim flanges and wipe clean with a moist rag.

(3) Clean off the tyre beads, moisten tyre beads, rim surfaces and tyre levers with clean water or soap solution.

(4) Fit the tyre in the normal way, use narrow levers and taking small bites to avoid strain and damage to the beads. Avoid damage at all times as the sealing quality of the tyre is determined by the condition of the bead.

(5) Fit the second bead so that the part of the bead nearest the valve goes over the rim flange last.

NOTE: Do not use hammer or mallet to fit tubeless tyres. Ensure that the balance mark on the tyre is adjacent to the valve.

TO INFLATE

(1) Holding the assembly upright, bounce the tread of the tyre on the ground at several points around its periphery. This will help to seat the beads on the tapered rim seats and provide a partial seal.

(2) With the valve core removed, connect the air hose and inflate the tyre until the beads have sealed correctly. It may be necessary to bounce the tyre while inflating.

(3) Remove the air hose, fit the valve core and inflate the tyre to 2.81 kg/cm² (40 psi). Test the tyre for leaks and deflate to the normal pressure.

TO INFLATE USING A TOURNIQUET

(1) Inflate the tyre with the assistance of a tourniquet use Dunlop tool No TT/1 or its equivalent, follow the fitting instructions included in the kit.

(2) With the valve core removed, inflate the tyre until the beads are sealed against the flanges. Remove the hose, fit the valve core and inflate the tyre to 2.81 kg/cm² (40 psi). Test the tyre for leaks and deflate to normal pressure.

NOTE: As an alternative method a tourniquet can be made by using a piece of rope and a suitable lever e.g. a bar, tyre lever or a piece of wood.

4. TYRE WEAR DIAGNOSIS

1. Abnormal wear on both sides of tread.

Possible cause

(a)   Under inflation of tyres.
(b)   Over-loading.

Remedy

— Check and inflate to recommended pressures.
— Reduce maximum loading.

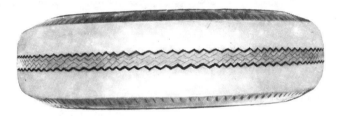

2. Abnormal wear in centre of tread.

Possible cause

(a)   Over inflation of tyres.

Remedy

— Check and reduce to recommended pressures.

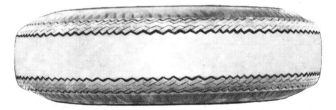

3. Abnormal wear on inside of tyres.

Possible cause

(a)   Insufficient camber angle.
(b)   Sagging front coil spring(s).
(c)   Loose or worn front hub bearings.
(d)   Bent stub axle.
(e)   Loose or worn suspension arm components.

Remedy

— Check front end alignment and adjust as necessary.
— Check and renew faulty spring(s).
— Check and adjust or renew hub bearings.
— Check and renew faulty components.
— Check and renew faulty components. Align front end.

4. Abnormal wear on outside of tread.

Possible cause — *Remedy*

(a)   Excessive camber angle.
(b)   Incorrect coil spring(s) fitted.

— Check front end alignment and adjust as necessary.
— Check and instal recommended replacement spring(s).

5. Spotty or irregular wear.

Possible cause — *Remedy*

(a)   Static or dynamic unbalance of wheel and tyre
         assembly.
(b)   Lateral run-out of wheel.
(c)   Excessive play in wheel hub bearing.
(d)   Excessive play in steering knuckle ball joints.

— Check and balance wheel and tyre assembly.

— Check and true-up or renew wheel.
— Check and adjust or renew hub bearing.
— Check and renew ball joints.

6. Lightly worn spots at centre of tread.

Possible cause — *Remedy*

(a)   Static unbalance of wheel and tyre assembly.
(b)   Radial run-out (eccentricity) of wheel.

— Check and balance wheel and tyre assembly.
— Check and renew wheel.

7. Flat spots at centre of tread.

Possible cause — *Remedy*

(a)   Eccentric brake drum.
(b)   Repeatedly severe brake application.
(c)   Lack of tyre rotation.

— Check and renew brake drum.
— Revise driving habits.
— Periodically change tyres by rotation of wheel/tyre
   assembly.

8. Heel and toe wear (sawtooth effect).

Possible cause — *Remedy*

(a)   Over-loading.
(b)   High-speed driving.
(c)   Excessive braking.

— Revise maximum loading.
— Avoid as far as possible.
— Revise driving habits.

9. Feathered edge on one side of tread pattern.

Possible cause — *Remedy*

(a)   Sharp inside edge — excessive toe-in.
(b)   One tyre sharp inside edge other tyre sharp outside
         edge.

— Check and adjust wheel alignment.
— Check for bent steering arm and renew.

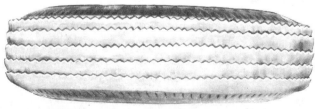

LUBRICATION & MAINTENANCE

CAPACITY AND GRADE

ENGINE
Capacity:
Oil change only . . . . 3.0 litres
Oil change and renew
filter . . . . 3.5 litres
Grade of lubricant:
Winter 10W/30
Summer 20W/40

MANUAL TRANSMISSION
Capacity:
Type 1 . . . . 1.35 litres
Type 2 . . . . 0.9 litres
Type 3 . . . . 0.9 litres
Type 4 . . . . 1.9 litres
Grade of lubricant . . . . . . SAE 80 EP

AUTOMATIC TRANSMISSION
Capacity . . . . 6.4 litres
Grade of lubricant . . . . Donax T7

REAR AXLE
Capacity:
Type A . . . . 1.0 litres
Type B . . . . 1.1 litres
Grade of lubricant . . . . . . SAE 90 EP

STEERING BOX
Capacity . . . . 0.14 litres
Grade of lubricant . . . . SAE 90 Hypoid

COOLING SYSTEM
Capacity:
1300 . . . . 5.8 litres
1600 . . . . 6.4 litres
2000 . . . . 7.1 litres

FUEL TANK
Capacity . . . . 54.0 litres

LUBRICATION SCHEDULE

	EACH 1000	5	10	15	20	25	30	35	40	45	50	55	60
ENGINE (1) Check the oil level on the dipstick each time the fuel tank is topped or every 1000 km. Top up as necessary with MS engine oil as recommended.	●												
(2) Drain the crankcase and renew the oil filter every 10,000 km or six months. Refill the crankcase with the oil recommended.			●		●		●		●		●		●
(3) Clean the crankcase emission valve and oil filler cap in solvent and blow dry every 10,000 km or six months. Re-oil the filler cap gauze and drain off surplus oil.			●		●		●		●		●		●
COOLING SYSTEM (1) Check the water level in the radiator every 1000 km and top up as necessary. *NOTE: If the vehicle is at normal operating temperature use care when removing the radiator cap to avoid scalding.*	●												
(2) Inspect the radiator and heater hoses for deterioration every 10,000 km or six months.			●		●		●		●		●		●
(3) Drain, flush and refill the cooling system every 20,000 km or twelve months. Add conditioner or anti-freeze as necessary.					●				●				●
FUEL SYSTEM (1) Clean the fuel pump and carburettor filter every 10,000 km or six months. Ensure that all sediment is removed from the fuel pump.			●		●		●		●		●		●
(2) Renew the in-line fuel filter (where fitted) every 48,000 km. Check for fuel leakage after installation.											●		

	EACH 1000	5	10	15	20	25	30	35	40	45	50	55	60
(3) Remove the air cleaner element and clean every 10,000 km or six months by tapping it lightly on a bench to remove dirt.			●		●		●		●		●		●
(4) Renew the air cleaner element every 48,000 km.											●		
MANUAL TRANSMISSION (1) Check the transmission lubricant level every 10,000 km and top up as necessary with recommended lubricant.			●		●		●		●		●		●
AUTOMATIC TRANSMISSION (1) Check the oil level in the transmission case every 5000 km and top up as necessary with the recommended automatic transmission fluid.		●	●	●	●	●	●	●	●	●	●	●	●
(2) Renew the fluid every 40,000 km and clean the filter.									●				
FRONT SUSPENSION (1) Remove, clean and repack the hub bearings every 29,000 km with a high melting point lithium base grease.							●						●
(2) Lubricate the front suspension ball joints using a molybdenum based grease every 48,000 km.											●		
STEERING (1) The steering box is filled on assembly and must not be overfilled. Periodically check the steering gear for leaks and if excessive remove and rectify. Refill with the correct amount and grade of lubricant.													
REAR AXLE (1) Check the rear axle lubricant level every 10,000 km and top up as necessary with recommended lubricant.			●		●		●		●		●		●
BRAKE FLUID RESERVOIR (1) Check and top up with heavy duty hydraulic brake fluid as necessary or at least every 5000 km.		●	●	●	●	●	●	●	●	●	●	●	●
(2) Flush and refill the fluid reservoir at the master cylinder overhaul using clean hydraulic fluid as specified.													
TYRES (1) Test and inflate to the recommended pressure as required.	●												
BATTERY (1) Check and top up the electrolyte with distilled water as required or at least monthly.	●												
BODY (1) Check and lubricate the following components as required with a dry lubricant: Door lock, rotor and strikers, bonnet catch plate, luggage compartment lock and striker.													

THOUSAND KILOMETRES

	EACH 1000	THOUSAND KILOMETRES											
		5	10	15	20	25	30	35	40	45	50	55	60
(2) Lubricate the following components with a few drops of engine oil as required: Door hinges, bonnet catch bolt and hinges, luggage compartment hinges, door locks on replacement and handbrake linkage.													
ALTERNATOR (1) Pack the bearings with a high melting point grease at overhaul.													
GENERATOR (Where applicable) (1) Sparingly lubricate the generator rear bearing with engine oil every 10,000 km or six months.			●		●		●		●		●		●
DISTRIBUTOR (1) Remove the rotor and insert a few drops of engine oil every 10,000 km approximately.			●		●		●		●		●		●
(2) Place a smear of high melting point grease on the distributor cam when the contact points are cleaned and adjusted or renewed.													
(3) Clean and set the ignition contact points every 10,000 km. Renew as found necessary.			●		●		●		●		●		●
SPARK PLUGS (1) Clean and gap the plugs every 10,000 km.			●		●		●		●		●		●
(2) Renew the plugs at intervals of approximately 20,000 km.					●				●				●

CONVERSION TABLES
SOME METRIC UNITS FOR EVERYDAY USE

Quantity	Imperial Unit	Metric Unit	Conversion Factors (Approximate)	
			Imperial to Metric Units	Metric to Imperial Units
LENGTH	inch (in)	millimetre (mm) or centimetre (cm)	1 in = 25·4 mm	
	foot (ft)	centimetre or metre (m)	1 ft = 30·5 cm	1 cm = 0·394 in
	yard (yd)	metre (m)	1 yd = 0·914 m	1 m = 3·28 ft
	furlong (fur)	metre (m) or kilometre (km)	1 fur = 201 m	1 m = 1·09 yd
	mile	kilometre (km)	1 mile = 1·61 km	1 km = 4·97 fur
	(for navigation)	international nautical mile (n mile)	1 n mile = 1852 m	1 km = 0·621 mile
MASS	ounce (oz)	gram (g)	1 oz = 28·3 g	1 g = 0·0353 oz
	pound (lb)	gram (g) or kilogram (kg)	1 lb = 454 g	1 kg = 2·20 lb
	stone	kilogram (kg)	1 stone = 6·35 kg	1 kg = 0·157 stone
	ton	tonne (t)	1 ton = 1·02 t	1 t = 0·984 ton
AREA	square inch (in²)	square centimetre (cm²)	1 in² = 6·45 cm²	1cm² = 0·155 in²
	square foot (ft²)	square centimetre (cm²) or square metre (m²)	1 ft² = 929 cm²	1 m² = 10·8 ft²
	square yard (yd²)	square metre (m²)	1 yd² = 0·836 m²	1 m² = 1·20 yd²
	perch (p)	square metre (m²)	1 p = 25·3 m²	1 m² = 0·0395 p
	rood (rd)	hectare (ha)	1 rd = 0·101 ha	1 ha = 9·88 rd
	acre (ac)	hectare (ha)	1 ac = 0·405 ha	1 ha = 2·47 ac
	square mile	square kilometre (km²)	1 square mile = 2·59 km²	1 km² = 0·386 square mile
VOLUME	cubic inch (in³)	cubic centimetre (cm³)	1 in³ = 16·4 cm³	1 cm³ = 0·0610 in³
	cubic foot (ft³)	cubic metre (m³)	1 ft³ = 0·0283 m³	1 m³ = 35·3 ft³
	cubic yard (yd³)	cubic metre (m³)	1 yd³ = 0·765 m³	1 m³ = 1·31 yd³
	bushel (bus)	cubic metre (m³)	1 bus = 0·0364 m³	1 m³ = 27·5 bus
VOLUME (fluids)	fluid ounce (fl oz)	millilitre (ml)	1 fl oz = 28·4 ml	1 ml = 0·0352 fl oz
	pint (pt)	millilitre (ml) or litre (ℓ)	1 pt = 568 ml	1 litre = 1·76 pt
	gallon (gal)	litre (ℓ) or cubic metre (m³)	1 gal = 4·55 litre	1 m³ = 220 gal
	acre foot	cubic metre (m³) or megalitre (Ml)	1 acre foot = 1230 m³ = 1·23 Ml	1 Ml = 0·811 acre foot
FORCE	pound-force (lbf)	newton (N)	1 lbf = 4·45 N	1 N = 0·225 lbf
	ton-force (tonf)	kilonewton (kN)	1 tonf = 9·96 kN	1 kN = 0·100 tonf
PRESSURE	pound per square inch (psi)	kilopascal (kPa)	1 psi = 6·89 kPa	1 kPa = 0·145 psi
	atmosphere (atm)	kilopascal (kPa) or megapascal (MPa)	1 atm = 101 kPa	1 MPa = 9·87 atm
	ton per square inch (ton/in²)	megapascal (MPa)	1 ton/in² = 15·4 MPa	1 MPa = 0·0647 ton/in²
	psi	kg/cm²	1 kg/cm² = 14.22 psi	1 psi-0.070 kg/cm²
VELOCITY	mile per hour (mph)	kilometre per hour (km/h)	1 mph = 1·61 km/h	1 km/h = 0·621 mph
	(for navigation)	knot (kn)	1 kn = 1·85 km/h	
TEMPERATURE	temperature (°F)	temperature (°C)	$°C = \frac{5}{9}(°F - 32)$	$°F = \frac{9 \times °C}{5} + 32$
DENSITY	pound per cubic inch (lb/in³)	gram per cubic centimetre (g/cm³) = tonne per cubic metre (t/m³)	1 lb/in³ = 27·7 t/m³	1 t/m³ = 0·0361 lb/in³
	ton per cubic yard	tonne per cubic metre (t/m³)	1 ton/yd³ = 1·33 t/m³	1 t/m³ = 0·752 ton/yd³
ENERGY	British thermal unit (Btu)	kilojoule (kJ)	1 Btu = 1·06 kJ	1 kJ = 0·948 Btu
	therm	megajoule (MJ)	1 therm = 106 MJ	$1 MJ = 9·48 \times 10^{-3}$ therm
	(for electrical energy)	kilowatt hour (kWh)	1 kWh = 3·60 MJ	
POWER	horsepower (hp)	kilowatt (kW)	1 hp = 0·746 kW	1 kW = 1·34 hp
TIME		second (s)		
		minute (min)	1 min = 60 s	
		hour (h)	1 h = 3600 s	
FREQUENCY	cycle per second (c/s)	hertz (Hz)	1 c/s = 1 Hz	1 Hz = 1 c/s
ANGULAR VELOCITY	revolution per minute (rpm)	radian per second (rad/s) revolution per minute (rpm)	1 rpm = 0·105 rad/s	1 rad/s = 9·55 rpm
TORQUE	lb/ft	kg/m	1 kg/m = 7.233 lb/ft	1 lb/ft = 0.138 kg/m

CONVERSION TABLES

INCHES	DECIMALS	MILLI-METRES	INCHES TO MILLIMETRES — Inches	m.ms.	MILLIMETRES TO INCHES — m.ms.	Inches	°F	°C	°C	°F
1/64	.015625	.3969	.0001	.00254	0.001	.000039	−20	−28.9	−30	−22
1/32	.03125	.7937	.0002	.00508	0.002	.000079	−15	−26.1	−28	−18.4
3/64	.046875	1.1906	.0003	.00762	0.003	.000118	−10	−23.3	−26	−14.8
1/16	.0625	1.5875	.0004	.01016	0.004	.000157	−5	−20.6	−24	−11.2
5/64	.078125	1.9844	.0005	.01270	0.005	.000197	0	−17.8	−22	−7.6
3/32	.09375	2.3812	.0006	.01524	0.006	.000236	1	−17.2	−20	−4
7/64	.109375	2.7781	.0007	.01778	0.007	.000276	2	−16.7	−18	−0.4
1/8	.125	3.1750	.0008	.02032	0.008	.000315	3	−16.1	−16	3.2
9/64	.140625	3.5719	.0009	.02286	0.009	.000354	4	−15.6	−14	6.8
5/32	.15625	3.9687	.001	.0254	0.01	.00039	5	−15.0	−12	10.4
11/64	.171875	4.3656	.002	.0508	0.02	.00079	10	−12.2	−10	14
3/16	.1875	4.7625	.003	.0762	0.03	.00118	15	−9.4	−8	17.6
13/64	.203125	5.1594	.004	.1016	0.04	.00157	20	−6.7	−6	21.2
7/32	.21875	5.5562	.005	.1270	0.05	.00197	25	−3.9	−4	24.8
15/64	.234375	5.9531	.006	.1524	0.06	.00236	30	−1.1	−2	28.4
1/4	.25	6.3500	.007	.1778	0.07	.00276	35	1.7	0	32
17/64	.265625	6.7469	.008	.2032	0.08	.00315	40	4.4	2	35.6
9/32	.28125	7.1437	.009	.2286	0.09	.00354	45	7.2	4	39.2
19/64	.296875	7.5406	.01	.254	0.1	.00394	50	10.0	6	42.8
5/16	.3125	7.9375	.02	.508	0.2	.00787	55	12.8	8	46.4
21/64	.328125	8.3344	.03	.762	0.3	.01181	60	15.6	10	50
11/32	.34375	8.7312	.04	1.016	0.4	.01575	65	18.3	12	53.6
23/64	.359375	9.1281	.05	1.270	0.5	.01969	70	21.1	14	57.2
3/8	.375	9.5250	.06	1.524	0.6	.02362	75	23.9	16	60.8
25/64	.390625	9.9219	.07	1.778	0.7	.02756	80	26.7	18	64.4
13/32	.40625	10.3187	.08	2.032	0.8	.03150	85	29.4	20	68
27/64	.421875	10.7156	.09	2.286	0.9	.03543	90	32.2	22	71.6
7/16	.4375	11.1125	.1	2.54	1	.03937	95	35.0	24	75.2
29/64	.453125	11.5094	.2	5.08	2	.07874	100	37.8	26	78.8
15/32	.46875	11.9062	.3	7.62	3	.11811	105	40.6	28	82.4
31/64	.484375	12.3031	.4	10.16	4	.15748	110	43.3	30	86
1/2	.5	12.7000	.5	12.70	5	.19685	115	46.1	32	89.6
33/64	.515625	13.0969	.6	15.24	6	.23622	120	48.9	34	93.2
17/32	.53125	13.4937	.7	17.78	7	.27559	125	51.7	36	96.8
35/64	.546875	13.8906	.8	20.32	8	.31496	130	54.4	38	100.4
9/16	.5625	14.2875	.9	22.86	9	.35433	135	57.2	40	104
37/64	.578125	14.6844	1	25.4	10	.39370	140	60.0	42	107.6
19/32	.59375	15.0812	2	50.8	11	.43307	145	62.8	44	112.2
39/64	.609375	15.4781	3	76.2	12	.47244	150	65.6	46	114.8
5/8	.625	15.8750	4	101.6	13	.51181	155	68.3	48	118.4
41/64	.640625	16.2719	5	127.0	14	.55118	160	71.1	50	122
21/32	.65625	16.6687	6	152.4	15	.59055	165	73.9	52	125.6
43/64	.671875	17.0656	7	177.8	16	.62992	170	76.7	54	129.2
11/16	.6875	17.4625	8	203.2	17	.66929	175	79.4	56	132.8
45/64	.703125	17.8594	9	228.6	18	.70866	180	82.2	58	136.4
23/32	.71875	18.2562	10	254.0	19	.74803	185	85.0	60	140
47/64	.734375	18.6531	11	279.4	20	.78740	190	87.8	62	143.6
3/4	.75	19.0500	12	304.8	21	.82677	195	90.6	64	147.2
49/64	.765625	19.4469	13	330.2	22	.86614	200	93.3	66	150.8
25/32	.78125	19.8437	14	355.6	23	.90551	205	96.1	68	154.4
51/64	.796875	20.2406	15	381.0	24	.94488	210	98.9	70	158
13/16	.8125	20.6375	16	406.4	25	.98425	212	100.0	75	167
53/64	.828125	21.0344	17	431.8	26	1.07362	215	101.7	80	176
27/32	.84375	21.4312	18	457.2	27	1.06299	220	104.4	85	185
55/64	.859375	21.8281	19	482.6	28	1.10236	225	107.2	90	194
7/8	.875	22.2250	20	508.0	29	1.14173	230	110.0	95	203
57/64	.890625	22.6219	21	533.4	30	1.18110	235	112.8	100	212
29/32	.90625	23.0187	22	558.8	31	1.22047	240	115.6	105	221
59/64	.921875	23.4156	23	584.2	32	1.25984	245	118.3	110	230
15/16	.9375	23.8125	24	609.6	33	1.29921	250	121.1	115	239
61/64	.953125	24.2094	25	635.0	34	1.33858	255	123.9	120	248
31/32	.96875	24.6062	26	660.4	35	1.37795	260	126.6	125	257
63/64	.984375	25.0031	27	690.6	36	1.41732	265	129.4	130	266

wheels ROAD TEST

This road test panel courtesy Wheels Magazine, from its November, 1971, Sydney report.

FORD CORTINA 2000 XL GS

MAKE . . . . .Ford
MODEL . . . . .Cortina 2000 XL GS
BODY TYPE . . . . .Four-door Sedan
PRICE . . . .$2650 plus options
OPTIONS:
Heavy duty battery $4
GS Pack $120
Radio $94
Radial Tyres $49
Electric Aerial $29.61
Laminated Screen $51
COLOR . . . . .Jewel green
MILEAGE START 1353
MILEAGE FINISH 2196
WEIGHT . . . .(1025 kg) 2260 lb
FUEL CONSUMPTION:
Overall . . . .(9.5 kpl) 26.7 mpg
Cruising . . . .(8.9-9.9 kpl) 25-28 mpg
TEST CONDITIONS:
Weather . . . . cold, dry
Surface . . . . hot mix
Load .two persons
Fuel . . . . premium
SPEEDOMETER ERROR:

Indicated mph	30	40	50	60	70	80	90
Actual mph	31	41	52	63	74	85	95

PERFORMANCE

Piston speed at max bhp . . . . (926.6 m/min) 3040 ft/min
Top gear mph per 1000 rpm . . . . . .(32.1 kph) 19.95
Engine rpm at max speed . . . . .5500 rpm
Lbs (laden) per gross bhp (power-to-weight) . . (9.1 kg) 20.1
MAXIMUM SPEEDS:
Fastest run . . . .(182.9 kph) 113.6 mph
Average of all runs . . . .(176.2 kph) 109.5 mph
Speedometer indication, fastest run . . (173.8 kph) 108 mph
IN GEARS:
1st . . . .(51.5 kph) 32 mph (6200 rpm)
2nd . . . .(94.9 kph) 59 mph (6200 rpm)
3rd . . . .(138.4 kph) 86 mph (6200 rpm)
4th . . . .(176.2 kph) 109.5 mph (5500 rpm)

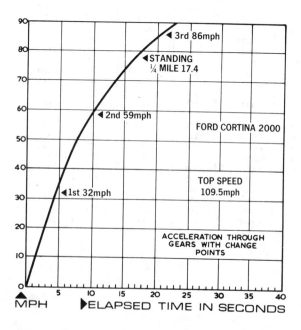

FORD CORTINA 2000

3rd 86mph
STANDING ¼ MILE 17.4
2nd 59mph
TOP SPEED 109.5mph
1st 32mph
ACCELERATION THROUGH GEARS WITH CHANGE POINTS

MPH ▶ELAPSED TIME IN SECONDS

ACCELERATION (through gears):
0-30 mph . . . . .3.5 sec
0-40 mph . . . . .5.2 sec
0-50 mph . . . . .7.8 sec
0-60 mph . . . . .10.3 sec
0-70 mph . . . . .13.6 sec
0-80 mph . . . . .17.8 sec
0-90 mph . . . . .23.4 sec

	2nd gear	3rd gear	4th gear
20-40 mph	4.1 sec	6.0 sec	8.4 sec
30-50 mph	4.4 sec	6.0 sec	8.3 sec
40-60 mph	5.5 sec	6.3 sec	8.7 sec
50-70 mph	—	7.2 sec	9.7 sec

STANDING QUARTER MILE:
Fastest run . . . . .17.2 sec
Average all runs . . . . .17.4 sec
BRAKING:
From 30 mph to 0 . . . . .1.8 sec
From 60 mph to 0 . . . . .3.4 sec

SPECIFICATIONS
ENGINE:
Cylinders . . . . .four, in-line
Bore and stroke . (3.575 in.) 99.8 mm x (3.02 in.) 76.95mm
Cubic capacity . . . .(121.6 cu in.) 1998 cc
Compression ratio . . . . .9.2 to 1
Valves . . . . .belt driven, overhead cam
Carburettor . . . . .Weber 2-barrel
Fuel pump . . . . mechanical
Oil filter .full flow
Power at rpm . . . . 112 bhp at 6000 rpm
Torque at rpm . . . .(16.9 kg/m) 122 lb/ft at 3500 rpm
TRANSMISSION:
Type . . . . four-speed, all syncromesh
Clutch . . . . .single dry plate
Gear lever location . . . . .central
RATIOS:

	Direct	Overall	mph per 1000 rpm
1st	3.65	13.505	5.4
2nd	1.97	7.289	10.1
3rd	1.37	5.069	14.5
4th	1.00	3.700	19.95
Final drive	3.7		

CHASSIS AND RUNNING GEAR:
Construction . . . . unitary
Suspension front . . . . .upper and lower arms,
coil springs, anti-roll bar
Suspension rear . . . . .4-link, coil springs,
Lateral arms
Shock absorbers . . . . .telescopic
Steering type . . . . rack and pinion 18.7
Turns l to l 3.6
Turning circle . . . .(10.18 m) 31 ft 8 in.
Brakes type . . . . .disc/drum
Dimensions . . . . disc 9.6 in. diameter,
drum 9 in. diameter
Friction area . . . . (1893.3 sq cm) swept area 293.4 sq in.
DIMENSIONS:
Wheelbase . . . .(257.8 cm) 101.5 in.
Track front . . . .(142.2 cm) 4 ft 8 in.
Track rear . . . .(142.2 cm) 4 ft 8 in.
Length . . . .(426.7 cm) 14 ft
Width . . . .(170.2 cm) 5 ft 7 in.
Height . . . .(132.1 cm) 4 ft 2 in.
Fuel tank capacity . . . .(54 litres) 12 gallons
TYRES:
Size . . . . 175 x 13
Pressures . . . . .(F2.0/R 2.0 kg/cm²) F 28 psi, R 28 psi
Make on test car . . . . .Dunlop SP 41
GROUND CLEARANCE:
Registered . . . .(12.7 cm) 5.5 in.

INDEX

SUPPLEMENT

The following specifications and information relate to items not covered by the main manual and changes in specification from late 1973.

Variations only are given and reference should be made to the main manual for specifications not given in this supplement.

Operational procedures in the main manual are applicable unless shown otherwise in this supplement.

Prepared by Scientific Publications, Co. Durham, England, as a special supplement to Scientific Publications Pty Ltd. Workshop Manual Series Number 60 Cortina.

ENGINE

SPECIFICATIONS – 1600 OHC

ENGINE ASSEMBLY

Type .... 4 cyl in line – ohc
Bore .... 87.65 mm
Capacity .... 1576 cc
Stroke .... 66 mm
Ignition timing – static .... 6 deg. btdc

VALVES

Valve head diameter:
  Inlet 1600 HC .... 38.3 – 38.7 mm
  Inlet 1600 GT .... 41.8 – 42.2 mm
  Exhaust 1600 HC .... 29.8 – 30.2 mm
  Exhaust 1600 GT .... 33.8 – 34.2 mm
Valve length – inlet – 1600 HC ..... 112.6 – 113.4 mm
Valve timing – 1600 HC:
  Inlet opens .... 16 deg. btdc
  Inlet closes .... 60 deg. abdc
  Exhaust opens .... 58 deg. bbdc
  Exhaust closes .... 18 deg. atdc
Valve timing – 1600 GT:
  Inlet opens .... 18 deg. btdc
  Inlet closes .... 70 deg. abdc
  Exhaust opens .... 64 deg. bbdc
  Exhaust closes .... 24 deg. atdc
Assembled spring load – valve open:
  1600 HC .... 74 – 80 kg
  1600 GT .... 77 – 83 kg

CYLINDER BLOCK, PISTONS

Standard bore .... 87.680 – 87.690 mm
Standard piston .... 87.630 – 87.655 mm

DESCRIPTION

The 1600 cc overhead camshaft engine is similar in design and operation to the 2000 cc OHC described in the main manual.

With the exception of the variation in specifications all service and repair operations given in the main manual for the 2000 cc OHC are also applicable to the 1600 cc OHC.

COOLING SYSTEM

Cooling system capacity including heater:
  1600 OHC .... 6.5 litre

HEATER CONTROLS

To Remove and Instal

(1) Disconnect the battery earth terminal.

(2) Remove the tray from the transmission tunnel.

(3) Remove the dash lower trim panel and the steering column shrouds.

(4) Withdraw the rheostat knob from the instrument panel and remove the six screws securing the panel. Withdraw the panel sufficiently to allow the speedometer cable and electrical multiblock connectors to be disconnected from the panel.

NOTE: When a radio is fitted it will be necessary to remove the control knobs and trim to facilitate the withdrawal of the instrument panel.

(5) Remove the instrument panel.

(6) Disconnect the heater distribution operating cables from the heater distribution unit beneath the dashboard.

(7) Disconnect the operating cable from the heating control lever and bracket beneath the dashboard.

(8) Remove the three screws securing the heater control assembly, disconnect the electrical connections and remove the control assembly complete with the operating cables noting the position of the insulators.

Installation is a reversal of the removal procedure with attention to the following points:

Check all operating cables for free movement and signs of chafing or binding and renew where necessary by detaching the defective cable(s) from the heater control assembly.

Ensure the correct and secure fitment of all electrical connections on assembly.

Check the operation of all the heater controls and adjust the operating cables where necessary.

FUEL SYSTEM

SPECIFICATIONS

FORD CARBURETTOR

Type . . . . Single barrel downdraught

*Model applications:

1600 OHV low compression,
auto choke 71–1W–9510–BNA

1300 OHV high compression,
emission control, manual choke 71–1W–9510–RA

1600 OHV high compression,
emission control, manual choke . . . 71–1W–9510–ANA

1600 OHC high compression,
auto choke 71–HW–9510–AJA
71–HW–9510–AGA

1600 OHC high compression,
emission control, auto choke 71–HW–9510–YA
71–HW–9510–AHA

Venturi diameter:
71–1W–9510–RA . . . . 25 mm
All other models . . . . 28 mm

Main discharge jet:
71–1W–9510–RA 125
71–1W–9510–ANA
71–1W–9510–BNA 145
71–HW–9510–AJA
71–HW–9510–AHA
71–HW–9510–AGA
71–HW–9510–YA 137

Float level:
71–1W–9510–RA . . . . 27.43 mm
All other models . . . . 27.93 mm
Float travel, all models . . . . 6.60 mm

Choke plate pull down clearances:
71–1W–9510–RA . . . . 3.30 mm
71–1W–9510–ANA . . . . 3.55 mm
71–1W–9510–BNA
71–HW–9510–AJA
71–HW–9510–AHA
71–HW–9510–AGA
71–HW–9510–YA . . . . 3.81 mm

De-choke setting (auto choke only):
71–1W–9510–BNA . . . . 7.62 mm
71–HW–9510–AJA
71–HW–9510–AHA
71–HW–9510–AGA
71–HW–9510–YA . . . . 5.33 mm

Accelerator pump stroke:
Except 71–1W–9510–ANA
and 71–1W–9510–BNA . . . . 2.54 mm
71–1W–9510–ANA
71–1W–9510–BNA . . . . 2.66 mm

Automatic choke models only:
Vacuum piston link hole . . . . Outer
Thermostat spring slot . . . . Centre

Idle speed:
71–1W–9510–RA, ANA, BNA . . . . 700 rpm
Except RA, ANA, BNA . . . . 730 – 770 rpm

Fast idle speed:
71–1W–9510–RA . . . . 1400 – 1600 rpm
71–1W–9510–ANA . . . . 1000 rpm
71–1W–9510–BNA . . . . 2050 – 2250 rpm
71–HW–9510–AJA
71–HW–9510–AHA . . . . 2000 – 2200 rpm
71–HW–9510–AGA
71–HW–9510–YA . . . . 1650 – 1850 rpm

*Identification number can be obtained from the identification plate attached to the carburettor top cover.

WEBER CARBURETTOR

Type . . . . Dual barrel downdraught

Model applications:–

1600 OHV – GT.
high compression, manual choke . 71–1F–9510–FA

1600 OHV – GT.
high compression, auto choke 71–1F–9510–GA

1600 OHC – GT.
high compression, manual transmission,
auto choke 71–HF–9510–BA

1600 OHC – GT.
high compression, auto transmission,
auto choke 71–HF–9510–CA

Primary venturi diameter . . . . 26 mm
Secondary venturi diameter . . . . 27 mm
Main jet – primary venturi 140
Main jet – secondary venturi 135

Air correction jet – primary venturi:
71–1F–9510–FA
71–1F–9510–GA 165
71–HF–9510–BA 170

Air correction jet – secondary venturi:
71–1F–9510–FA
71–1F–9510–GA 160
71–HF–9510–BA 140

Emulsion tube type:
Primary F50
Secondary F6

Idling jet:
Primary 55
Secondary, 71–1F–9510–FA, GA 50
Secondary, 71–HF–9510–BA 45

Accelerator pump jet:
71–1F–9510–FA
71–HF–9510–BA . . . . 50 Special
71–1F–9510–GA 50

Needle valve . . . . 2.0 mm

Float level – cover vertical;
Except 71–HF–9510–BA . . . . . . 38.75 – 39.25 mm
71–HF–9510–BA . . . . 35.00 – 35.5 mm

Float drop — cover horizontal:
    Except 71–HF–9510–BA .... 50.0 – 51.5 mm
    71–HF–9510–BA .... 50.5 – 52.0 mm
Choke plate pull down:
    71–1F–9510–FA .... 4.45 mm
    71–1F–9510–GA .... 3.50 mm
    71–HF–9510–BA .... 4.50 mm
Secondary throttle valve
    adjustment .... 0.051 – 0.076 mm
Idling speed:
    Except 71–HF–9510–BA .... 800 rpm
    71–HF–9510–BA .... 700 rpm
Fast idle speed:
    Except 71–1F–9510–GA .... 3200 rpm on High cam.
    71–1F–9510–GA .... 3000 rpm on High cam.
Fast idling speed setting:
    Except 71–1F–9510–GA .... 0.85 mm
    71–1F–9510–GA .... 0.80 – 0.85 mm

CLUTCH

SPECIFICATIONS

Driven plate outside diameter:
    1600 OHC .... 189 mm
    1600 OHC GT .... 215 mm
Cushion springs:
    1600 OHC 4
    1600 OHC GT 6

DRIVE LINE

On later models, modifications were introduced to obtain correct drive line alignment. This alignment is correct when a straight line can be sighted from the centre of the front universal joint, through the propeller shaft(s) and through the pinion centreline. Where a one-piece propeller shaft is fitted the adjustment is obtained by serrated plates at the lower radius arm to axle mounting bolts. Where a two-piece propeller shaft is fitted adjustment is provided by the serrated plates and additional spacing washers fitted to the centre bearing mounting bolts, see illustration.

Drive line alignment and adjustment is necessary when either the two piece propeller shaft or the rear axle has been disturbed. The operation should only be carried out with the weight of the vehicle on all four wheels and the handbrake firmly applied.

TO ADJUST DRIVE LINE

(1) Slacken but do not remove the lower radius arm to axle housing bolts to release the serrated plates.

(2) Manoeuvre the axle and also add to, or subtract from the centre bearing spacer washers to obtain correct alignment.

(3) Securely tighten all the mounting bolts.

FRONT SUSPENSION

SPECIFICATIONS

Castor angle .... 1 deg. 45 min – 3 deg. 45 min
                      positive.
              Maximum castor variation
              between each side must not
              exceed 0 deg. 45 min.
Camber angle .... 0 deg. 53 min – 1 deg. 43 min
                      positive

REAR SUSPENSION

SPECIFICATIONS

Spring free height — standard:
    1600 OHC. HC .... 279 mm
    1600 OHC. GT .... 273 mm
    1600 OHC. Estate .... 290 mm
Spring installed height:
    1600 OHC. HC .... 215.7 mm
    1600 OHC. GT .... 217 mm
    1600 OHC. Estate .... 215.6 mm

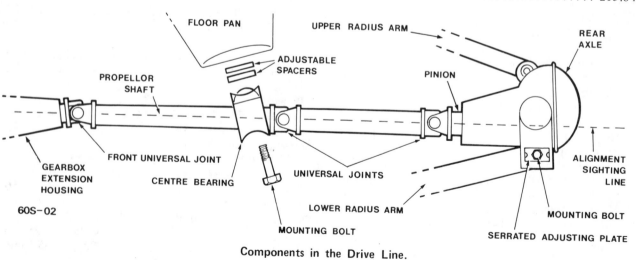

60S-02

Components in the Drive Line.

DESCRIPTION

Later model vehicles are fitted with a stabiliser bar on the rear suspension. Should removal of the lower radius arms be required, the stabiliser bar must be removed. The rear axle to lower radius arm mountings have also been modified to allow adjustment of the drive line. If the rear suspension has been disturbed, drive line alignment and adjustment must be carried out, refer to Rear Axle — Drive Line Adjustment in this supplement.

The coil spring lower seat on the lower radius arm has also been modified and no longer requires a bolt and plate to secure the spring. To remove and instal the coil springs, follow the procedure given in the main manual but disregard the spring retaining bolt and plate.

STABILISER BAR
To Remove and Instal

(1) Remove the four bolts and nuts securing the stabiliser bar to the lower radius arms and remove the stabiliser bar.

(2) Should the stabiliser bar insulators require renewal proceed as follows:

(a) Remove the self locking nuts and washers from the ends of the stabiliser bar.

(b) Withdraw the insulators and brackets from the stabiliser bar.

(c) Remove the internal spacers from the insulators and prise the insulators from the brackets.

(d) Renew any unserviceable insulators using a soap solution to aid installation to the brackets.

(e) Insert the spacers, and instal the assemblies and washers to their original position on the stabiliser bar securely tightening the self locking nuts.

(3) Instal the stabiliser bar to the lower radius arms and securely tighten the bolts with the nuts fitted to the outside of the radius arms.

STEERING

STEERING COLUMN

TO REMOVE AND INSTAL

(1) Raise the bonnet and fit covers to both front wings.

(2) Disconnect the battery earth terminal.

(3) Release the lock tabs on the universal joint coupling clamping plate, remove the retaining bolts and disconnect the universal joint coupling from the upper steering shaft.

(4) Remove the instrument panel as described under INSTRUMENT PANEL — To Remove and Instal.

(5) Take out the screws securing the dash lower trim panel and remove the panel.

(6) Disconnect the combination switch multiblock connector, take out the bolts securing the combination switch to the steering column and remove the switch.

(7) Remove the ventilation hose fitted across the steering column.

(8) Disconnect the wires from the ignition switch.

(9) Unscrew the column mounting bolts and manoeuvre the entire column assembly upward and withdraw it from the vehicle.

Installation is a reversal of the removal procedure with attention to the following points:

Before installing the column assembly it may be checked for collapse by measuring the overall length of the upper steering shaft which should be 790 – 791 mm. If the shaft has collapsed or shows signs of looseness or backlash the shaft must be renewed.

Instal the column mounting bolts but do not tighten at this stage. Position the steering column until a measurement of 73 – 77 mm can be obtained between the front face of the dash panel and the rear face of the steering wheel boss. Securely tighten the mounting bolts. Ensure that the road and steering wheels are in the straight ahead position and the weight of the vehicle is on the wheels.

Assemble the universal joint coupling and clamping plate to the upper steering shaft and manoeuvre until the whole of the white sealing plug in the upper shaft is just visible from the lower end of the clamping plate.

NOTE: Ensure that the clamping plate does not cover any part of the sealing plug and the flexible coupling is correctly aligned.

Tighten the retaining bolts on the clamping plate and bend over the lock tabs.

The above installation procedures relating to the steering column and lower steering shaft must be carried out if either of the two components are disturbed.

ELECTRICAL SYSTEM

SPECIFICATIONS

GENERATOR REGULATOR

Type . . . . Autolite
Mechanical adjustments:
Voltage regulator armature
to core air gap . . . . 0.61 – 0.71 mm
Current regulator armature
to core air gap . . . . 0.36 – 0.48 mm
Cut out armature to
core air gap . . . . 0.64 – 0.94 mm
Cut out armature to core,
points just touching . . . . 0.38 – 0.64 mm
Electrical adjustments:
Cut out – cut in voltage . . . . 12.6 – 13.4 volts
Cut out opening voltage . . . . 9.25 – 11.25 volts
Current regulator load setting . . . . 22 amps
Voltage regulator open circuit
setting . . . . 14.4 – 15.6 volts
at 20 deg. C

STARTER MOTOR

Make and pinion operation:

Bosch .... EF 0.7 PS pre-engaged
GF 1.0 PS pre-engaged
Number of poles 4
Commutator .... Barrel type
Brush length – min ....10 mm
Brush spring tension .... 900 – 1300 gm
Armature end float .... 0.1 – 0.3 mm
No load current draw – max:
EF 0.7 PS .... 45 amp
GF 1.0 PS .... 54 amp

DISTRIBUTOR

Type and make:
1600 OHC HC model –
Type .... 71 HM – SA
Ident. colour .... Black
Make .... Bosch
1600 OHC GT model –
Type .... 71 HM – DA
Ident. colour .... Blue
Make .... Bosch
1600 OHC GT model –
Type .... 71 BB – UB
Ident. colour .... Red
Make .... Motorcraft
Direction of rotation .... Clockwise
Drive .... Auxiliary shaft
Firing order 1, 3, 4, 2
Shaft end float .... 0.20 mm
Breaker point gap – Bosch .... 0.4 – 0.5 mm
Breaker point spring tension – Bosch ..... 430 – 530 gm
Dwell angle – all models .... 38 – 40 deg.
Initial advance .... 6 deg. btdc

DISTRIBUTOR

DESCRIPTION

The Bosch distributor is fitted as standard on the 1600 cc HC OHC models and may also be fitted to the 1600 cc OHC GT models as an alternative. The Bosch distributor is similar in construction and operation to the Motorcraft distributor fitted to OHC models described in the main manual. The routine servicing procedures are similar to the Motorcraft distributor. The Bosch distributor can be readily identified by the capacitor fitted externally to the distributor body.

TO REMOVE

(1) Mark the distributor body and crankcase to facilitate correct re-assembly.

(2) Remove the distributor cap.

(3) Rotate the engine until the rotor button aligns with the segment for No. 1 cylinder plug lead and so that the appropriate timing mark on the crankshaft pulley is in line with the pointer on the timing cover.

(4) Mark the initial position of the rotor arm on the distributor body, remove the low tension lead, vacuum advance pipe, remove the mounting bolt and withdraw the distributor from the engine.

(5) Mark the final position of the rotor arm after withdrawing the distributor.

TO DISMANTLE

With the distributor removed from the vehicle, the dismantling procedure is as follows:

(1) Remove the distributor cap and rotor.

(2) Disconnect the low tension lead at the terminal inside the housing, remove the retaining screw and detach the contact breaker point assembly.

(3) Remove the 'E' clip, when fitted, from the vacuum advance unit pull rod pivot pin, unscrew the vacuum advance unit and capacitor retaining screws, lift the vacuum advance unit sufficiently to clear the pivot pin and separate the vacuum advance unit and capacitor from the distributor body with the primary lead assembly.

(4) Remove the screw holding the breaker plate retaining bracket, earth wire and distributor cap clip.

(5) Remove the retaining screw and clip on the opposite side of the distributor body.

(6) Lift out the breaker plate, remove the damping spring screw, spring and steel ball.

(7) Mark the fitted position of the drive gear relative to the shaft.

(8) Drive out the drive gear securing pin and withdraw the drive gear from the end of the shaft. Remove the shims and washer from the end of the shaft.

(9) Withdraw the shaft assembly from the top of the housing and collect any shims and washers that may be adhering to the shaft and action plate or at the top end of the housing bore. Keep the shims and washers in their relative positions to facilitate assembly.

NOTE: Prior to dismantling the cam, centrifugal weights and action plate assembly, mark all the components with quick drying paint to facilitate assembly.

(10) Remove the felt pad and circlip from the upper end of the cam, disconnect the centrifugal weight control springs from the action plate and withdraw the cam assembly from the distributor shaft, complete with springs and washers.

NOTE: Observe the fitted position of the centrifugal weight control springs.

(11) Remove the 'E' clips from the centrifugal weight pivots on the action plate and lift off the weights and thrust washers.

(12) Clean all the components excluding the capacitor and vacuum unit in cleaning solvent and inspect for wear or damage after blowing dry with compressed air.

TO ASSEMBLE

(1) Check the breaker plate and base plate assembly for wear and distortion. Check the ball bearing for flat sections and the spring tension of the ball retainer. Replace as necessary and lubricate with high melting point grease.

(2) Check the distributor housing bush and distributor shaft for wear. Replace as necessary and lubricate with high melting point grease.

(3) Check the cam for wear or scoring and renew as necessary.

(4) Check the centrifugal advance control springs for weakness, compare with new springs if possible, renew as necessary.

(5) Place the thrust washers on the pivot pins.

(6) Position the centrifugal weights on the pivot pins the correct way up and in their original position, ensure that the markings correspond with those on the action plate and secure with the 'E' clips.

(7) Place the control springs on the base of the cam in their correct positions.

(8) Align the mark on the cam with the marks on the action plate and centrifugal weight, instal the cam on the distributor shaft and connect the two control springs to the action plate.

(9) Secure the cam on the distributor shaft with the circlip and instal the felt pad.

(10) Instal the upper shims and washer on the shaft in the order in which they were removed, oil the shaft and body and insert the shaft in from the top of the distributor.

(11) Place the lower shims and washer on the end of the shaft and instal the drive gear according to the marks made prior to dismantling.

(12) Push the drive gear onto the shaft far enough to insert the securing pin. Check that the end float does not exceed 0.20 mm. If necessary remove the drive gear and adjust the end float by removing or adding shims between the end of the body and the drive gear.

(13) Instal the securing pin.

(14) Instal the vacuum unit, capacitor, breaker plate and contact points in the reverse order of dismantling. Adjust the contact breaker points, see To Adjust Contact Breaker Points in the main manual.

(15) Apply a smear of high melting point grease to the cam lobes and a small amount of grease on the heel of the contact points, insert one or two drops of engine oil down the centre of the cam onto the felt pad. Apply one drop of engine oil to the top of the breaker arm pivot pin.

NOTE: Do not allow grease or oil to contaminate the contact points as this will produce arcing or burning of the points.

(16) Instal the distributor as described in Distributor – To Instal.

TO INSTAL

(1) If the engine has been turned while the distributor was removed it must be re-timed by turning the engine until No. 1 piston is on the compression stroke, No. 1 cylinder cam lobes face upwards when viewed through the oil filler neck. Observe that the appropriate timing mark on the crankshaft pulley is in line with the pointer on the timing cover.

(2) Align the rotor button with the final mark on the distributor body made after removal. Instal the distributor to the engine aligning the marks made on the distributor body and crankcase. With the distributor fully installed check the rotor button which should align with the initial mark made on the body before removal.

(3) Instal and securely tighten the distributor mounting bolt.

(4) Refit the vacuum advance pipe, low tension lead and distributor.

(5) Check and adjust the ignition timing, see – To Adjust Ignition Timing in the main manual.

SWITCHES AND CONTROLS

COMBINATION SWITCHES

On later model vehicles the combination switch on the steering column has been moved to the opposite side of the steering column to accommodate a further combination switch controlling the lighting and windscreen wiper operations. For removal and installation procedure of the switches see – COMBINATION SWITCHES – To Remove and Instal contained in the main manual.

INSTRUMENT CLUSTER

To Remove and Instal

(1) Raise the bonnet, fit covers to both front wings and disconnect the battery earth terminal.

(2) Remove the steering column lower shroud securing screws and remove the upper and lower shrouds.

(3) Withdraw the rheostat knob from the instrument panel and remove the six retaining screws from the panel.

NOTE: Where a radio is fitted it is necessary to remove the control knobs and trim to facilitate the withdrawal of the instrument panel.

(4) Withdraw the instrument cluster sufficiently to allow the speedometer cable and electrical multiblock connectors to be disconnected from the rear of the panel.

(5) Disconnect the electrical connections from the cigar lighter, hazard warning switch and the heated rear window switch, where these items are fitted.

(6) Remove the instrument cluster from the vehicle.
Installation is a reversal of the removal procedure.

LAMP UNITS

HEADLAMPS (RECTANGULAR)
To Remove and Instal

(1) Remove the radiator grill securing screws and remove the grill.

(2) Remove the headlamp securing screw, withdraw the headlamp assembly to enable the bulb holder and bulb to be removed from the rear of the headlamp.

Installation is a reversal of the removal procedure. The headlamp focus or adjustment should be checked after installing new components.

SCIENTIFIC PUBLICATIONS MANUAL SERIES

MOTOR CARS

	Book No.	Pages	Illustrations
Chrysler/Mitsubishi			
Galant/Colt 1300, 1600	05	192	202
Datsun			
1000, 1200	87	224	208
510: 1300, 1400, 1600 (1968-72)	88	256	241
180B, 160B	110	224	208
Sunny, 120Y	111	224	278
Ford			
Capri 1600, 1600 GT	82	173	108
Consul/Zephyr Mk II (1956-62)	08	184	124
Cortina 1200, 1500 1600, Mk I & II (1964-71)	68	288	192
Cortina Mk III 1600, 2000 (1971-74)	60	240	239
Cortina Mk III, 6 cyl. (1972-74)	59	176	135
Escort 1100, 1300, 1300 GT (1970-75)	81	192	172
Falcon XK to XW 6 cyl. (1960-1970)	62	290	188
Falcon XY to XB 6 cyl. (1970-76)	155	272	226
Falcon XR to XY V8 (1966-71)	154	272	190
Falcon XA and XB V8 (1971-76)	156*		
Hillman			
Hunter/Arrow HB, HC (1967-70)	79	188	121
Avenger	80	176	267
Holden			
Gemini	113	160	215
FX, FJ, FE, FC, FB, EK, EJ, EH, HD, HR (1948-68)	67	286	128
HK, HT, HG V8 (1968-71)	85	272	215
HK, HT, HG 6 cyl. (1968-71)	86	224	188
HQ, HJ 6 cyl.	146	208	194
HQ, HJ V8	147	256	240
Torana LC, LJ 6 cyl. (1969-74)	84	192	172
Torana LH 6 cyl. (1974-76)	58	192	200
Torana HB	72	192	120
Torana LC, LJ, TA 4 cyl. (1969-75) ohv	56	196	287
Torana LC, LJ, TA 4 cyl. (1969-75) ohc	145	196	295
Torana LH 4 cyl. (1974-76)	16	180	197
Honda			
Civic Hondamatic	139	176	350
Civic Manual	140	176	339

	Book No.	Pages	Illustrations
Leyland			
Marina 1.3, 1.8 (1971-75)	142	192	277
Marina 1500, 1750	03	160	291
P76: V8	04	180	274
P76: 6 cyl.	141	180	324
Mazda			
Capella 616: 1600 (1970-73)	89	160	134
1500, 1800	90	212	196
RX2, R100 Rotaries	91	200	199
1000/1300	92	160	305
MG			
TC to MGB Mk I	70	320	204
Morris			
Minor MM, II	23	142	161
Minor 1000	24	96	96
Marina see Leyland			
Mini Cooper and 'S' Mini 1100, Moke (1961-73)	64	236	187
1100	65	146	106
1800 Mk I, Mk II	66a	224	174
BMC Complete Mini, 1100, 1800	71	606	467
Peugeot			
403, 404	31	122	171
Renault			
12	32	160	317
Dauphine	34	134	158
R8 and R10	74	164	97
Rootes Group			
Hillman, Humber, Husky, Cob (1958-66)	36	390	399
Toyota			
Corolla 1100	73	176	107
Corolla 1200	93	190	170
Corona 2R, 12R	83	224	186
Corona 2000 16R, 18R	120	176	256
Corona 12R, RT80/81	123	160	220
Valiant			
AP6, VC, VE, VF V8 (1965-70)	69	174	95
R, S, AP5, AP6, VC, VE, VF 6 cyl. (1962-70)	78	280	145
Hemi VG, VH, VJ 6 cyl. (1970-74)	52	224	183
Galant: see under Chrysler			
Vauxhall			
Viva HA, HB, 90 1964-67	76	200	140
Viva HC 1159, 1256 (1970-76)	57*		
Chevette 1256 cc	114	160	239

	Book No.	Pages	Illustrations
Volkswagen			
"Superbug" 1302S, 1600 (1971-73)	45	224	188
Beetle 1100, 1200, 1200A, 1300, 1500 (1954-71)	46	260	240
Fastback Type 3, 1600	47	232	167
Transporter (1954-72)	48	272	205
Volvo Series 140			
With Carbies	53	212	172
With Fuel Inject.	54	196	147

HARD TO GET AND VINTAGE MANUALS

	Book No.	Pages	Illustrations
Austin			
A40 Devon, Dorset	00	106	89
A40 Somerset	01	100	84
Jaguar			
Mks VII, VIII, IX, XK120, 140, 150	21	274	237
Mk I, II: 2.4, 3.4, 3.8	22	274	281
E Type 3.8, 4.2 (1962-69)	77	202	124
Standard			
8-14 (1939-46)	40	82	51
Ten (1955-58)	41	148	134
Spacemaster II	42	126	105
TR2, TR3, TR4	44	168	130

MOWERS AND SMALL ENGINES

	Book No.	Pages	Illustrations
Rover Series to 1973	101	128	151
Small Engines	112	160	231
Victa Series to 1972	100	80	89
Victa Series to 1974	102	96	112

MOTOR CYCLES

	Book No.	Pages	Illustrations
Honda			
QA50 Minibike	129	64	95
SL70, CT90	130	128	224
C/S:50, 65, 70	131	96	182
Street/Trail 175	132	112	341
125 Vertical Twin	133	112	346
250, 350	134	128	376
100-125 Vertical Single	135	112	374

OUTBOARDS

	Book No.	Pages	Illustrations
Evinrude-Johnson			
3-4 hp (1964-72)	105	64	92
5-6 hp (1965-74)	106	96	177
9½ hp (1964-73)	107	80	198
18, 20, 25 hp (1960-73)	108	112	260
33-40 hp (1965-74)	109	128	300
40 hp Lark (1965-74)	104	112	250

* In Production.

OVERSEAS REPRESENTATIVES

Canada: Repco Auto Parts (Canada) Ltd, 325 West 6th Avenue, Vancouver, 10 BC.

New Zealand: M.E.P. Bookshop, 82 Taranaki St., Wellington.
Publishers Services, 13 Eden St. Newmarket, Auckland.
E. Sime and Co., 82 Tory St., Wellington; and 140 Target Rd, Glenfield Auckland.

South Africa: Australian Industries (Export) Pty Ltd, PO Box 2016, Johannesburg.

United Kingdom: Alltech Distributors, 15 High St., Hampton, Middlesex.
Frederick Muller Ltd., Victoria Works, Edgware Road, London
Scientific Publications, P. O. Box 11, G.P.O., Durham.

U.S.A.: Repcoparts U.S.A. Inc., 6281 Chalet Drive, Commerce, California. 90022.
Repco Auto Parts (U.S.A. East), 161 W. State Street, Doylestown, Pennsylvania. 18901.

Printed by Times Printing Sdn. Bhd., Singapore.